I0418960

Mastering Composition

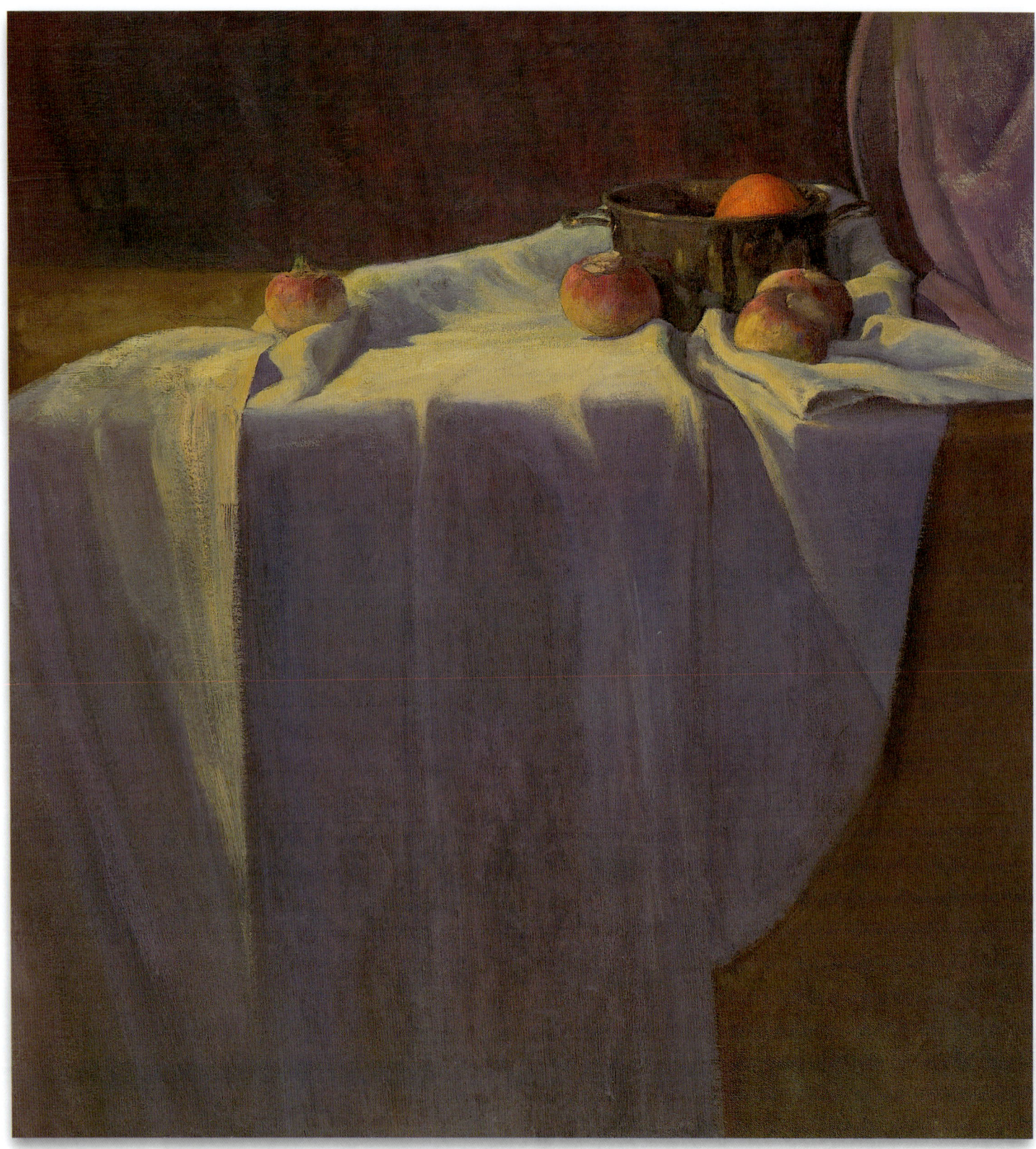

DARK SILVER
Oil on canvas
32" × 30" (81cm × 76cm)

mastering
composition

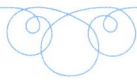

techniques and principles to
dramatically improve your painting

Ian Roberts

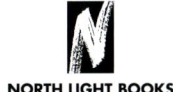

NORTH LIGHT BOOKS

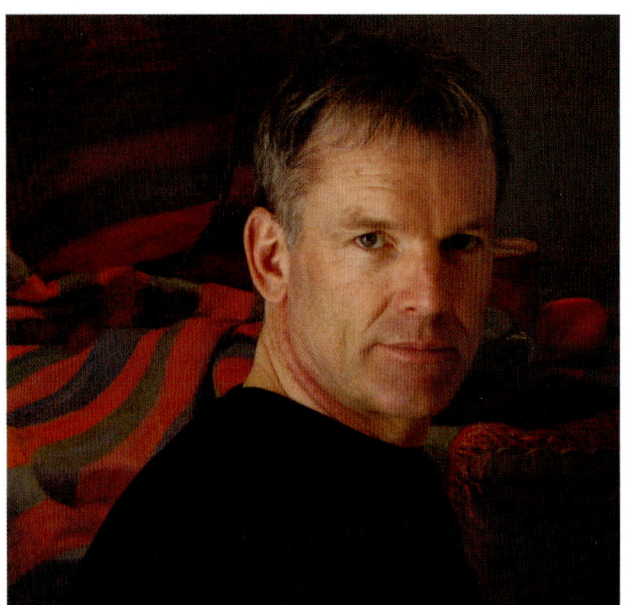

About the Author

Ian Roberts began accompanying his father on landscape painting trips when he was eleven. He has been painting full-time for over 40 years.

Ian attended the New School of Art and the Ontario College of Art in Toronto, and studied figure painting in Florence, Italy.

He taught plein air painting workshops in Provence, France for 25 years, through his school Atelier Saint-Luc, named after the patron saint of painters. He now teaches online courses on composition, drawing, brushwork and color.

He is the author of *Creative Authenticity: 16 Principles to Clarify and Deepen Your Artistic Vision* and an illustrated novel, *A Land Apart.* He lives in Los Angeles with his wife, the painter, Anne Ward.

NORTH LIGHT BOOKS

An imprint of Penguin Random House LLC
1745 Broadway, New York, NY 10019
penguinrandomhouse.com

Copyright © 2008 by Ian Roberts
Penguin Random House values and supports copyright. Copyright fuels creativity, encourages diverse voices, promotes free speech, and creates a vibrant culture. Thank you for buying an authorized edition of this book and for complying with copyright laws by not reproducing, scanning, or distributing any part of it in any form without permission. You are supporting writers and allowing Penguin Random House to continue to publish books for every reader. Please note that no part of this book may be used or reproduced in any manner for the purpose of training artificial intelligence technologies or systems.

ISBN 978-1-58180-924-4

Printed in China
23

Library of Congress Cataloging in Publication Data
Roberts, Ian
  Mastering composition : techniques and principles to dramatically improve your painting / Ian Roberts.
      p. cm.
  Includes bibliographical references and index.
  ISBN 978-1-58180-924-4 (hardcover : alk. paper)
  1. Composition (Art) 2. Space (Art) 3. Painting--Technique. I. Title.
ND1475.R625 2007
751.4--dc22   2007021350

Edited by Mary Burzlaff
Designed by Guy Kelly

The authorized representative in the EU for product safety and compliance is Penguin Random House Ireland, Morrison Chambers, 32 Nassau Street, Dublin D02 YH68, Ireland, https://eu-contact.penguin.ie.

Metric Conversion Chart

To convert	to	multiply by
Inches	Centimeters	2.54
Centimeters	Inches	0.4
Feet	Centimeters	30.5
Centimeters	Feet	0.03
Yards	Meters	0.9
Meters	Yards	1.1

Acknowledgments

I'd like to thank those at North Light Books: Jamie Markle and Jennifer Lepore for suggesting and believing in the idea, and my editors, Mona Michael, Kelly Messerly and particularly Mary Burzlaff, for keeping track of everything and pulling it all together.

Over the years I've met and become friends with some very good artists. In the course of conversations about painting, a few of these artists have sparked real insights into the painting process for me. The most significant and relevant to this book were: Tom Darro (edges), Dan Pinkham (color temperature), Mark Daily (transition colors) and Dan McCaw (attitude). Thank you all.

Another significant learning experience for me has been giving workshops. I thank my students for posing the questions that forced me to think about and give expression to the ideas in this book.

Thanks to Mary Landa, curator at the Brandywine River Museum, for getting Andrew Wyeth's permission to include his image in the book. The ideas for the compositional structure of the paintings by Rogier van der Weyden and Francisco de Goya are from Charles Bouleau in his book, now long out of print, *The Painter's Secret Geometry*.

The before-and-after paintings were kindly donated for me to play with by four local artist friends.

Without Jon Gillette I have no idea how I would have done any of the digital images.

Lindsey Gillard brought her broad range of skills in digital manipulation, animation, film and editing to the video project. I was lucky to find one person who could coordinate all that so competently and agreeably. Thanks to Rob Lillo and John Hickey for filming, Shane Cloutier for composing and playing the music, and Trevor MacKenzie for recording and mixing it.

Finally, I'd like to thank Laura Hickey for her constant support, encouragement and help throughout the whole project.

Dedication

I dedicate this book to that lively creative core in each of us and to our giving it meaningful and engaging expression.

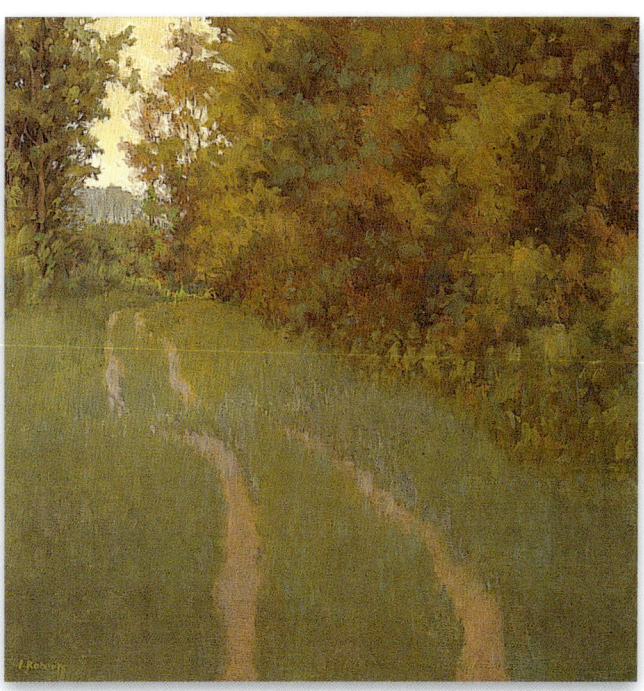

THE HILL NEAR ST. MEDIER
Oil on canvas · 24" × 24" (61cm × 61cm)

Table of Contents

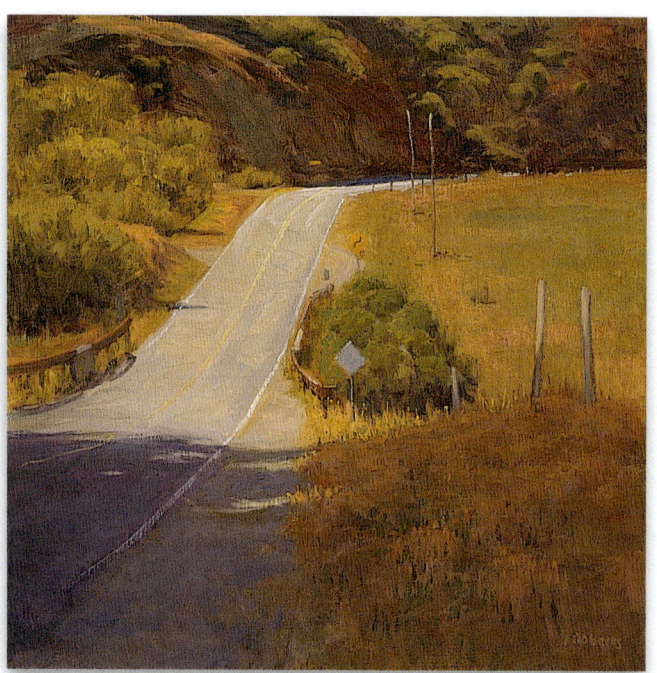

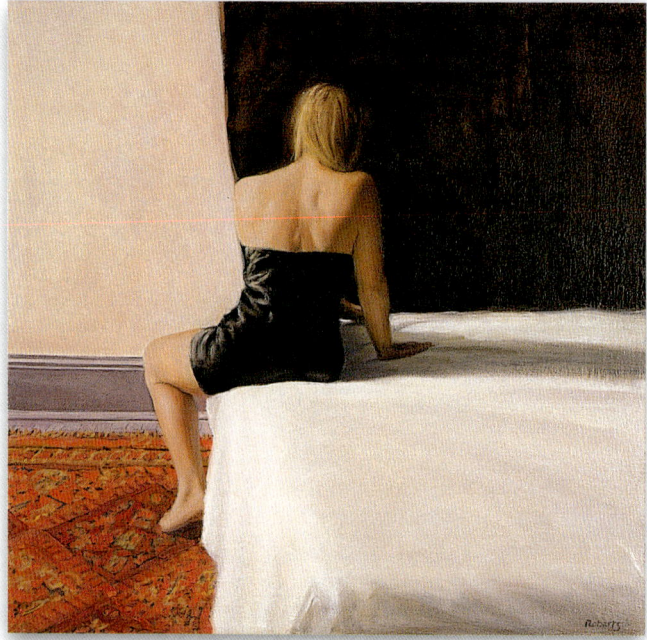

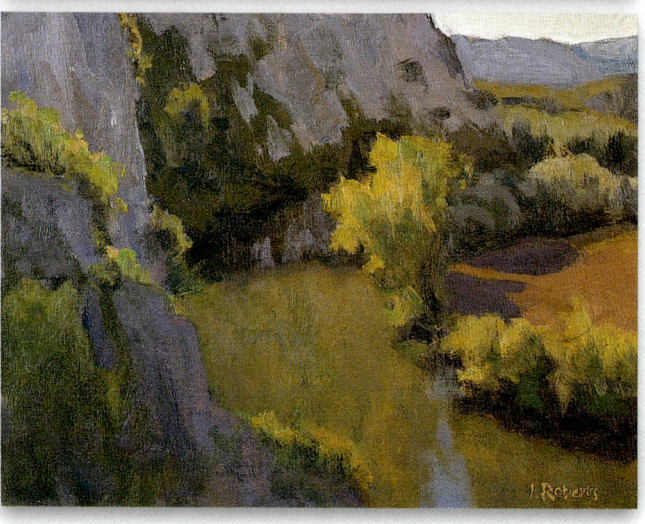

Introduction

When I was eleven years old, I accompanied my father, a professional landscape painter in Canada, along with several of his artist friends, on their annual painting trip to Cape Ann, Massachusetts. I had been allowed to come and paint, but only small 8" × 10" (20cm × 25cm) panels in oils. The most vivid memory I have of that trip—and others, as they became more frequent for me—was the painters' discussion and critique at the end of the day.

We'd prop the paintings up against rocks or lobster traps. I remember the discussion almost never concerned subject matter. It was as if it didn't exist. The comments would be: "I love the way you've got us moving past all that stuff on the left to come in on that hint of color on the right," or "I think the way you've got that huge dark gray shape holding all that space just for that little piece down in the bottom really works," or "That whole foreground area's too complicated; I'm getting hung up there and can't move back into the painting."

That's the way they thought about painting. It is the way I think any accomplished representational painter thinks about painting. In any case, it's how I learned to think about it, and I suppose, how I came to write this book.

Years later, I started teaching outdoor landscape painting workshops. I would, and still do, take groups to Provence, Tuscany, Maine and Taos, places that have really great potential for painting. But what I find interesting, particularly in Europe, is that the "subject"—the cypresses, the lavender fields (the worst culprit), the organic majesty of the old villages perched on a hillside—is so enticing that, at first, everyone's paintings look like postcards. They are painting "Provence." I can't tell you the number of wrought-iron street lamps I have seen in paint.

For the first day or two, when we arrive at a new place to paint, everyone gets out of the van and immediately sets up their easels to start painting—assuming, I suppose, that since they are on a painting trip they better get brush to canvas. So I spend my time as a teacher getting students to slow down and think "behind" the subject matter: think first about shapes, their arrangement on the

> To understand the whole, it is necessary to understand the parts. To understand the parts, it is necessary to understand the whole. Such is the circle of understanding.
> **Ken Wilber**

picture plane, and the visual flow being created in the painting. That is the subject of this book. The book probably could have been called *Shapes, Shapes, Shapes*—although that would need the subtitle *And Their Arrangement, Interaction and Flow on the Picture Plane*, which I admit is a bit clumsy.

While writing this book, I had to think much more deeply into a subject I had already been thinking about for years, breaking it down and creating exercises so that you could access the ideas simply and directly. What I hadn't expected was how much I learned, how much this project has affected my own understanding and spilled over into my own paintings.

The great thing about painting is that you can do it all your life and still be getting major revelations and ideas of where you want to go next. I hope this book offers you a revelation. Certainly it can help you build paintings more successfully and consistently—which is exciting and inspires you to want to paint more. Which leads to more insights and breakthroughs. Which leads to more inspiration. Which leads to better painting. Which leads to . . . well, you get the idea. A life spent in creative pursuit of your unique inspired vision. And what could be better than that!

Working Method

All the paintings in this book are oils on canvas, or canvas glued to board. All the landscapes 24" × 24" (61cm × 61cm) or smaller were done en plein air, that is, outdoors, from life. Anything larger was done either from a smaller oil sketch or a photograph. All the still lifes are from life. All the figures are from life, except *At the Café* (page 49), *Leanne* (page 6) and *Hailey* (page 97).

Looking at the steps of each demo is a bit misleading. The entire first block-in takes just thirty minutes to an hour, yet represents perhaps three steps in the demo. The refining of that block-in can then take several hours.

HIGHWAY #1, TOMALES
Oil on canvas · 24" × 24" (61cm × 61cm)

LEANNE
Oil on canvas · 24" × 24" (61cm × 61cm)

EVENING ON THE LOT
Oil on canvas · 9" × 12" (23cm × 30cm)

What Is Composition?

All art forms have the need for *composition*, or structure. Think of a musician playing a Bach fugue. He is conforming to a very specific arrangement and to the rules of harmonics. A writer, to syntax and grammar. For a painter, it is the visual dynamics of contrasts on the picture plane. Those dynamics function whether or not you believe them, see them or want them to, and they affect the success of every painting you make. Learning to work with and master those dynamics is composition.

Really great composition is a mystery. How did Rembrandt do *The Company of Frans Banning Cocq and Willem van Ruytenburch* (*The Night Watch*), or Velázquez *Las Meninas*? How did they even think of it? I don't know. And this book won't teach you that. But one thing is for certain: strong, engaging composition does not appear miraculously at the end, when you are putting the finishing touches on a painting. Strong compositions are built in considered steps right from the beginning. "Well begun is half done" really applies here.

When you are really grabbed by a painting you see across a room in a gallery, what are you responding to? Details, highlights or fine brushwork? You probably can't see those from that far away. Is it the medium, oils or watercolor? Again, you may not be able to tell. Is it the subject matter? Even this probably wasn't what really grabbed your attention; there might be a painting with a similar subject next to it that you didn't even notice. You respond to a few simple value masses arranged on a picture plane. That's what you see and respond to across a room—big shapes and their contrasts. You may then go up closer, finding more and more to engage you. Or not. But if the big design sense isn't clear, it's unlikely that you'll go up to it for a second look. A painting succeeds or fails because of its arrangement of major abstract value masses.

I use the word *abstract* here carefully. When listening to a symphony by Mozart, you don't listen for the sounds of birds and wind and rustling leaves and get confused when you don't hear them.

Music is abstract; its subject is structure and relationships. Painting is the same. Sometimes we refer to certain paintings as "abstract," but it is less confusing to call these paintings nonrepresentational. All painting is abstract, even a photorealistic painting. It is abstracted from the three-dimensional into a series of shapes on a two-dimensional plane. The more engaging those abstract shapes in relation to the picture plane, the more engaging the painting.

Learning to master composition means learning to see abstractly. One of the definitions of *abstract* is "to draw away from." You've chosen something to paint because it excites you. But you have to "draw away from" the world of boats and horses, flowers and faces, and respond to what you've chosen to paint in terms of light and dark color shapes. If you paint in terms of subjects, your focus becomes too narrow too early. When you think in terms of shapes, you don't worry about the subject until the major arrangement and flow of shapes is working. Ironically, when you give enough attention to the shapes—their color and how they fit together—the subject will appear automatically.

Learning to paint can be frustrating if you concentrate on subjects. No matter how much time you spend and how much reworking you do, so many paintings will remain unresolved and unresolvable. However, if you concentrate on shapes and flow, you will "see" your painting, see the actual visual dynamics on your canvas, which you can respond to and adjust consciously and effectively.

Seeing composition in terms of shapes and flow is not an intellectual idea you apply; it's a perceptual shift. It is something you can learn on the level of experience and performance through exercises. It isn't tricks or gimmicks for a quick fix. It is the foundation that all great representational painting rests on, and it will dramatically improve the way you paint.

As music is the poetry of sound so is painting the poetry of sight, and the subject matter has nothing to do with harmony of sound or color.

James Whistler

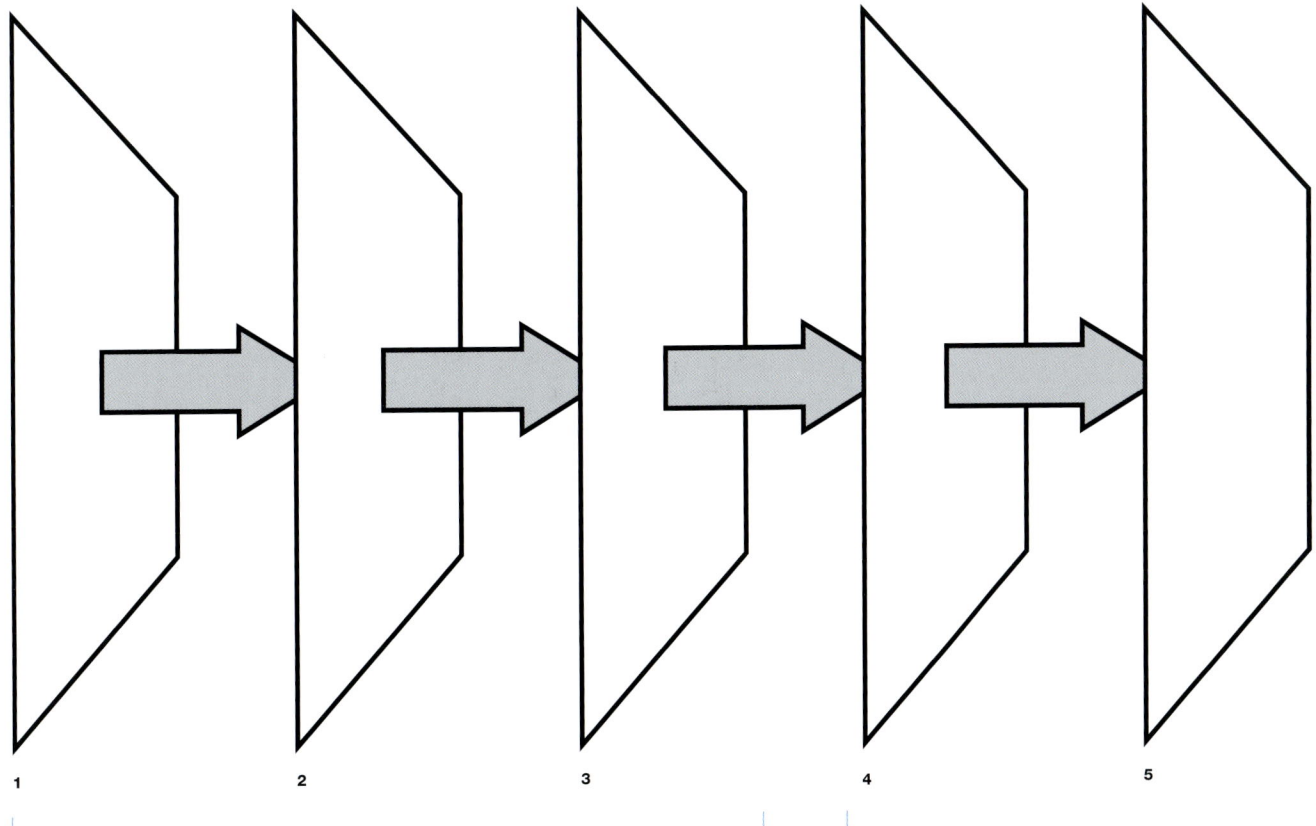

1   2   3   4   5

This is where the real artistic thinking has to occur before you start to paint.

This is so often where inexperienced painters focus their attention. The result is a lack of artistic clarity and drama in their paintings.

The Foundation of the Painting

1. The Dynamics of the Picture Plane. Each proportion and scale of every painting—square, vertical or horizontal—has its own special dynamic that affects and is affected by every mark or shape you put on it. The edges of your picture plane are the four most important lines in your composition since they, in the most basic sense, define the foundation you are starting with.

2. Armature. The fundamental lines of direction or flow that connect the main compositional movement to the picture plane.

3. Abstract Shapes. The building blocks of the painting. Each shape is interacting with every other shape. Resolving this interplay is the main arena of painting. This really is where the success or failure of the painting lies.

4. Subjects. Bottles, mountains, kids on beaches.

5. Details. Highlights, wrought-iron street lamps and almost anything else painted with a little pointed brush.

Most students come in at step 4, gripped immediately by the subject. Now you do need to get excited about what you want to paint. To structure a painting means taking that idea and seeing it in relation to step 1, then steps 2 and 3. That may not take long. Perhaps you're lucky and most of what you need is available. However, an experienced painter will often abandon an idea because, although interesting and engaging, there's no way to get it to work as a composition. Subjects do not make compositions. Compositions are made through the arrangement of abstract value masses on a picture plane.

Remember that a picture—before being a battle horse, a nude woman, or some anecdote—is essentially a plane surface covered with colors assembled in a certain order.
Maurice Denis

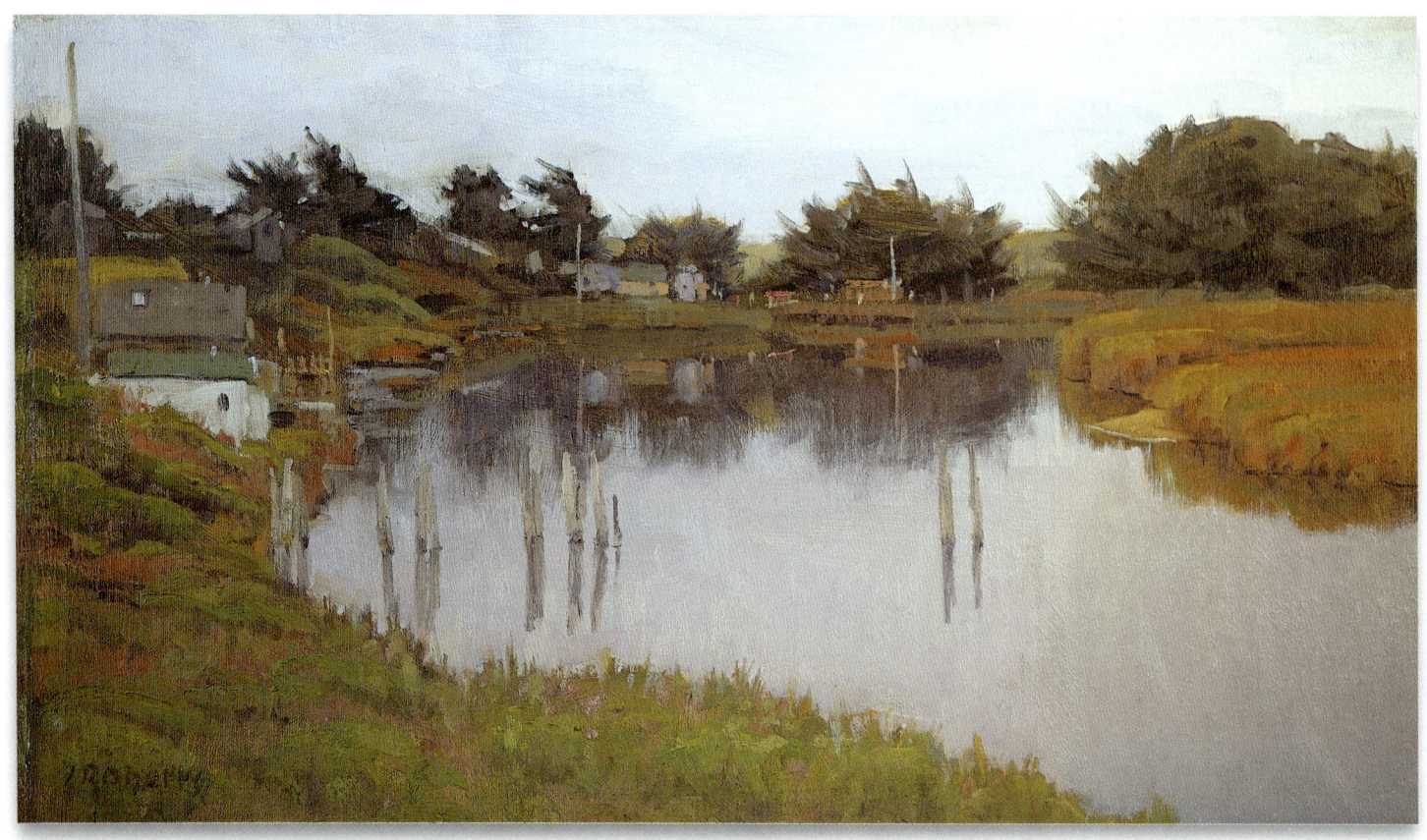

SALMON CREEK
Oil on canvas · 13" × 24" (33cm × 61cm)

Composition is so fundamental to the creation of pictures that a list of the world's greatest pictures would overlap a list of the greatest compositions in a majority of titles. Yet of all the elements in the art of painting, composition is the one least recognized by the average observer, even when it is playing a major part in his reaction to a picture.

John Canaday

If you can remember learning to drive a car, particularly if it was a stick shift, you will remember how overwhelming it was to think about all those actions at once. It felt as if your brain were seizing up in confusion. With practice, driving became easier and smoother. Now you could probably drive, talk on the phone and eat chips all at the same time (although I wouldn't recommend it). The component skills of driving the car are so integrated, they've become second nature.

Learning to paint is a similar experience. At first, there are so many things to think about, you get overwhelmed and confused. The brush is moving, but the brain has stopped.

If your paintings are to work consistently, you must juggle a lot of skills simultaneously. However, there are a finite number of these skills, and they can be mastered far more easily in isolation. Then, later, when you are painting, you'll see how one newly mastered skill connects to another and then to another. Before long, you will have integrated them all. You need these skills to convincingly give voice to your own expressive nature. Skills and expression are bound together.

So that you get the maximum benefit from this book, I propose you conduct a period of self-directed study, without feeling pressured to make great art. As artists, we're always having to rethink and reassess. Setting up this study period gives you a chance to go through the process without feeling that the product defines you, whether good or bad.

This book has both intellectual concepts and practical exercises for each of the various skills needed to master painting. Do the exercises that interest you the most. You could work through them systematically, but you will know or feel ones that attract you and would benefit you the most.

When you're working on a new painting, think in terms of value masses and color shapes. Work with the major shapes. If you just can't seem to pull off a visually arresting arrangement, rethink it or start another painting. Don't waste your time adding details to a composition whose major masses don't interest or engage you.

The other important aspect of this period of study is to stay attentive. Like a tennis player who must keep an eye on the ball at all times, painting requires being present. Slow down, plan your painting and be patient with yourself.

The exercise I would really encourage you to be disciplined about is the "composition-a-day" drawing (see page 62). It is a very functional tool that will help you grow and expand as a representational artist. You can do it anywhere, anytime with a minimum of equipment. Practice daily; that's where progress happens. Practice creates neural pathways in the brain, making what you are practicing easier and more effortless. With time, you'll have more and more attention free for the moment-to-moment flow of creativity when you paint. This exercise also engages you holistically with the perceptual shift of seeing in terms of shapes and the picture plane. Do one a day for a year and you'll be in a different league as an artist. You will be producing design-driven rather than subject-driven compositions.

You'd never question the need of a musician, regardless of talent, to spend at least an hour or two practicing daily. Somehow there's this idea that painters don't need to practice. Painters are born with talent, and you've either got it or you don't. It's not true. To get better at painting, you must practice.

This book has been designed to break the mastery of painting into its component parts so that your practice becomes most effective, productive and enlightening.

The Road to Mastery

Unconscious incompetence

Conscious incompetence

Conscious competence

Unconscious competence

Anonymous

Talent is the ability to do hard work in a consistently constructive direction over a long period of time.

James Whistler

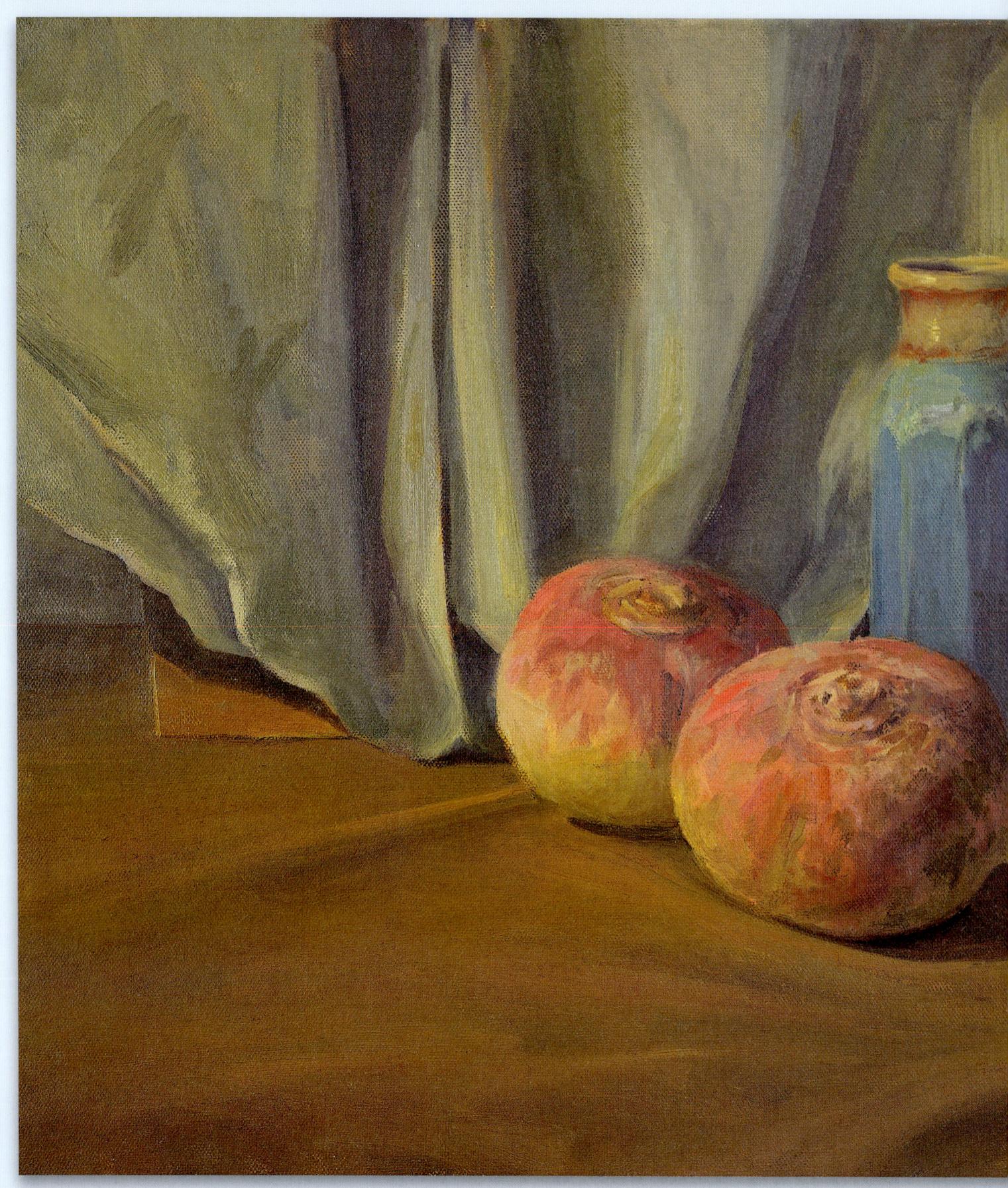

TURNIPS AND BLUE
Oil on canvas · 16" × 20" (41cm × 51cm)

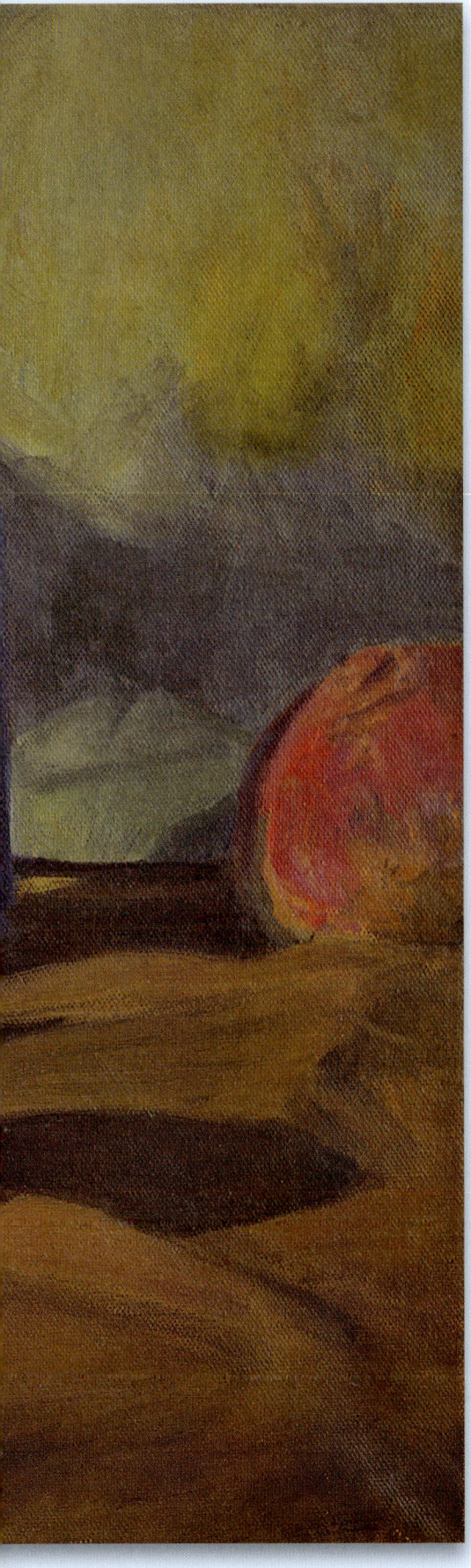

CHAPTER ONE

Armatures

Shapes make the painting. However, those shapes need to be arranged and adjusted to create a coherent flow. That flow is what I call the *armature*. It is the backbone of the painting.

Just as the picture plane has dynamics, the armature is the first and perhaps most important dynamic you create on the picture plane. It is the overriding theme of movement and structure in the painting. Often, when you are looking for something to paint, it's the armature that presents itself first. It then will help define the proportions of the major shapes and how you will lead the viewer's eye into and through the painting.

Study the Masters

When we think of the Old Masters, we don't think of people like you and me. Rather, we think of someone mythical, elevated and unapproachable. But, fundamentally, they were doing exactly what we're trying to do—only they brought an extraordinary level of tradition, craft and vision to their art.

Nevertheless, there is good reason to look at their work carefully. The Old Masters really understood composition, the dynamics of the picture plane and the need for planning and preparation. When you recognize the amount of preparation that went into their work, you start to understand that their process was a bit more human and accessible. They didn't leave much to chance. They put a lot of thought and drawing into their compositions before they ever came close to touching brush to canvas.

Even with all that preparation, they still found parts that didn't work, figures that had to be removed or shifted around. If we learn only one thing from the Old Masters, let's learn this: Don't be in a hurry to get your brush into the paint. Slow down and plan your composition before picking up your brushes. The great artists of the past knew what they were doing.

In these three examples, by Peter Paul Rubens, Rogier van der Weyden and Francisco de Goya, you will see that the artists:

1. Built an armature to "hold" their complex figure compositions within the picture plane.
2. Based their armature on the proportions of that picture plane.

The good news is that most of the paintings you're likely to paint won't be as large or nearly as complex as these are. So you're not likely to need such elaborate armatures.

The point is the Old Masters did use armatures. They spent a lot of time planning them. Then they built their paintings on top. In most pieces the armature is largely hidden, yet it's influence is still clearly felt. If this technique was good enough for the Old Masters, it's probably good enough for us.

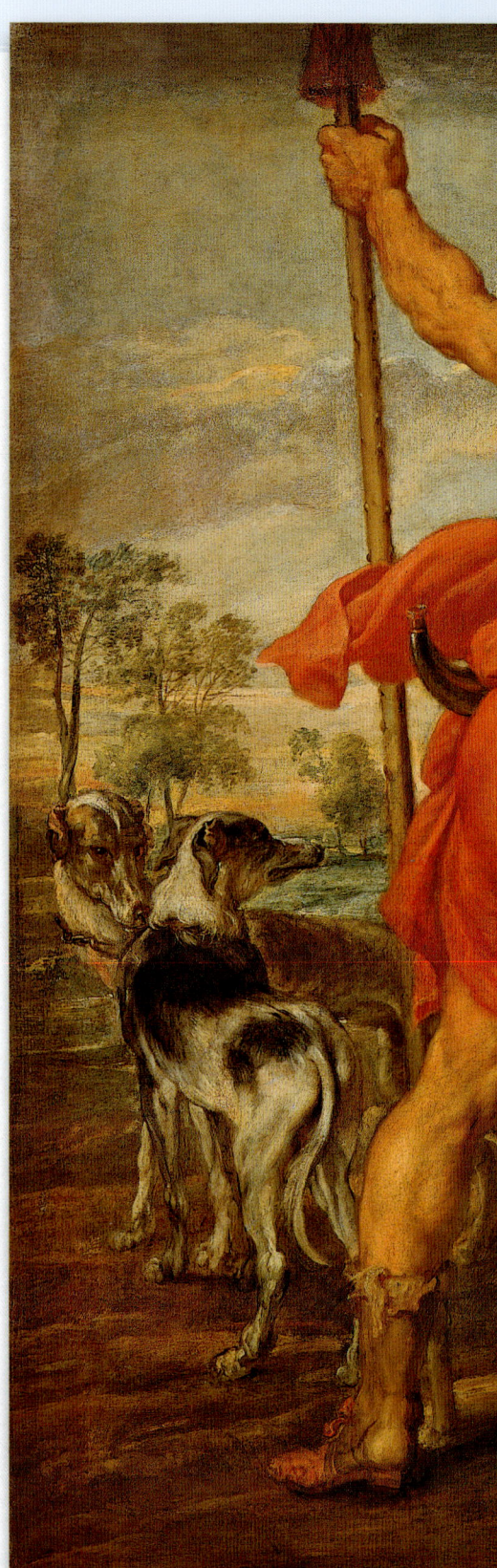

Peter Paul Rubens (1577–1640). Venus and Adonis (1635). Oil on canvas, 77¾" × 95⅝" (197cm × 243cm). The Metropolitan Museum of Art, gift of Harry Payne Bingham, 1937 (37.162), New York, New York, U.S.A. Photograph © 1983 The Metropolitan Museum of Art

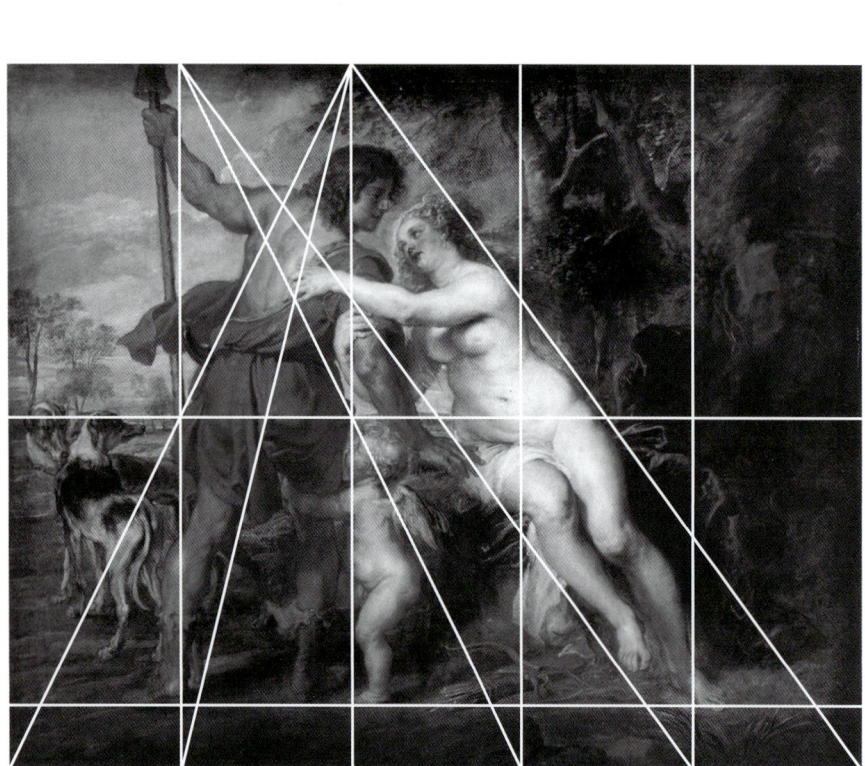

The Metropolitan Museum of Art, reproduced with permission

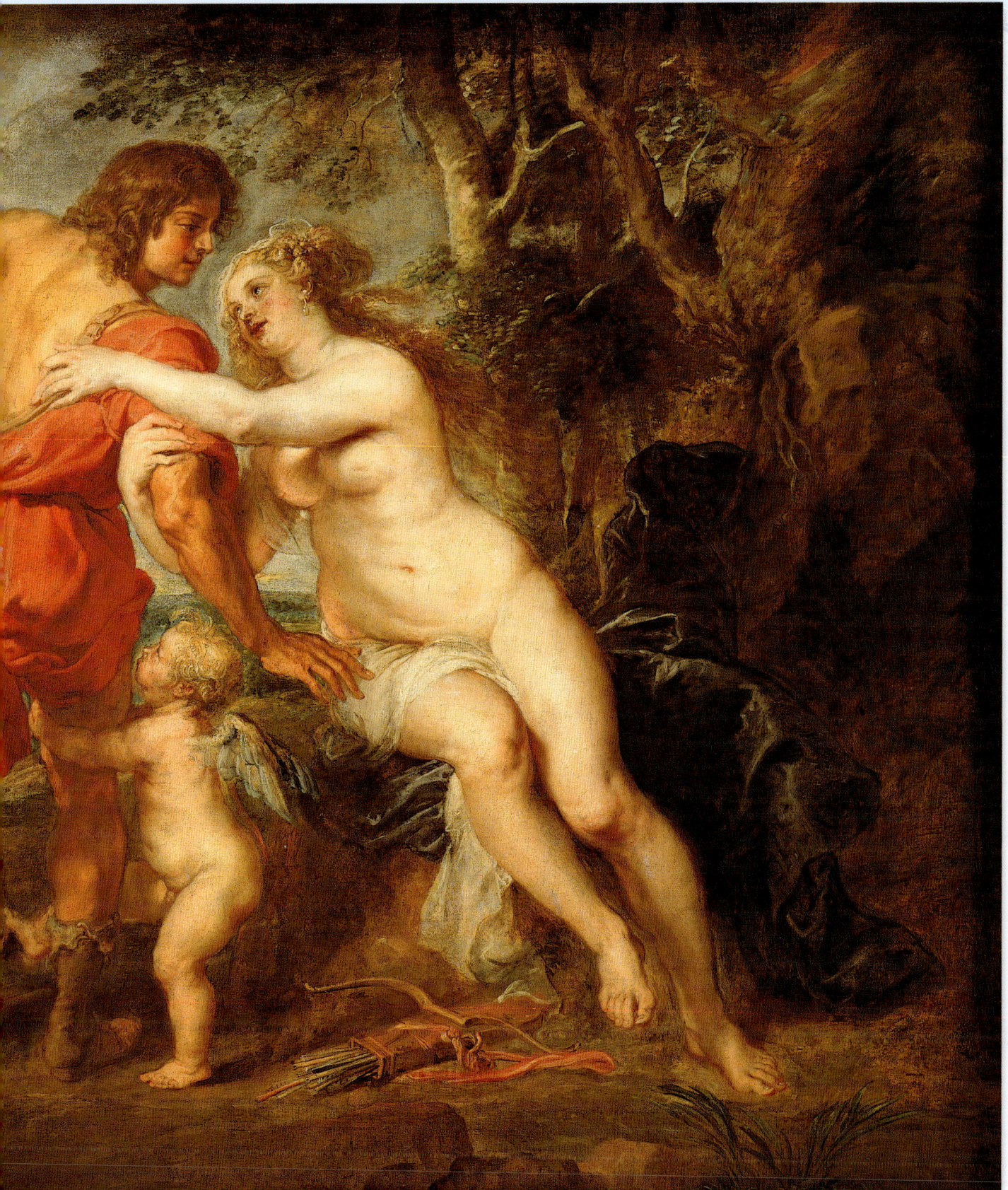

Using Structure for Placement

We have no record of the exact structure Rubens used for this painting. Whether it's this structure (which seems likely) or a variation isn't as important as how obvious it is that a structure was established. Rubens appears to have divided the canvas vertically into fifths. Dropping verticals from those points between the top and bottom edge, it isn't hard to see the major structural lines—the *armature*—he used to house his figures on the picture plane.

Notice the second vertical from the right. It lines up with the edge of the tree at the top, disappears behind Venus's body and then reap-

pears lining up with the drapery below Venus's knee. You can create a structural line, but it doesn't need to continue all the way through the painting visually.

You can also see the three-dimensional circle of attention Rubens created around Venus's hips, through the head of the *putto* (cherub), along the back of the dog and then curving right along its nose on to the horizon—which, interestingly, divides the canvas in half—and then again wrapping forward around Venus.

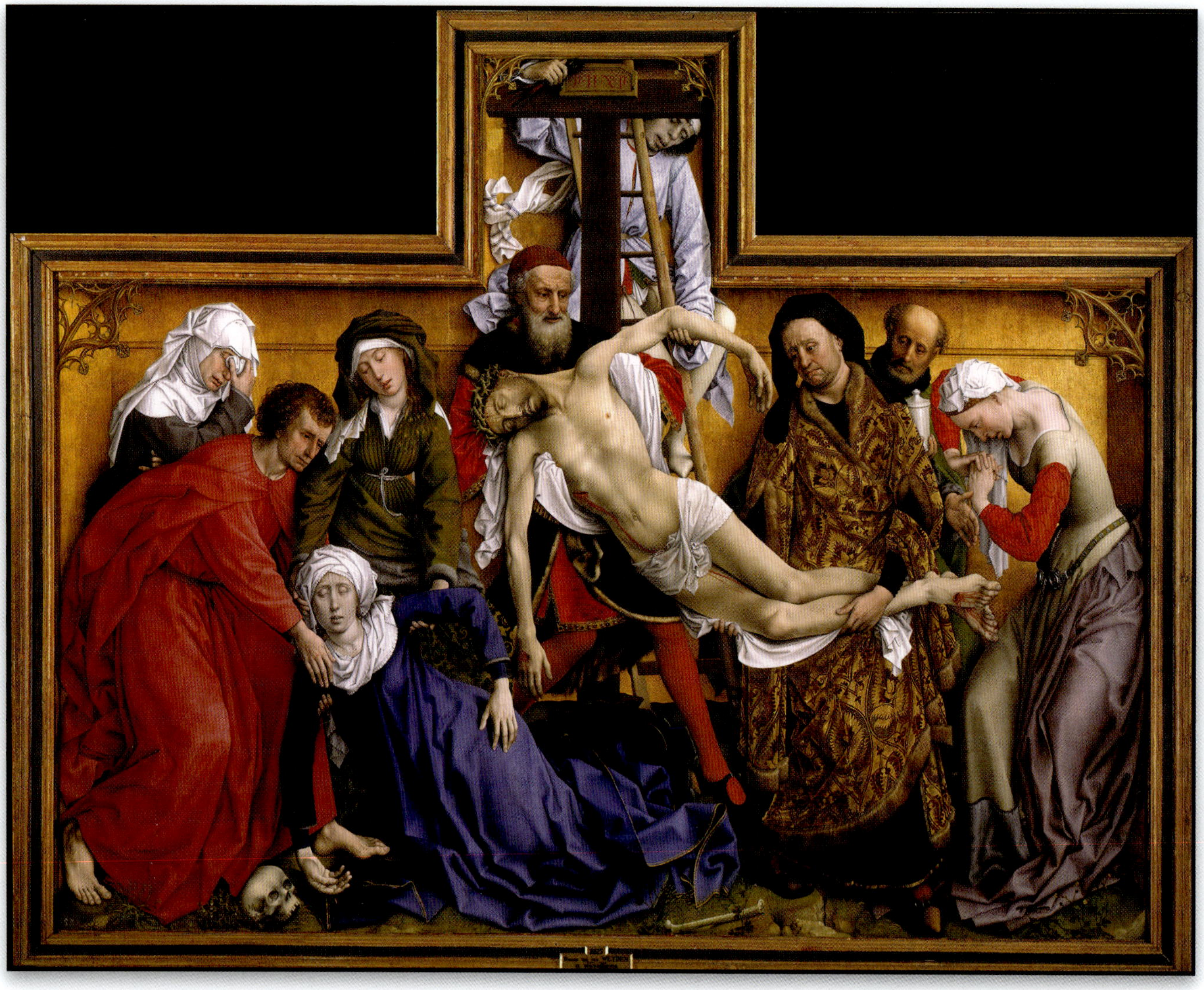

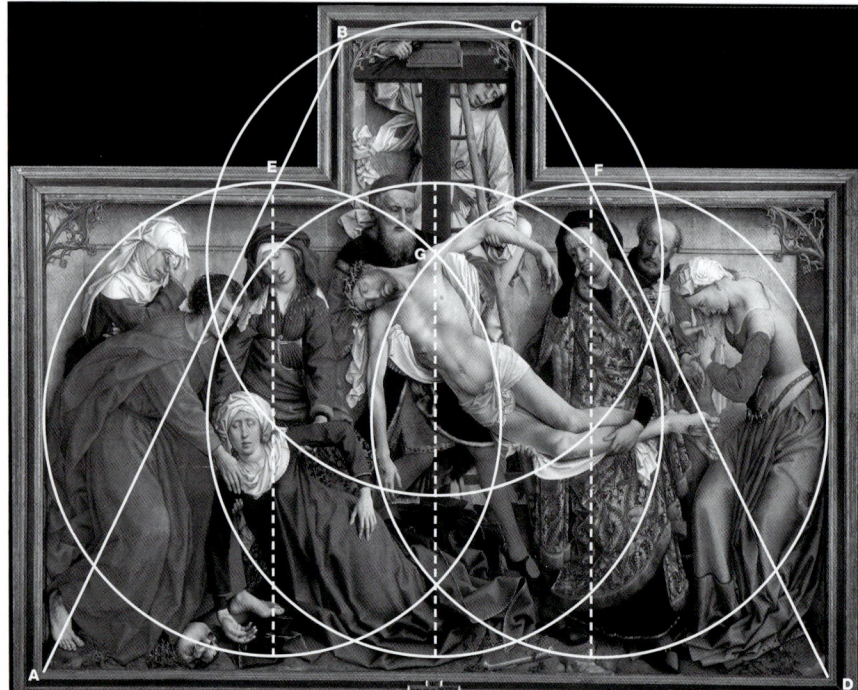

Rogier van der Weyden (1399–1464). *Deposition From the Cross* (1440). Oil on panel, 86⅝" × 104" (220cm × 262 cm). © Museo Nacional del Prado, Madrid, Spain

Museo Nacional del Prado, reproduced with permission

Structure and Fluidity

Standing in front of this piece is a rich lesson in what painting is capable of achieving. Its formal structure is elaborate and precise, and yet Van der Weyden has used it with such creativity and fluidity that you never feel he's forcing it.

The small rectangle at the top of the painting falls on the golden section of the width of the larger rectangle. A line drawn through AB and CD creates points E and F at their intersection with the top edge of the main rectangle. Verticals dropped from those points form the centers of two of the circles in the composition. The intersection of those two circles at G forms the center of a third circle and the center line of the rectangle forms the center of the fourth circle.

OK, you're thinking, he must have been a mathematician. But look at the painting. You can feel the armature forming the figures in the picture plane, yet, for all that structure, it seems so natural and flexible. It is created and then sucked back in behind the picture so it isn't intrusive. It supports without distracting us.

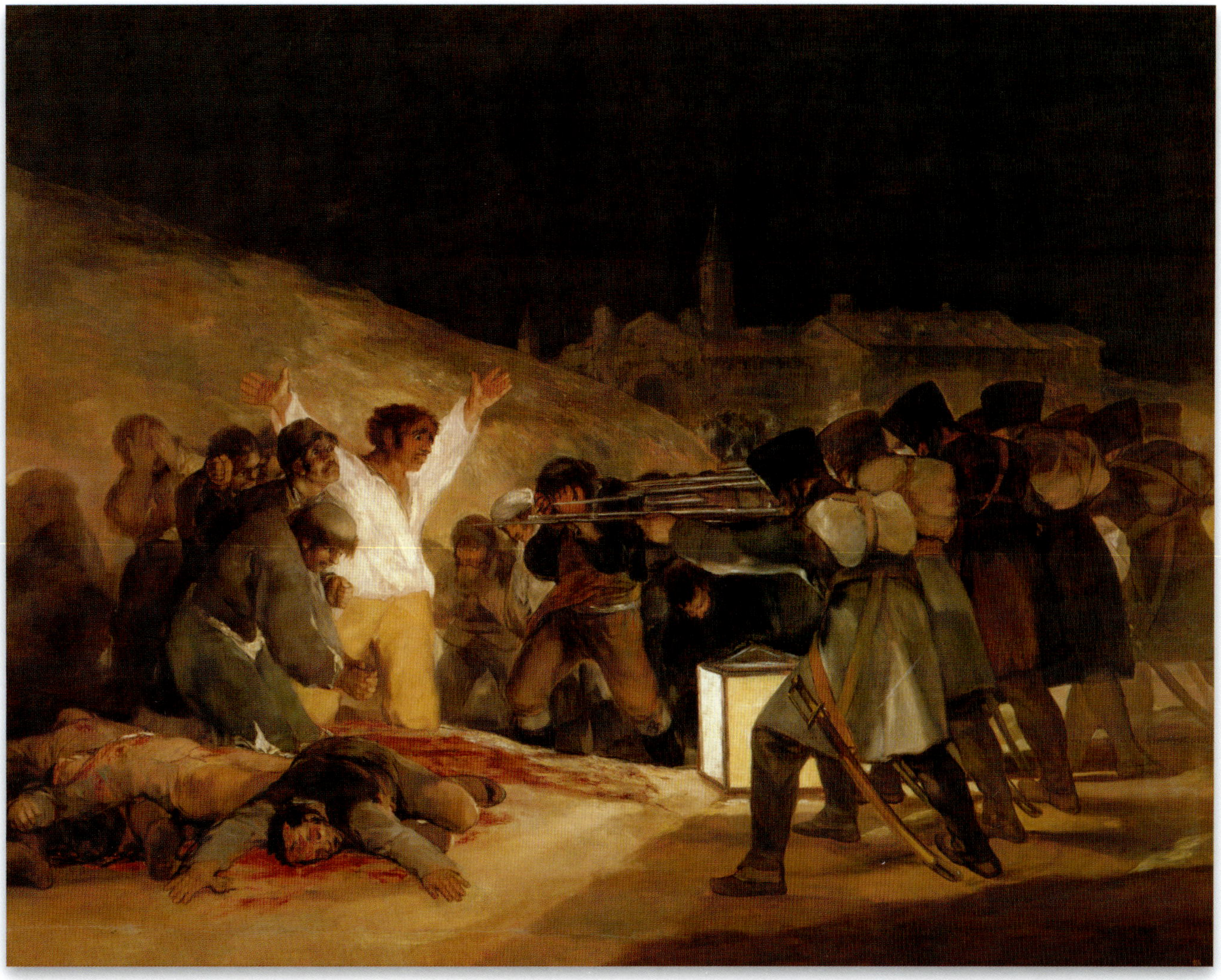

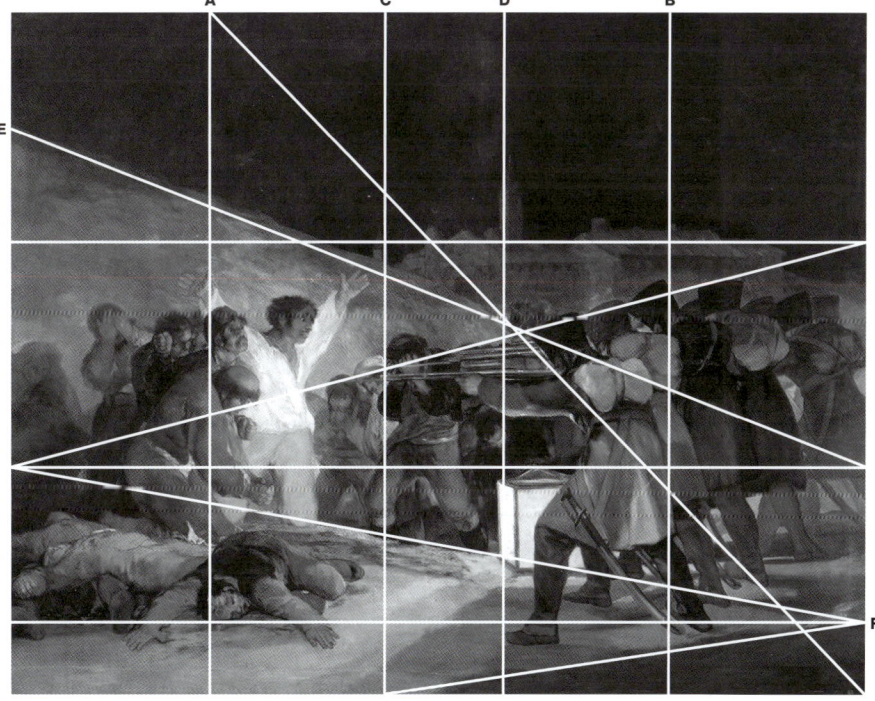

Francisco de Goya (1746–1828). *Executions of the Third of May, 1808* (1814). Oil on canvas, 104¾" × 135⅞" (266cm × 345cm). © Museo Nacional del Prado, Madrid, Spain

Creating Drama

This painting has punch, especially when you're standing in front of it. It's huge. Goya used the ratio of the proportions of the rectangle to create the armature. This was a common practice, dating back to pre-Renaissance artists. The verticals at A and B are the height of the canvas set along the width from both the left and right. Both C and D intersect the width of the painting in the same ratio as the height is to the width (OK, so he's a mathematician too). Notice again how the structural line D defines the left side of the tower, disappears, and then reappears at the left edge of the lantern.

Horizontally the painting is divided into thirds. The top third divided in half is the starting point of the wall on the left and forms the line of the town in the distance. The bottom third divided in thirds gives the line of the shadow along the bottom right and the line of the top step. Diagonals between the thirds create the structure for the powerful movement across the canvas. Again, it isn't a rigid "I can't move" structure. It allows Goya to design the drama and the movement with the assurance that it's resting on something substantial.

Museo Nacional del Prado, reproduced with permission

The Four Most Important Compositional Lines

Before you think about putting any mark on your paper or canvas, you must consider the four most important lines in your composition: the four that define the boundaries of your painting or drawing. To call them the four most important lines may seem like an exaggeration as you look at a still life and see all those wonderful shapes and shadows and highlights and think how enticing it will be to paint them.

But slow down a minute. Let's think about this. Each rectangle has a proportion of height to width. Each proportion affects the dynamic of everything happening within the piece. How are the abstract shapes you will be using in your composition going to interact with the proportions you have chosen for your canvas? This question is

fundamental; the success of your painting depends on it.

Once we have proportions, we have a picture plane. Once we have a picture plane, we have created a dynamic field of play.

You may think this is self-evident. However, in my experience, it is not unusual to work with a student on a thumbnail, sorting out the proportions, planning a composition and encouraging him or her to begin painting, only to come back an hour later and find the almost-square drawing that held such promise now jammed and stretched to fit into a 12" × 16" (30cm × 41cm) canvas. There's a lot to think about when you start a painting, but it's very unlikely that that composition, and therefore that painting, will improve with unconscious transformation.

Creating better paintings is more than just developing better painting skills. You are isolating the world within a rectangle. What you are looking at, whether a landscape, still life or figure, is going to be translated into a series of shapes that interacts directly and intimately with that rectangle. Choosing those shapes and learning to see how their arrangement affects the viewer's eye movement through that rectangle is a major challenge to you, the artist. This is not the time to worry about how to paint the highlight on a bottle. First you must determine how to transform what you've found "out there" in the world into a dynamic, engaging composition that works.

The Most Common Proportions

1:1 All squares
1:2 10" × 20" (25cm × 51cm), 12" × 24" (30cm × 61cm)
2:3 20" × 30" (51cm × 76cm), 24" × 36" (61cm × 91cm)
3:4 9" × 12" (23cm × 30cm), 12" × 16" (30cm × 41cm), 18" × 24" (46cm × 61cm)
4:5 8" × 10" (20cm × 25cm), 16" × 20" (41cm × 51cm), 24" × 30" (61cm × 76cm)
5:6 10" × 12" (25cm × 30cm), 20" × 24" (51cm × 61cm)

Most of these sizes are available commercially in watercolor blocks and stretched canvases. I used to be more of a purist in my search for the perfect proportions for a composition. However, I ended up with too many frames, specially made for some painting that never sold, with odd dimensions like 16½" × 19¼" (42cm × 49cm). So now I stick to commercially standard sizes.

Note that the metric dimensions provided here are simply conversions of the English system measurements. In countries where the metric system is in use, the standard dimensions will be more regular (20cm × 30cm, for example), but these conversions will give you the general idea of the sizes you're looking for.

Eight Common Armatures

The eight armatures in this section appear over and over again in representational painting. I am providing fairly obvious examples to make the point, but you can see how they are working behind the scenes to support the composition.

You don't need to be dogmatic about using armatures. You could have a composition that combines two types of armature. The demonstration at the end of this chapter (see pages 37–41) is a good example of an S armature and the use of horizontals and verticals. I have seen students, new to the idea, agonizing over whether their composition is an S or an L, feeling bound and restricted by it. If it works, use a W or upside-down P.

The important point is to create a structure that will establish the placement of the major masses of your composition and the eye's movement through them. You want the armature to have a supporting role. It's the strong, silent type—like the wire structure hidden beneath a sculptor's clay. You can't actually see the wire, but its role is apparent in every gesture and line of the figure.

You want to use armatures that present themselves naturally in a composition. Use the big masses of what you are looking at to help you. The armature doesn't exist in isolation. It is created by the interplay of the major masses of what's in front of you.

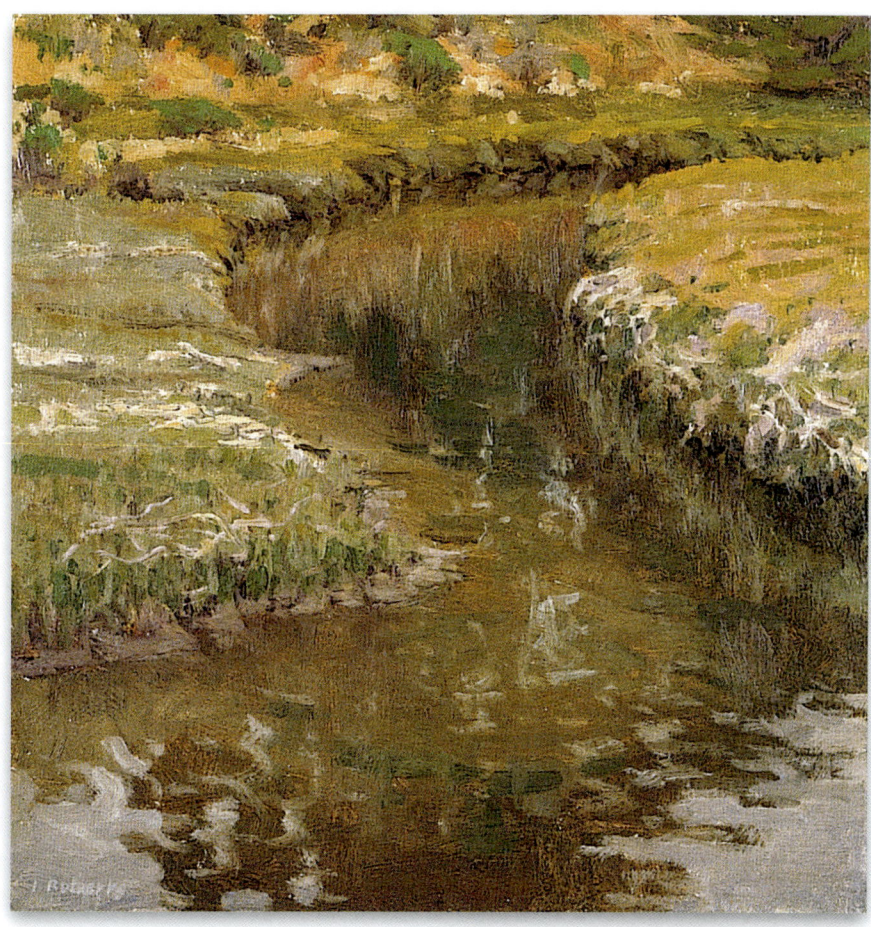

TOMALES ESTUARY
Oil on canvas · 12" × 12" (30cm × 30cm)

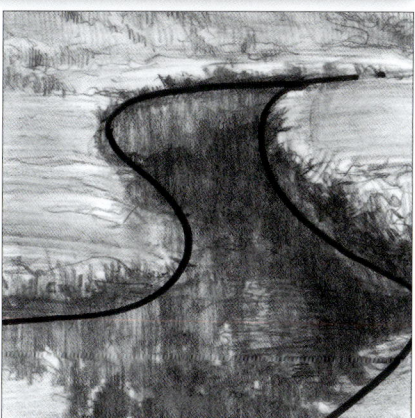

1. S

You find this type of armature in landscapes all the time because there are so many curves in nature. If the S moves beyond the edge of the picture plane, as it does here on the lower right, be careful that the visual motion of the armature doesn't shoot the viewer out of the painting. In the same way that the Old Masters used a line in the armature that disappeared and reappeared, you can de-emphasize the armature where you need to so it holds less attention. Here, the line of the armature becomes more hidden as it heads toward the upper right to ensure that we don't follow the line right out of the picture.

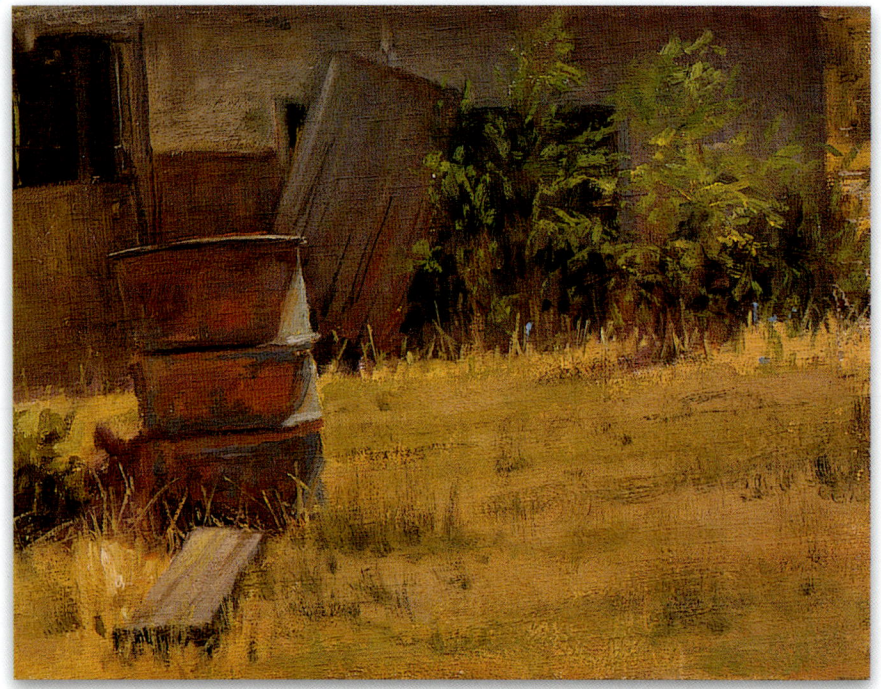

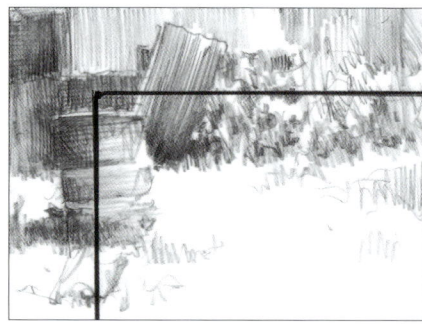

FARM SCENE
Oil on canvas · 9" × 12" (23cm × 30cm)

2. L

With the L you'll find your center of interest usually along one of the arms near the L's intersection. Both arms of the L should hold less and less attention as they move out toward the edge of the picture plane. You can configure the L four different ways, upside down or back to front.

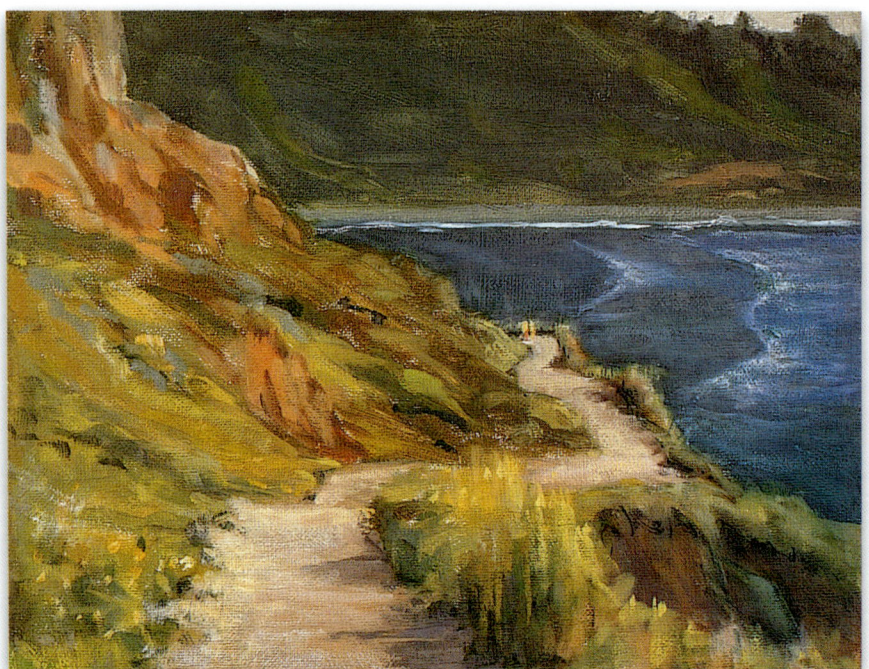

PALOS VERDES SURF
Oil on canvas · 9" × 12" (23cm × 30cm)

3. Diagonal

Be careful with this one because the angle of the diagonal tends to gain momentum, particularly if it's moving top left to bottom right. That's because the diagonal has the most dynamism in relation to its rectangular frame. So the armature needs to be de-emphasized at both ends as it nears the edge of the painting, as I've done here. You'll often find that a good horizontal or vertical will help break that momentum, too.

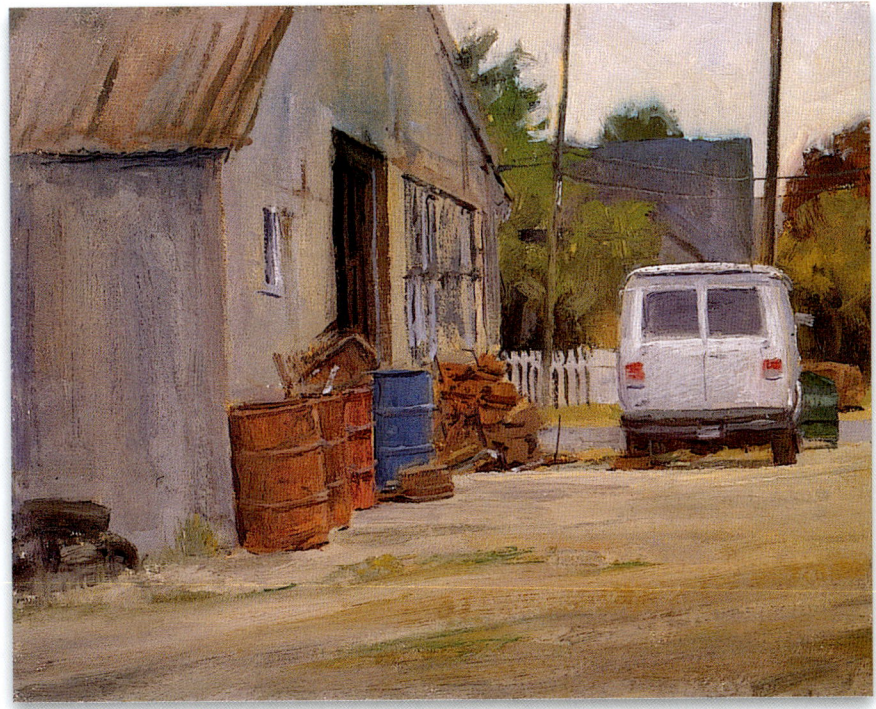

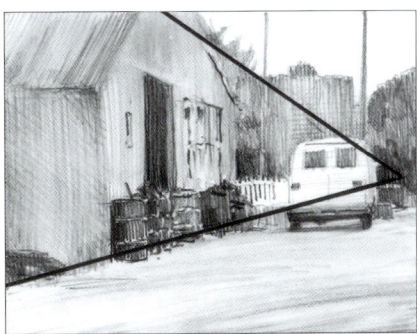

STEVE'S WELDING SHOP
Oil on canvas · 11" × 14" (28cm × 36cm)

4. Triangle

Perspective lines often create the triangle. Most commonly, the center of interest is near or on one of the angles of the triangle. If it isn't in your composition, you might ask yourself why you're using a triangle. What role it is playing then? Again, you want to make sure that the lines of the structure don't gain so much momentum that the eye shoots past your center of interest and out of the painting.

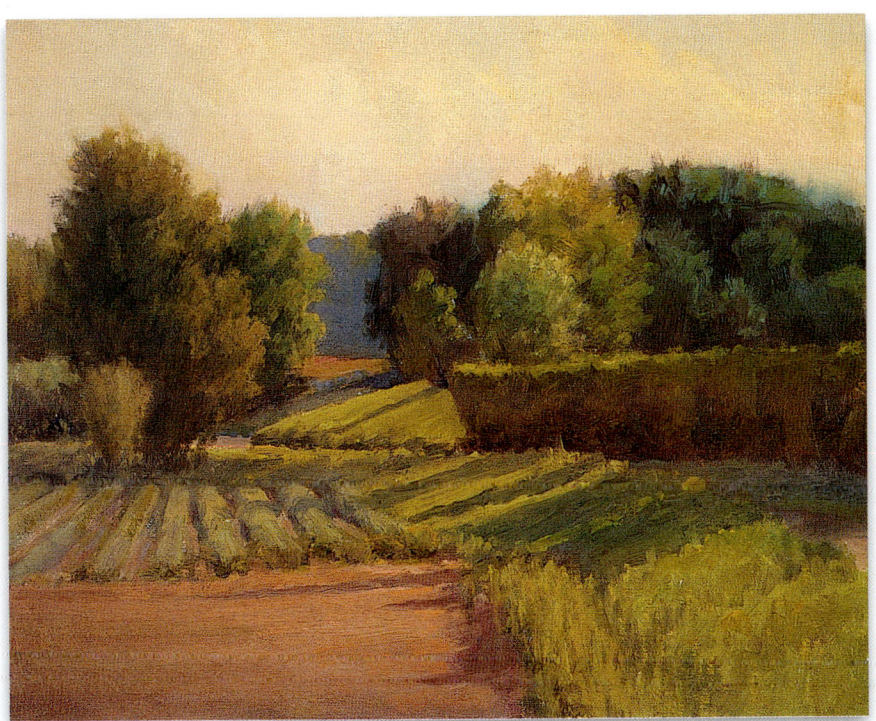

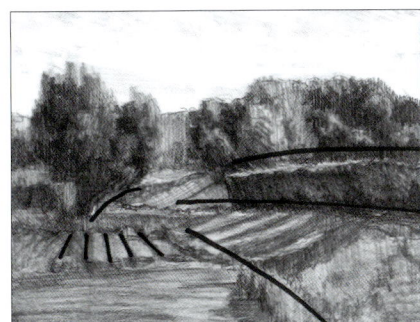

EVENING LIGHT IN GRIGNON
Oil on canvas · 12" × 15" (30cm × 38cm)

5. Radiating Lines

An obvious example of radiating lines is one-point perspective, where everything in the picture converges on one point. The problem with this is that you may get our attention to that point so fast we have no time to linger and meander around your painting. Give us the chance to enjoy the journey you're creating in your painting. You can use radiating lines to pull us in, and opposing, weaker lines (as in the field in the foreground) to slow us down.

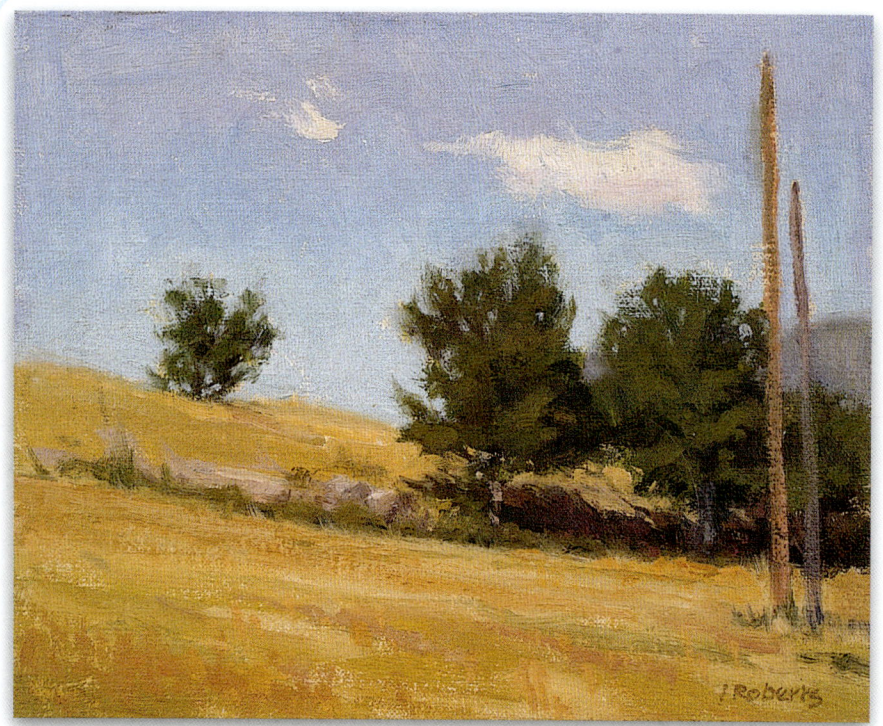

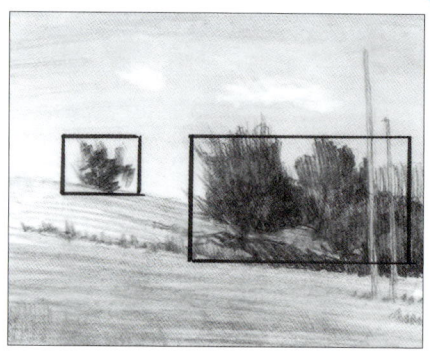

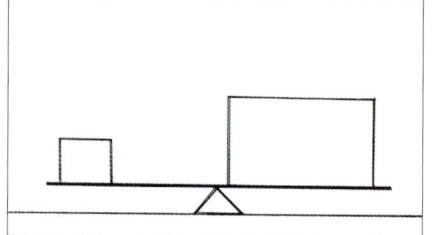

AFTERNOON IN AUREL
Oil on canvas · 8" × 10" (20cm × 25cm)

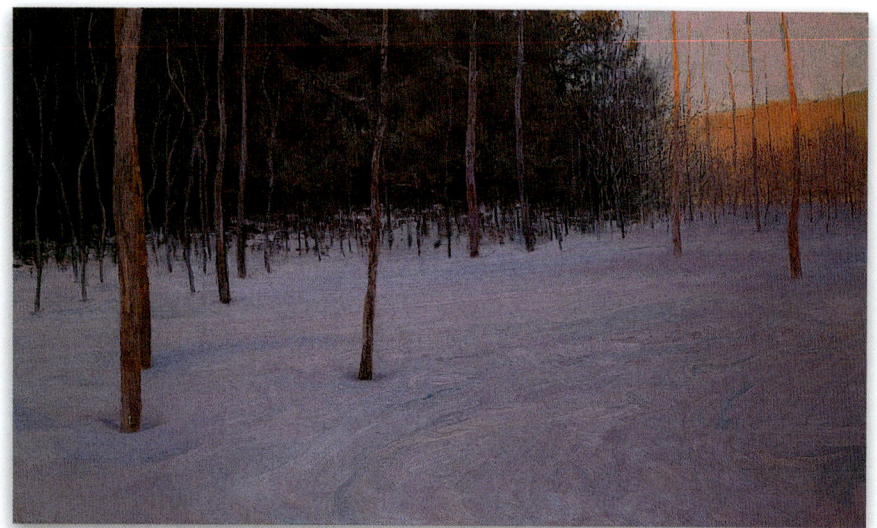

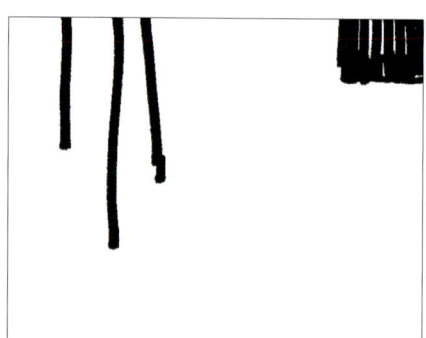

FIRST LIGHT AT KOLAPORE
Oil on canvas · 48" × 72" (122cm × 183cm)

6. Fulcrum

The idea of the fulcrum is interesting because, in fact, all of painting is a balancing act of large to small, light to dark, warm to cool, detailed to simple. It's all a question of balance.

As an armature, the fulcrum allows for a balancing of the major masses, usually smaller against larger, as it is here, to create a dynamic balance. If the two masses are too close in size, they will create a static balance, which is less engaging. Try a composition using the fulcrum and see how far you can push the dynamism of that balance.

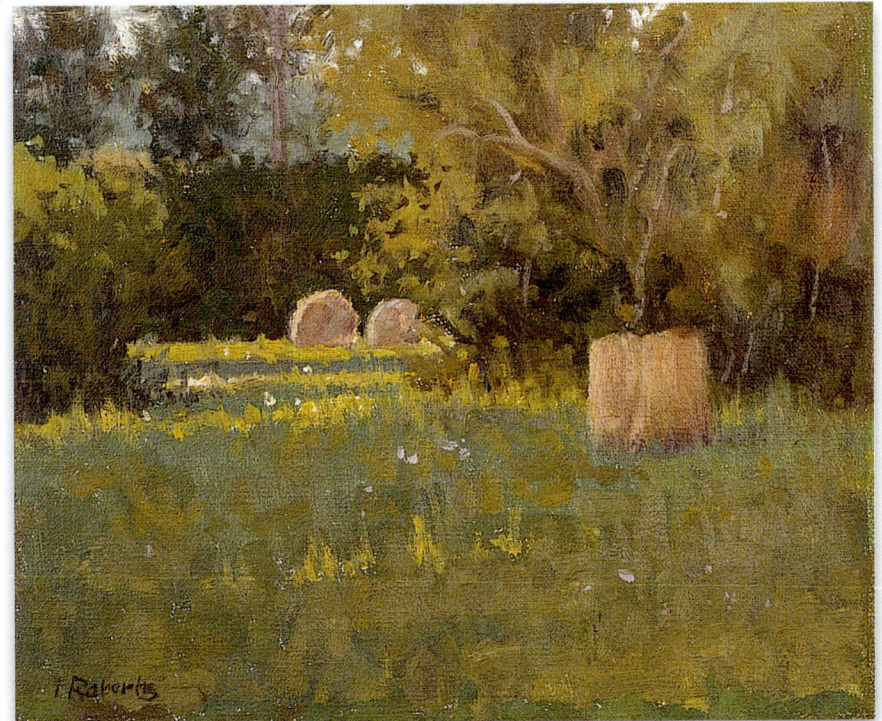

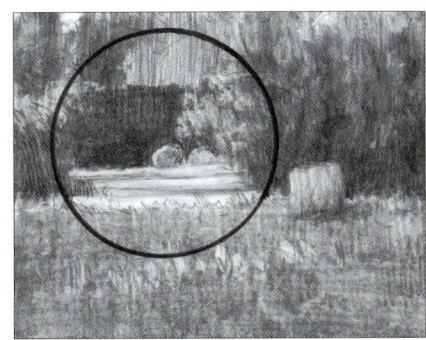

LATE SUMMER IN THE PAYS DE SAULT
Oil on canvas · 8" × 10" (20cm × 25cm)

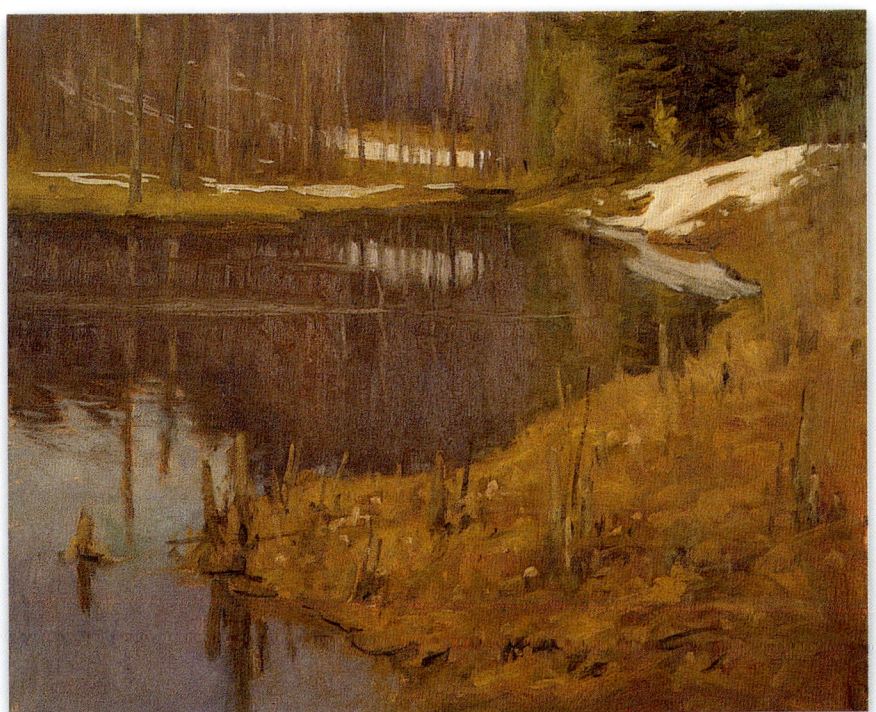

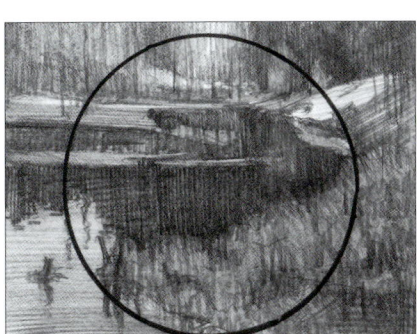

LAST SNOW IN THE VALLEY
Oil on canvas · 16" × 20" (41cm × 51cm)

7. O

There are two types of O armatures. One uses the O as a framing device for the center of interest, as in *Late Summer in the Pays de Sault* (above, top). The larger hay bale in the foreground forms a hurdle that prevents us from running into the center of interest too quickly. We move in and back out again. You don't want the center of interest to be too dominant, or it will create an "eye-trap" you can't get out of.

In the second O armature, the eye is led around the outside of the picture plane. The center of interest lies on the O at some point (in the top right in *Last Snow in the Valley*, above), but the momentum of the armature keeps us moving and exploring the different parts of the painting.

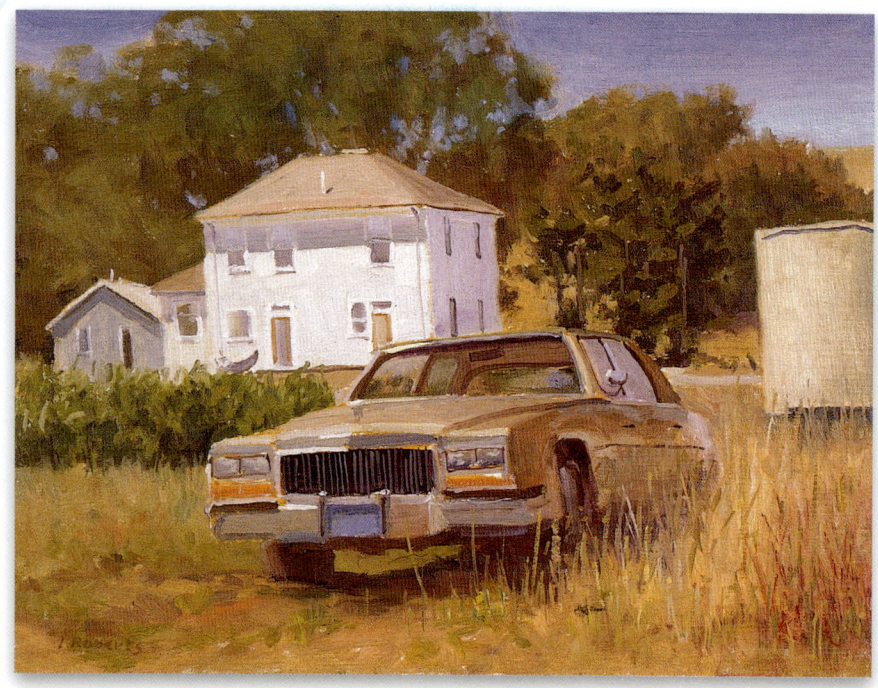

RICHARD'S CADILLAC
Oil on canvas · 12" × 16" (30cm × 41cm)

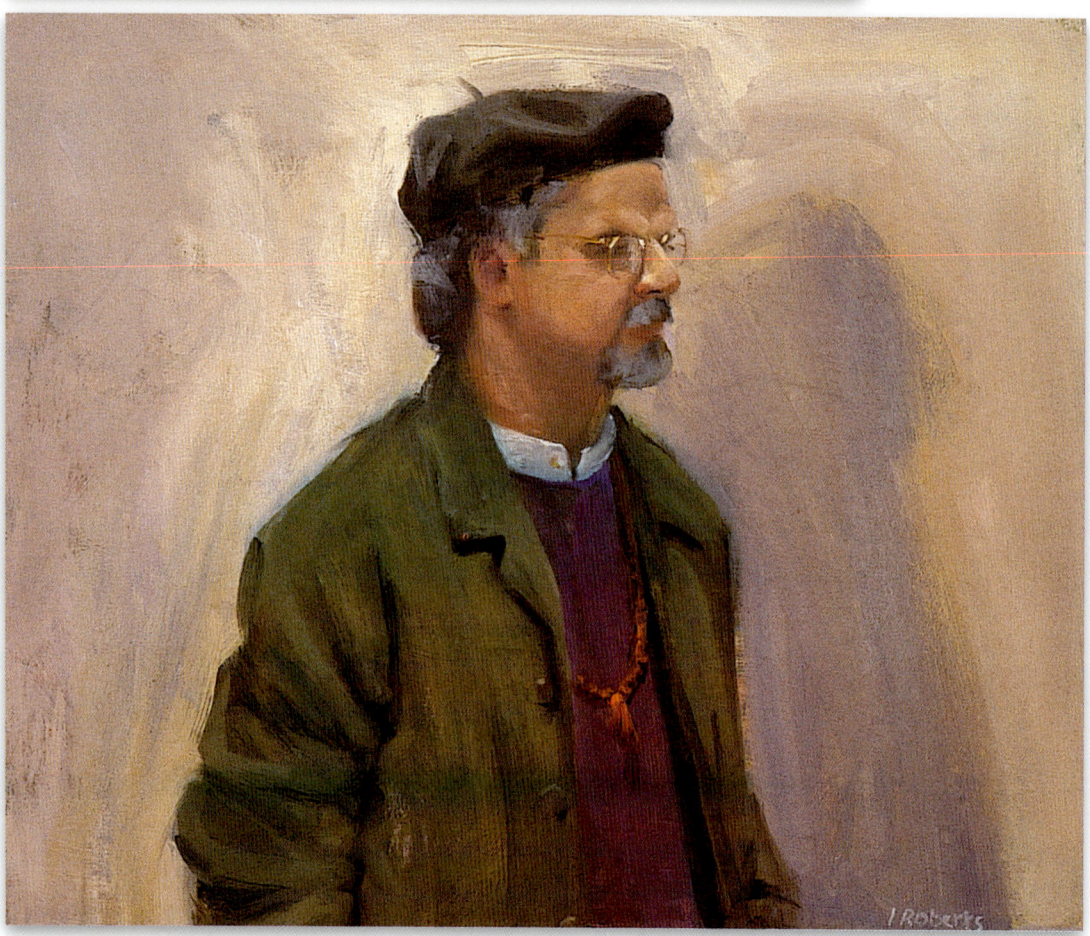

8. Portrait

Whenever you are attracted to something you just want to paint—a person, a boat, a vase of flowers—think of it as a portrait. You need to be aware of the spaces, or negative shapes, around it and the way they interact with what you are portraying. You still need to think in terms of structure, but your center of interest will naturally fall within the thing you are portraying. In the case of a person, that will be the face, unless you decide to really de-emphasize it by putting it in shadow or having the figure turn away from us. In the portrait of *The Poet* (above), you follow the body up to the face, which also has the areas of highest contrast.

THE POET
Oil on canvas · 16" × 20"
(41cm × 51cm)

Horizontals and Verticals

When you use horizontals and verticals to create an armature, you can immediately engage the entire picture plane. You start to think in terms of the whole composition. The horizontals and verticals can often frame the center of interest as well.

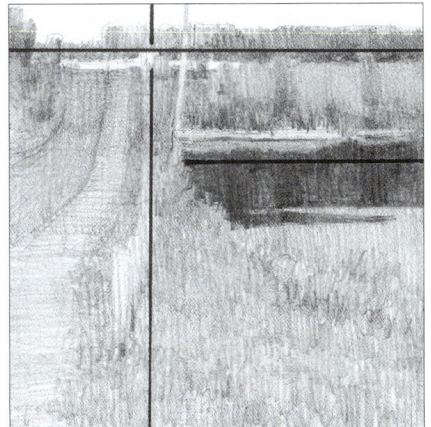

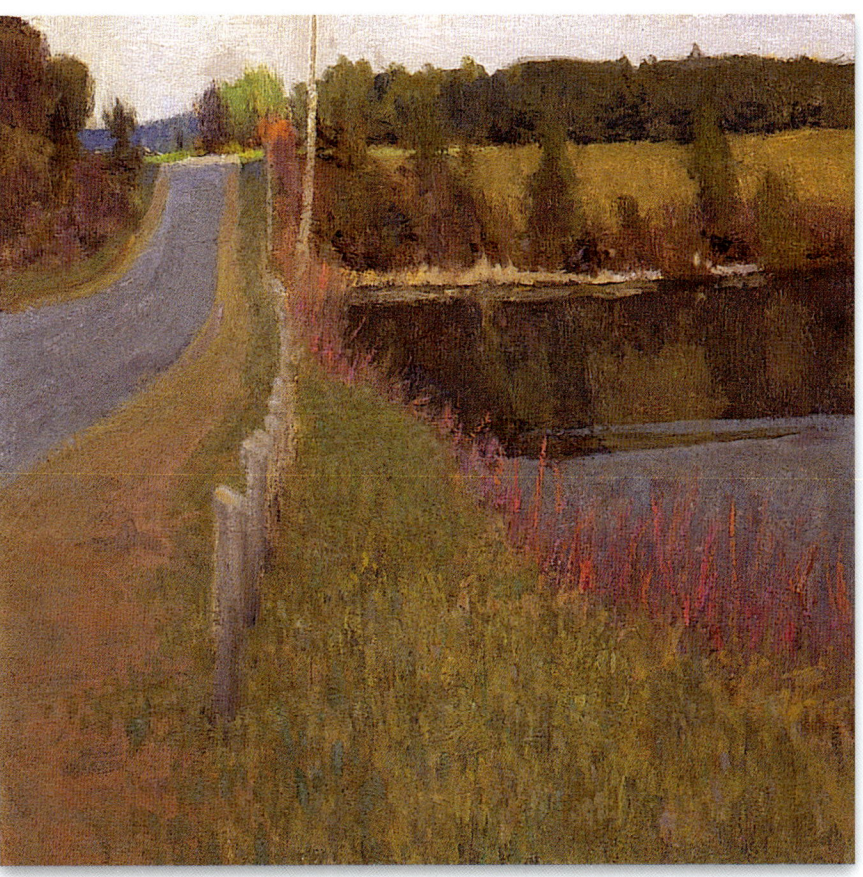

Add Verticals to Balance the Horizon
In landscapes, the horizon often becomes a dominant horizontal. You need to look for verticals to balance it. Telephone poles, for example, create strong verticals. I often hear, "I don't like telephone poles." But, if I see a good vertical to anchor and secure my composition, I don't worry whether it's made of wood, metal or plastic; I just use it.

THE ROAD TO
BILL'S PLACE
Oil on canvas · 12" × 12"
(30cm × 30cm)

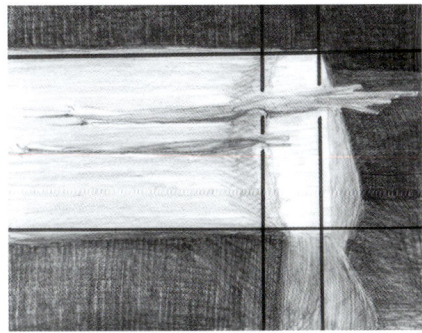

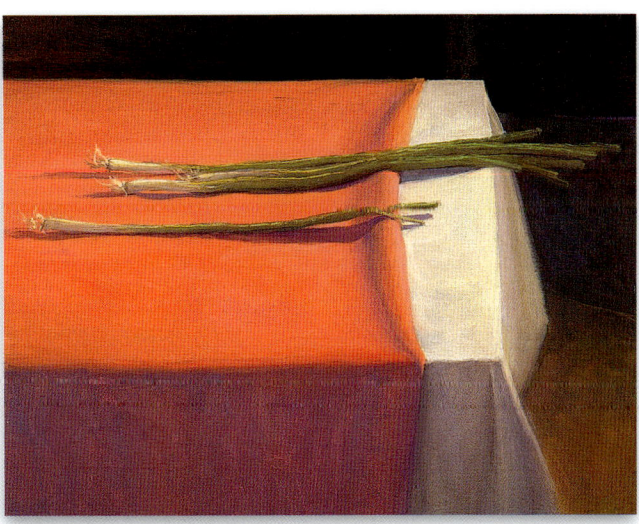

GREEN WITH RED
Oil on canvas · 16" × 20"
(41cm × 51cm)

Create Interest With Simplicity
This armature is almost all horizontals and verticals. Notice the contrast of a small amount of green with a large amount of its complement. Try stripping the composition down to just a couple of contrasts. There's a lot of power in a simple yet dramatic design.

The Cruciform

The *cruciform* (from the same root as *crucifix* or *cross*) is another way to use horizontals and verticals. These examples give you a good idea of how effective a cruciform can be. You can immediately see the way it engages all sides of the picture plane.

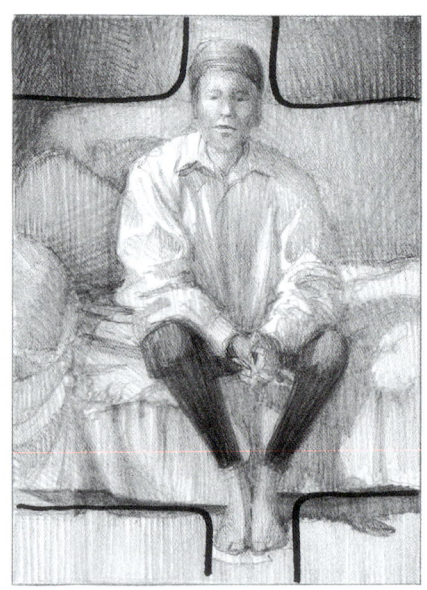

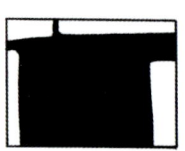
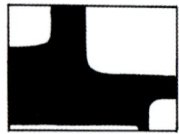
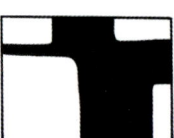
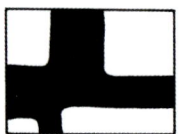

The Many Forms of the Cruciform
This diagram shows how endlessly flexible and adaptable the cruciform is. The diagram is not to suggest that everything within the cruciform needs to be a dark value. It just shows the cruciform's versatility and helps to get you thinking about how abstract masses can interact with the picture plane.

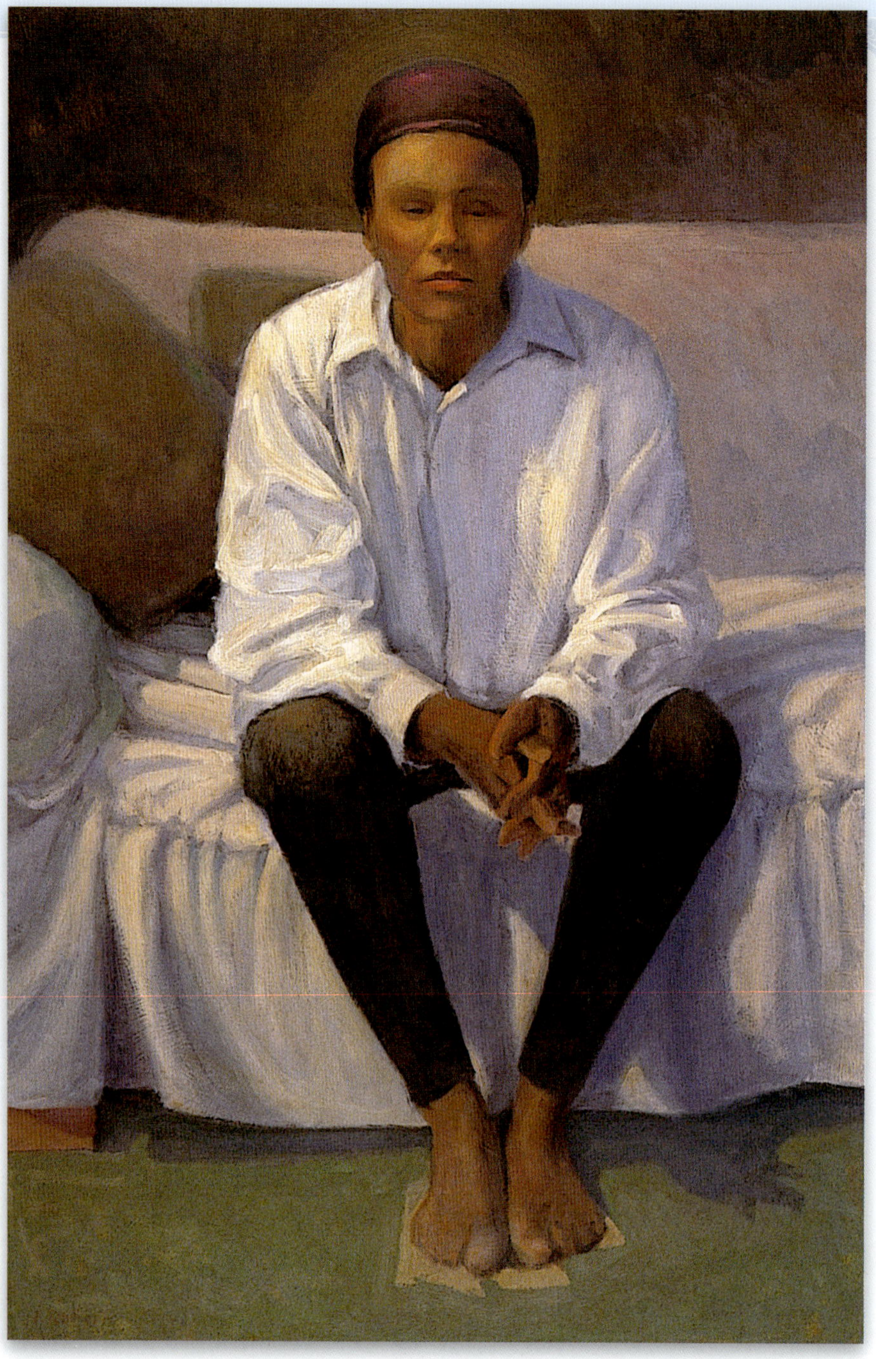

Let the Eye Complete the Structure
Notice that the ends of each arm of a cruciform don't have to touch the edge of the picture. The figure has such a strong vertical force and the head and feet are close enough to the top and bottom of the canvas that your eye completes it. You get the feeling that she sits securely grounded and isn't about to start rotating on the picture plane.

VIRGINIA
Oil on canvas · 36" × 24"
(91cm × 61cm)

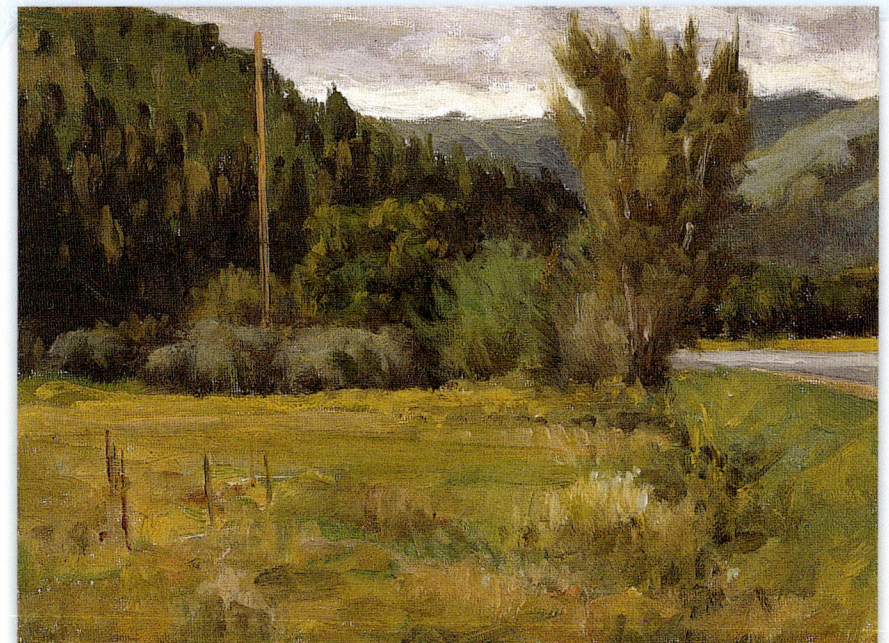

Engage the Whole Picture Plane
Find verticals in the top and bottom of your composition that interact and intersect with the horizontal to get the whole picture plane involved. The cruciform automatically gets you thinking that way.

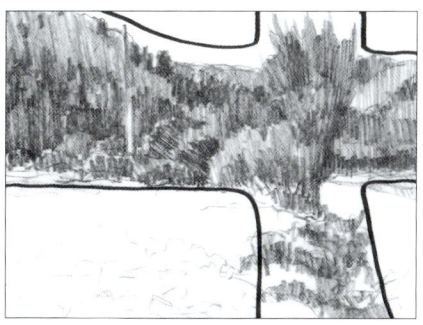

EVENING IN COLORADO
Oil on canvas · 9" × 12" (23cm × 30cm)

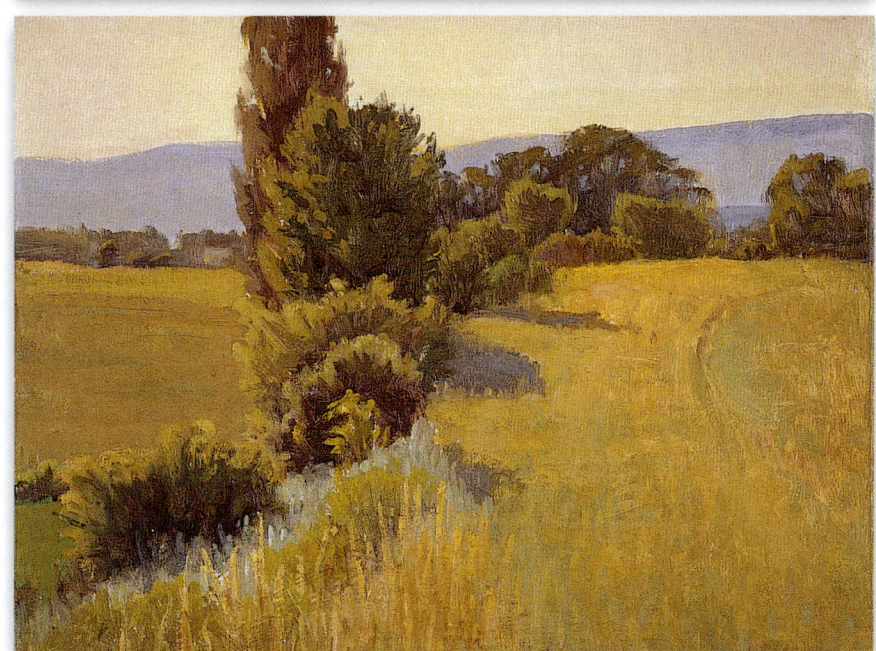

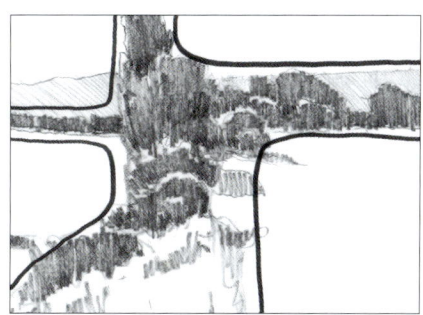

FALL IN PROVENCE
Oil on canvas · 12" × 16" (30cm × 41cm)

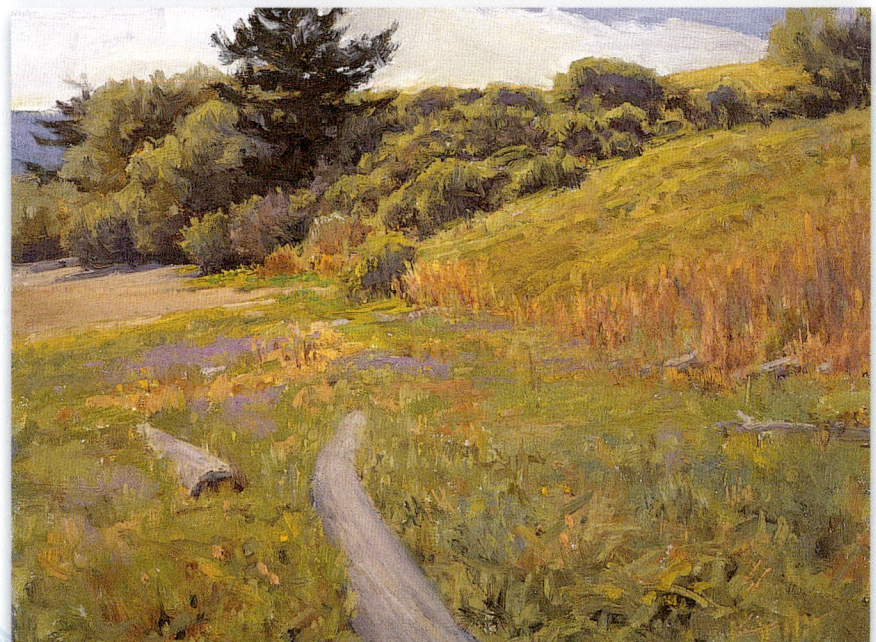

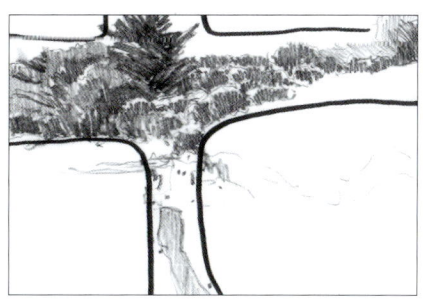

STORM APPROACHING, TOMALES BAY
Oil on canvas · 12" × 16" (30cm × 41cm)

27

Twelve Composition Basics

If you have ever taken a two-dimensional design class, you will remember the exercises. The main point of those exercises was to help you learn that the moment you put a mark on a picture plane, something happens. Things start to react within the rectangle. You create dynamism. You create tension. Those exercises also taught that you can create so much tension at the edge of the picture plane that you break out of its boundary.

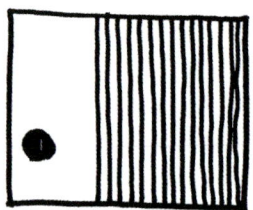 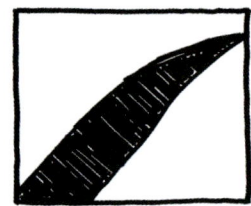 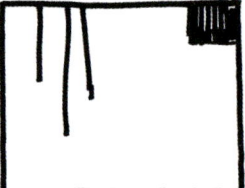

"Designing" the Rectangle

Try making some diagrams with a fat marker. Get a feel for how different shapes affect and alter the movement in the rectangle. How does your attention get pulled by those shapes? You'll quickly get the feeling of "designing" the rectangle with masses.

In the left example above you can feel the tension being created on the circle between the left side of the rectangle and vertical lines. Try using a large mass as a foil for a smaller one, or a dark shape as a foil against which to put a light one.

Notice how in the middle example it is very difficult to stay in the rectangle at all. You keep falling out the bottom. Visually you break out of the picture plane.

The right example gives a very simple design, which in fact is the basic design for the painting on page 22. The fulcrum uses two masses of different density or size to create a dynamic balance.

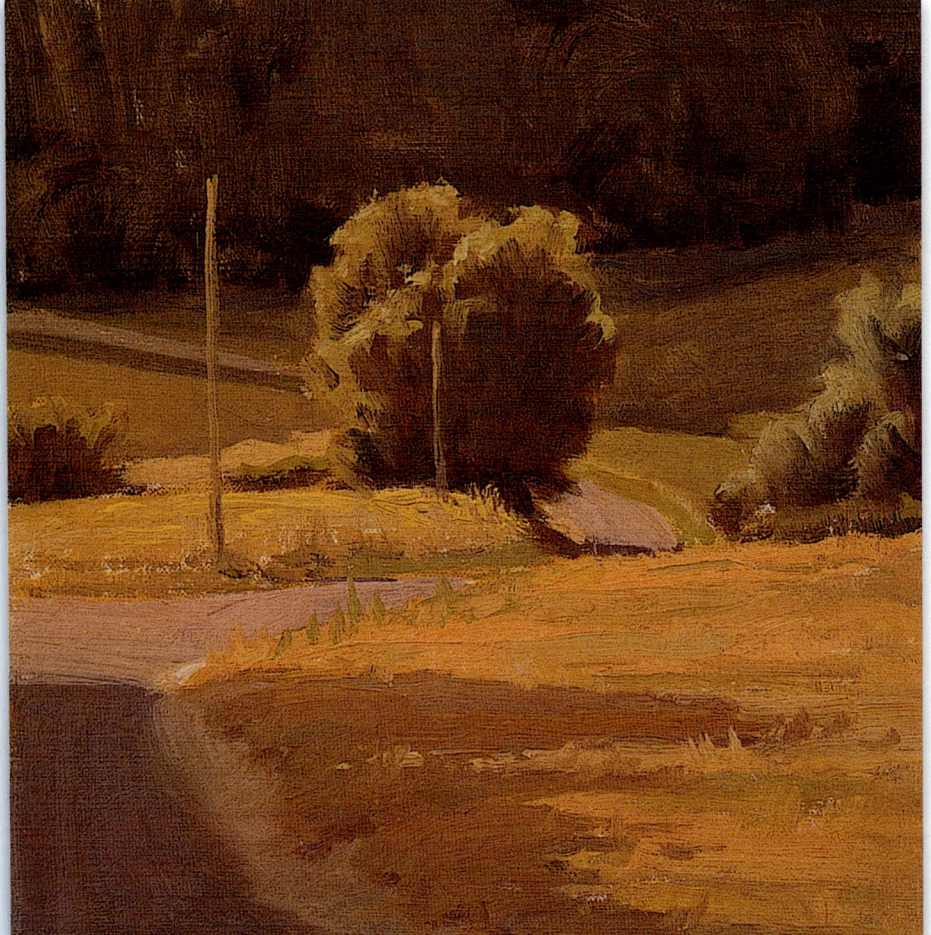

Breaking the Rules

You've heard of course that you should never put your center of interest in the middle of your canvas. It's a sound principle because your eye tends to get rooted there. Here I put the main mass in the center on purpose and then got the movement of the road in front of it and behind it to make sure the eye moves to, around and past the tree. So, you can break even the most basic conventions. But, for the time being, think about applying the following ideas and principles until they become second nature.

THE ROAD TO MANAS
Oil on canvas · 12" × 12" (30cm × 30cm)

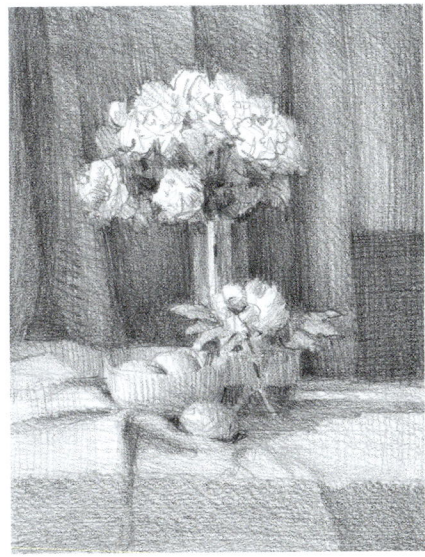
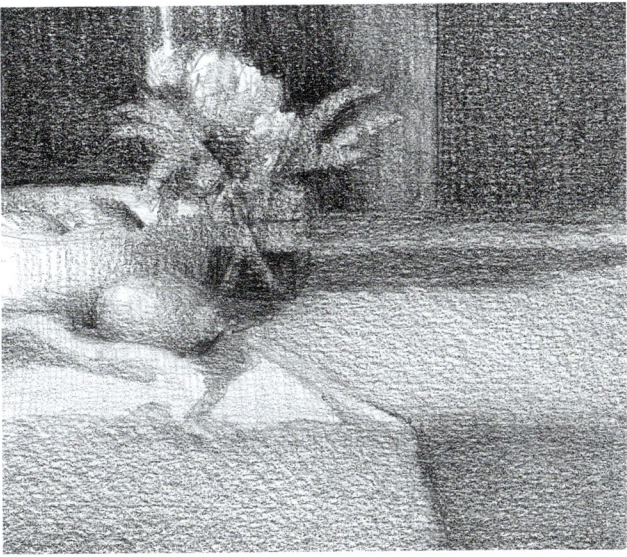

1. Crop for Drama

If you go to a local art show, invariably you'll see paintings of objects. Be it a vase of flowers or a barn, the object will be placed politely on the canvas with almost no relationship, tension or dynamism between the object and the masses in the rest of the picture plane. When you paint, think drama: a play of shapes in the picture plane. However, be careful that your dramatic crop doesn't become just strange or incomprehensible.

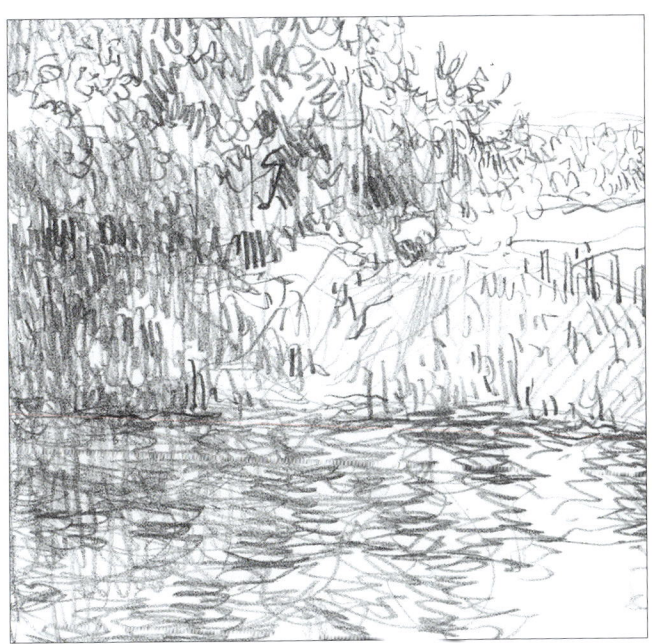
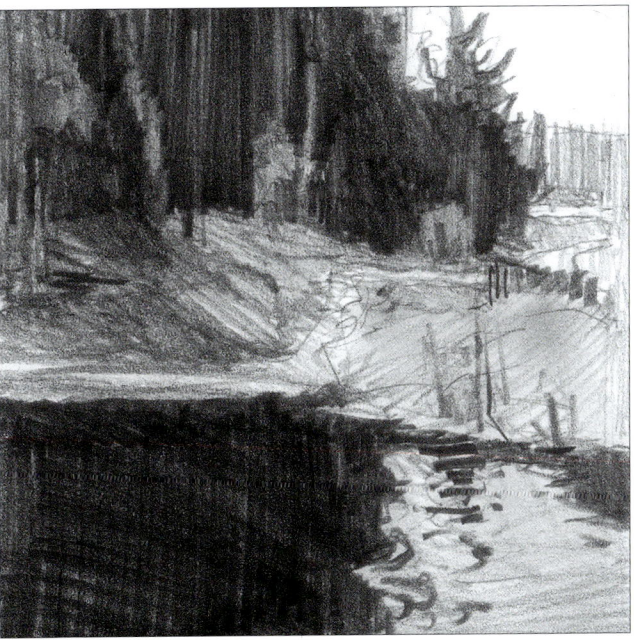

2. Look for the Value Masses

Creating engaging compositions is perhaps first and foremost when learning to see and paint in terms of value masses. Look at the two landscape examples here. The amount of information found in nature can be overwhelming. Squint to simplify and see masses. Otherwise, you get so distracted by all the details, you can't get to the meat of the matter. The example on the left focuses on details at the expense of the masses. The one on the right, on masses at the expense of details. If, when squinting at a potential composition, you can't see a few simple value masses, move on to something else.

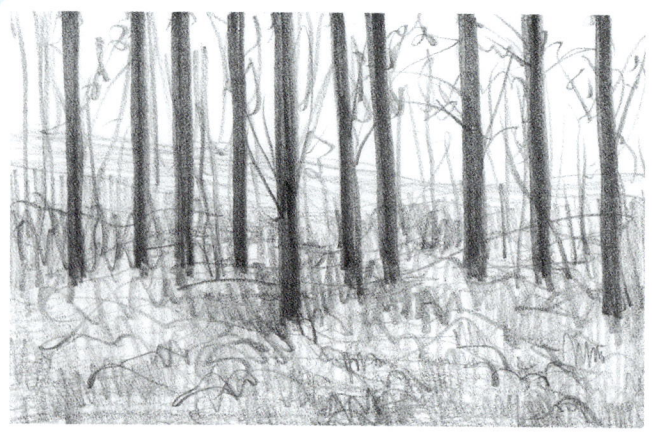

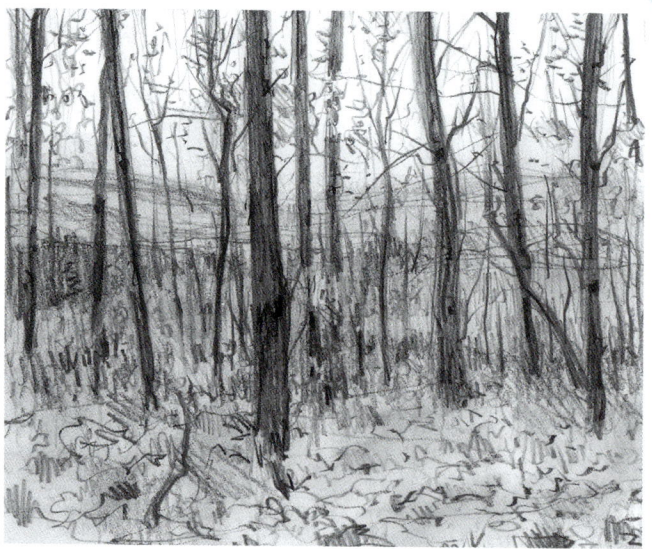

3. Design Divisions With Rhythm

I know you know this point. But somehow, in painting, things have a way of ending up in the middle, or in neat rows, or all the same size.

If you find that happening in your work, slow down a bit and pay more attention to rhythm and variety when you're designing your composition. Unfortunately, you have to keep coming back to check this point while you paint because as you get immersed in everything else, things start creeping back to the middle and lining up again.

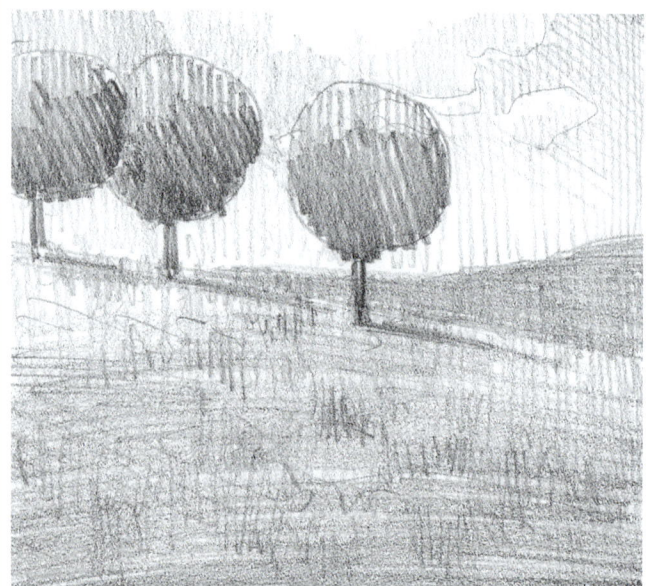

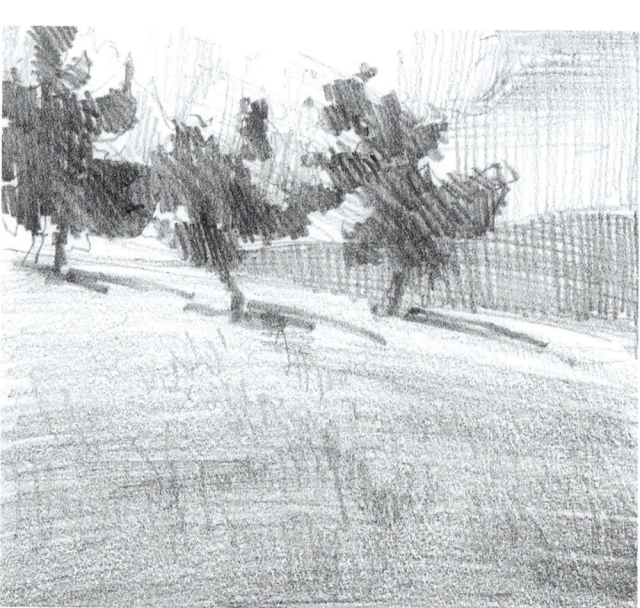

4. Keep Your Shapes Interesting

Be attentive to the character of your shapes. Think of everything as little portraits. Find the unique proportions and angles of things to make them come alive. As with the last principle, when you're painting, things have a way of sliding toward the generic if you're not careful.

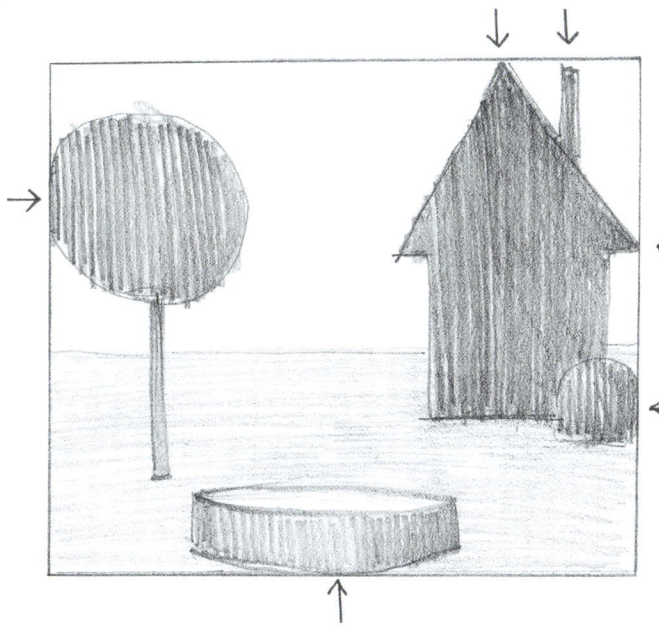

5. Avoid Attracting Attention to the Edges of the Picture Plane

An object ending right on the edge of the picture plane will rivet the viewer's attention. It also gives the impression you ran out of room. It makes the composition look unplanned.

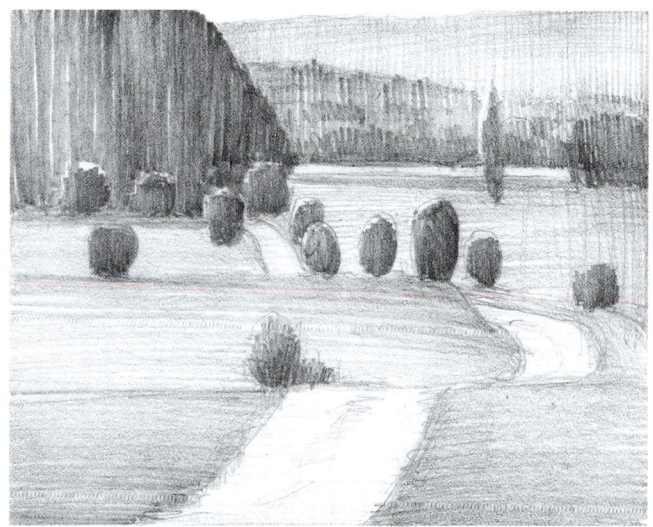

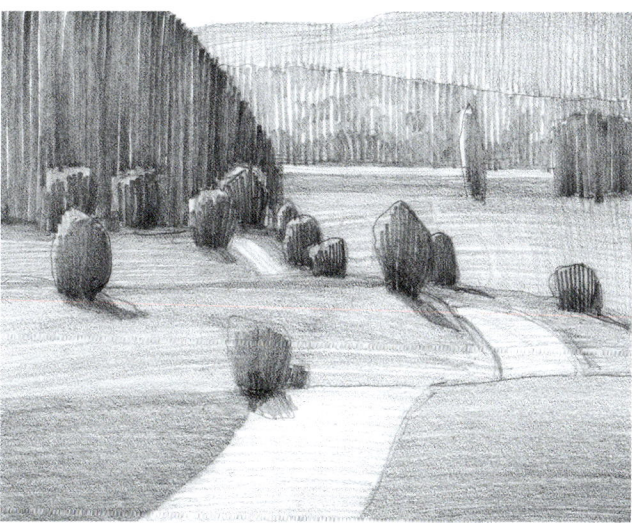

6. Create Depth With Overlaps

With a representational painting, we sculpt depth into the picture plane when we paint. Nothing creates that sense of depth as easily and as clearly as overlapping. The overlap says: This is behind that, obviously farther back in space.

Without overlaps, you may find objects hovering in space in your painting. This is a particular problem with fruit in still lifes and bushes in landscapes. An overlap will solve the problem immediately.

In the left example, notice how the road and the hills create a clear sense of distance. The trees are another matter. Where do they sit? Some you can tell; others are more ambiguous.

In the example on the right, overlaps have clarified where everything is, as have the shadows of the trees. Notice how the use of gradation at the bottom of the picture plane pushes the viewer up into the drawing.

You obviously don't need to have everything in a painting overlap. It's a tool for clarification and, therefore, very useful.

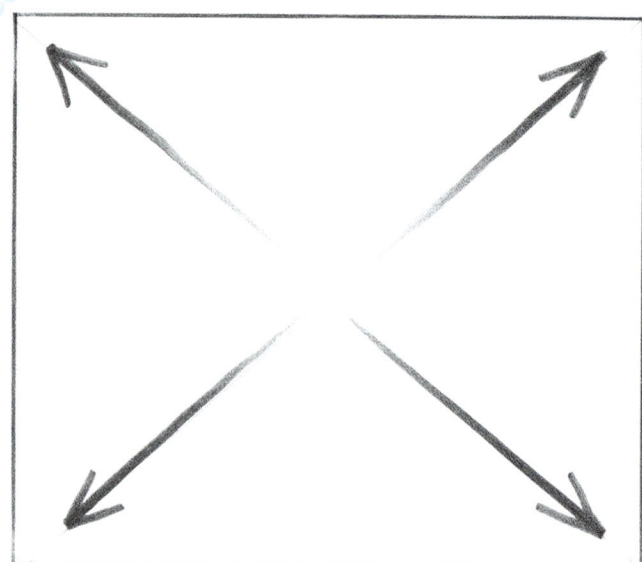

7. Watch the Corners

You want to watch the attention you create in the corners of your composition so that the viewer doesn't end up watching them too much. The diagonals of the rectangle create the most dynamism because they are the most opposed to the rectangle's horizontal and vertical. Consequently, running the edge of a strong contrast out to the corner will tend to take the eye there, and unless there's somewhere else for it to go, right out of the picture plane.

If you have a major design element going out a corner that you can't do much about because of other considerations, reduce the contrast as you move out to the corner so the eye will in fact get pulled into the painting.

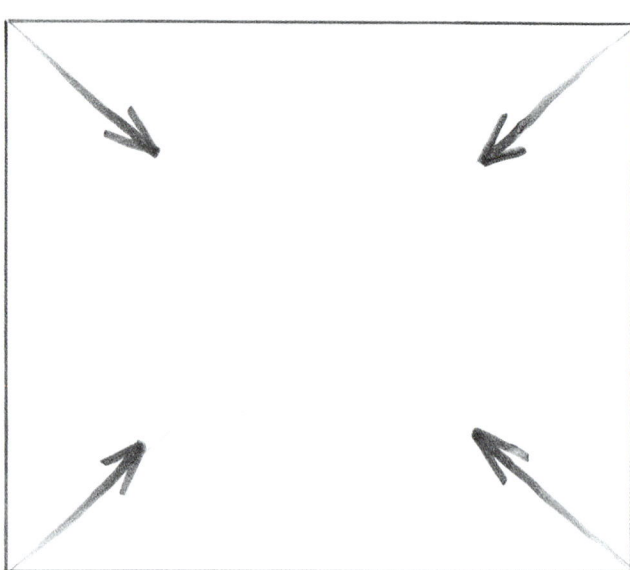

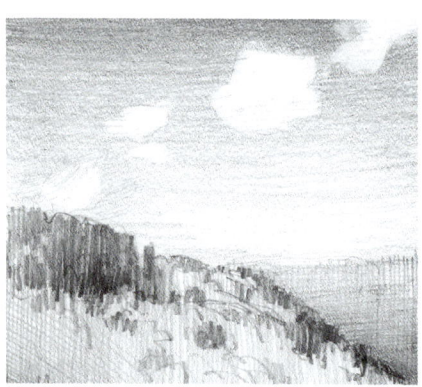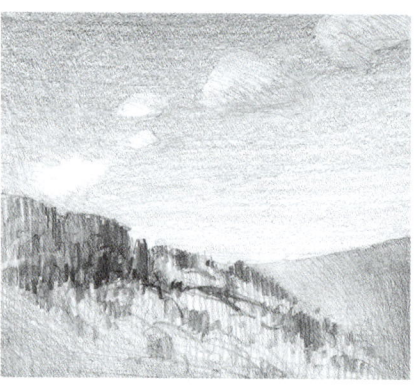

Adjust for Emphasis

This example shows how you can redirect the eye without changing the shape of your masses by de-emphasizing contrast. In the left example, the viewer is pulled out of the drawing at the top and bottom right, and really doesn't come back. In the example on the right, he gets pulled into a center of interest and his eye stays moving within the picture plane.

We can create a line to pull the eye into the painting just as easily as out of it. The adjustment of edges and emphasis in your painting is a fundamental composition tool. I'll come back to it in chapters three and four (see pages 87–89 and 99–106).

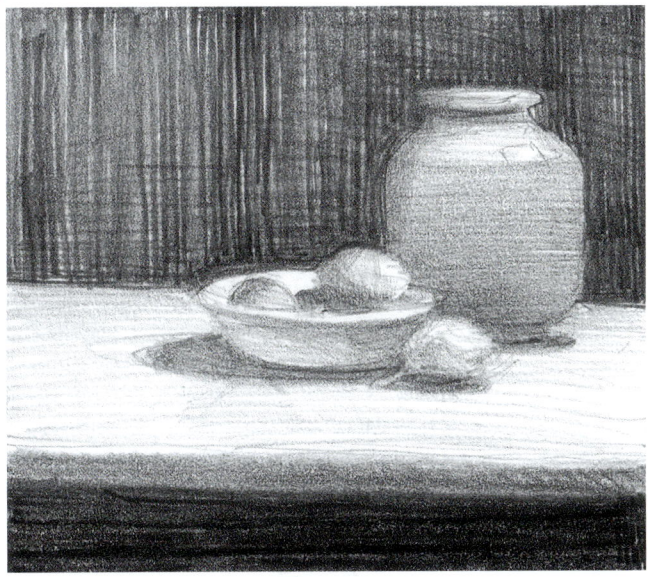

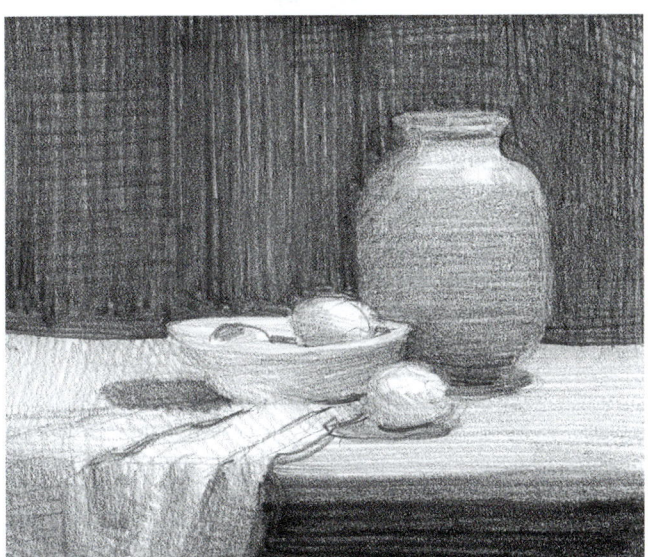

8. Create an Entrance

Invite the viewer into the picture plane by creating an entrance along the bottom edge. The point of entry doesn't need to be obvious, but it needs to be there. Don't block your entrance with a hedge or a building or the edge of a table. We will have to visually hurdle it before we can enter the painting.

In the top example, you can feel how isolated those still-life objects are. It's hard to visually cross the dark mass at the bottom of the drawing. In fact, we don't cross it at all; we just start viewing the drawing above it. In the bottom example, the eye moves easily toward those same objects. The whole picture plane is involved.

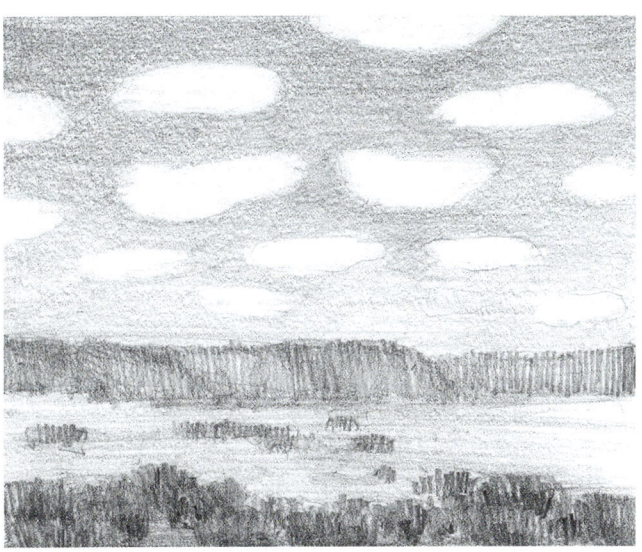

9. Organize Your Masses

You can control the elements of a still life, but nature doesn't always give us a neatly organized composition. With landscapes, you must impose order. Keep looking until some arrangement of masses really grabs you. Then, make necessary adjustments. Clouds, patterns of light and dark, water reflections and other parts of the landscape need to be simplified.

The top drawing is an exaggerated example of the kind of pattern you might see in nature. No emphasis, drama, or direction. Notice the mass of bushes in the foreground hindering the entrance to the composition. In the bottom drawing, all the cloud masses have now been orchestrated to swing the viewer from the top right to mid-left and back to the right again along the horizon. The bushes are now arranged to swing the viewer left into the landscape, then over to the right.

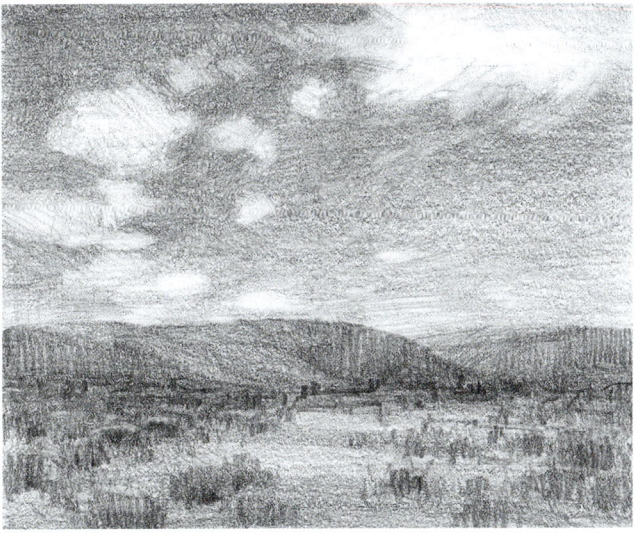

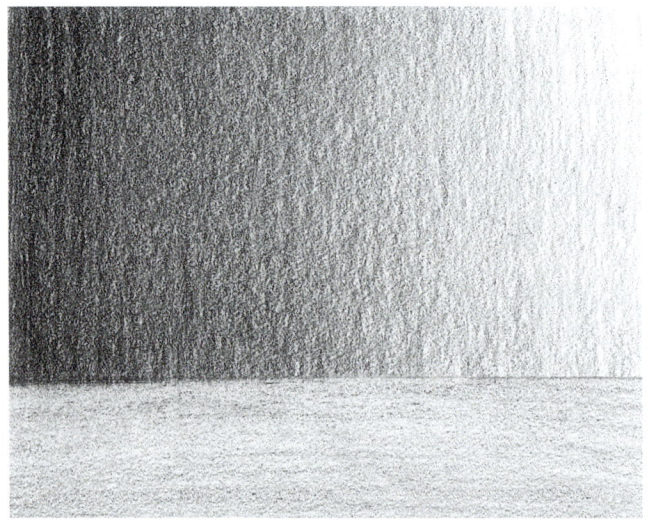
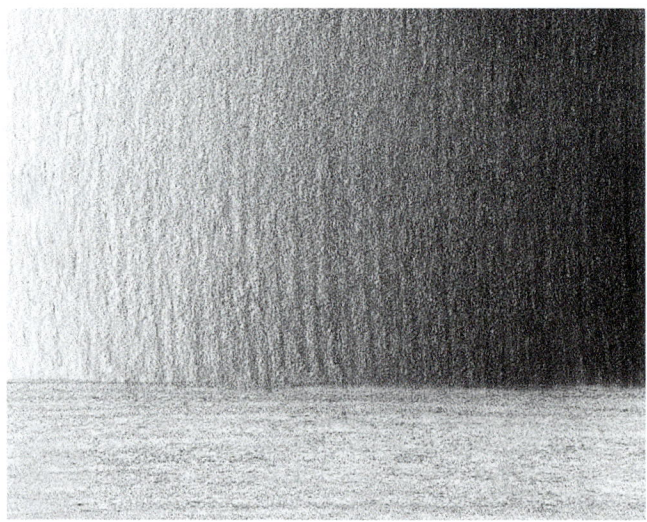

10. Orchestrate the Masses for Good Eye Movement With Gradation

I don't think any tool is as valuable and versatile for orchestrating balance and the movement of the eye among the abstract masses in a painting as gradations. You can see examples of its use in points 1, 4, 6 and 7. You can see in the illustrations above that your eye is pulled to the light side; you move right in the left example and left in the right example. My experience is that gradations always work this way, pulling your eye from dark to light.

Whenever you seem to paint and repaint a mass that isn't the center of interest and find that you can't get it right, try simplifying the whole mass to one simple gradation to move the eye across that mass toward your center of interest.

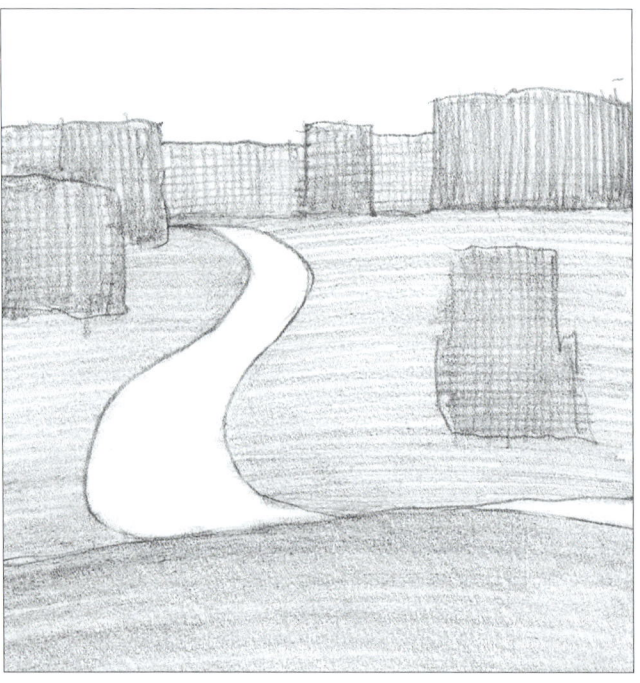
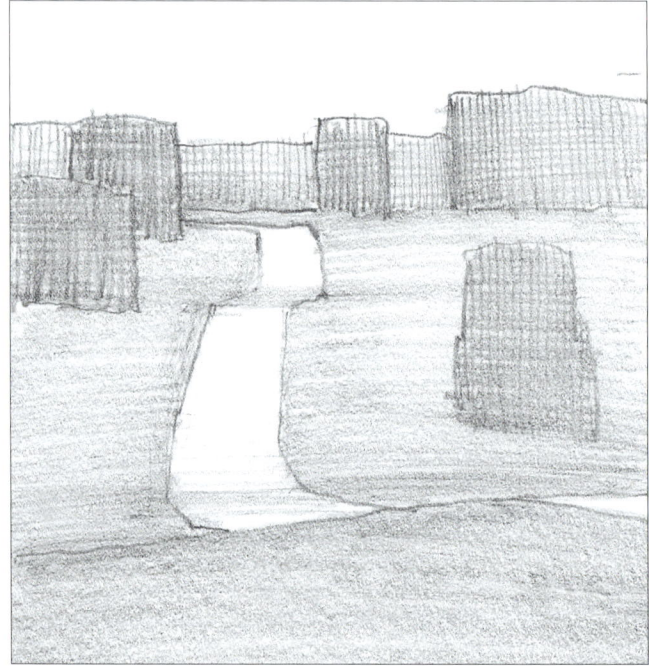

11. Use Straight Lines

Obviously I don't mean paint a sphere with straight lines. But long, loopy curves of roads and clouds and drapery give those objects a detached, floating quality. Look carefully and you'll see that most curves are sections of straight lines that change direction. Look for the reasons for those shifts in direction—a rise in the land, for example—so your forms will all fit together in space as an integrated whole.

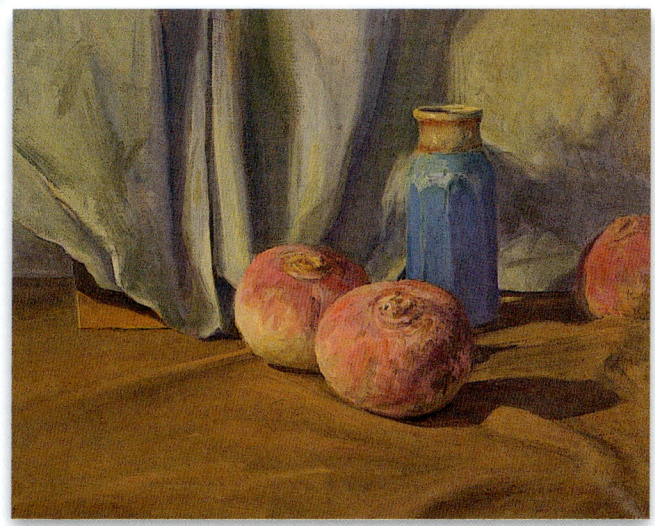

TURNIPS AND BLUE
Oil on canvas · 16" × 20" (41cm × 51cm)

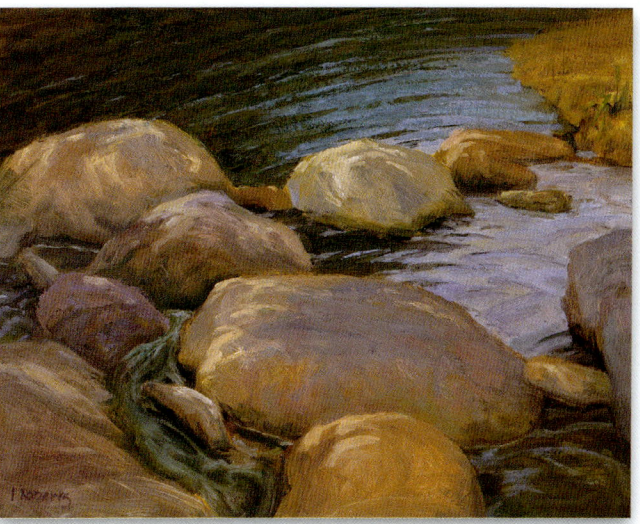

SUMMER LIGHT ON THE POND
Oil on canvas · 12" × 16" (30cm × 41cm)

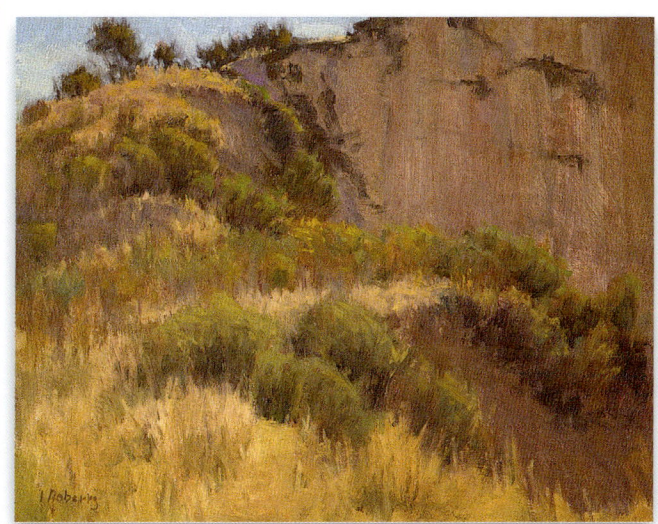

IRVINE LAND
Oil on canvas · 12" × 16" (30cm × 41cm)

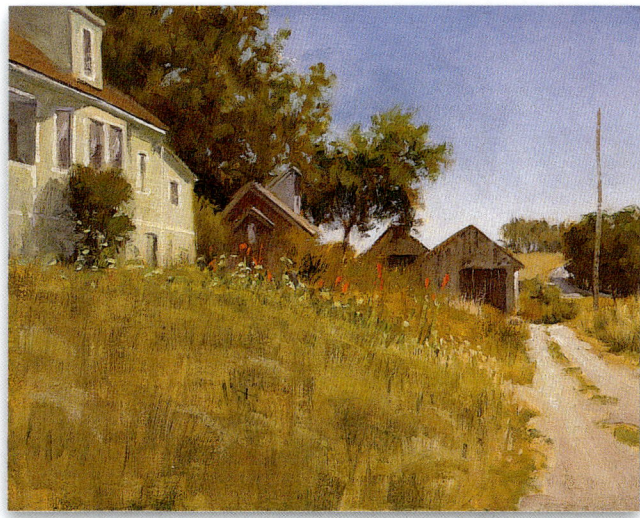

THE GREEN HOUSE
Oil on canvas · 12" × 16" (30cm × 41cm)

12. Think Foreground, Middle Ground and Background

Linear perspective (in which objects recede toward a vanishing point), *atmospheric perspective* (in which distant objects become lighter and bluer as they recede) and *overlaps* are three major tools for creating depth. Your subject may range from a still life with a front-to-back depth of 18" (46cm), or a close-up of a landscape with a depth of 20' (6m), a landscape that goes back 200' (60m), or one that goes back a mile (1.6km) or more. You'll find it easier to structure depth if you think in terms of a foreground, a middle ground and a background. Usually you will create more density of information in the middle ground. The foreground acts as an introduction to the middle ground, while the background creates a sense of space for the middle ground to sit in. Not all paintings have all three spaces. But, when you're planning your composition, identifying and effectively utilizing these areas will help you plan the visual movement back into the depth of your painting.

The Emphasized-Edge Sketch

The armature is a fundamental tool for structuring a composition. But it's important to realize that armatures lie behind the scenes. Throughout this book we are relating several ideas that need to converge into a whole. For example, the lines of the armature may need to coexist with lost edges that may run right along through part of the armature.

Using what I call "emphasized-edge" sketches will clarify the way armatures work with the other elements in your painting. Emphasized-edge sketches show only the degree of contrast along the edges in a painting, from lost edges to hard, high-contrast ones. These sketches indicate the lines of attention or the lines of direction you want your viewer to follow. These are the main lines of the composition plus any secondary lines used to create more interest and movement through the picture plane.

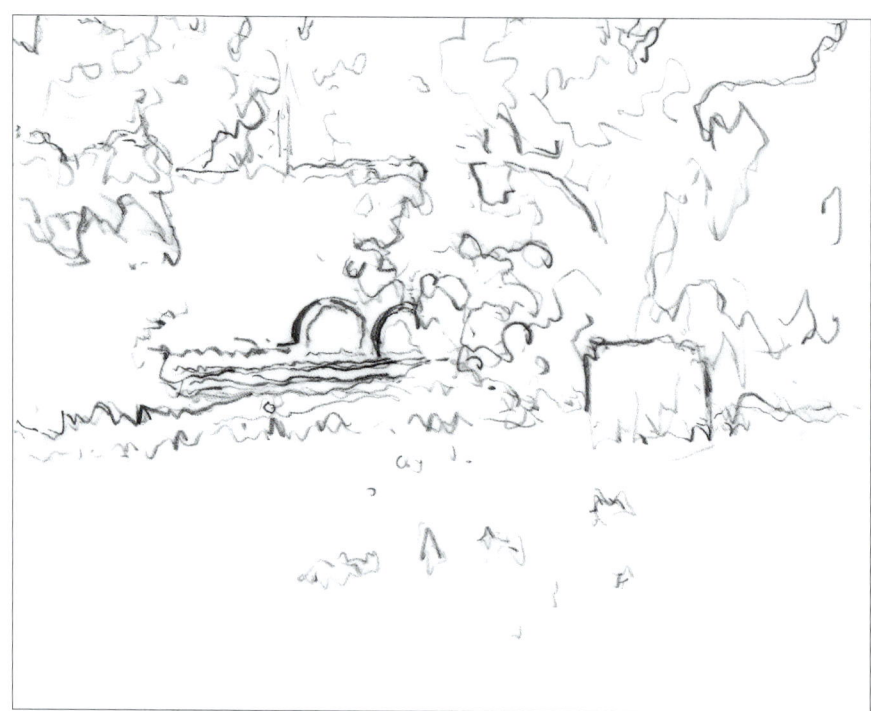

Exercise

Choose half a dozen paintings you really like, preferably by well-respected masters of representational art. Lay a piece of tracing paper over a reproduction of one of those paintings. Lightly trace all the edges in the painting and then, with the painting in front of you, carefully draw the relative strength of all the edges that you traced. As you do this, feel how those edges are pulling your attention or letting it go. A painter's control of edges is a pretty clear indication of his mastery of painting.

Control and Nuance Edges

The two drawings above are the emphasized-edge sketches of the L and one of the O armatures we saw on pages 20 and 23. Although all the edges in the painting may be present in the drawing, they are weighted, light or dark, by how much attention they attract when we look at the painting. The antithesis of this type of drawing would be a coloring book where all the lines—the edges—have equal weight. We will talk about the control and nuancing of edges throughout this book because it's an idea that needs to become prominent in your visual awareness. Nothing indicates a student painter so quickly as brush marks that show a confusion of unconsidered edges. Mastering edges will dramatically change the way you paint.

develop a sound working method

For the demonstrations in this book I'll suggest a working method to build your awareness of how to structure a strong composition, and then, a systematic method to achieve it in a finished painting. You will then have greater control of the painting at each step along the way. Once you get a good sense of how to build dramatic compositions that work, you will inevitably develop a working method that evolves to suit you best.

My method works like this. After finding a still-life arrangement you like and having done a thumbnail of it, you will:

1. Do a simple block-in—one color for each color shape.
2. Do a second block-in, adjusting each shape for halftones and reflected lights, modulating colors and edges, pulling the eye into the center of interest.
3. Continue modifying each color shape until the painting is working as a whole.
4. Finally, add highlights and details only at the very end.

The tendency is to want to put in details and highlights far too early. Using this method, the painting can stand on its own without any details. The structure of the color shapes carries it.

MATERIALS

Surface
Oil-primed canvas, 20" × 20" (51cm × 51cm)

Brushes
Nos. 4, 8 and 10 hog bristle filberts, no. 6 sable or synthetic rigger

Pigments
Titanium White, Cadmium Yellow Light, Cadmium Yellow Deep, Yellow Ochre, Cadmium Orange, Cadmium Red Light, Alizarin Crimson, Quinacridone Violet, Dioxazine Purple, Ultramarine Blue, Phthalo Blue, Phthalo Green, Chrome Oxide Green

Other supplies
Smooth drawing paper, B and 2B pencils, kneaded eraser, mineral spirits

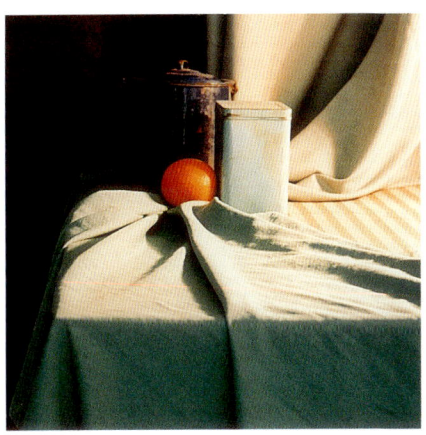

Still-Life Setup
When you set up a still life, be deliberate about creating the armature—the structure your painting will hang from. Use simple objects and not too many of them. Light the still life from one source and consider the shadow shapes being created by that light source as an integral part of the composition. Think in terms of masses and lost edges. If you use drapery, I recommend not using patterned or decorated material for now.

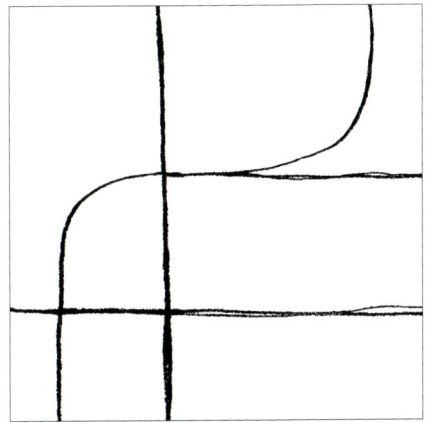
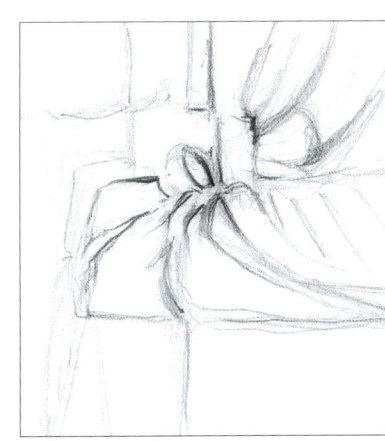

Armature Defines Structure
The armature (left) contains the underlying structure. The line created vertically through the edge of the light cloth in the background extends in the fold of the cloth that runs forward across the table and then down to the bottom edge of the painting. The big sweep from top right to bottom left is an S armature.

The emphasized-edge sketch (right) shows what edges and contrasts we will use to pull the eye into the center of interest. That strong vertical in the armature is still there as structure, but now it is "buried" in the painting—yet its support is still felt.

Think Value Masses in Your Thumbnail

Try setting up a still life with shadows that force you to think in value masses: big light and dark shapes. When you do your thumbnail, draw value masses, not objects.

Look at the top-left mass: one large, dark shape that includes a piece of dark cloth with a few highlights, a pot, and the shadow of that pot on the cloth to the left of it that continues down to the bottom left of the picture plane. Also notice the final adjustments to the proportion of the picture plane on the bottom and right side of the drawing.

Also, spend time arranging the cloth the way you actually want to paint it. Smooth out folds you don't want, hang folds so you can read their structure clearly. If you just drop the cloth down any old way and imagine you will figure it out in the painting process, you will get buried by it. Believe me. If you've set up a still life and you're fiddling with little adjustments over and over and are really not sure if you even like it, then take it apart. Start again. Rethink it. I set up three before deciding on this one.

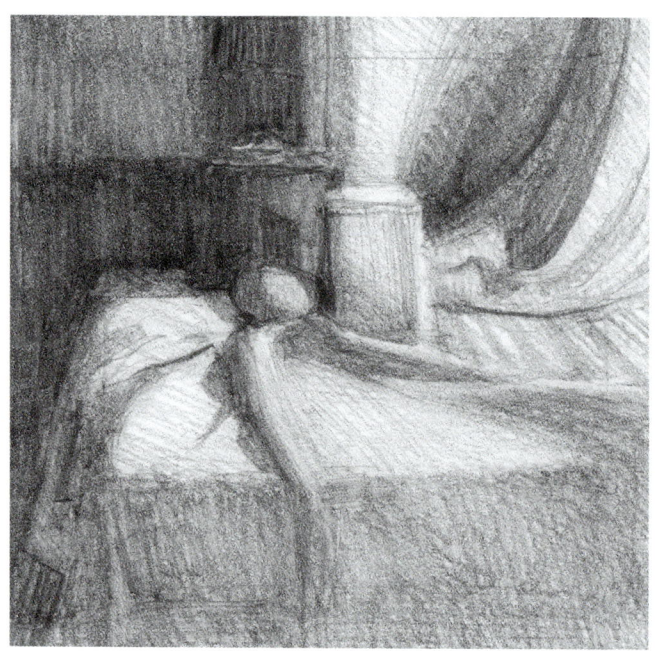

1 Establish Proportions and the First Simple Color Shapes

To establish your composition on the canvas be sure the proportions of your thumbnail are the same as your canvas (see page 18 for more information on proportions). Use Yellow Ochre, a no. 4 filbert and enough mineral spirits to make the paint thin enough to draw with. Yellow Ochre doesn't stain so you can keep wiping it out until you have everything where you want it. Notice the residual ochre tint on the canvas, left over from wiping out and redrawing some areas. Don't rush. Get each line where you want it; don't just accept it where it ends up. You're the boss.

Look at your still life and choose two or three color shapes that are close in value and low in color intensity. Start there. Remember, your first color will look darker against the white canvas than it will once it's surrounded by other colors.

Use a no. 10 filbert for the entire first block-in. Use Phthalo Green and Alizarin Crimson for the dark of the cloth and the side of the pot. Using that as a base color, add Cadmium Red Light for the lit side of the dark cloth and Ultramarine Blue and Yellow Ochre for the shadow of the tablecloth.

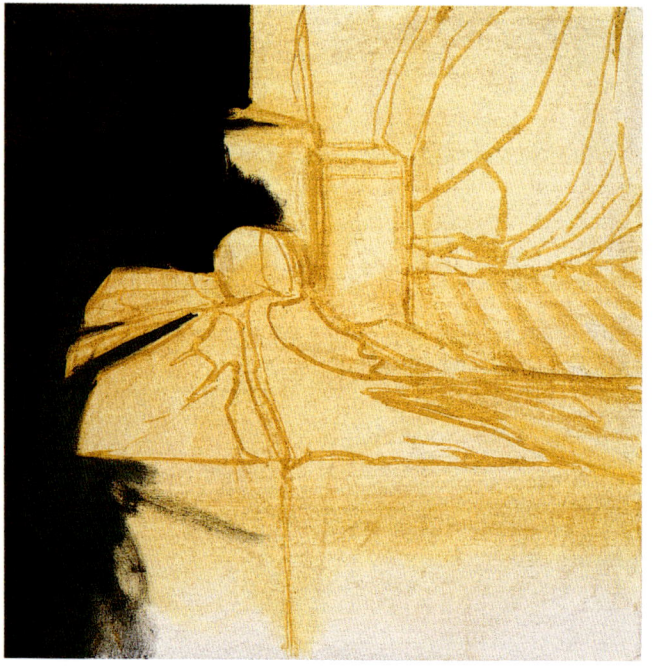

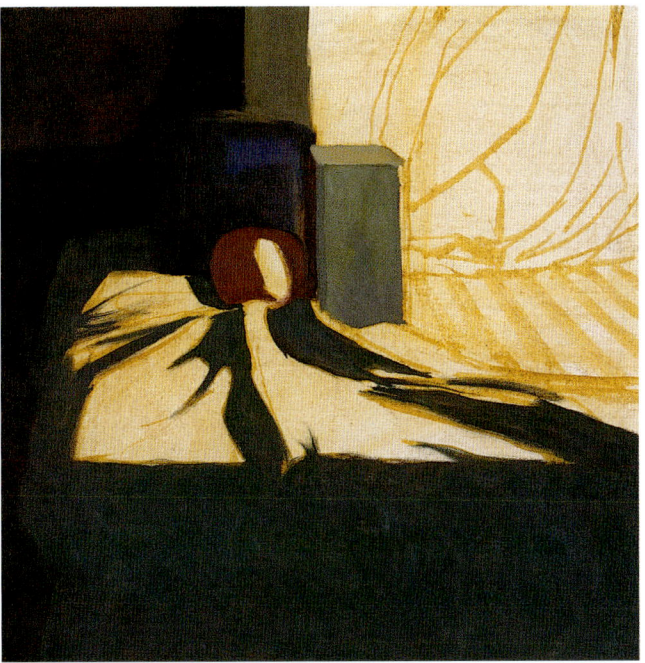

2 Block In Shape by Shape

Choose the next color shape to paint adjacent to the one you've already painted in. That way you're always comparing colors in relationships you can actually see. Paint in a mark for the next color shape right beside another already established color. You can test it and adjust it. Don't paint in the whole shape and then ask yourself if it's working. You might test a color several times before being satisfied. You may also find that you need to go back to adjust an earlier color in order to make all the relationships work as you proceed.

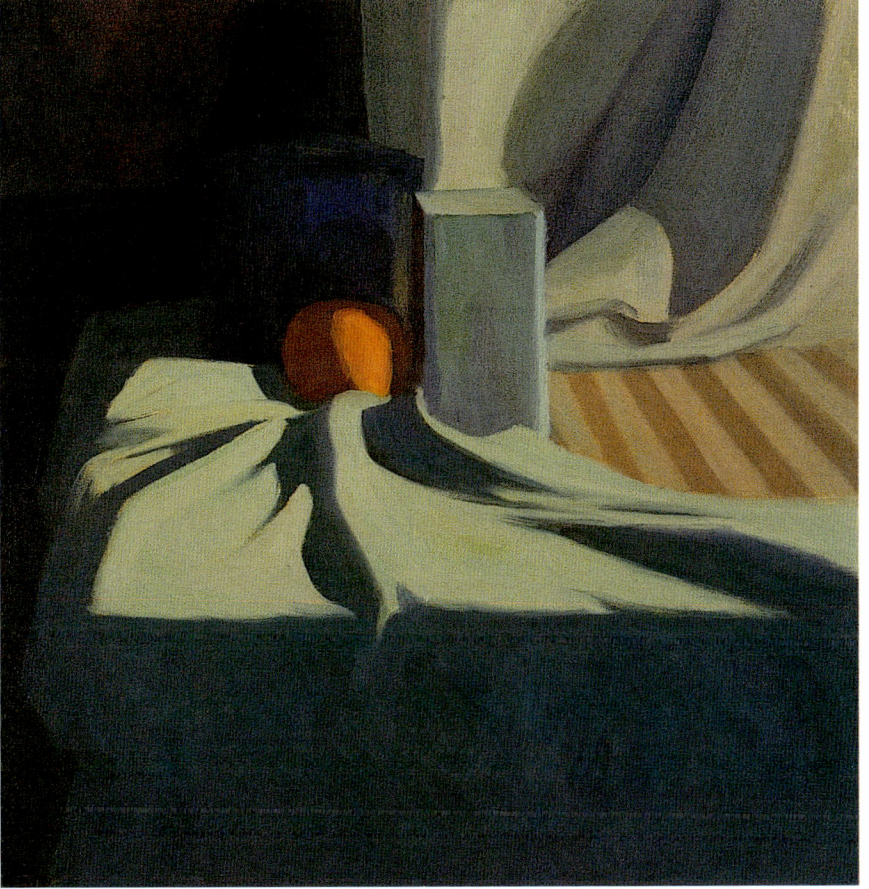

3 Refine the Light and Dark Areas

Find one color after another as accurately and simply as possible. There are no color modulations or transition colors.

If you have a strong, warm light source, be sure that you get a good warm-cool shift between the lit and shadow shapes, not just a value shift. It's usually much stronger than you imagine. In the green cloth across the tabletop, use Cadmium Yellow Light, Yellow Ochre and just a hint of Cadmium Orange, Ultramarine Blue and Titanium White.

Look for colors in the darks. The shadow on the orange is Cadmium Red Light, Ultramarine Blue and Dioxazine Purple. Dark doesn't necessarily mean dull.

When you block in like this, you will have a very good feel for where the painting is going. Compare this step with the finished painting. The armature is giving a structure and holding all the color shapes of the painting together in relation to the picture plane. You have a sound foundation on which to continue.

This has taken 40–50 minutes to block-in. From here you can work "all over" as you advance and adjust the painting.

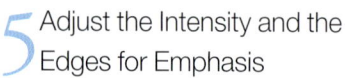

4 Add Halftones and Reflected Light in the Fabric

The first block-in created only two values for each object: the lit area and the shadow. Now, with the second block-in, it's time for halftones on the lit side and reflected lights for the shadow. Where the folds of the drapery face the light source will be lightest, the highlight. The light rakes across the tabletop on more of an angle, so the light isn't as strong, creating a halftone. Paint the halftones in a step darker (on a ten-step gray scale) by adding more Ultramarine Blue and Yellow Ochre to the mixture you used on the highlights.

Do the same for the darks. Paint in the reflected light on the front face of the table-cloth and in the shadows, adding a little Yellow Ochre to the shadow mixture you used in step 1. These are a step or two lighter than the dark shadows. You can do a lot with these four values, two for the lights, two for the darks.

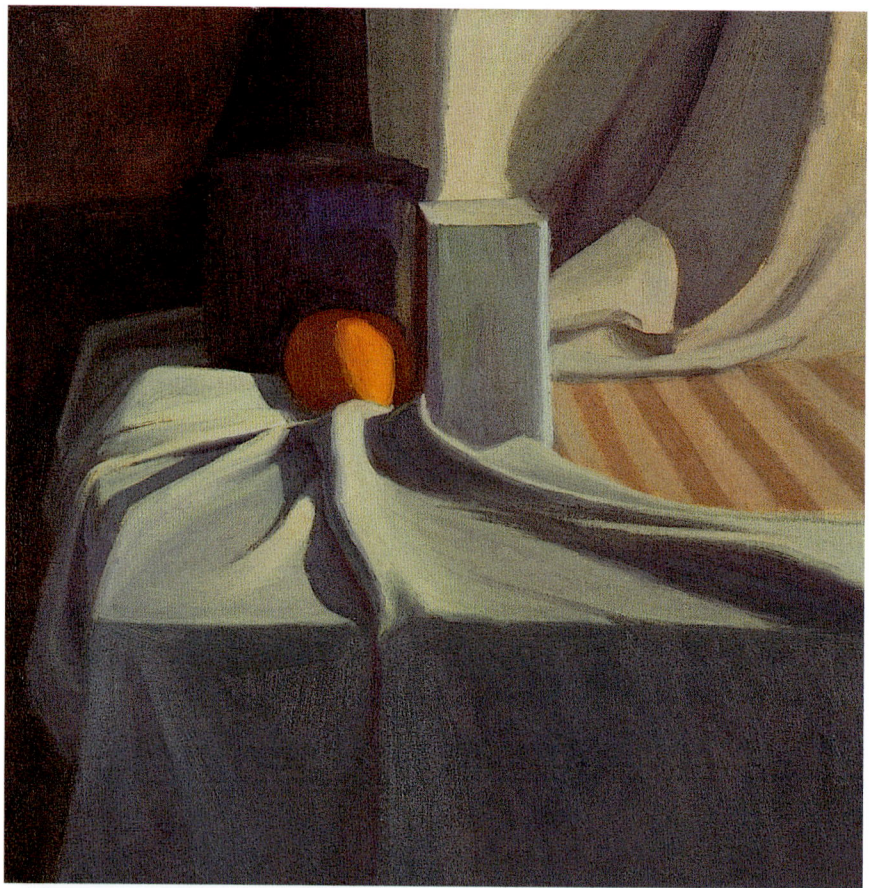

5 Adjust the Intensity and the Edges for Emphasis

Begin using a no. 4 filbert to adjust the color intensity and the edges to pull the eye toward the center of interest. Look at the striped cloth on the right. Increase the color intensity of the stripes as they move left across the picture plane by adding more Cadmium Orange to each stripe. That shape pulls the viewer into the picture.

Notice also the brush marks over the right edge of the blue tin. Don't try to stop each stroke right at the edge of the next shape. Go over it with one clean vertical stroke of paint and clean up the blue tin later.

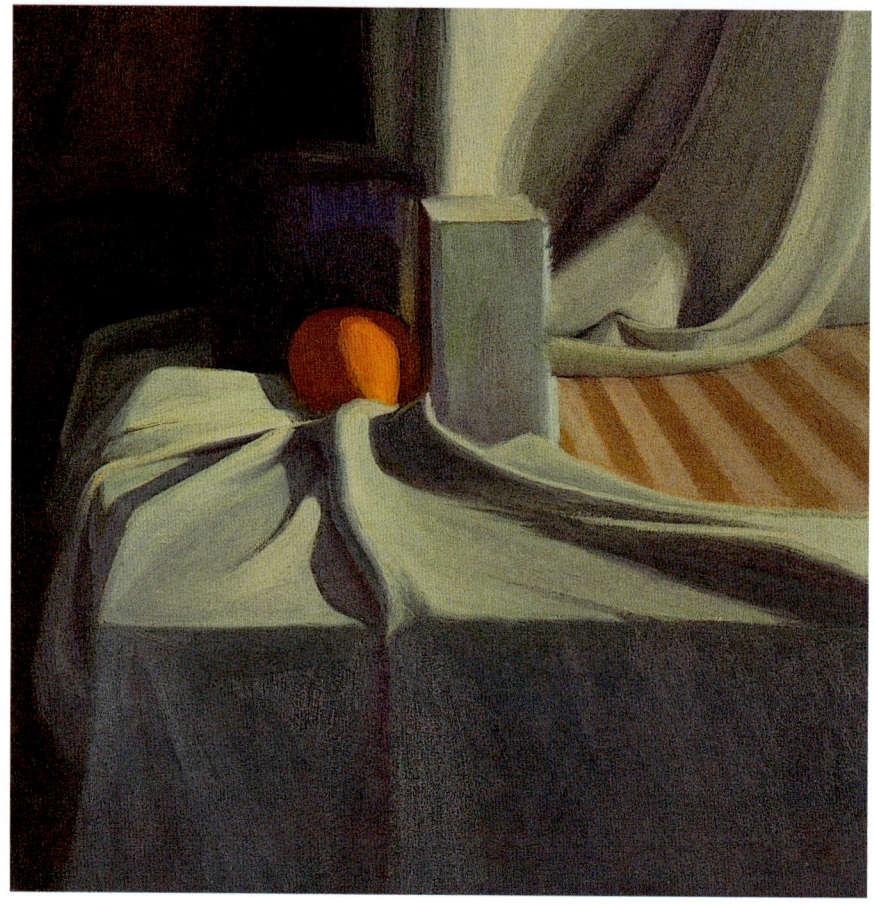

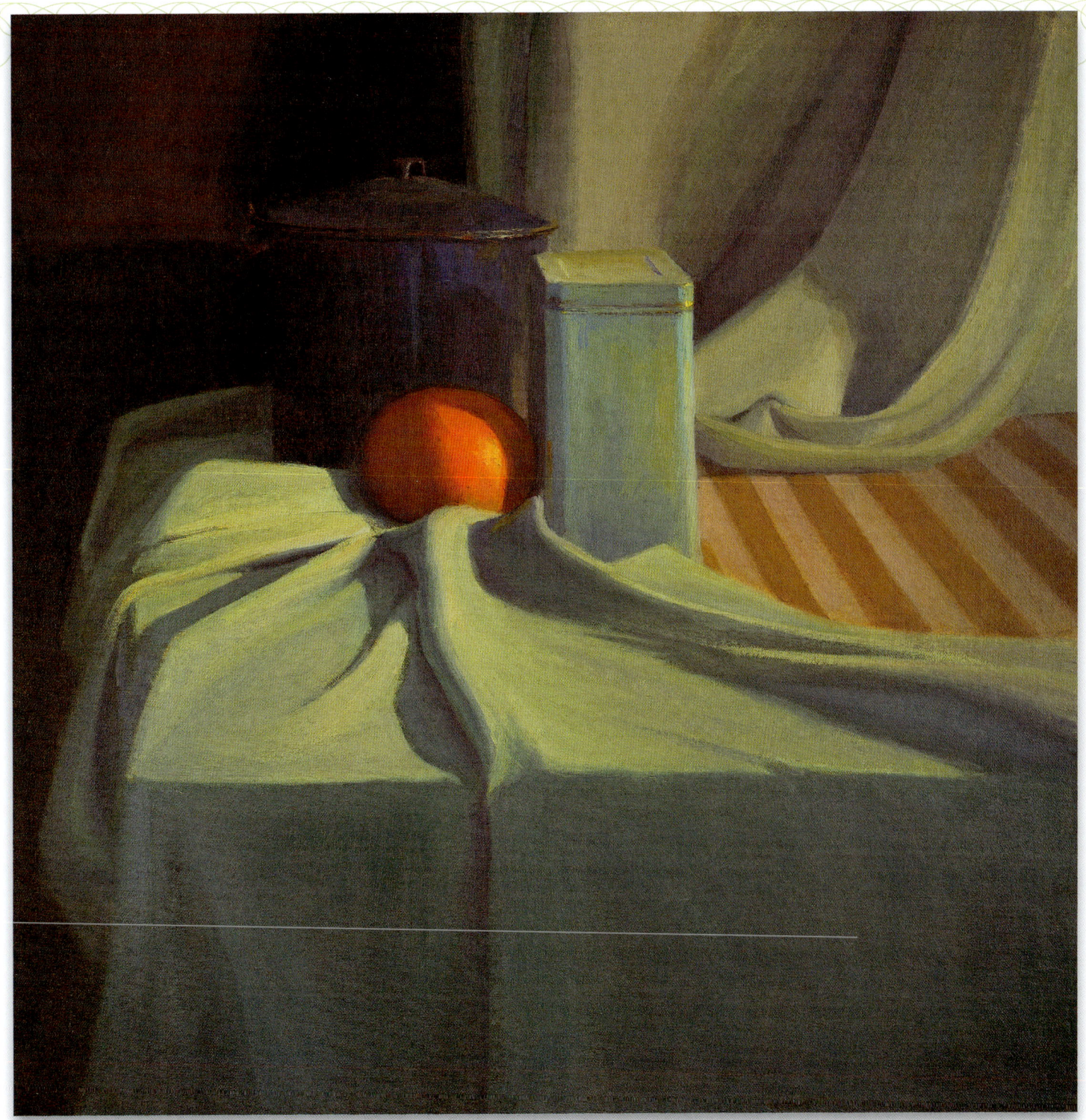

6 Pulling It All Together

Now spend more time looking than painting. Examine every color shape, edge and color transition to make sure that your eye is being led to the center of interest. At the same time, your armature structure will create movement away from the center of interest, into the rest of the picture plane and then back toward the center of interest again. Study your painting from a level of pure visual response. Where does your eye get distracted? What catches your attention as your eye moves about the painting that might disrupt the flow you had in mind? Look at it in a mirror. Turn it upside down—anything to see it with a fresh eye.

When you're satisfied, the painting is basically finished. The big shapes define the painting. Color modulation creates interest. It's all in the structure. Look at the two photos of this painting on page 92, showing before and after the details were added. Clearly the structure carries the painting—not the detail.

STILL LIFE IN ORANGE AND BLUE
Oil on canvas · 20" × 20" (51cm × 51cm)

41

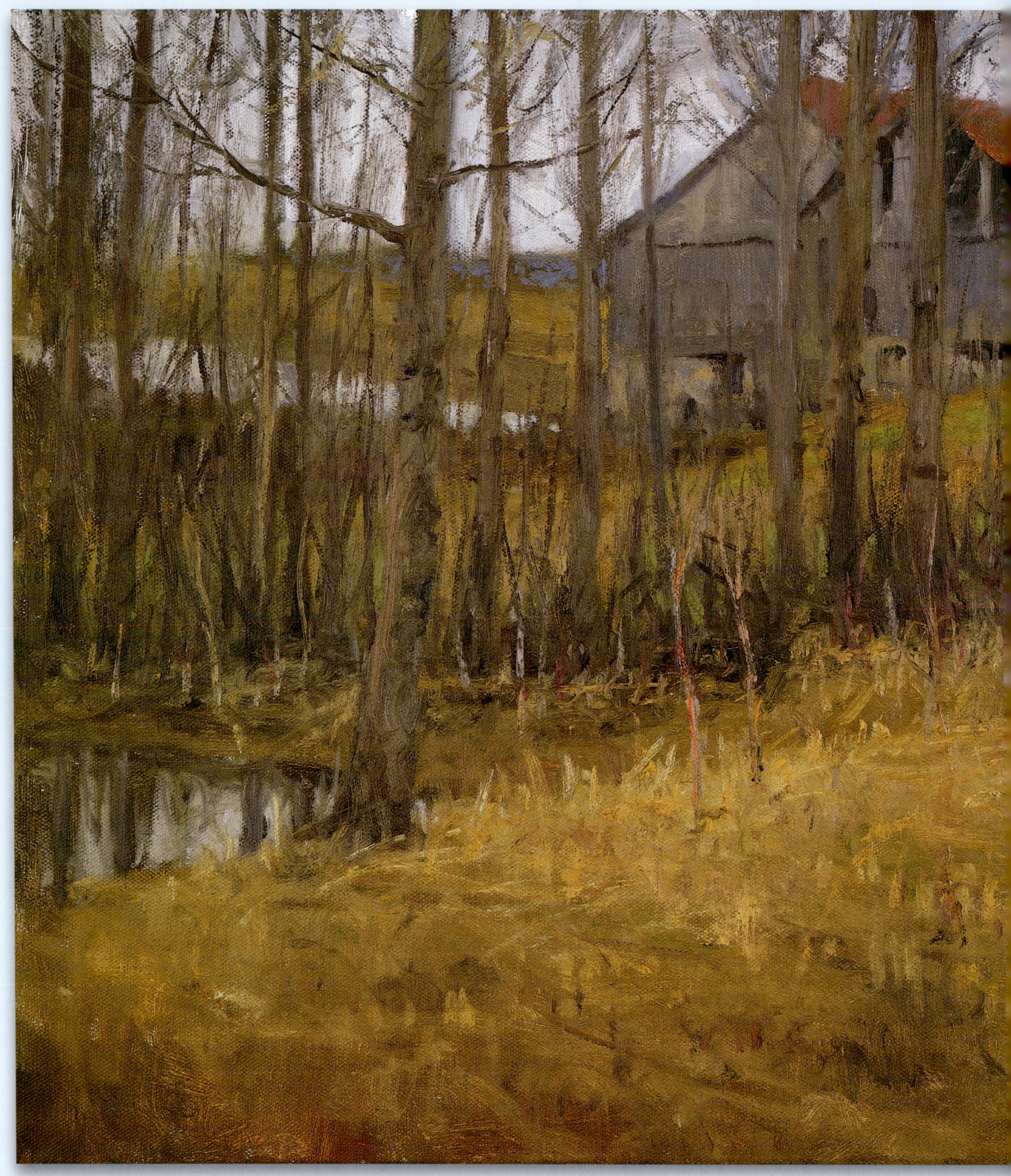

EARLY SPRING IN THE VALLEY
Oil on canvas · 16" × 20" (41cm × 51cm)

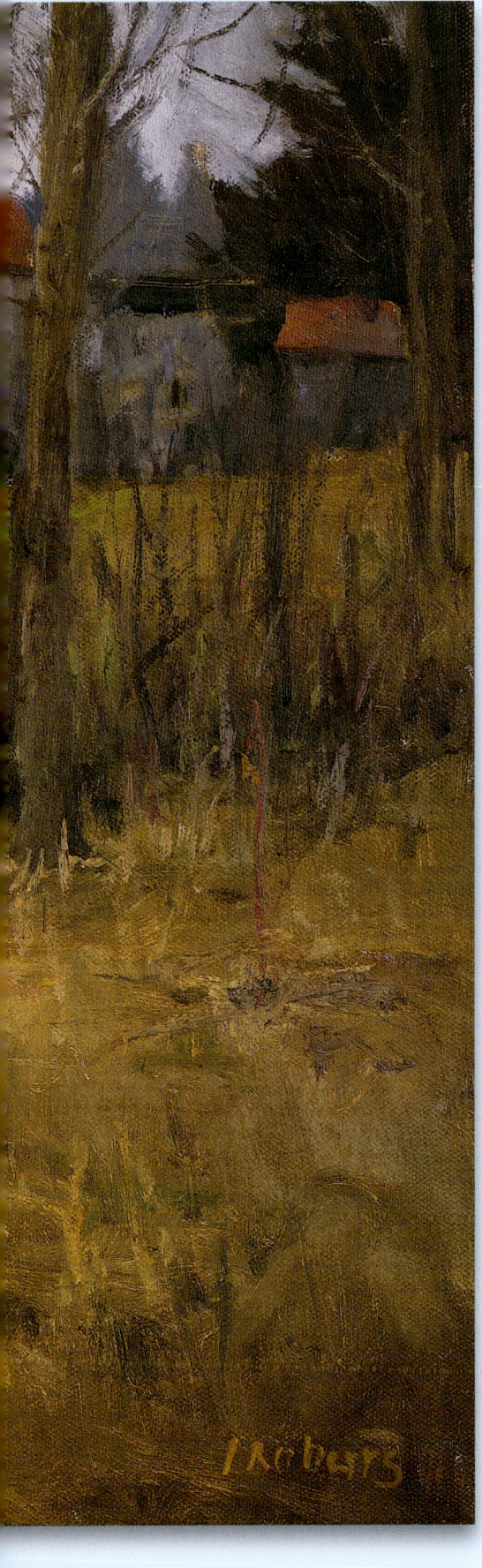

CHAPTER TWO

Abstract Masses: Cropping and Framing

You'll notice the title of this chapter has two ideas: abstract masses and cropping and framing. Together. How you approach and frame your idea for a painting has a lot to do with whether you are thinking in terms of abstract masses or seeing it just as a subject.

The French poet Paul Valéry observed, "To see is to forget the name of the thing one sees." This is a perfect expression of the mind-set for painting. Something has to shift. Maybe it's a shift from left brain to right brain; but that shift seems absolutely necessary to create consistently strong compositions. Until that shift is made and you start thinking in abstract masses on a picture plane, you are, in a sense, on the outside of the painting process looking in.

At first, thinking in masses is a bit confusing. That tree is a mass, and that one next to it is a mass, and the one next to it. The shadow those trees cast across the land is a mass, where it hits the dark water is a mass. But if you squint, you may find that actually you can hardly see any difference in value between all those masses; their edges disappear. This is seeing in abstract value masses—squinting and conceiving of the composition in terms of three or four big value masses. Just as the picture plane has proportions, so the major masses have proportions in relation to the picture plane. Choosing and arranging those few major masses is where your painting goes from acceptable to really engaging—right here, at its conception, before you start to paint.

Create Interest and Drama With Value Masses

The crux of good composition lies in seeing what you are painting in terms of abstract masses and their relationship to the picture plane. Yes, you need an armature. Yes, you need nuanced and modulated color and so on. All the other parts are necessary. But if this part—seeing in abstract value masses—doesn't happen, your painting will be like a play without leading actors. There will be no dramatic theme.

You may say, "I don't want to create loud paintings." Drama doesn't have to be loud; it can be quiet. If you don't have drama, you're going to put us to sleep. In painting, drama is another word for effective design.

Design lies in the arrangement of the major abstract value masses you use in your painting. Whether you're working from life or a photograph, you need to squint to see those masses. Otherwise, you will get distracted by details. By squinting, you can see the big shapes of light and dark.

As you survey a scene, try to see those big shapes in relation to a rectangle—your picture plane. With pencil or paint, translate those abstract masses into light and dark shapes, arranged within a rectangle.

By focusing primarily on designing several value masses, the variety of their sizes and the flow between them, you can improve your painting dramatically. You may master every skill imaginable, but, without design, you won't have a way to make consistently engaging paintings. Learn to see and arrange value shapes and your painting will take a quantum leap forward. Master this concept and your success rate will soar.

Remember

The value masses carry your painting more than anything else. They are what the viewer will see from across the room.

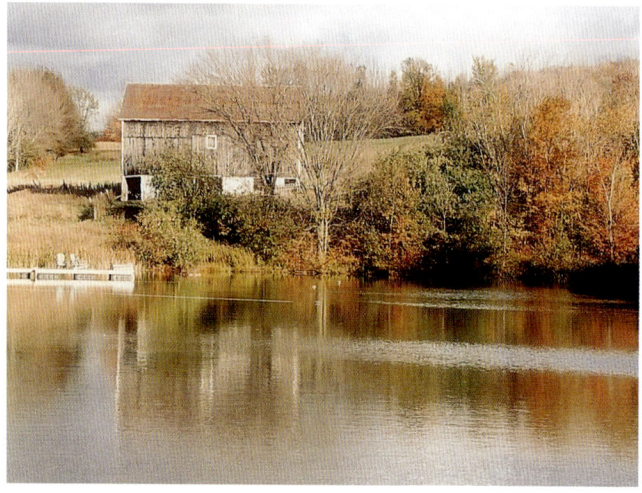 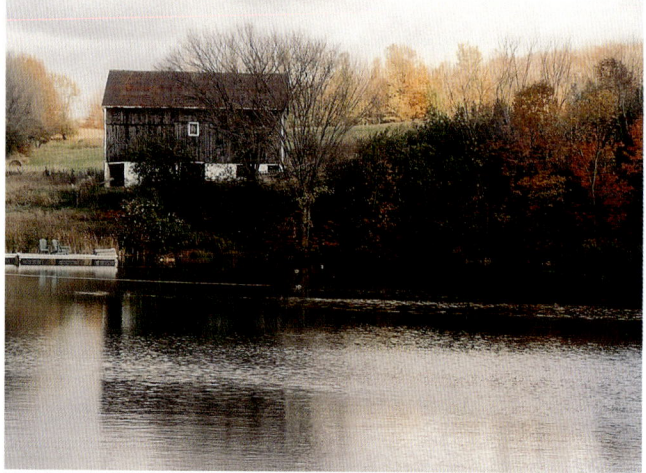

Drama Begins With Effective Design
Let's look at two photos of the same subject. The one on the left is a pleasant country scene. But there's no design, no drama, no simplicity to the value masses. In fact, there are no major value masses, just lots of little shapes. Compare that with the photo on the right and you can see immediately how this one could be translated into a bold, broadly painted landscape. Or you could paint it with lots of details. Either way, the main value masses would carry it. Squint at them both. The one on the left has nothing to help you get started. It's just a jumble of little shapes. The one on the right is strong and simple. If you imagine creating a strong warm-cool temperature shift between what's in shadow and what's in the light you would see this could be fun and dramatic to paint.

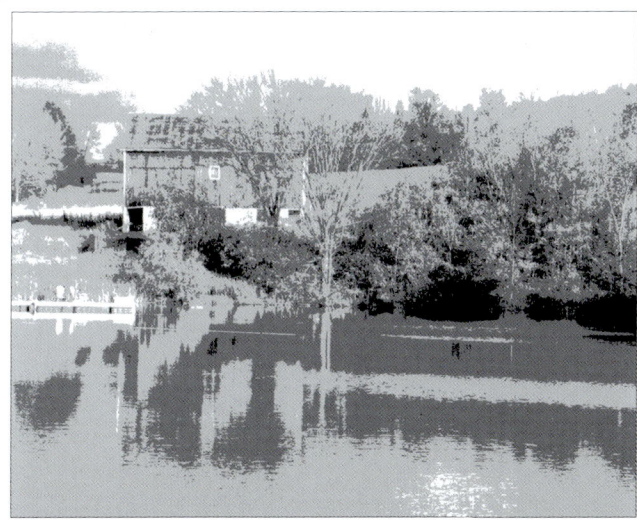
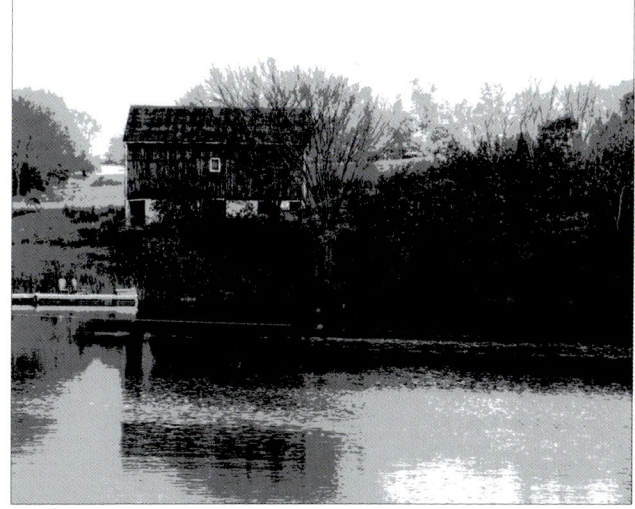

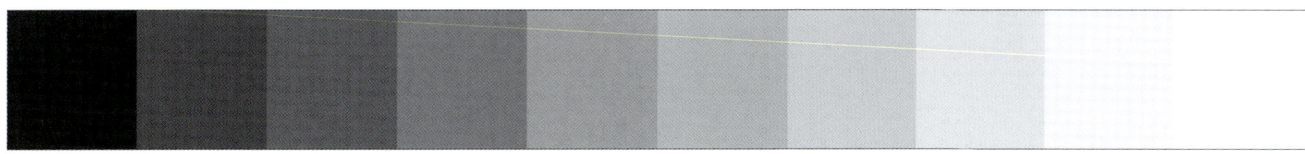

Think in Terms of Values

Here are the same images from the previous page, posterized into three values of gray and white. Through this manipulation, the one on the right becomes even more obviously dramatic. The image on the left is mostly mid-gray, and none of the elements are very well defined. On the right, you can see immediately how three value masses would define the foundation and drama of the painting. Even through we often see a ten-step gray scale, think in terms of using only three, or at most four values, in developing your composition.

You might respond: "Well it's easy if you're using such obvious examples." But that is precisely the point. You must learn to see—or create—obvious contrasts between your value masses. That is why this type of preparation is so necessary. Don't start painting until you do find something that will translate into a few abstract masses like this.

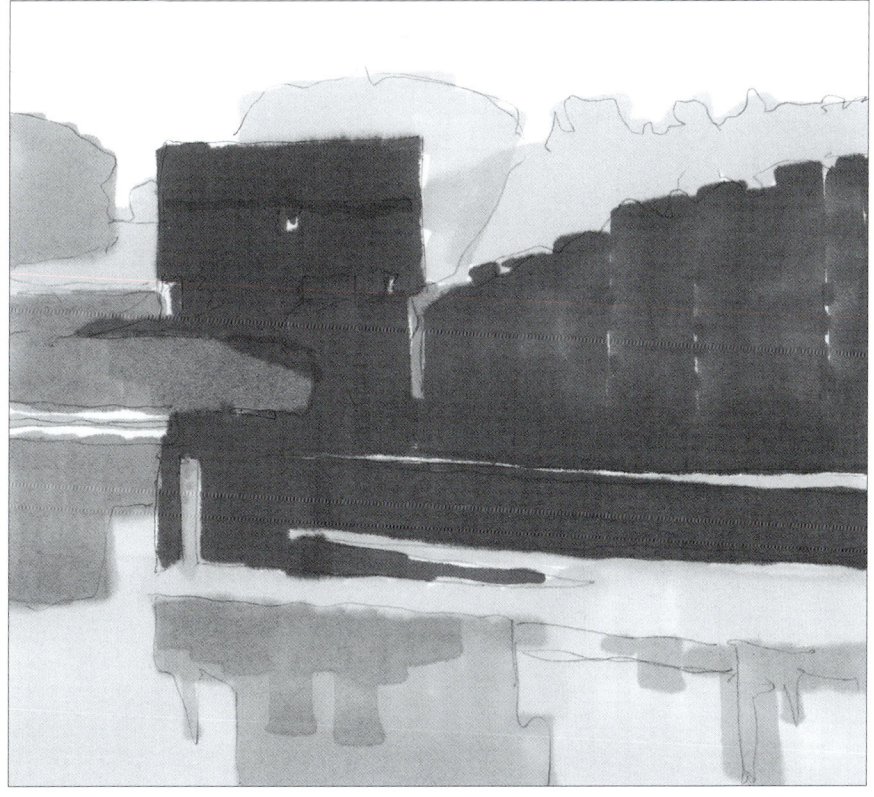

Exercise:
Simplify With Three Gray Markers

Try working out the three or four major value masses of your next painting with three gray markers and see how it changes the way you think about abstract shapes. Gray markers come in a range of values, 1 through to black. You could get 1, 3 and 5 for example (my 5 is actually closer to a 7 on the gray scale). The nibs are fat and clumsy to use, which is the point. If yours come with markers at both ends, one fat, the other a sharp point, pretend the sharp one doesn't exist. Then you'll have to think and draw in simple masses and shapes, not details. You'll definitely find it clumsy at first. Try it on bond paper, which bleeds a bit. You're not trying to create a beautiful drawing; you're using the markers to see if your composition can be reduced to three or four value masses, and to force yourself to render those masses simply.

Think in Value Masses, Not Subjects

The idea of thinking in value masses rather than in subjects is a bit difficult to explain. I often repeat this idea to students every day over the course of a couple of workshops. Invariably, after several days, someone will say, "Oh, I see. Why didn't you tell me that before?" The idea, which until then simply hadn't registered, suddenly clicked in. It is a perceptual shift, a different way of thinking. It's a question of emphasis and focus.

Of course, every representational painting has a subject, but if you let the subject matter rather than the large value masses carry the painting, you'll lack drama and probably get buried in details. When you think in masses, you see the big light and dark shapes as the real subject of the painting, and the objects in front of you are just the inspiration for the painting.

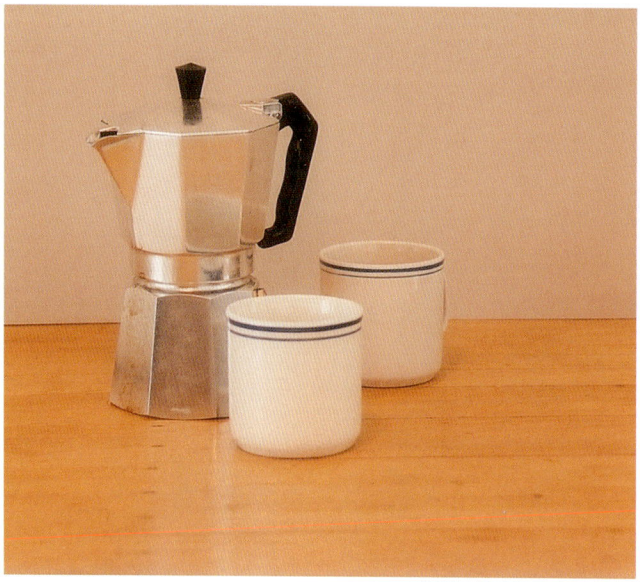

Do I Really Want to Paint This?
The light is coming in from several directions, shadow shapes are minimal and there is no overall design of light and dark. The handle and knob of the coffee pot create the darks in isolation. It's flat and uninspired.

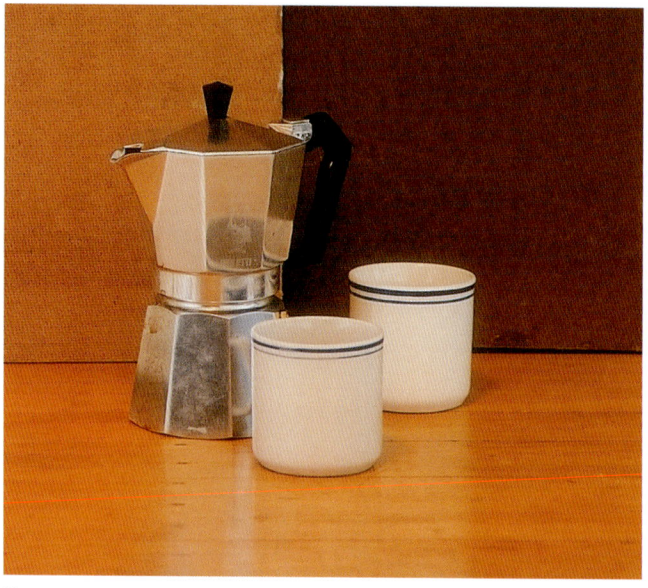

Hmmmm . . . Not Yet
Two darker shapes in the background begin to establish a sense of design. There is now a large value mass on the right that contains the handle of the coffee pot. But the lighting is still too uniform.

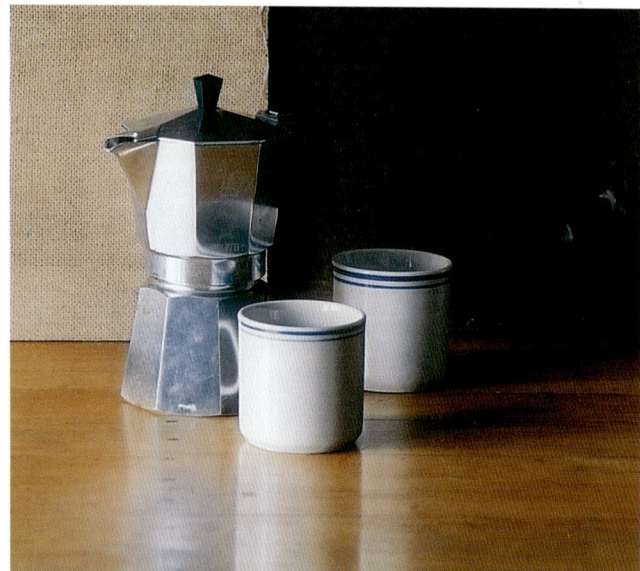

Now We've Got Some Abstraction
With a single light source on the left, we get masses. Notice all of the things that are now incorporated into the dark mass on the right. The front cup's shadow runs straight into its reflection as one shape. The image is about light and dark value masses.

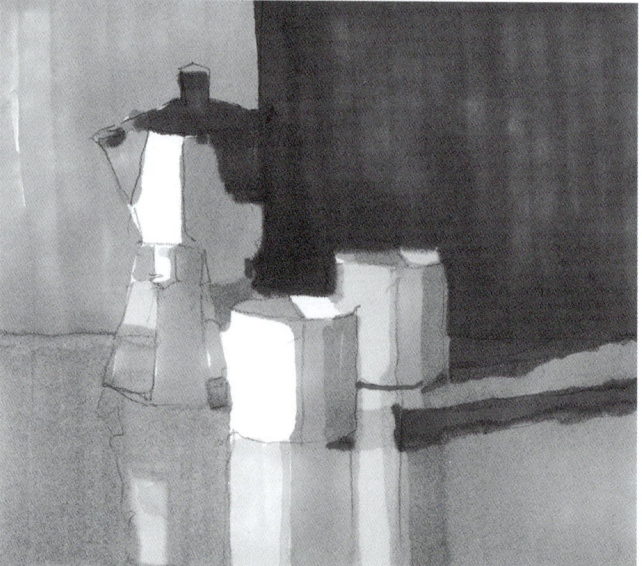

Shapes, Shapes, Shapes
The three-value marker exercise will force you to think simply or you'll soon realize you've got yourself caught in a mess of little marks leading to frustration. Try planning your next few paintings this way. When you've created a composition with some big dramatic lights and darks, you'll see how much bolder and more confident you can be when you paint.

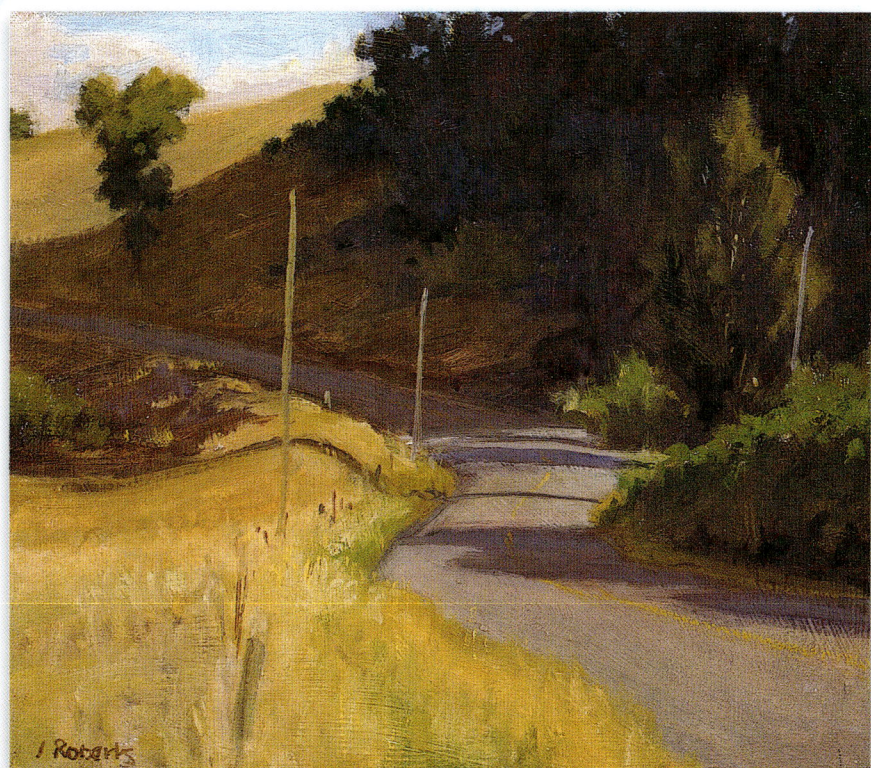

Establish Major Value Masses Early

For a *plein air* landscape, decide on your major light and dark shapes at the beginning and stick with them. You can't keep changing the shadow shapes as they move. As the shadow shapes change, you will still have reference for the color in the area where shadow and light meet. Work fast, but if you spend time at the beginning to create a good design, you'll find you can paint with greater speed and boldness.

HIGHWAY NEAR TOMALES
Oil on board
9½" × 11" (24cm × 28cm)

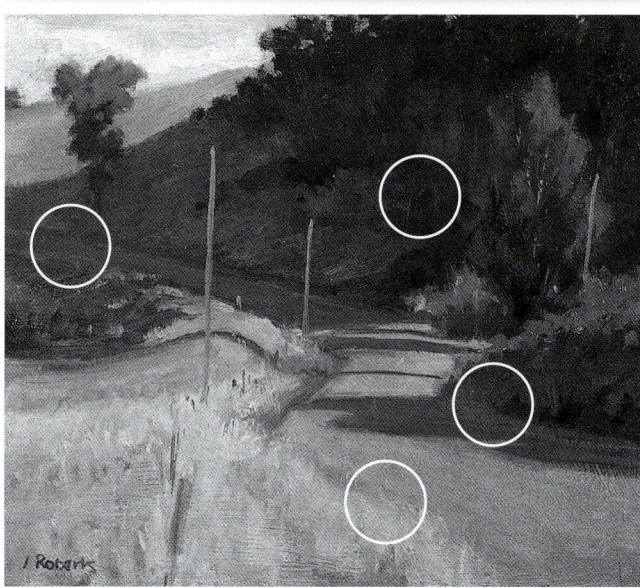

Design With Light and Dark Shapes

In black and white it's easy to see the emphasis this painting has on light and dark masses and abstract shapes. Notice the values are the same in each circle. Next time you look at a scene in evening light, squint and look for the large shadow shapes and the patterns of light and dark, then imagine those as your subject—not the trees and fields and so on that cause them.

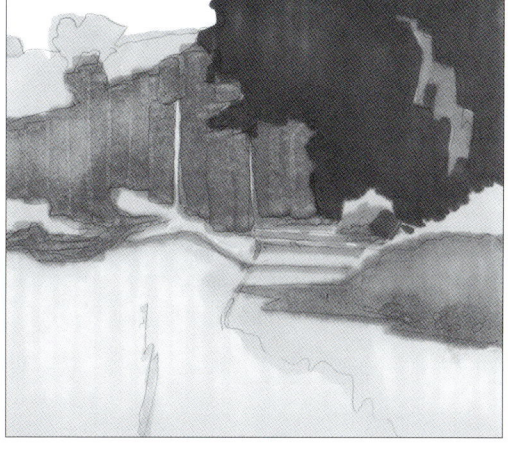

Three-Marker Drawing

Eliminate all the details and color to see how the composition can be expressed as three value masses.

Better Design = Better Painting

John Carlson aptly expresses the problems associated with painting objects without a simplifying design idea:

"The eye is greedy. There is always too much material seen, with not enough synthesis."

"If you approach nature without some idea, she is merciless in the way in which she piles lumber in your way."

Seek Strong Abstract Shapes

If you look at the work of the best early black-and-white photographers, you'll see that they really understood the value of strong abstract shapes. It was all they had to work with. They also had to make decisions before taking their photos since there was only so much they could do in the darkroom. Have a look at the work of Edward Steichen, James Craig Annan, Paul Strand, Henri Cartier-Bresson and Edward Weston. They were using photography as an art form, not just as a means to record data. Because black-and-white photography is so limited, they really had to push the abstractness and drama of their designs.

You can learn three important lessons from those photographers:

1. Think about the visual strength and beauty of your shapes. This will affect how you crop or frame your image.
2. Think about those shapes in terms of light and dark value masses.
3. Plan those shapes before you start to paint.

It's not that you see only simple shapes and no longer see details. When you squint, you simply subdue their importance so they won't distract. Then, when you come to paint the details after you've established the major shapes of your composition, you'll see that the shapes are already carrying the painting. Then you'll be able to choose which elements to eliminate and which to integrate. Thus the details will mesh with rather than conflict with the abstract shapes.

Look at the three paintings on these pages. Notice how they are conceived abstractly. A black-and-white copy of each painting only emphasizes this quality. If you study the great paintings of the past, you will see that they, too, are carried by abstract value masses.

As an exercise, try painting several paintings in just black and white to force you to establish interesting value shapes. Try focusing on this one idea so that it becomes second nature.

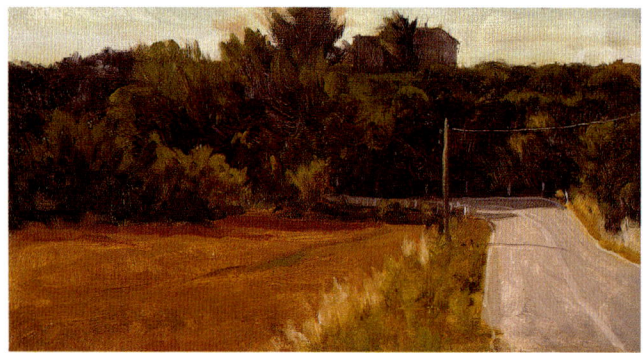 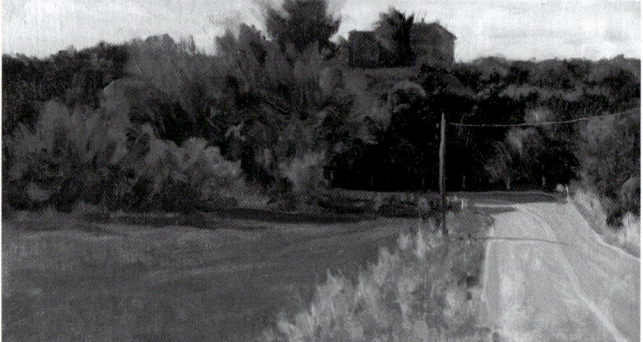

Squint to See the Main Masses
This painting was done late in the day in about thirty minutes. I concentrated on portraying shapes in relation to the picture plane and took no time for details. When you think this way, you get a feeling for what is relevant and needs to be included, and what is just going to complicate the painting and bog you down.

PROVENÇAL EVENING
Oil on board
8" × 15" (20cm × 38cm)

What counts is your eye, your sensitivity and the strength of the shapes you make.

Henri Cartier-Bresson

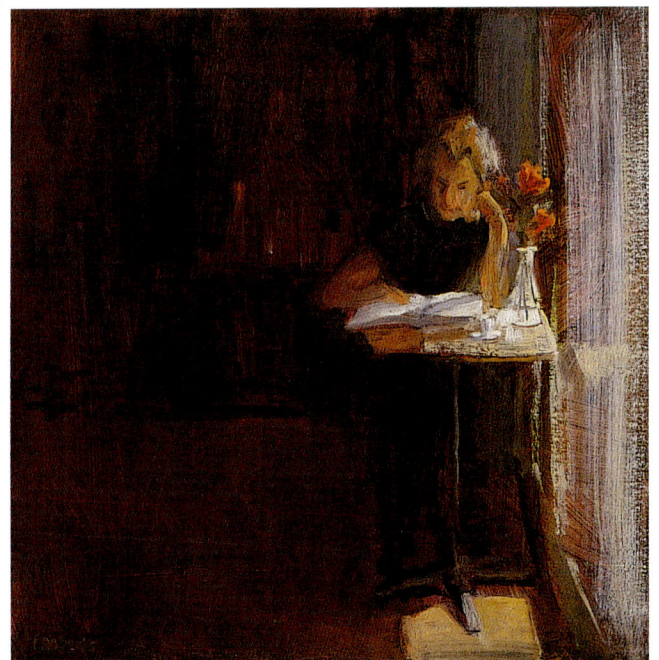 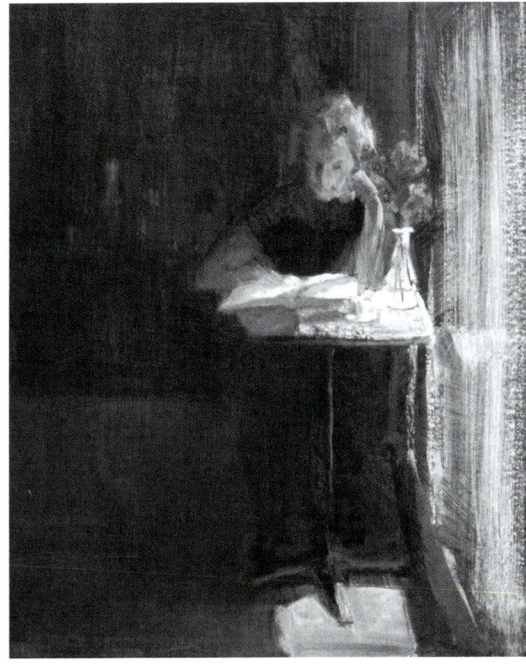

Concentrate on Design, Not Detail

This is a dramatic asymmetrical design. It's the unusual cropping that makes this painting engaging. You can see it's painted loosely, letting the design carry it.

AT THE CAFÉ
Oil on canvas
20" × 20" (51cm × 51cm)

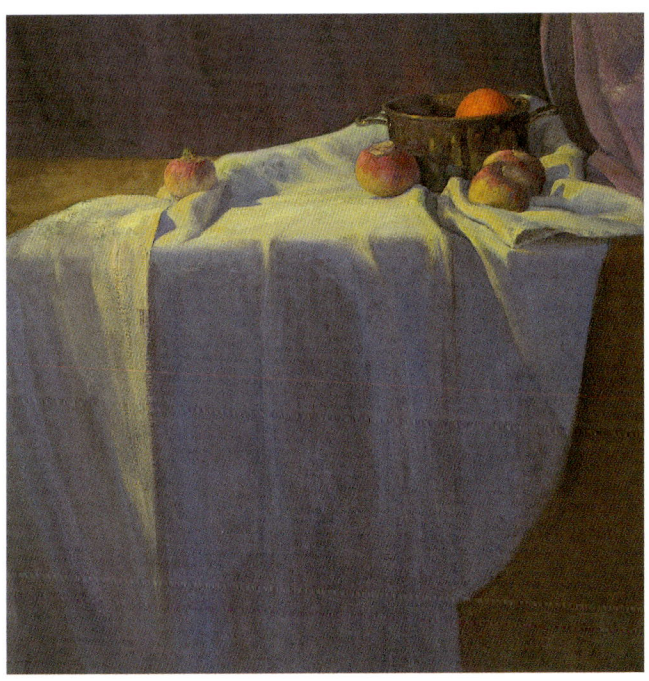 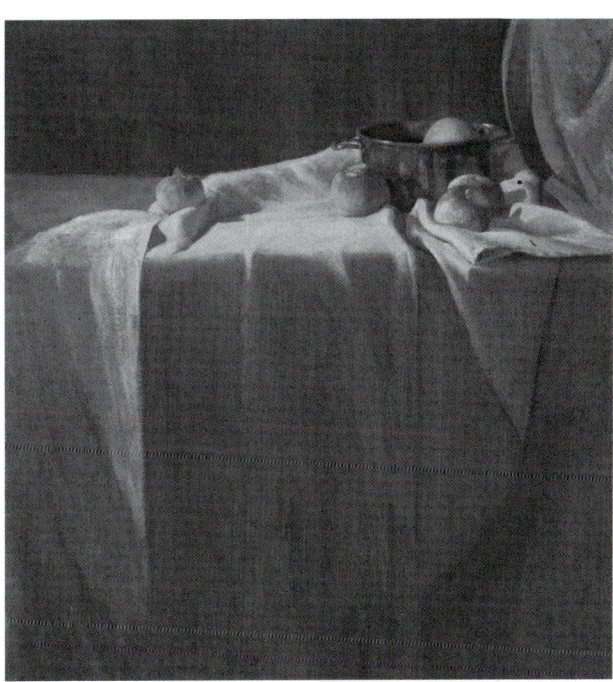

Use Lighting to Create Drama

This piece only works because of the light and dark shapes. If it were lit more evenly, it would be much less engaging. The inverted L armature leads us up to the rich center of interest at the tarnished silver pot and turnips.

DARK SILVER
Oil on canvas
32" × 30" (81cm × 76cm)

Use a Viewfinder

The easiest way to find a pleasing arrangement of abstract shapes is with a viewfinder. A viewfinder is a simple device that allows you to isolate or "crop" a scene within a rectangular area. You can adjust the viewfinder back and forth, left and right, and up and down, looking for the most dramatic and engaging composition. Use it to find big, simple shapes against small ones, light ones against dark ones. As you locate these shapes and value masses, you start the process of translating the three-dimensional world into two dimensions.

You can also adjust the proportions of height to width. Would your composition be better in a square, a horizontal or vertical format? The viewfinder allows you to quickly play with dozens of options.

Some viewfinders divide the area of the rectangle into thirds. You can place major masses along those lines. They create pleasing visual divisions and will help you immeasurably in drawing accurately. Without the thirds-indicators to help us, we inevitably tend to let things drift toward the middle into very static and conventional placement. That wonderful dark shape you saw way over on the left side, dividing the left third of the composition in half, somehow ends up occupying more than a quarter of the space instead of only one-sixth, and the whole dynamic of your composition is lost.

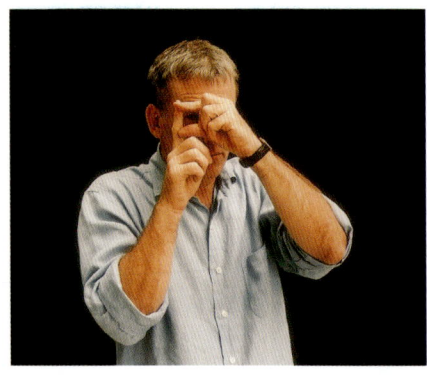

If You've Nothing Else
When you're just walking around looking for something to paint, you can get a feeling for a composition, for the shapes, by simply using your fingers as a viewfinder.

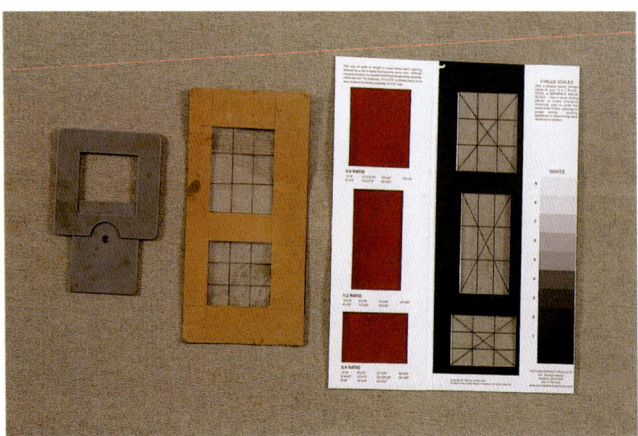

The Division of Thirds and The Golden Section

The division of thirds is very close to the golden section (a line segment divided so that the ratio of the shorter part to the longer part is equal to the ratio of the longer part to the whole line), which artists use both consciously and unconsciously because that division is naturally pleasing. For example, on a 10" (254mm) canvas the third falls at 3⅓" (85mm) while the golden section would be at 3⅔" (93mm). It is close but not exact. However, if you're talking about, say, the placement of a tree, the shape will cover both divisions anyway. The division of thirds is a convention. It's been around a long time because it's helpful. It's not a rule; it's a possibility.

Types of Viewfinders
Commercially-made and homemade viewfinders come in many variations. I think these three types are the most useful. I like the sturdy plastic one on the left (ViewCatcher, available at http://www.colorwheelco.com/viewcatcher) because it's easy to carry in a pocket or pack without bending or crushing it. You can slide the inner piece back and forth to create any variation of height or width.

The middle one is homemade. I like square compositions, so I made one with a square and with a 3:4 rectangle (9:12, 12:16). I glued two pieces of card together, inserting a sheet of acetate marked in thirds with a permanent marker between the pieces of card. The size of the square is 2¼" (6cm).

The third viewfinder (available at www.pictureperfectviewfinder.com) has three rectangles with 1:2, 3:4 and 4:5 ratios divided in thirds. It also has red acetate, which is useful for determining value masses. Sometimes when students first use a viewfinder they feel limited by how much they can get into the frame. It doesn't take much practice before you realize that by adjusting the distance from the viewfinder to your eye, you can control how much to include or exclude.

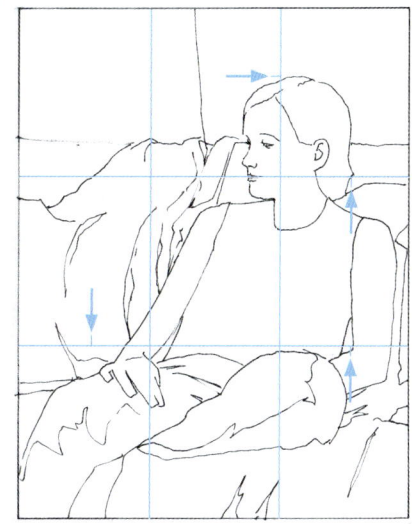

A Grid

If you've found a composition you like in a view-finder that isn't divided into thirds, you have very few reference points for placing the drawing in the rectangle. In fact, you just have four: the edges of the rectangle itself. With a grid of thirds, you have thirty-six reference points: the edges of each of the nine rectangles created by the grid. You can see the placement of several key elements of the figure within their respective squares. You can make reference marks for all the main elements, so the proportions and boundaries will be established when you start to draw them.

Exercise: With and Without a Grid

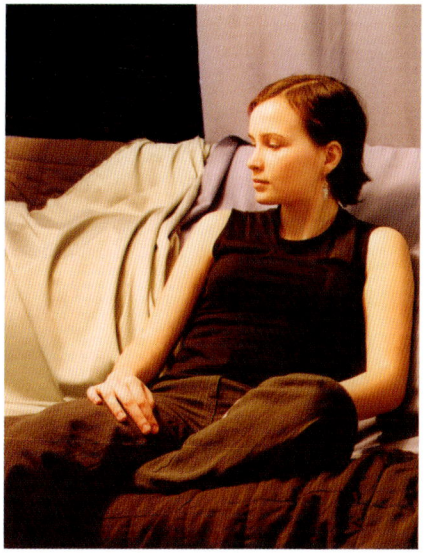
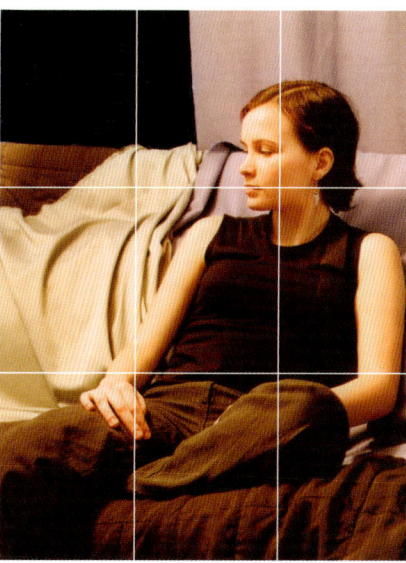

Draw a rectangle 5" × 4" (13cm × 10cm) and, covering up the gridded photo on the right, draw the figure on the left as accurately as you can. Then draw another rectangle and divide it into thirds each way and draw the figure again using the gridded photo. You can see how much easier it is to achieve accurate proportions and placement when you have a grid.

Build Your Drawings Structurally

When you draw any object or scene, look for aspects that line up horizontally and vertically and notice their proportions to get started. With those established, you can find other large angles more easily. You will have much more success drawing if you build a drawing this way than if you just start in on the "outlines" of the figure or object. With practice, your brain gets habituated to "seeing" that grid of horizontals and verticals. It allows you to line things up, to see proportions and judge distances.

This drawing was copied from the Bargue drawing course. Most of the academy type schools today use it. Charles Bargue developed it with Jean-Léon Gérôme in the 1860s, and, if you are interested in really drawing the figure, it is worth studying. You copy cast drawings and some really wonderful figure studies like the one shown here. Gerald M. Ackerman has gathered the course materials together in *Charles Bargue With the Collaboration of Jean-Léon Gérôme: Drawing Course*.

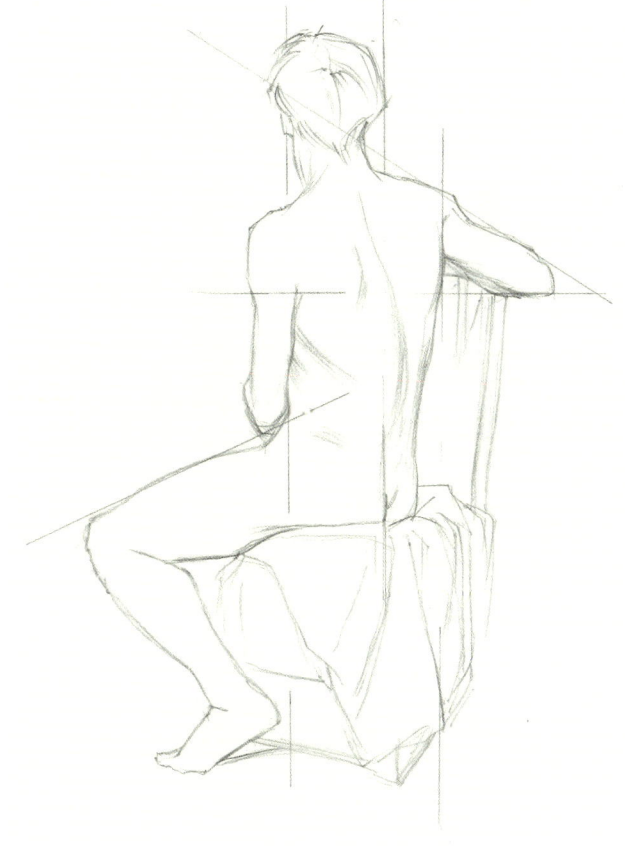

Start With Good Photographic References

A designer friend of mine once told me that your painting will only be as good as your reference. With enough experience, you may be able to make a successful painting, no matter how good the reference is. However, until you're making consistently strong, engaging paintings, take this idea as gospel: start with good photographic references.

Taking Good Photographs

Often, when my students wonder why they're struggling with a painting, I'll ask them to show me the reference. The reason then becomes obvious: the reference photo is creating more questions than it's answering. Don't think that art will somehow magically appear or that because you are an artist you should be able to transform an uninspired photo. You need good reference material.

Keep a couple of things in mind when taking photographs:

1. Think about those abstract shapes filling the viewfinder when you shoot. They won't automatically appear when the film is developed. Get a camera with a good zoom lens so you can do a lot of the cropping and framing before you shoot.

2. Photographs have nowhere near the value range that your eyes have. With a strongly lit subject, the lights will bleach out or the darks will get lost in blackness. You can bracket a subject by taking one shot the way your light meter recommends and then a shot two stops either side of that. The overexposed photo will give you information in the shadows, and the underexposed one will give you information in the highlights. Ask your photo store to develop the photos accordingly. If you don't ask, their machine will override the bracketing and all your photos will come out looking the same.

3. Photography cannot match the natural range of subtle color. Slides offer better color resolution than prints, but still can't duplicate the range of color in nature.

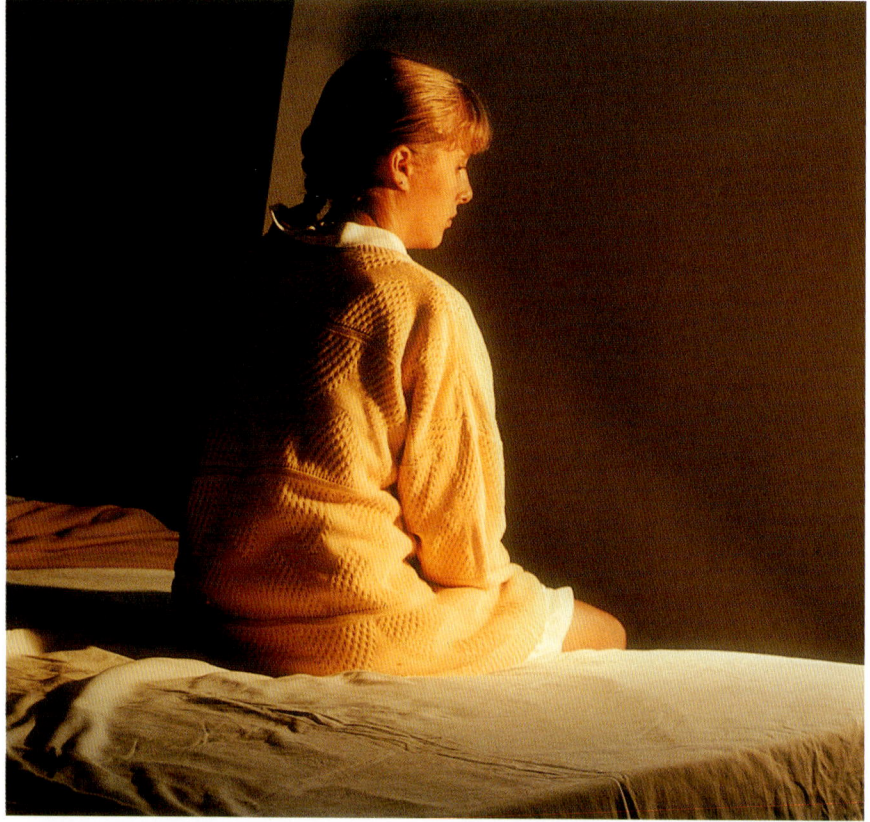

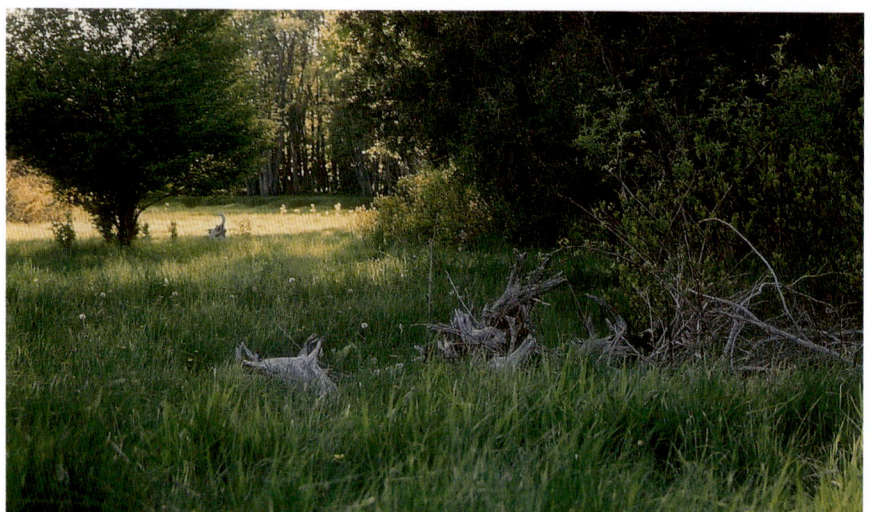

Get Good Reference Photos
Both of these images are good reference photos. You might say, well, it's easy if you have photos like that. But that is exactly the point. You need to have good references to paint successfully from photos. How do you get good reference shots? Take lots of pictures. For landscapes, my ratio is about one usable photo for every thirty-six photos taken. Not much better for figures. I don't use photos for still lifes. If you get two or three rolls of film back and really don't see anything that's working, so be it. You just have to try again. If you get the photos back from your vacation in Greece and find that they're lousy, forget trying to make paintings from them; you'll just create frustration and further disappointment.

4. Photographs distort perspective and reduce vertical dimension in the distance (you know this if you've ever shot photos of mountains). The more you work from life, the more experience you'll have to know how to fill in gaps in color information and overcome distortion issues.

If you have a lot of experience with Adobe Photoshop and digital cameras you can make adjustments to eliminate some problems. I don't adjust photos digitally, but there are painters I respect a lot who do.

WORKING WITH PROPORTIONS

When you use a photo, make sure your canvas has the same height to width proportion as the photo. Buy a circular proportional scale from a photography store, or use the following formulas:

a = photo vertical dimension

b = photo horizontal dimension

c = painting vertical dimension

d = painting horizontal dimension

To find a: c × b ÷ d = a

To find b: a × d ÷ c = b

To find c: a × d ÷ b = c

To find d: c × b ÷ a = d

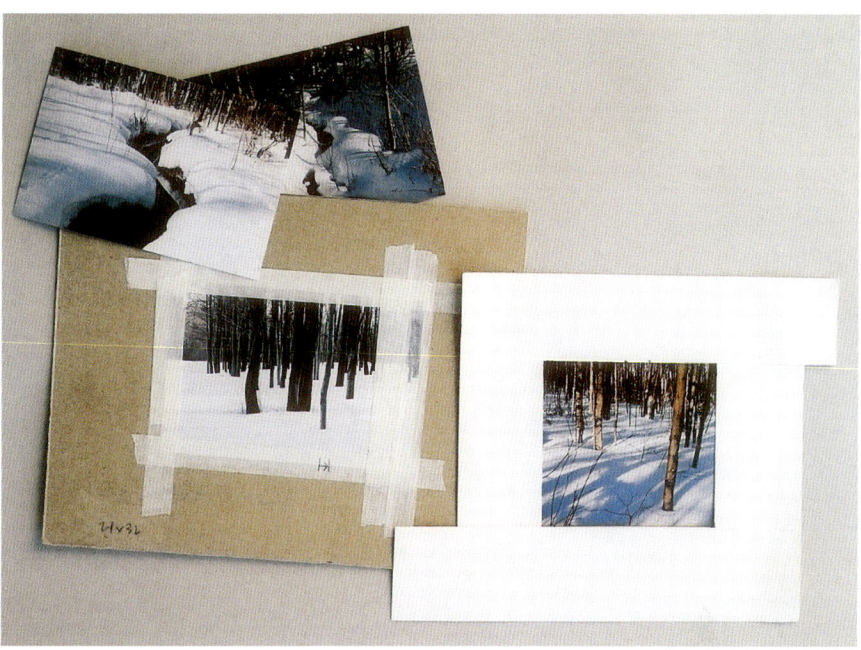

Cropping
You can use two L-shaped pieces of card, cut so the inside dimensions are 5" × 7" (13cm × 18cm), to crop and frame your photos. Play with the cropping and don't just settle on the first idea you get. Once you're sure of an idea, mount the print on cardboard and use masking tape to crop it to the proportions you liked for painting.

Search Out the Composition

Sometimes ideas for compositions just come to you, fully formed. Other times you have to build them from scratch. In both cases, you still need to play with the idea to develop it.

Approach the framing of a composition with an open mind. Coax it. Exaggerate it. Dramatize it. Start fluidly, so the boundaries aren't fixed. This is the process that leads to great composition. Be open to an unusual or unexpected possibility. A small shift to one side or another can suddenly make all the difference, so don't commit too soon. When you find a subject that's worth pursuing, do a value sketch to evaluate its potential. If, after exploring an idea, you aren't excited by it, move on and try something else.

Don't feel that all this experimentation is just busywork before you get down to the real creative process of picking up your brush and starting to paint. This is a vital part of the process, and can be just as engaging as applying the paint.

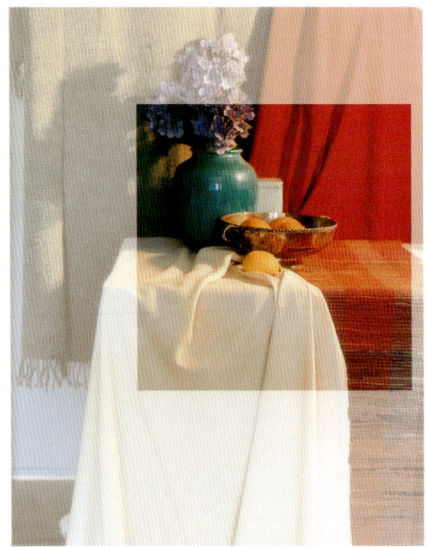

Cropped Photo Reference
Any still life has a lot of possibilities for cropping and emphasis. Even when your painting will be done from life, it's useful to observe the setup and determine the final crop with a viewfinder.

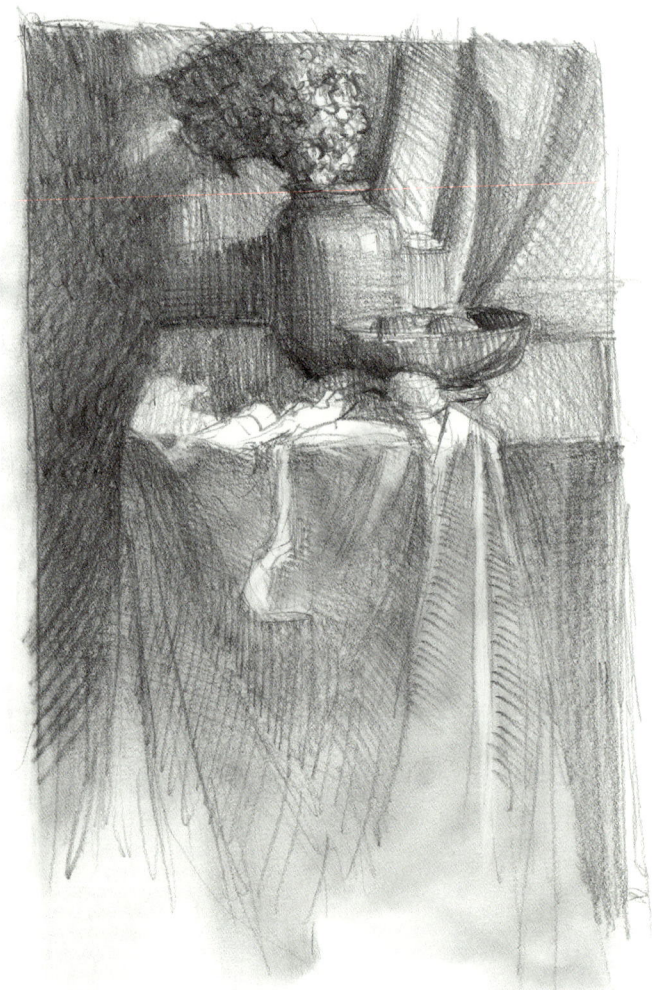

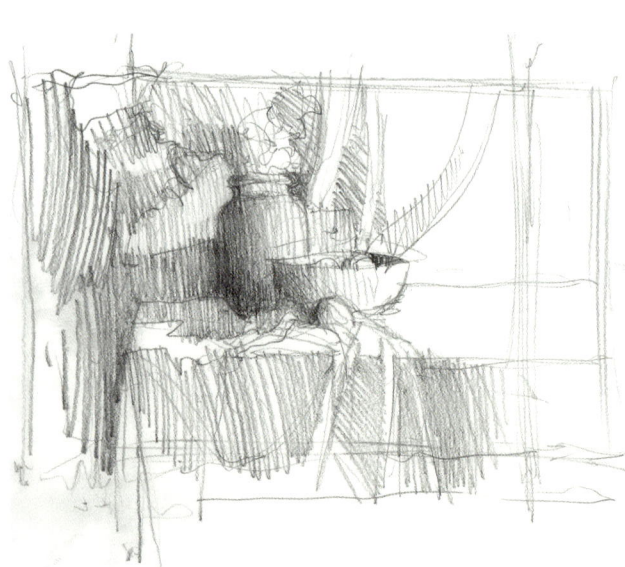

Keep the Boundaries Fluid
Notice the boundary changes in this sketch. The left side has been expanded beyond the original border. The right side has been cropped in and the bottom extended down. The boundaries are fluid; anything is possible at this point.

Try a Different Format
This sketch examines the possibility of a strong vertical composition. It's not clear yet how close to the bottom the composition should be cropped. Try running your hand up the drawing to see where you might crop it.

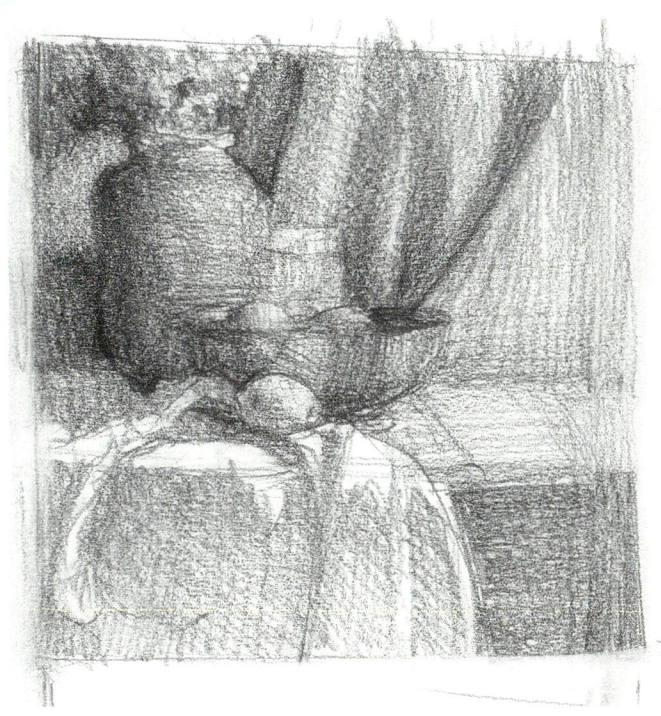

Final Crop
Here is the final thumbnail. Notice that the left side has been further cropped and the right extended. Solve as many compositional problems as you can before you start to paint. Once you do start to paint, there are so many other things to think about that you may not notice serious compositional flaws until too late. Once you have committed a lot of time and effort to developing the painting, you may be very reluctant to go back and make significant fundamental changes.

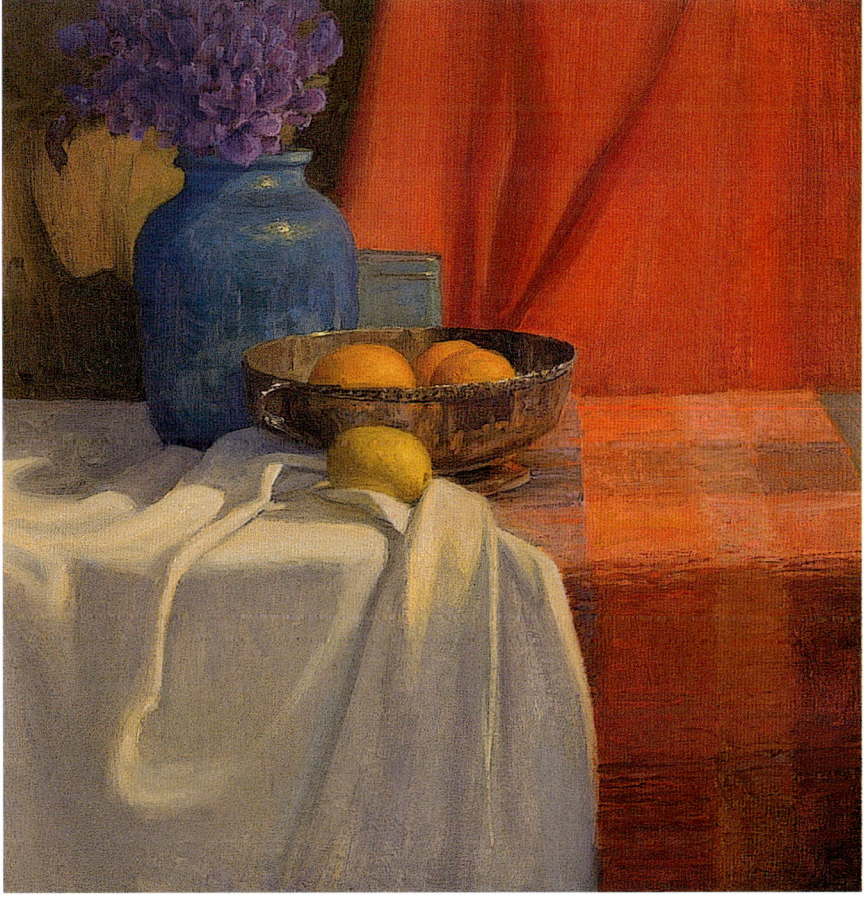

Finished Painting
Even though the color intensity is quite high in this painting, you can still see the abstract value masses that define it. The shadows, lost edges and reduced contrast encourage your eye to travel out to various parts of the painting, but they then swing back to the center of interest, the fruit and silver bowl.

RED, BLUE AND TARNISHED SILVER
Oil on canvas · 20" × 20" (51cm × 51cm)

Do not be afraid that too much labor

over a composition is going to kill

the spontaneity.

John Carlson

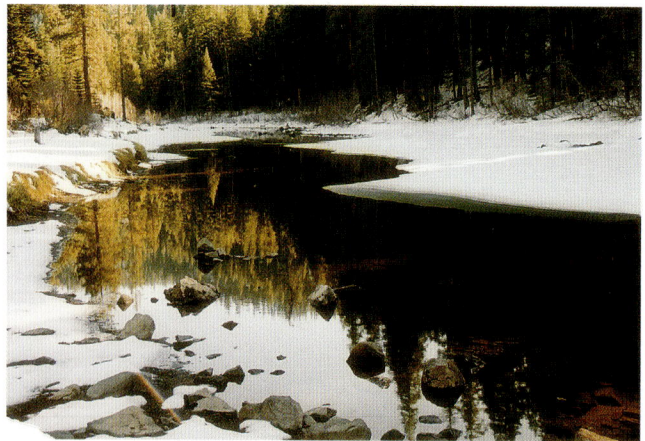

Uncropped Photo
Although I may have seen the right side as more interesting, the camera always takes photos in the same proportions. So even if you have a clear idea for a composition, you may get a lot of extra material on one side or the other in a reference photo that you know you'll have to crop.

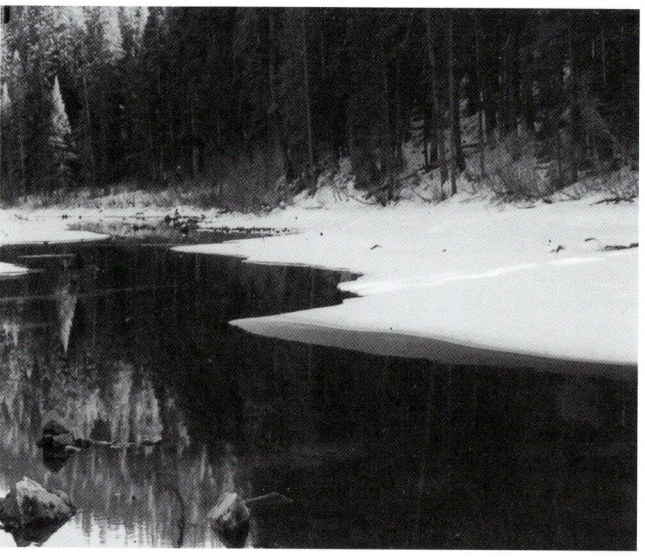

The Design Idea Becomes Clear
You can see the big design shapes leading to the small yellow tree immediately now. The foreground area on the left is distracting, so it will be necessary to simplify it.

In black and white, the abstract shapes are more pronounced. With a composition idea like this, you could paint it roughly, even quite crudely, yet the design would still carry it as a painting.

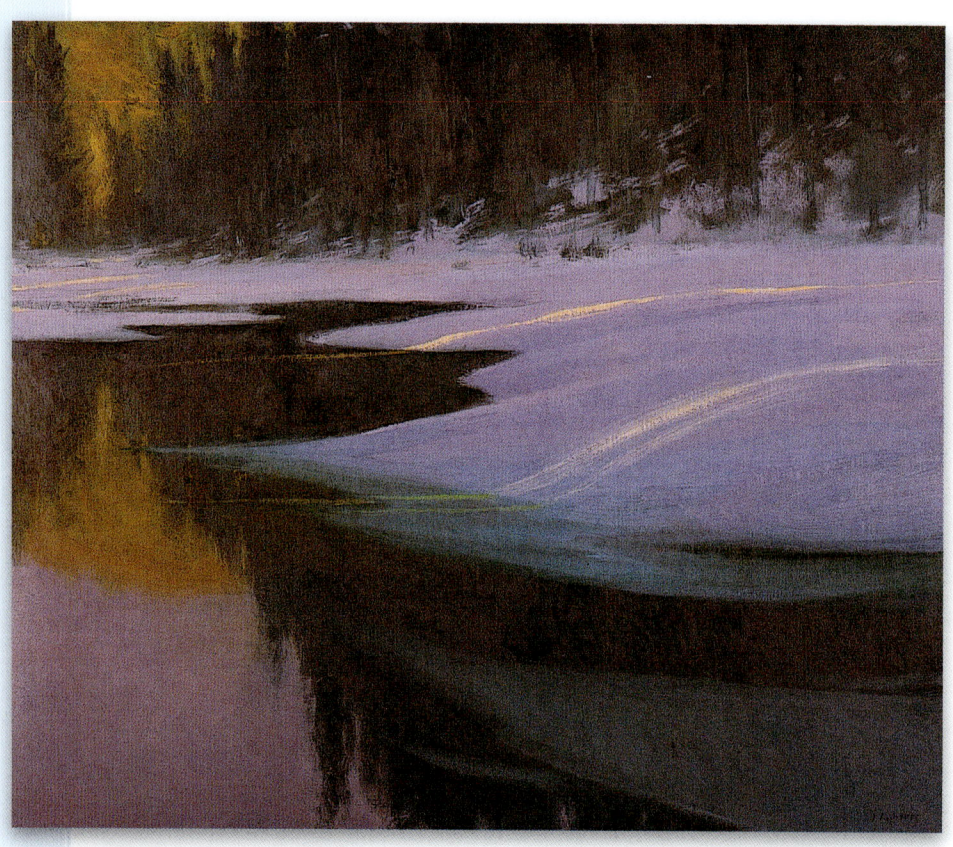

EVENING ON THE TRUCKEE
Oil on canvas · 40" × 48" (102cm × 122cm)

Adding Emphasis to the Design
Notice how the information in the lower-left corner has been simplified and the value contrast subdued so it would not fight with the lit area above it. I added the green shape in the water on the right because the dark area of the reflected water seemed empty without it. The shape is designed to move you back into the painting, toward the small lit tree. Each element was adjusted to reinforce the design idea seen in the photo.

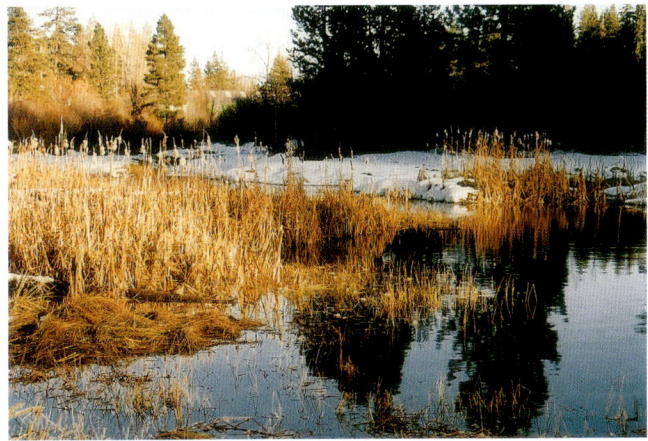

Uncropped Photo
The lighting in this scene is beautiful, but the left side of the photo is too busy. The right side is less cluttered and has some big simple shapes with high contrast.

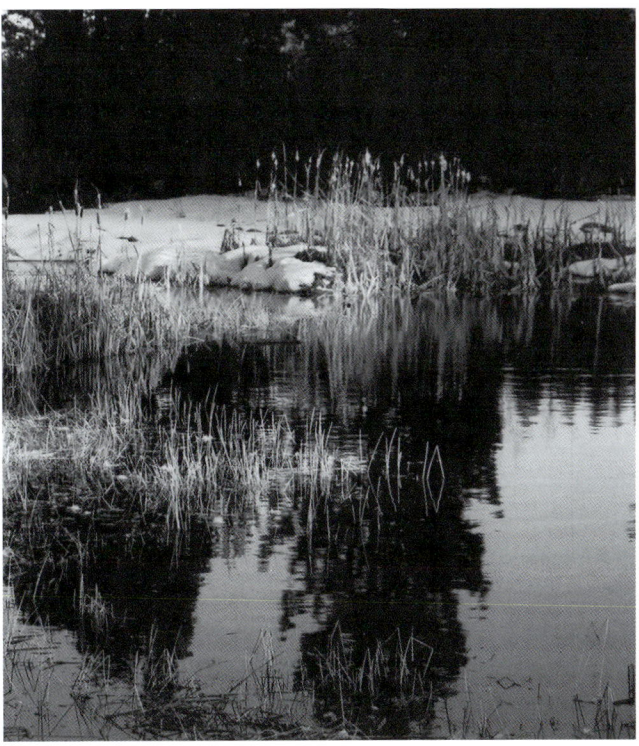

Big Simple Shapes
Now three or four value masses dominate the composition. You can see that it is now design driven.

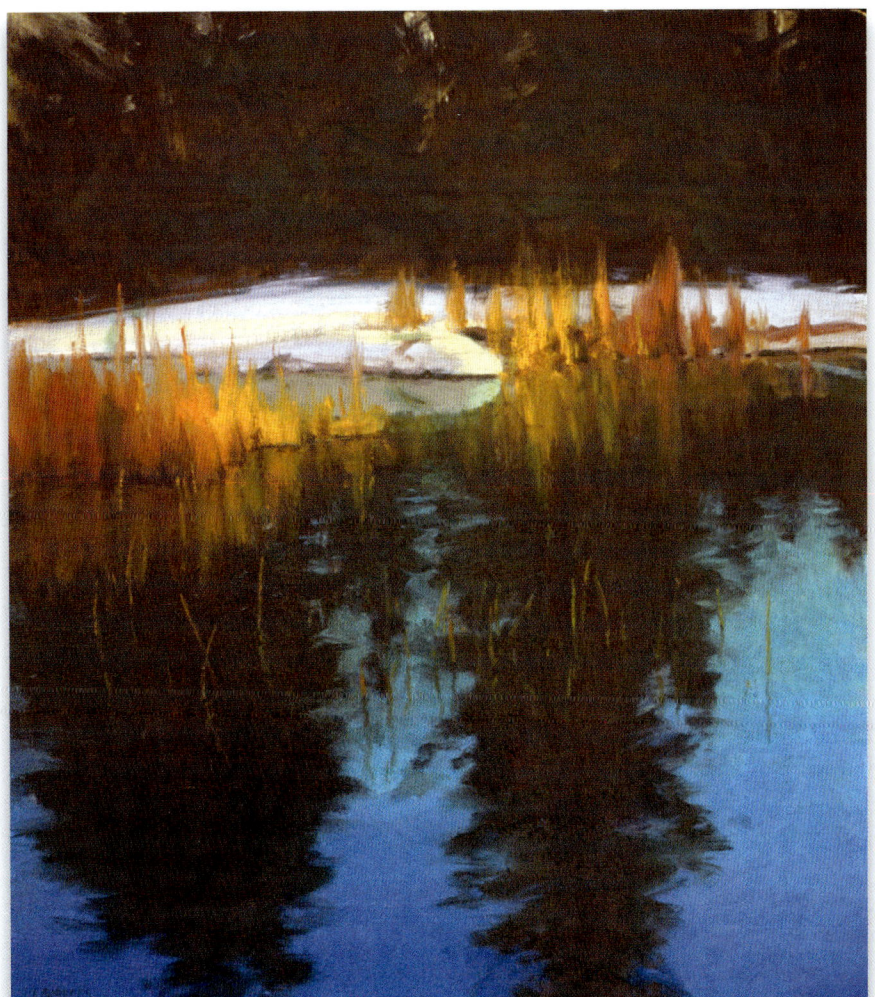

Simplicity and Emphasis
The warm evening light in this painting is beautiful, particularly when contrasted with the blue of the water and the snow. Nevertheless, the composition is held together first and foremost by the abstract value shapes—the light and dark patterns.

GOLDEN REFLECTIONS
Oil in canvas · 36" × 32" (91cm × 81cm)

Change Your Viewpoint

If ten people set up to paint the same thing, you'll get ten very different paintings. Teaching workshops you see this all the time; people see from different points of view, both literally and figuratively. Sometimes you can take a wildly different viewpoint simply by moving slightly to the left or right. But a significant change may be as much or more about an inner shift of framing, emphasis, exaggeration or omission.

Everyone has clichéd ways of looking at things. Breaking those habits and taking a fresh viewpoint is important to the artistic process. You know the experience of seeing something familiar as if for the first time; it seems alive and exciting. That's the way you want to try to see things before you paint.

In landscape painting, the best way to achieve a fresh point of view is to just "be" with the landscape for a while. Walk around without actively trying to find a subject to paint. You may have already done this on another day and decided that a particular view at four in the afternoon on a cloudy day in mid-October is what you want to paint. That's different.

When you're looking for something to paint, slow down, absorb nature, quiet your mind and appreciate the nuances and variety of what's around you and your opportunity to be there and paint it. Then, just be attentive to your feelings until something arrests your attention. You'll find a subject with your heart, not your head. Maybe you'll find two or three possibilities. Go from one to the next. Using a viewfinder to isolate your subject, do thumbnails of the major shapes. Decide which one has the most engaging and dramatic shapes. Which one excites you the most? Which one can you look at and visualize with the colors and brushwork that you might use in a painting?

If you slow down and let the landscape speak to you, you'll be less likely to filter the scene through your usual clichés of what a good painting or subject is. You'll respond

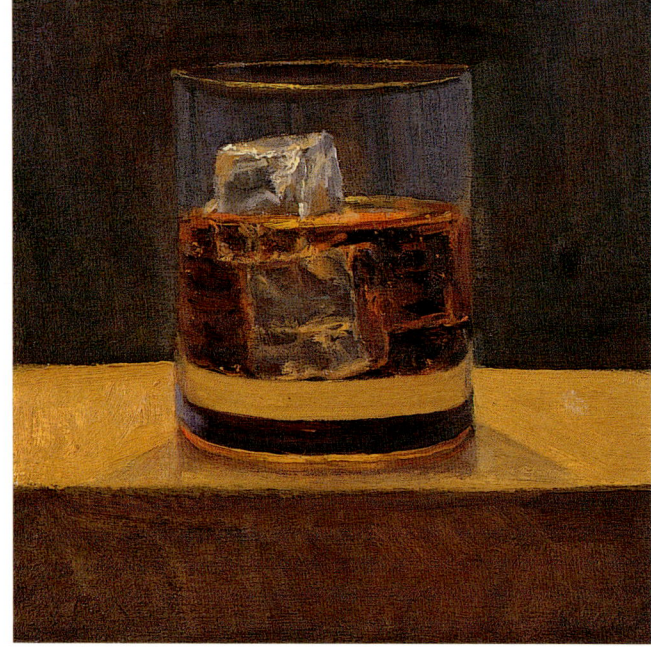

Find Something Engaging
I saw this glass with acrylic ice cubes and scotch and loved the way the light came through it. I knew it would make a good series painting.

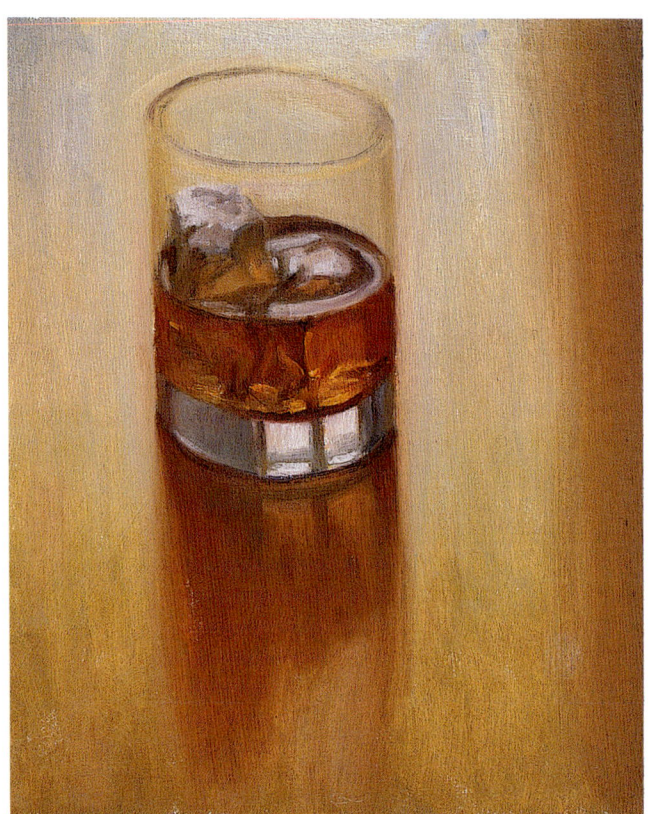

Investigate It Further
If you find an object engaging, it's a good exercise to paint it several times. Try to set it up and see it in a fresh light each time. Slow down and really extract all of its expressive potential.

with a fresher vision of shapes and their arrangement.

You can do this exercise with still lifes, too. In many ways, still life is the most meditative form of representational painting. You have so much control over it, and—as long as you're not painting in direct sunlight—it won't change while you're working. Set one up. Study it. Take it apart and try another—just like walking around in the landscape. The tendency is to set something up and then become too attached to it, making just tiny adjustments. Take it apart. Set up another. I tell students to use a variety of objects, backdrops and lighting to set up several different still lifes. If you find something really promising, make a sketch so that you can come back to it.

Go through the same process to set a pose with a model. Be really attentive to the lighting, to what it emphasizes and how it helps to define form and create shadows. Often you'll try several poses, settle on something and draw for thirty minutes; then, during the break, the model settles into a more natural and engaging pose. If the new pose really excites you, go for it while you have the chance. Make whatever sketches or notes you can to capture it.

If you find a model, a still life or a landscape that inspires you, be sure to consider different viewpoints. Try changing the lighting, the time of day, the season, the angle, and so on. You can always dig deeper in your exploration of engaging shapes on a picture plane. Often, it's by examining something

several times that we find a way to see it in a new light.

Kevin D. Macpherson's book *Reflections on a Pond: A Visual Journal* includes 365 paintings of practically the same view seen from his home. It, too, is a testament to how much attention and vision can be extracted from one subject—a beautiful communion with a favorite spot in different seasons and times of day. Spend whatever time you need to find a fresh viewpoint of your subject. This is as important as applying the paint to the canvas. In the end, it's the only way you'll create an engaging body of work. It's your vision ultimately that will hold us.

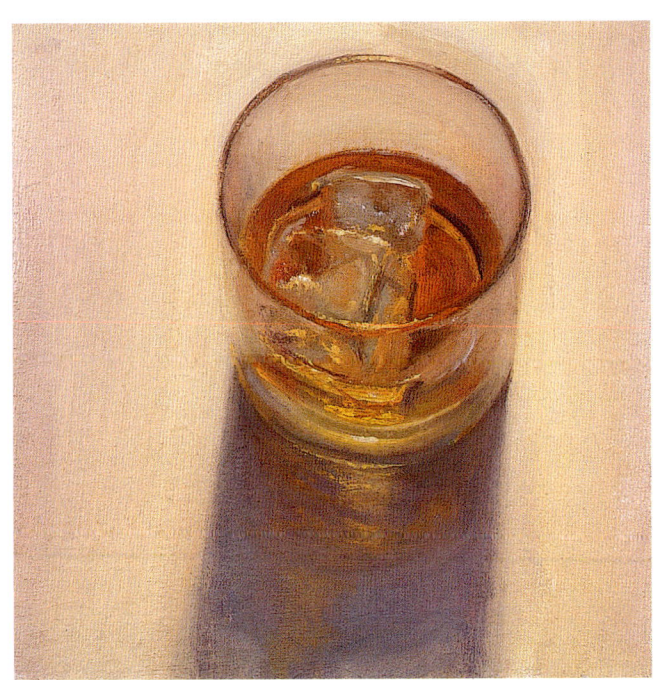

Try a Different Viewpoint
Each time you paint the same object, you get more practiced at rendering the constants. You see the subject and express it more and more as shapes. You start to notice new colors, qualities of edges and shape relationships that you hadn't seen before.

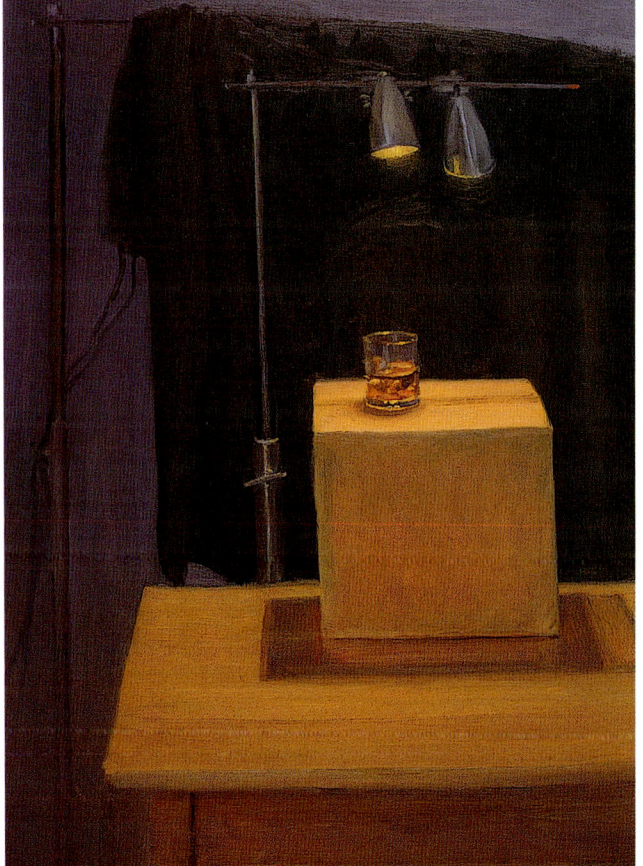

And Then You See Something Completely Different
You can be working on one thing, focusing in, arranging, rethinking, when all of a sudden you see the whole thing from a different point of view, which can start a whole new investigation.

Copy a Painting You Like

Often, when we look at art, we don't take time to discover what the artist has accomplished. But, if we like a painting, it is worth further exploration and analysis. You might say, "But I just want to respond simply to the painting. I don't want to analyze it." Yet, analyzing paintings you like helps you improve your own painting.

The artist probably used the same tools you have. He or she had the same range of colors you have (the Old Masters had even fewer), the same value range and the same types of brushes and canvas. Yet the great painters in history managed to extract a lot of juice from those materials, and it's worth some exploration to see how they did it.

There's nothing like copying a painting to focus your attention on finding out what the artist really did. When you copy, you discover information about value contrasts, edges and the arrangement and flow of value masses. You'll also see how the artist has created interest and emphasis and where he or she let it go. You really find out how the painting was composed.

The copying of great art used to be one of the primary learning tools for artists. The original function of museums, such as the Louvre, was to offer artists the opportunity to copy paintings in the collection. Only later did they open as public galleries. You can still see people copying in the Met, the Louvre and the Prado.

For the purposes of studying composition, you can learn a tremendous amount by simply copying a painting in pencil on paper. Choose a painting that really moves you. Start with reproductions of the work of historically great masters in books. Lay tracing paper over the artwork and use a grid of thirds to get the outlines on a similar grid very lightly indicated on your paper. You don't need to make them large. The examples here are about 5" × 4" (13cm × 10cm). Avoid paintings that are overly complicated (with dozens of figures, for example).

Above all, take your time, and try to discover what the artist has done. The masters can teach you a lot about shapes, value masses and edges. You're not trying to create a great finished copy; you are copying to discover.

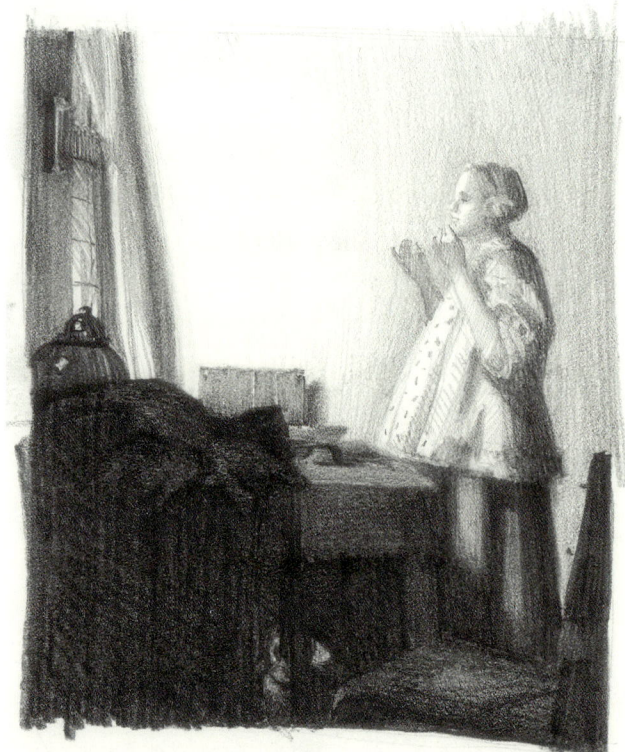

Woman With a Pearl Necklace
Jan Vermeer's mastery of composition, shapes and edges is evident in all his work. No matter how complex his subject, he seemed to express it effortlessly as simple color shapes.

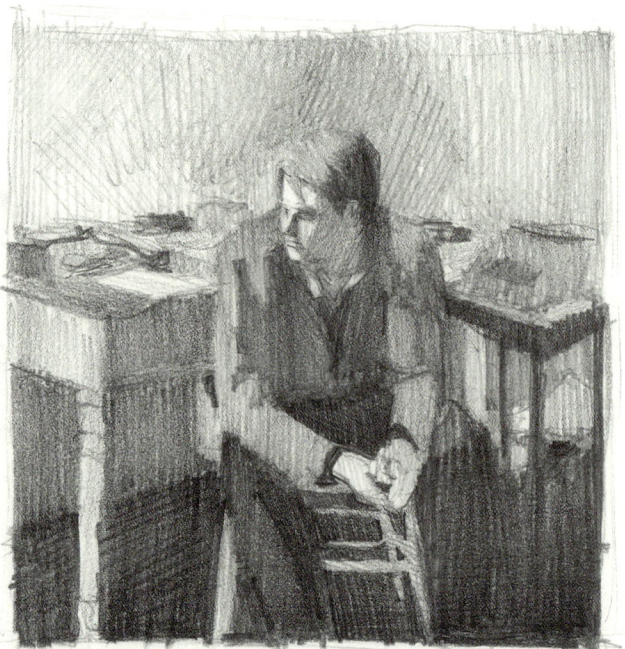

A Portrait by Fairfield Porter
The original painting expresses so much with just a couple of values. Simple shapes and a simple painting style convey a lot about this model.

Make the Most of a Museum Visit

We visit museums for different reasons. While traveling, we may visit a museum the same way we might see any attraction. However, you can also make a point of visiting a good museum as a specific part of your artistic education. Let me recommend an approach for visiting museums with the latter mind-set.

You should recognize two things. First, our eyes and brain can handle only about two hours of uninterrupted art viewing. After a couple of hours you begin to think of lunch or tea or fresh air, but not paintings. The other thing is that no matter how good the museum, there will be a lot of second- and third-rate paintings on view. Don't be swayed by the name of the artist: even the best had clunkers. If you're not careful, you'll use up your two hours on stuff that really isn't worth the effort. Also, don't waste your time with audio tours, which tend to highlight biographical information and won't be of much use to you artistically.

So, for a museum like the Met in New York or the National Gallery in Washington or London, this is what I recommend: Take two hours and go through the museum's entire collection of paintings on view. Go room by room and pay attention to the paintings that really grab you, regardless of who painted them or when they were painted. Don't worry about what anyone else would think of your choice or whether you've heard of the artist. Don't spend too much time with any one painting this time through. Just get a feeling for three or four paintings that you would really like to spend some time with. Then go have lunch. Take a break. Relax.

Later in the day, or perhaps the next day, go back and focus on the paintings you chose last time. Don't spend time on anything else. It's time to start drawing. Use a viewfinder with a grid and draw a grid on your paper. You aren't trying to make a

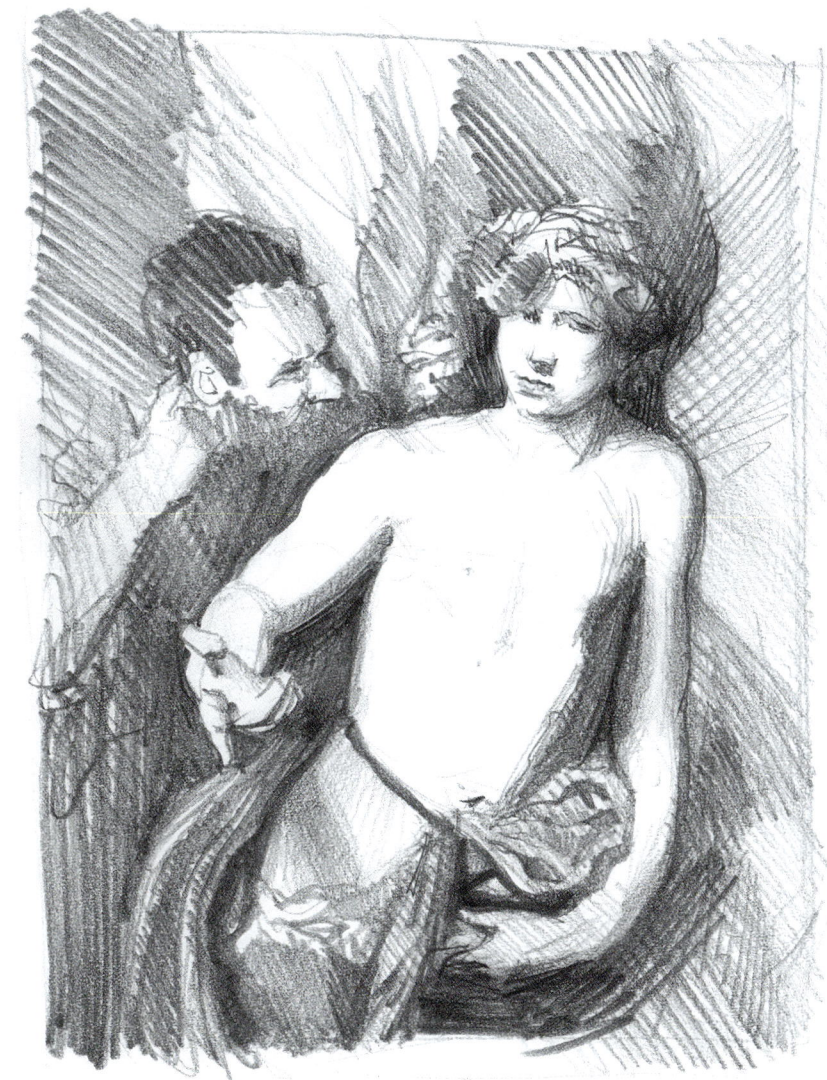

Daedalus and Icarus
This painting by Anthony van Dyck is in the Art Gallery of Ontario. I always have to visit it when I'm there. Notice that I've made no attempt to create a finished drawing. I'm interested only in shapes, edges, value shifts and how my eye is being pulled through the picture plane.

drawing anyone else will ever look at. This is your private drawing to help you see the shapes the artist used, how the masses fit together, the quality of the edges, armature, center of interest, value gradation and color nuance. As you draw, you will become aware of elements in the painting that you hadn't noticed before.

When you do this, you become engaged with the painting. Don't get discouraged if you feel your drawing isn't as good as the painting. Keep exploring how the artist has

structured the composition. You may find that you get absorbed in one painting and end up spending an hour or more on it. You may find there are points or observations you need to write about. When you've had enough, go to the next painting. You may be surprised to find that you're still going strong after two hours. When you're done, you will have come away with an intimate first-hand experience with several personally important works of art.

A Composition a Day

Earlier, I mentioned that the shift from thinking in terms of subjects to thinking in terms of shape and masses eventually just clicks. From that point on you will find you are constructing your paintings differently. It's one of those "aha" experiences.

No exercise will give you that breakthrough more surely than the composition-a-day exercise. Compare it to practicing scales on a piano. Nearly any piano teacher will tell you there is attentive practicing of scales and there is practicing by rote, which is defined as repeating mechanically without understanding (and, I'll add, without attention). Attentively practicing this exercise on a daily basis will give you a holistic way to hone your artistic skills.

The ability to make consistently good compositions can be mastered largely by doing this exercise. When I give workshops in Provence, France, I explain to the participants on the first morning that doing thumbnails is critical to the development of their compositions. They would learn so much in the eight or ten days ahead even if that was all they did: really work on thumbnails in pencil to develop design-driven compositions. Now I certainly wouldn't expect anybody to actually do that; they come to Provence to paint. But I do think it's true.

The basic idea is this: Every day draw a small 4" × 5" (10cm × 13cm) or so composition in pencil on paper. You don't need to go out and search for anything too elaborate.

Choose things that are right around you. The examples on these pages were done in my home and on my back porch. The point is to do it. Day after day. Make the emphasis of each composition the quality of the shapes, the abstract arrangement of the value masses and the edges between them. Think in terms of shapes rather than outlines of objects. Engage the whole picture plane with the masses.

The most important thing is to be attentive mentally to what you are doing. If you do a composition a day just because you're "supposed to," you'll find it is just a daily bother. But, if you slow down, you will find it is an effective way to master fram-

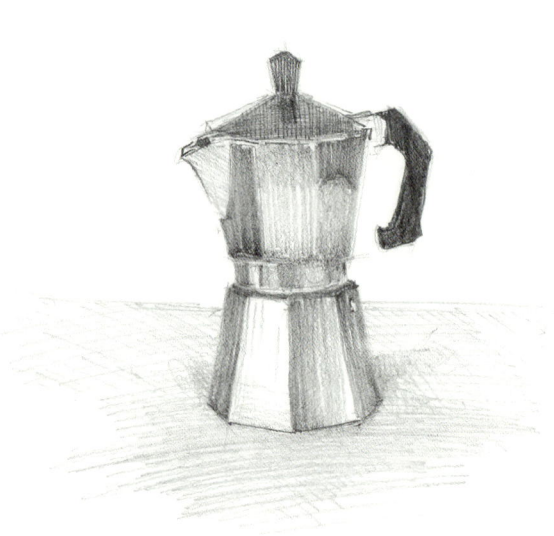

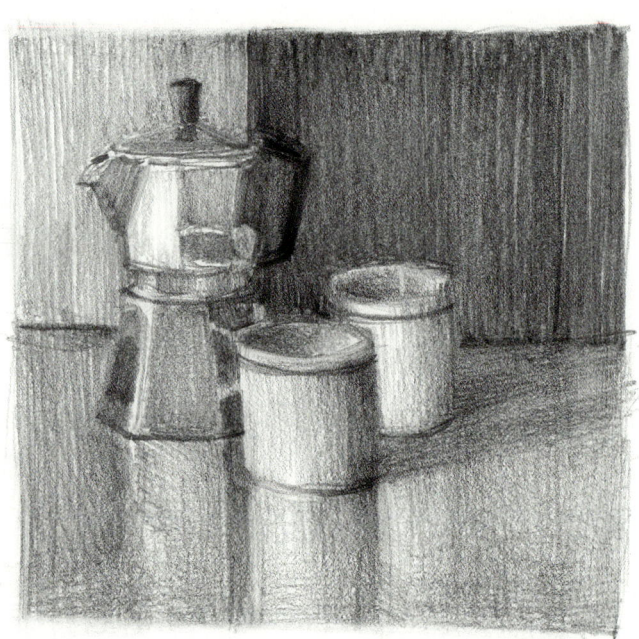

4½" × 4½" (11cm × 11cm)

Object-Driven Drawing
The drawing on the left isn't a composition a day; it's a drawing of an object. No matter how much time and attention might have gone into this drawing, it does not take into account a proportioned picture plane or the relationship of abstract masses to that plane. A more successful composition such as the drawing on the right includes these elements. Notice the range of values.

ing, armature, values, abstract masses, edge emphasis and so on.

Compared to painting, drawing feels like a quiet, private communion. Painting seems larger and more public, and thus it may tend to cause anxiety and fear. With drawing, you can be alone and explore. Also, because the investment in drawing materials and time is small compared to the outlay for painting, you can feel free to experiment. In painting, when we're working with more expensive materials, we tend to tighten up mentally. With a composition a day, you're working in a sketchbook with a pencil. You can try stuff—privately.

You may find this exercise slow at first. Look through the drawing tips on the following pages. As you become more fluent with your drawing skills and remain attentive to the idea of composing with shapes and values, you'll find it gets easier and faster to give expression to an idea. The learning curve as you get proficient at the various skills involved may at first seem a bit steep and sometimes discouraging. But nothing will allow you to master composition—and thus painting—more quickly than this exercise. Practice daily and your artistic skills will grow by leaps and bounds within the course of a year.

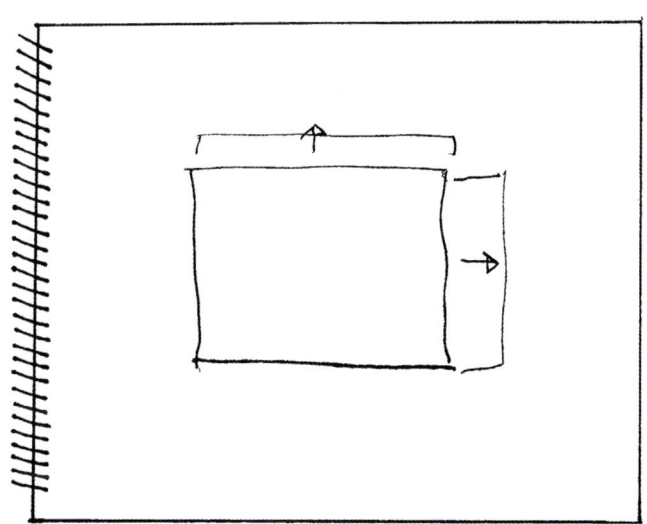

Keep the Boundaries Flexible
In doing a thumbnail or the composition-a-day exercise, work in the middle of the page so that you've got room to adjust and expand in any direction. Don't think of the size of the paper as the edges of the picture plane of your composition. If you do that, you're letting the paper manufacturer dictate the four most important lines of your composition, which limits your possibilities right from the start. Also, you'll end up making a drawing that's 6" × 8" (15cm × 20cm), 9" × 12" (23cm × 30cm) or even larger. Most of your time will be spent just trying to fill in large value masses. For this exercise, smaller is better.

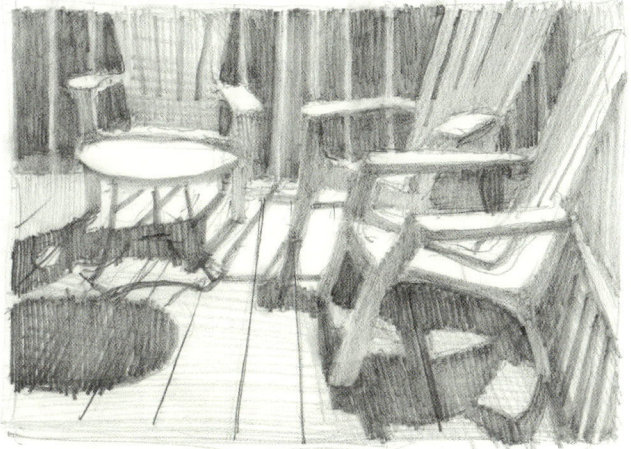

4" × 6" (10cm × 15cm)

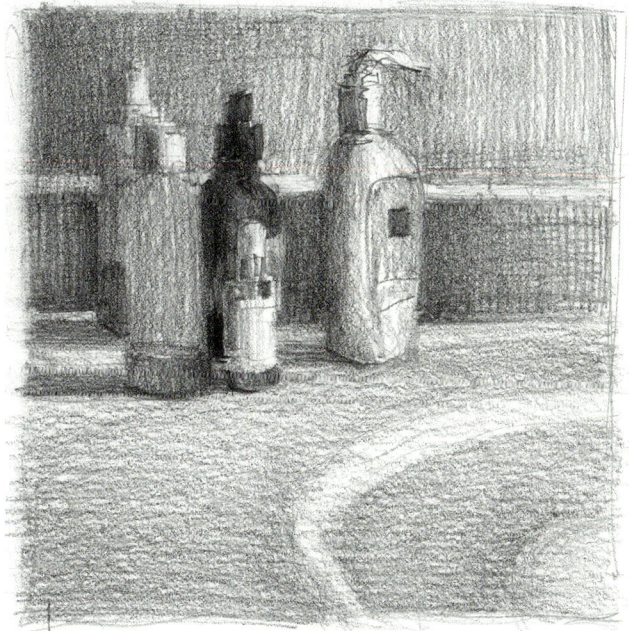

4" × 4" (10cm × 10cm)

Drawing Tips

Drawing is a very useful skill. The ability to fluently draw your idea for a painting allows you to quickly see whether the idea will work. If you find drawing to be a struggle, you will naturally tend to avoid it. However, with representational painting, you can't avoid it because drawing is one of your most basic painting tools. Ultimately, painting is just drawing with a brush.

The good news is that drawing can be broken down into several basic skills that can be practiced and mastered in isolation. Mastering these skills will affect your overall ability, enjoyment and success in both drawing and painting.

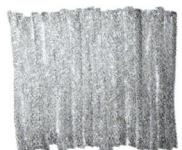 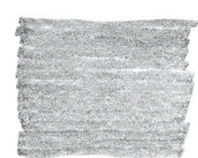  

Laying In Flat Value Masses

Two skills will immediately enhance your ability to draw. The first has already been discussed: using a viewfinder divided in thirds to establish the accurate proportions of your value masses (see page 50). The second skill is laying in flat value masses. Use a pencil. It's handy, versatile, erasable, and it offers a good range of values. Use B, 2B and 4B. Practice laying down value masses when you're doodling. Try making them horizontal and vertical, light and dark, and in gradations.

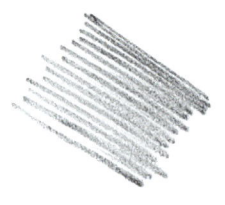
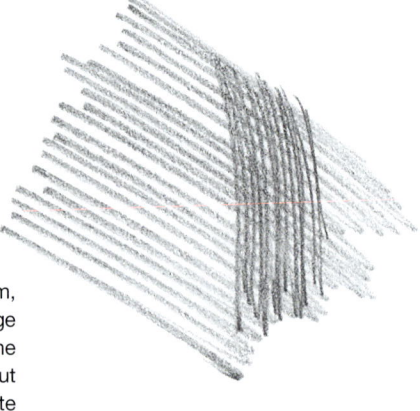

Drawing Even Value Masses

When we write, we use a combination of forearm, wrist and fingers to move the pencil across the page and form letters. To lay in masses evenly, hold the pencil the way you normally would for writing, but don't move your fingers. Use your wrist to create the motion, back and forth. If it's a broader area, use a sweep of your forearm. Then, with that motion, slowly move across the page. With a little practice, you will soon be able to create an even, smooth value mass in pencil.

Once you've laid in the mass, you can use the same motion to fill in any gaps and even out the whole value shape. If you need to crosshatch another value across the first, use the same motion but move your elbow out so that the lines are at a different angle to the first. You can also turn the page so you always have an easy sweep with your wrist or arm across the paper.

Learning to See

"Most people never learn to see well enough to draw." —Betty Edwards

Betty Edwards, in her revolutionary book *Drawing on the Right Side of the Brain*, was one of the first to recognize and teach that learning to draw involves learning perceptual skills rather than drawing skills. If you can't see it (a value shift, the proportion of one shape to the next, etc.), you can't draw it. Consequently, you can't paint it. Learning to draw involves a perceptual shift to the right-hemisphere of the brain—the spatial, non-verbal side. If you have trouble drawing, her book is worth a look.

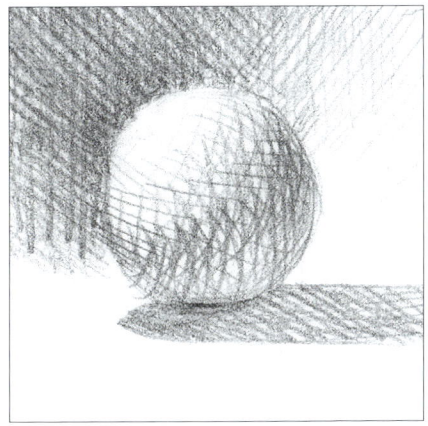

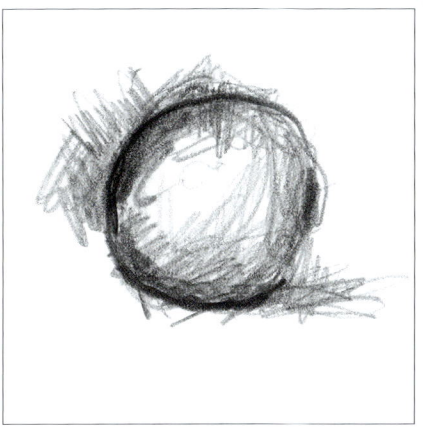

Crosshatching

Crosshatching allows you to build up values layer by layer, like washes in watercolor. Build up each layer of crosshatching evenly. Your hatching should carve into the picture plane so that you can feel the push and pull your drawing is creating on the paper. Notice that the lines of the hatching follow the form of the sphere (left).

If you don't lay in even value masses, your drawing will end up looking like the sphere on the right: no gradations in the density of the marks, and no illusion of depth. You get stuck looking at the marks themselves on the surface of the paper. The effect might be interesting in an expressionistic work, but it's distracting in a representational drawing.

The Kneaded Eraser

The kneaded eraser, like the pencil, is a versatile drawing tool. When you're drawing a flat, even value mass, you may need to fit your lines into a specific space. Inevitably, the beginning and end of each line will be darker. You can pinch the eraser into a point and dab softly at those darker marks to even the edge out (as in the upper-left side of the illustration above). You can also draw right over the edges and then erase the excess (as in the lower-left corner). You can also blot out lighter shapes within a mass (as in the lower-right portion) or pinch the eraser into a fine point and erase a line through a darker mass.

Vertical Hatching

You can also practice just using vertical hatching in a drawing, as in this example. You'll tend to draw with your forearm and wrist on a 90-degree angle to the paper, so you're actually drawing across the page. By using only one stroke direction you automatically create a greater sense of unity in the drawing.

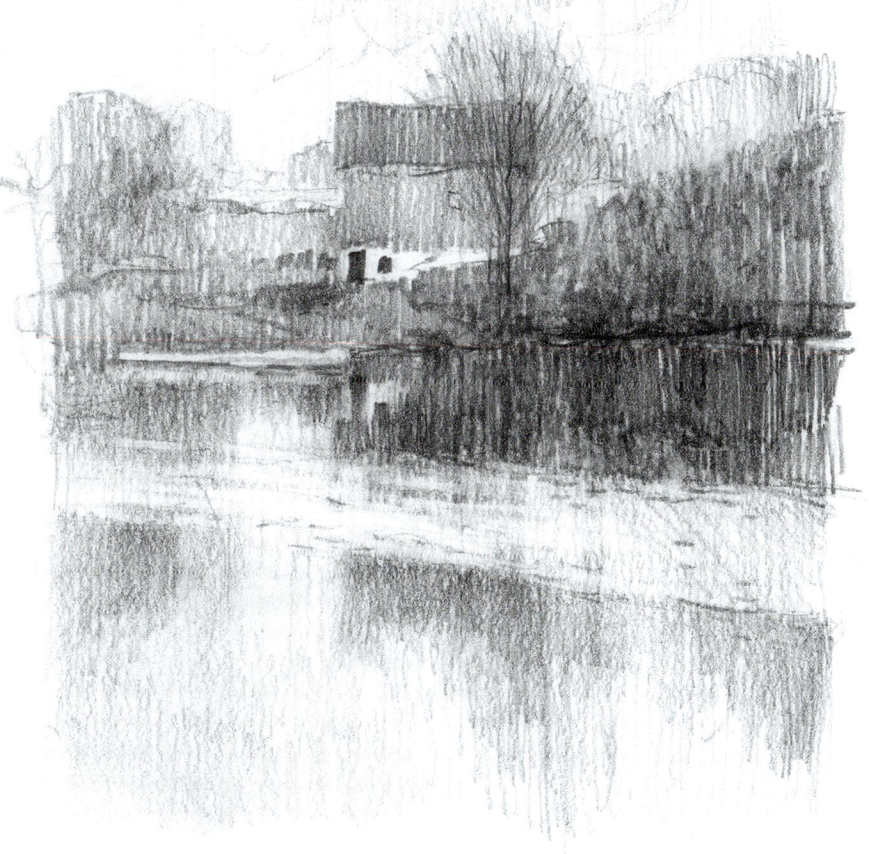

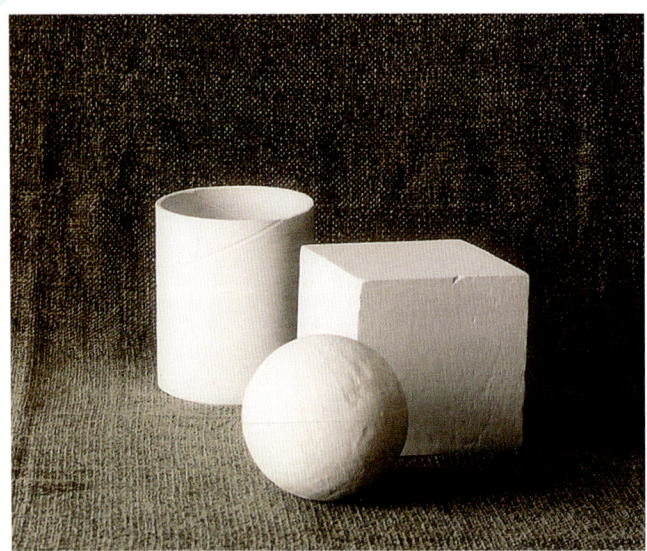

Cubes, Cylinders and Spheres
These shapes are the basic building blocks for everything we look at. You can make a good set of models from a 6" × 6" × 6" (15cm × 15cm × 15cm) block of wood, a piece of mailing tube and a plastic ball. Paint them white and use a single light source so that there are strong highlights and shadows.

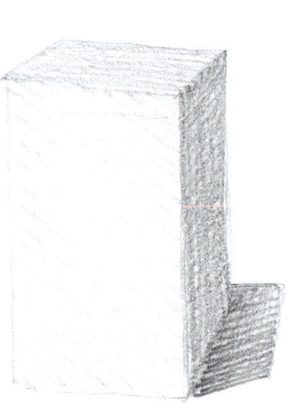

Avoid This
Don't just draw the object as if it were in a white, well-lit clinical setting.

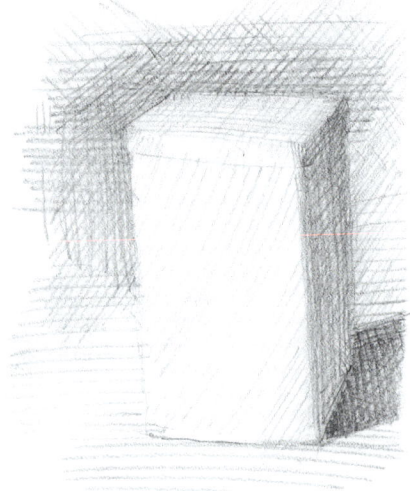

See Related Value Masses
Draw each object in relation to the values around it. How do those values interact with the edges of the object?

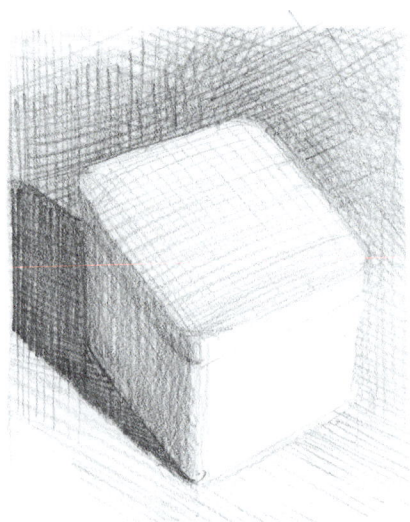

Vary Your Viewpoint
Draw the cube, cylinder and sphere from lots of different angles. Change the position of your light source as well. Strive for a sense of carving depth into your paper.

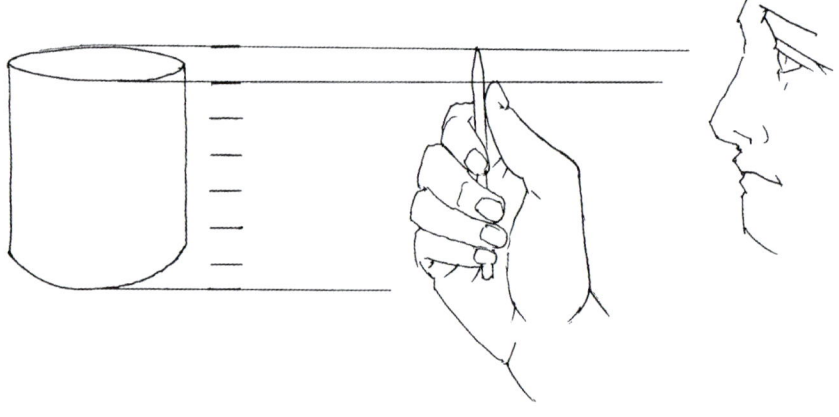

Cube and Cylinder Perspective
Unless you're standing and looking down on it, the top surface of a cube or cylinder almost always should appear much thinner than you think it should. Measure the top surface using the tip of your pencil. Line the tip up along the back edge of the object. Then slide the top of your thumb up the pencil until it lines up with the front edge of the object. Hold that measure and move down the front of the object. You'll see how much smaller the top edge of the object is compared to the vertical front surface.

Thumbnails

You've repeatedly heard, I'm sure, to do thumbnails before you paint. Most students in my workshops dash a few lines on a page, call it a thumbnail, and then start to paint.

Without a thumbnail, you're flying blind, and it will usually become obvious in the resultant painting. You may feel that the thumbnail is just holding you up. You want to paint. Ironically, it's the attention given to the thumbnail that saves both time and creative energy. You don't want to get into a painting and find it simply isn't working; that's discouraging and frustrating. If you just dive right in with painting you're relying too much on luck—and for consistency, luck's a bad partner.

Doing a thumbnail requires inquiry and attention. It is the point where you can really explore your possibilities creatively. As you explore one idea, you might get another idea that you realize would make a far more interesting painting. Even if you stay with the same idea, do the thumbnail attentively and you will discover the strengths and weaknesses of your composition. Reinforce what works. De-emphasize what doesn't.

If you find doing thumbnails frustrating, I recommend spending a couple of months drawing—exclusively. Do the exercises in this section and a composition a day. When you return to painting, you will be able to see how to structure paintings more effectively. You will see value masses interacting on your picture plane. You will understand how to get the eye to move where you want it. Then you will be able to translate your new skills to painting. In the long run, no other single skill will serve you as well.

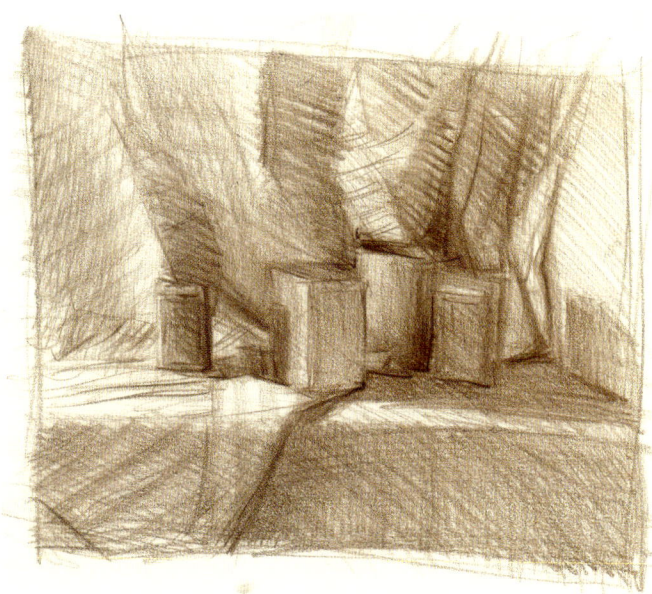

Draw Patiently
Really feel your way to understanding how the abstract value masses you're considering interact within the boundaries of your composition.

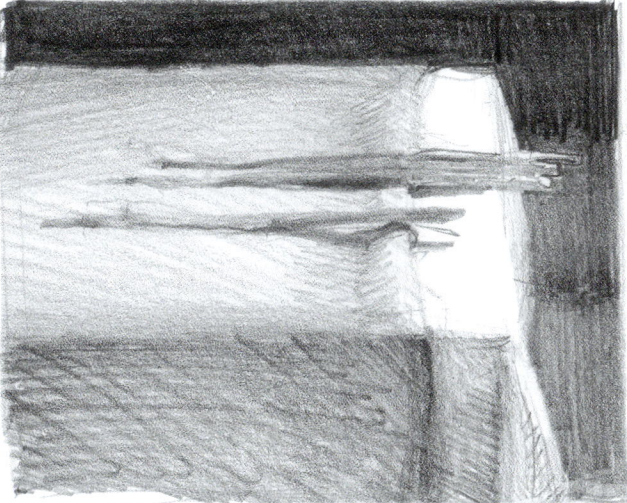

Lay In Masses
A thumbnail becomes a very quick and useful exploration tool when you lay in value masses.

My Sketchbook System

When I was in art school, I liked to use those black bound sketchbooks for all my drawings and notes. But, when I later turned back to those early drawings, all of the pencil sketches looked like dark gray snowstorms, with some vaguely discernible marks underneath the gray haze. Since I like to work in pencil, I decided to try something else. Now I cut large sheets of drawing paper down to 8½" × 11" (22cm × 28cm) and carry them in a clipboard folder. When I come home, I take any drawings from the day, three-hole punch them and put them in a binder. I can pull them out and use them for reference if I need them; otherwise, they rest there undisturbed, each binder filed by date.

plan big masses when you paint

Before you begin to paint, make sure you have several dramatic value masses clearly in mind. Then, as you paint, stand back often. Make sure they continue to hold your attention and don't fill up with distracting details. If the arrangement of major masses is strong and coherent, they'll carry the painting. You are then 90 percent of the way toward achieving a composition—and consequently a painting—that will work.

MATERIALS

Surface

Oil-primed canvas, 32" × 30" (81cm × 76cm)

Brushes

Nos. 4, 6 and 8 hog bristle filberts, no. 6 sable or synthetic rigger, 1½-inch (38mm) utility brush

Pigments

Titanium White, Cadmium Yellow Light, Cadmium Yellow Medium, Yellow Ochre, Cadmium Orange, Cadmium Red Light, Alizarin Crimson, Quinacridone Violet, Dioxazine Purple, Ultramarine Blue, Phthalo Blue, Phthalo Green, Chrome Oxide Green

Other supplies

Smooth drawing paper, B and 2B pencils, kneaded eraser, mineral spirits, two pieces of white card cut into an L-shape with inside dimensions of 5" (13cm) and 7" (18cm), rags, palette knife

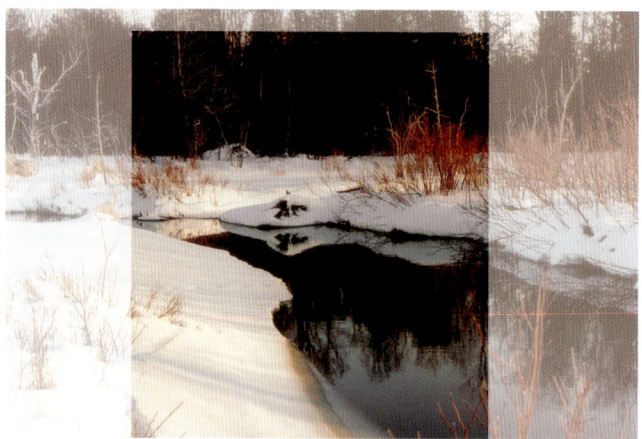

Cropping the Photo
Notice how the photo was cropped so it is now design driven, with three or four simple masses.

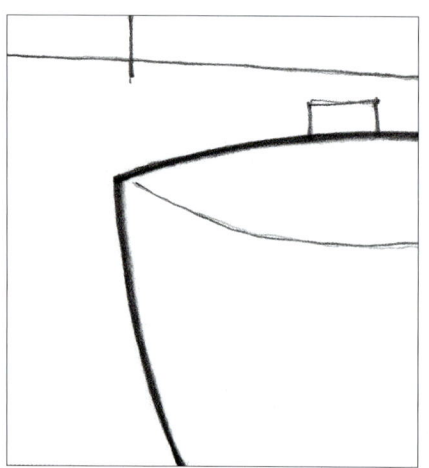
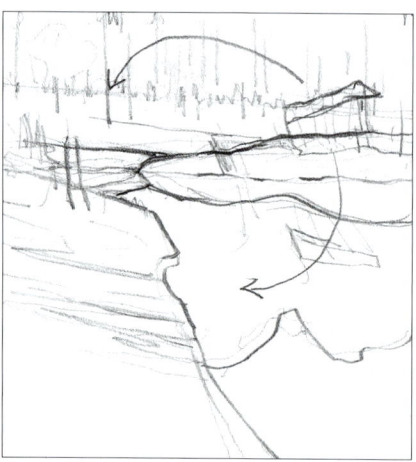

The Armature and Lines of Attention
Consider how you want the viewer's eye to move through your painting. The main line of the painting, following the armature, pulls the eye back to the lit snow bank and then over to the red dogwoods. There are also two return lines or secondary movements through the painting. The first moves down into the dogwoods' reflection and across the reflection to join the main line again. The second return line moves back into the woods and then down a tree to the sunlit bank. You want to keep the eye moving through your painting. Try to establish this kind of intention before you start. Sometimes return lines are obvious. Sometimes you have to create them.

68

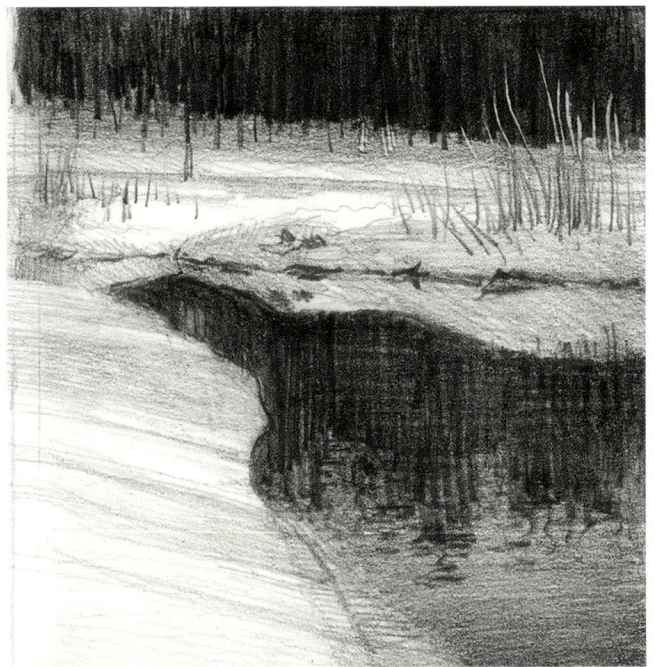

Find the Value Masses
Use a thumbnail drawing to get a good sense of the value of each of your masses. Make your values dense enough to approximate the values in front of you. Reduce the thumbnail to the large masses only. How do they work together? Do you see a problem? Perhaps the composition isn't dramatic enough, or there are too many little shapes. Maybe you need to crop tighter still. Determine whether you have a strong composition before you start to paint. You will save yourself from a lot of frustration and discouragement.

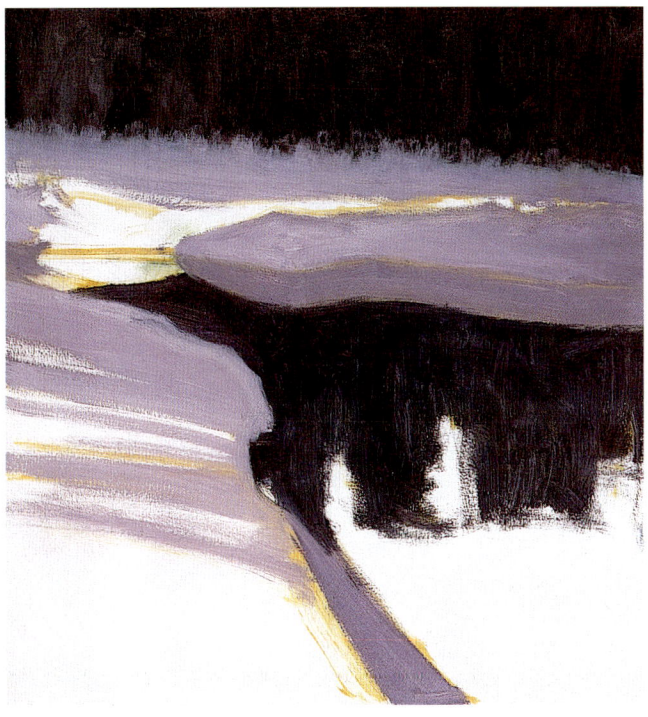

1 Paint Broadly at First

Using Yellow Ochre, mineral spirits and a no. 6 or 8 filbert, draw in the major shapes. Yellow Ochre wipes out easily, so keep adjusting the placement of the major masses until you've got them how you want them. Divide the photo and the canvas into thirds with grid lines if it will help you get the proportions right.

Block the masses in boldly. You want to see if those masses are going to carry the painting. For this size painting, use a 1½-inch (38mm) utility brush. Begin with the shape whose color and value seem easiest to find. In this case, start with the background forest (Alizarin Crimson and Phthalo Green with a touch of mineral spirits). In the area where the return line will pull us down into the painting over to the left, add some Ultramarine Blue and a hint of Titanium White. Wipe the bottom edge of the mass with a rag to soften it.

Continue painting in the simple value shapes with the utility brush. Squint to eliminate all the modulations, highlights and reflected lights that might distract you. Find the value and color that is the midpoint of all the variations in each mass. Test each new color against a mass you've already added. Don't just slap in a big area and then realize it's clearly not the right color. Paint boldly, but take your time on the color mixing.

The reflections of the trees in the water are Alizarin Crimson and Phthalo Green, the same as the forest. The shadow color of the snow is Ultramarine Blue, Cadmium Orange and Titanium White with a hint of Dioxazine Purple and Quinacridone Violet. Paint the snow back into the forest to start the interaction of two masses converging back into space.

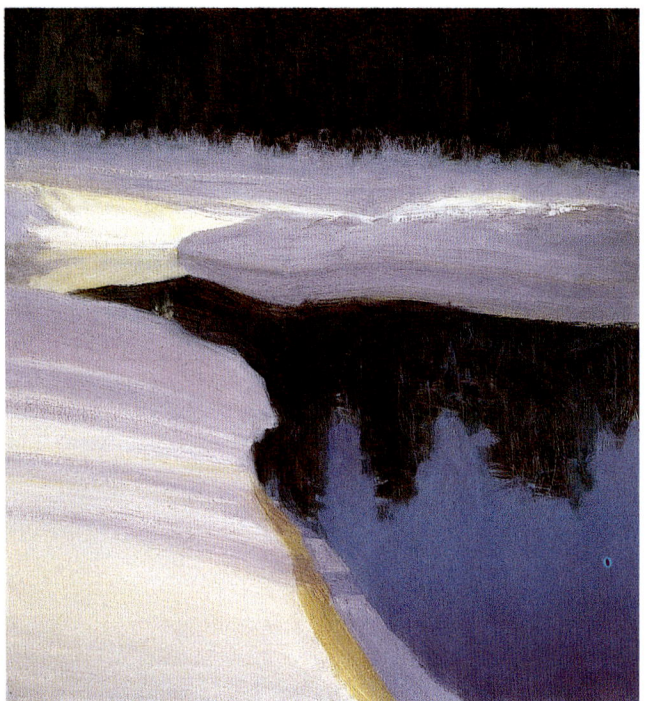

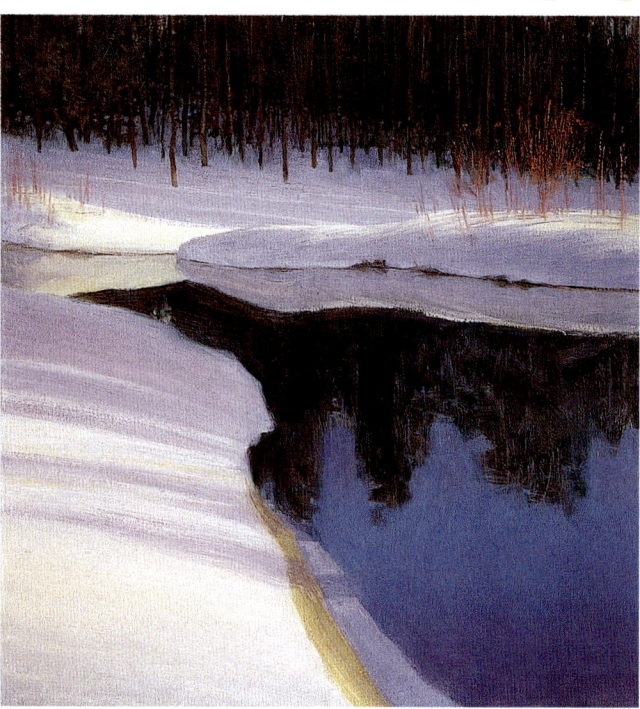

2 Keep It Simple

To paint the gradation in the water, use Ultramarine Blue, Phthalo Blue, Dioxazine Purple and Cadmium Orange, with a hint of Titanium White along the bottom edge. Wipe your brush and create a new mixture. Don't just add paint to the old one. Use the same colors as before, but reduce Dioxazine Purple and Cadmium Orange to just a hint. Brush each mixture next to the first color to see if it seems the right value for the level of gradation you want. You'll have four or five separate mixtures, so you'll have to judge each time. Brush the paint across the area, then blend it into the color below to soften the edge between the two colors. Mix a third color using Ultramarine Blue and Phthalo Blue with a bit more white and a hint of Cadmium Yellow Light, brush that color on above the last, then blend. The final color is the same as the last, only with a bit more white and yellow. Create several distinct "clean" mixtures and blend those if you want clean gradations.

Use Titanium White, Yellow Ochre, Cadmium Yellow Medium and Cadmium Orange for the sunlit snow. You may need to add a touch of Dioxazine Purple and Ultramarine Blue, so that the snow doesn't get too bright. You want it to look like sunlight but you also need to be able to add highlights later. Except for the gradation of the sky reflection and a touch of Ultramarine Blue and Cadmium Orange added to the snow at the very bottom of the picture plane, everything should be flat value masses.

Stand back and see how your masses are working. If they need adjusting, it is still easy to do so. Look at the painting in a mirror. You should be able to see how your armature is working and the main path your eye is taking through the painting.

3 Add Colors to the Main Masses

To turn that dark forest mass into a forest, you need tree trunks. Modulate the mass so that it reads as trees but doesn't distract. Mix colors close in value and intensity, but changing in hue. Using the base color of Alizarin Crimson and Phthalo Green, add Yellow Ochre, Cadmium Orange, Chrome Oxide Green and Quinacridone Violet—not all of them at once. Add some of one, a little of another. Load a no. 6 filbert with paint and drag it down in one stroke. If it's too light, mix something a little darker and drag it on top of the last stroke. You'll need some stronger darks too; the base mixture used more thickly will do. Make sure each mark means something—state it and leave it. When you stand back, you should be able to feel the sense of all those trees without a lot of jumpy vertical marks distracting you.

Create a mixture of Ultramarine Blue and Cadmium Orange with a hint of Dioxazine Purple a step or two darker than the one you used for the shadow color of the snow (step 1). Use this for the snow in the forest. That way when you paint it back into the more shadowed area of the forest it won't jump.

Use Alizarin Crimson, Quinacridone Violet and Yellow Ochre with a hint of Dioxazine Purple for the dogwoods. A couple of broad strokes with a no. 8 filbert will give the main mass. Use a no. 6 rigger for the rest. Load your brush and drag lightly in single strokes. Scrape back any that stand out too much with the tip of your palette knife.

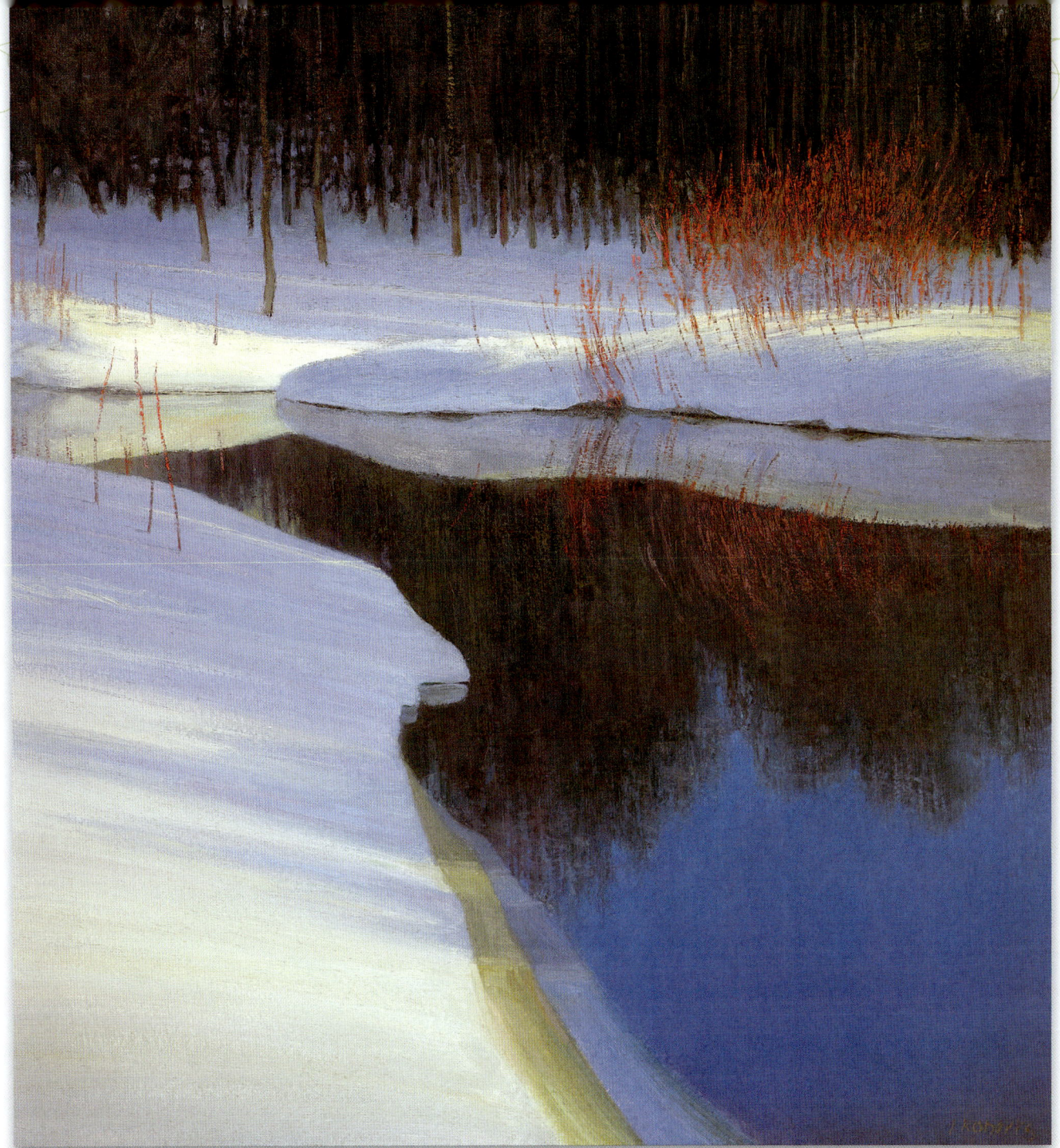

4 Refine the Shadows and Define the Dogwoods

Soften the edges of the foreground shadows on the snow. Mix the color of the lit snow (step 2) and the shadow color (step 1) and brush one up into the edge of the other. Use two brushes (one for each color) and go back and forth between the two colors to control the quality of the edge. These shadows are cast by the tops of trees that are forty or fifty feet out to the right of the picture plane, so their edges should be soft. The shadow cast right at the base of a trunk would be much more clearly defined.

You can use the same modulated colors you used for the tree trunks for their reflection in the water, but just hint at them in the reflection.

Define and refine the dogwoods using the rigger and the original dogwood color. Dull and darken the dogwood color (step 3) with Dioxazine Purple and a hint of Chrome Oxide Green, and brush that in with a few loose vertical strokes for the dogwoods' reflection in the water.

The three dogwoods on the left bank were put in at the end to ensure that the viewer's eye swings around for that return line, before going back again to the lit snow bank and over to the dogwoods on the right.

DOGWOODS AT KOLAPORE
Oil on canvas · 32" × 30" (81cm × 76cm)

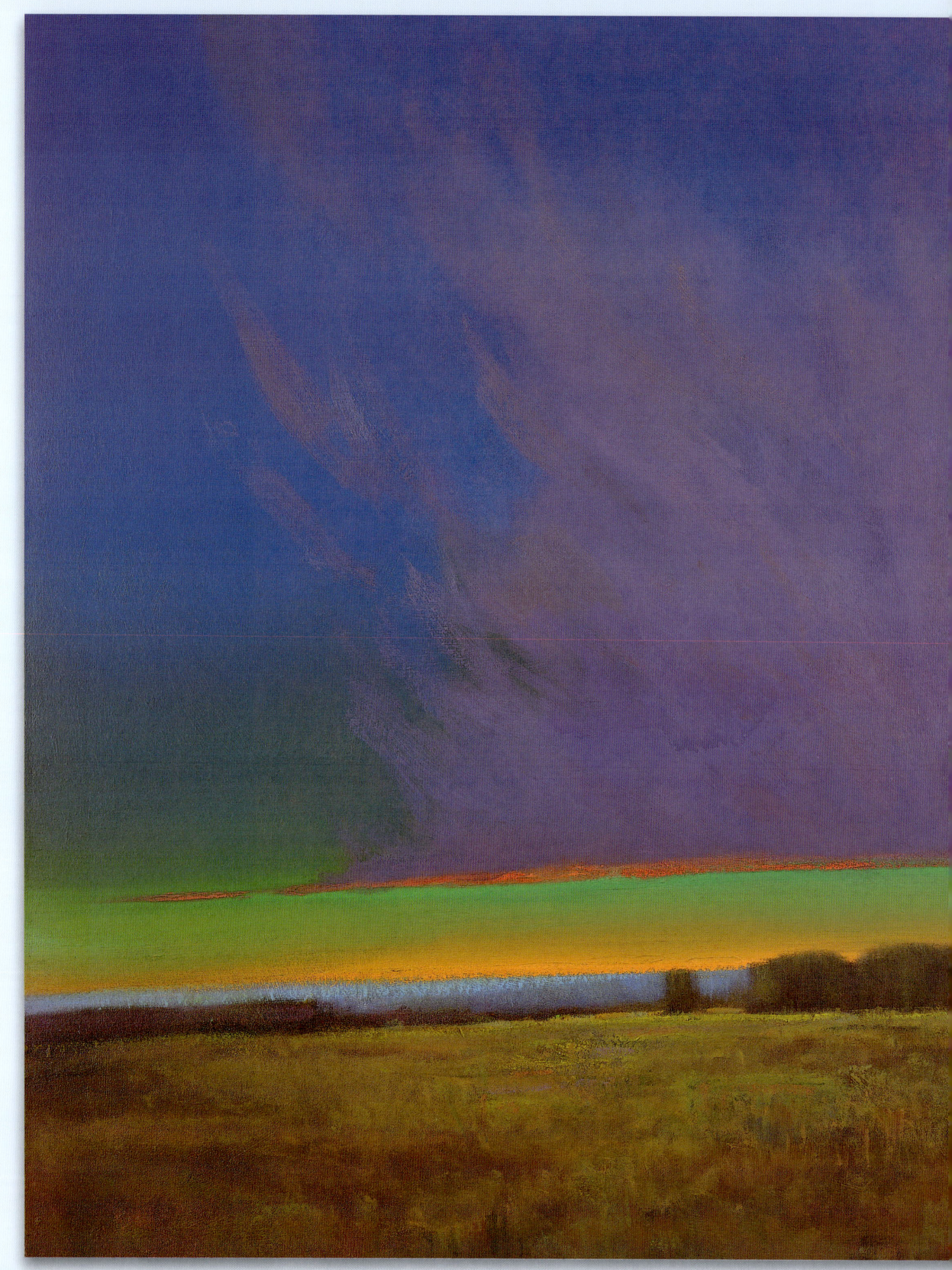

CHAPTER THREE

Color Shapes

The history of great representational painting in the West is the history of great shape making. This is the arena of negative and positive shapes— the shapes made by the spaces between things being as important as the shapes of the things themselves. When you see a painting you like (I recommend looking at the work of some artists from 150 or more years ago in addition to more recent ones, and really trusting your own instincts as to which paintings you like), study the shapes in that painting. Draw them. You can learn a lot through the study and assimilation of what has worked before.

As I've said before, the main abstract value masses are the foundation. If they don't work, you can't expect color to solve the problem. It is the placement of one color next to another and the interplay of those color shapes that makes the painting really come alive.

I shall always hold that the mixing of color—its desired hue, shade or nuance—is the real thrill of painting. The sheer delight and almost surprise of abstract color variations and vibrations and mass-harmonies.

John Carlson

WHERE SILENCE REIGNS
Oil on canvas · 36" × 36" (91cm × 91cm)

Color Shapes Are All You Have

When you look at a painting, all you see are color shapes on a two-dimensional surface. No matter how famous or magnificent the painting, that's what it is. In a sense, learning to paint is simply learning to put each color shape in your subject down on the canvas, one after the next. If you do that, the representation of your subject appears as a by-product.

However, if you're like most people, you probably have created a gap between the simple purity of what you actually perceive and what you *think* you see, and therefore what you paint on your canvas. Your "knowledge" of color—trees are green, lemons yellow, skies blue, clouds white—creates a mental filter that blinds you to the actual color shape in front of you.

With practice, of course, you can learn to see the color without that filter. As Betty Edwards said, most drawing problems are perceptual problems. So it is with color. If you break color down into its component parts, it will be easier to master.

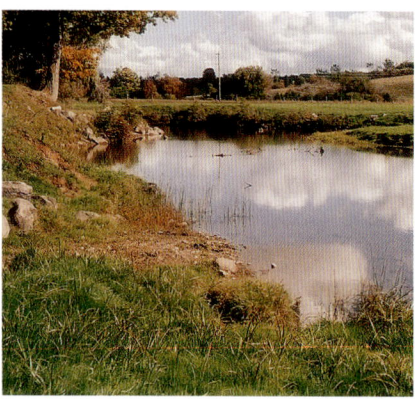
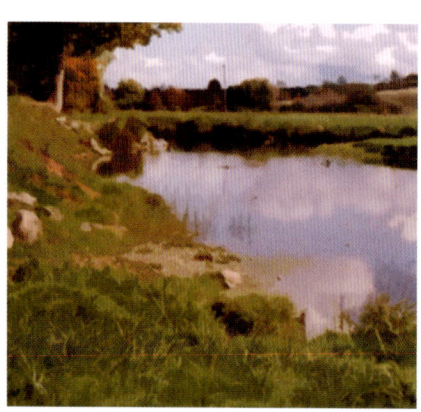

Seeing in Color Shapes
This photo and its digitized image show the difference between seeing the masses of detail that make up the world and seeing in simple color shapes. Notice how much easier it is to think about painting the digitized image. That perceptual shift, assisted by squinting, allows you to respond to color shapes alone.

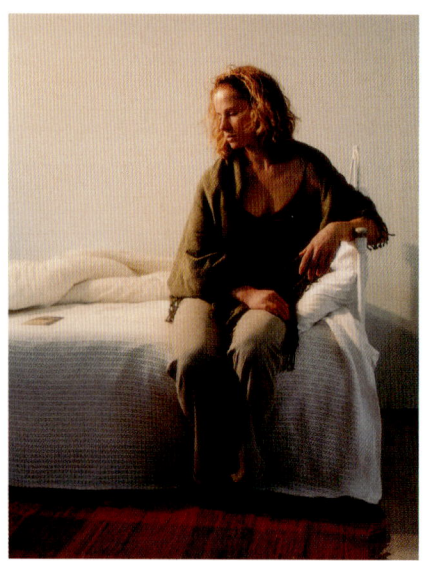
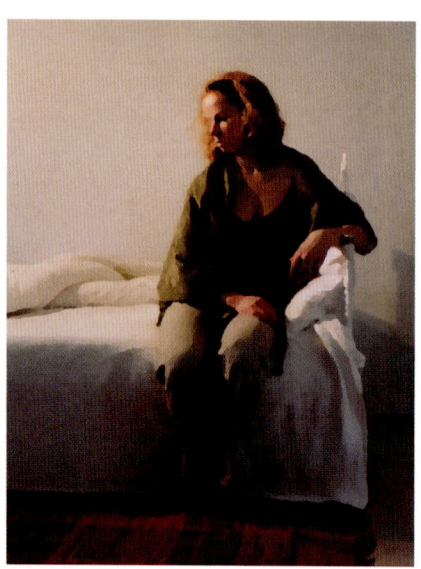

Find the Color Shapes Before You Start to Paint
Before you start to paint, study your subject until you can "see" the color shapes. If you choose a subject that isn't conducive to seeing in color shapes, you'll probably bury yourself in distracting detail and incidentals. Try to focus on the color shapes during every step of the painting. Yes, you create nuances in each shape, but don't let the shapes themselves get overwhelmed with highlights and incidental brush marks of color.

There is no model; there is only color.

Paul Cézanne

Three Qualities of Color

Each color has only three qualities: *hue*, *value* and *intensity*. That's the encouraging part. Release that color and its three qualities out into the world and surround it with other colors, however, and the challenges it presents can seem overwhelming. It is necessary to "see" a color in isolation so that you can mix it. Thus, you need to understand something of the science of color to have any hope of success.

No one has much trouble naming a rich, pure pigment: red, blue, yellow and green are easy to understand. The complexity begins when you add value (how light or dark the color is) and intensity (how bright or dull it is compared to its pure quality).

Consider not just the color of the object itself (*local color*), but also the light that is falling on that object, which changes the quality of the color. Every representational painter is a painter of light. Without light, there's nothing to see. Evening light casts a very different light than midday light, as does incandescent light compared to daylight. Colors in shadow change depending on the quality of light falling in the lit areas.

Reflected light bouncing into the shadows creates yet another color shift depending on what color is being reflected.

You get the idea. Color is complex. Get a good grasp of hue, value and intensity, then apply observation, careful mixing and patience. Mixing an individual color is not magic. The relationships between colors create the magic.

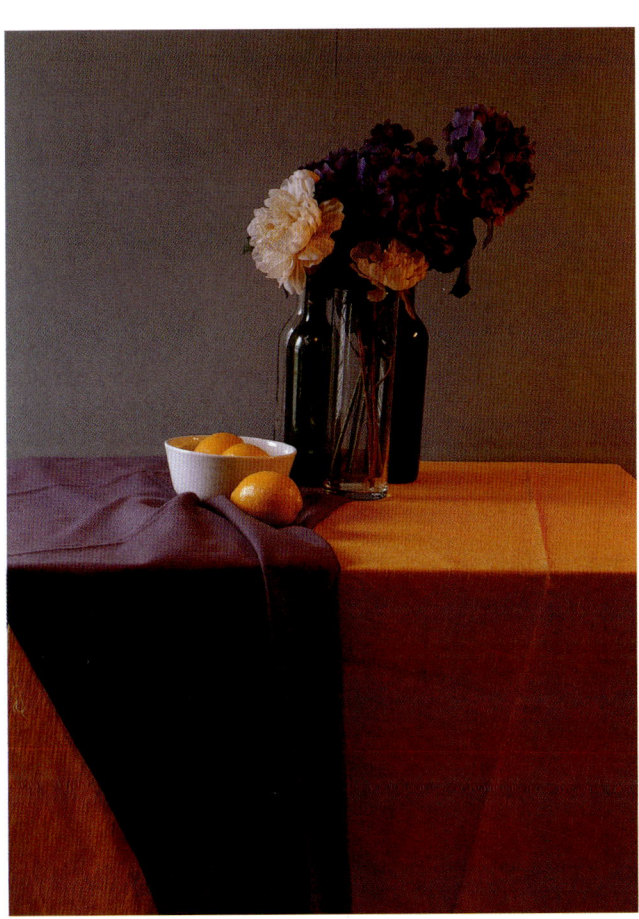 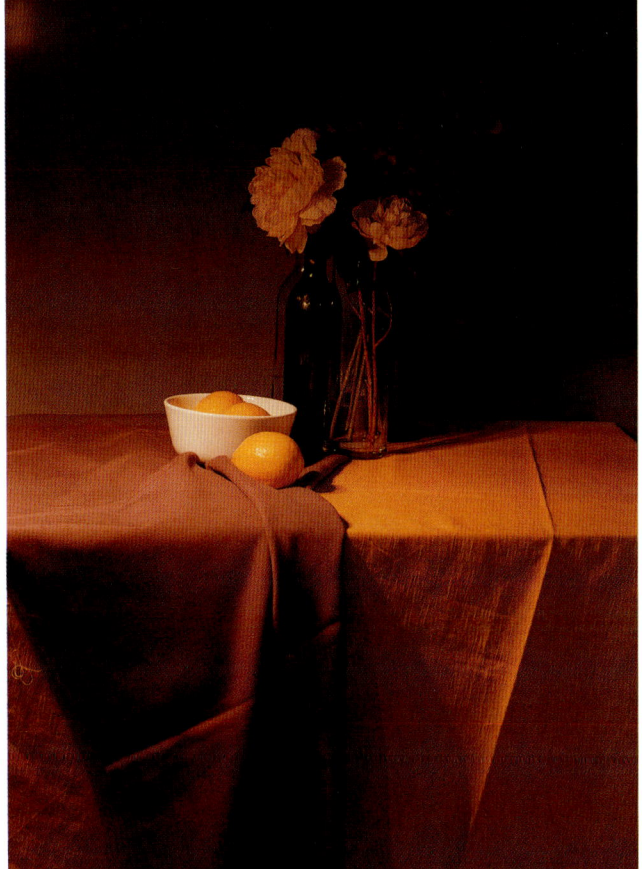

Lighting Changes Color Shapes
These two photographs were taken of the same still life. The lighting has been changed dramatically, making the colors and color shapes completely different. You are painting light, and the way the light falls on your subject affects everything.

When you go out to paint and things mean only spots of color to you, you have your painter's eye with you.

Charles Hawthorne

Understanding Color

Talk Your Way to Success

That's right, talk. When you mix a color, if you verbalize what you're trying to do, you will find the process much easier. Remember that color has three qualities: hue, value and intensity. That's it. When you mix a color, consider those qualities in that order, beginning with the broadest aspects of each and gradually refining them until you hone in on the color you want.

1. Start With Hue

Usually it isn't that hard to decide on hue. Where does the color fall in the color wheel? Sometimes, however, the hue won't be immediately obvious. What color is a rusted oil drum in shadow, the reflection of cedars in a silted mill pond, or tree trunks in a winter forest?

When the intensity of the color is very low—that is, the color is dull—you can find yourself calling it gray or brown. Neither name is very helpful in isolating hue except that grays tend toward cool (green to purple), browns toward warm (yellow to red).

But start by naming the hue; it's the easiest and broadest category of color to identify. Once you've established the hue, you can choose one or two colors on your palette to begin mixing.

2. Establish the Value

Of all color contrasts, value is the most important—yet most students find it very difficult at first to see value accurately. Colors of high intensity get confused with being light in value. If you continue to do a composition a day and to locate and draw in the correct value masses and their relationships to one another in your drawings, you will learn to isolate the values of the colors around you.

3. Adjust Intensity

The intensity of a color will often be affected automatically as you add colors to achieve the correct value, so it makes sense to finish here. You can reduce intensity by adding the complementary color. That will neutralize the hue. But if you want to warm the color you would also have to add a color one or two steps warmer on the color wheel as you reduced the intensity.

This color-mixing process may seem glacially slow at first, but there's really no other way. Experienced painters whose brushes seem to move effortlessly, mixing and applying paint, may seem to have some unattainable creative gift. In fact, they are using the same process that I've just described, but they have just gone through it so many times it now looks automatic.

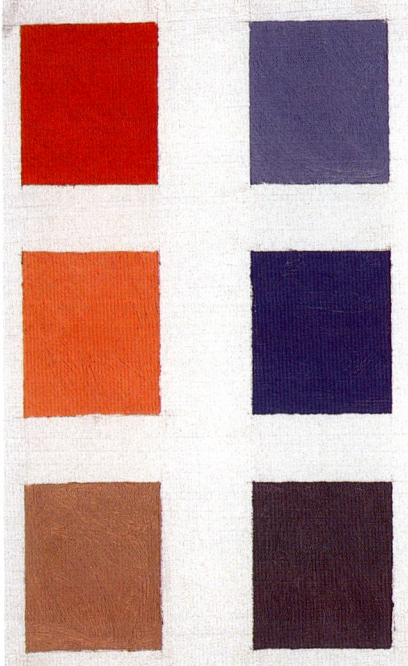

Hue, Value and Intensity
This chart shows changes in hue, value and intensity. The top row shows two swatches, one red and one blue. The red is pure Cadmium Red Light and the blue is Ultramarine Blue mixed with Titanium White. The hues are obvious. However, the white makes the blue lighter in value and lower in intensity than the red. The same hues appear on the second row, but this time the red is mixed with white, which lightens the value and reduces its intensity; the blue has less white, so the value is darker and the intensity has increased. The swatches on the bottom row have the same value as those on row two. In this case, the intensity of both colors has been reduced by mixing each with its complement. You can still tell what color they are, but they've moved a long way from the original tube color.

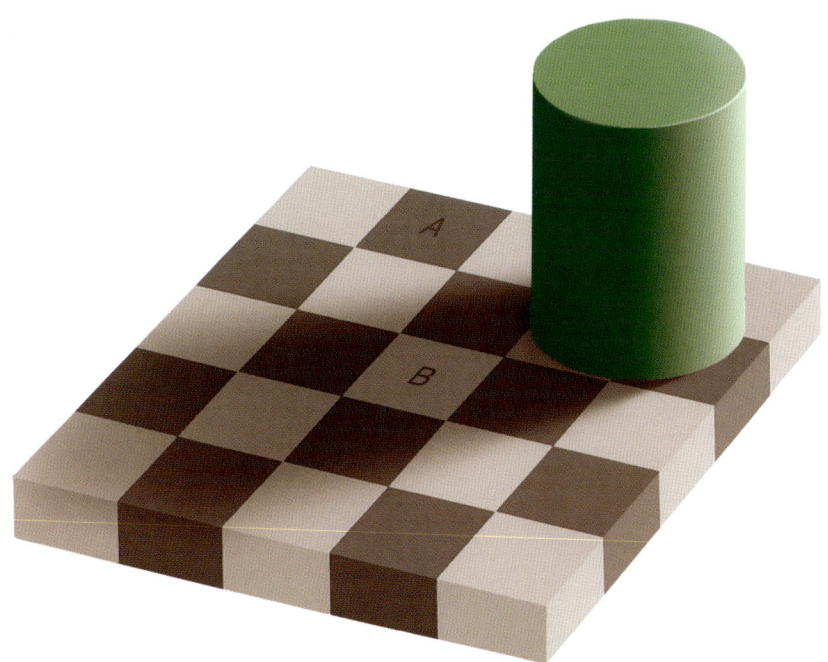

Which Is Darker?
The square marked A is the same value as the square marked B. No way, you say. That was my reaction too, but it's true. This illustrates how tricky even finding a value can be and how important it is that you learn to control and manipulate color.

Courtesy of Dr. Edward Adelson, Professor of Vision Science, Massachusetts Institute of Technology

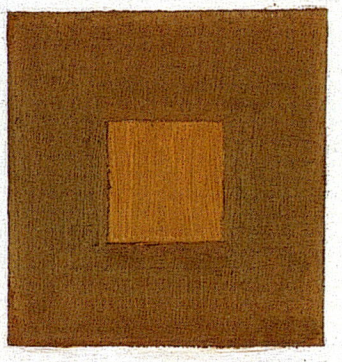 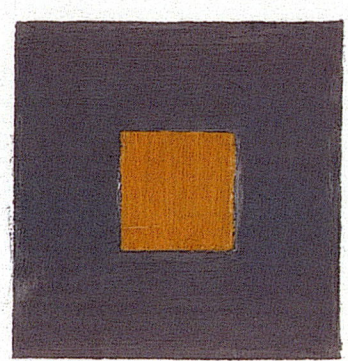 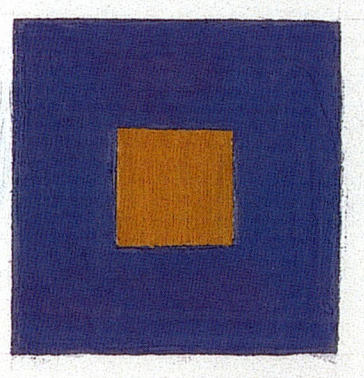

Color Works in Relationship
The orange on the left looks dull. It becomes lively when surrounded by gray, and livelier yet, surrounded by its complement, blue. It is interesting that the strongest color contrast comes from placing a color next to a color that is not its complement but the "complement-plus-one" (one step in either direction from the complement on the color wheel). In this case, the complement-plus-one would be blue-green or blue-purple.

Isolate Color With a Spot Screen

In his now (unfortunately) out-of-print book, *How to See Color and Paint It*, Arthur Stern suggests a useful tool for color mixing, which he calls a *spot screen*. You can make one out of stiff mid-gray cardboard cut to about 2" × 4" (5cm × 10cm) with a ¼" (6mm) hole punched about 1" (25mm) from the top. Look through the spot screen with one eye closed and isolate the color you want to mix. This will help you see the color just as it is, not surrounded—and therefore, influenced—by other colors. More importantly, you will see the color disassociated from the object. You won't automatically assume the color is green because the object is a tree or yellow because it is a lemon. When you see a color in isolation it may have so little to do with the green of a tree or yellow of a lemon that you won't believe what you're seeing. But trust your eye over what you "think" the color is.

The Color Wheel: Think 3-D

A standard color wheel—a ring of six or twelve pure colors—is a useful tool when considering color relationships and mixing, but it is obviously limited because it does not include the infinite variety of values and intensities possible for each hue. A standard two-dimensional wheel won't give you a complete picture of how to visualize and mix colors.

A better model is a three-dimensional color cylinder with a gray scale running down the center on the vertical axis. The color wheel does not sit perpendicular to the vertical gray scale because the pure colors around the outside edge of the wheel are not the same value; red is much darker than yellow, and blue and purple are darker still. The color wheel tilts on an angle so that the yellow is higher up the gray scale because it is lighter in value than the blue and purple. (Squeeze out Cadmium Yellow Light, Cadmium Red Light and Ultramarine Blue on your palette and you'll immediately see what I mean.)

For a painter, the most interesting part of this color cylinder is the whole area off that ring of pure color. That's the arena that you play in—the varied values and intensities. As you move away from the tilted color wheel either up and down the gray scale or in towards the center, the intensity of the color diminishes until along that central axis you have, in theory, a neutral gray. About 99 percent of the colors you put on your painting will not be from the pure hues you find on the color wheel itself but somewhere in the cylinder created by this three-dimensional color chart.

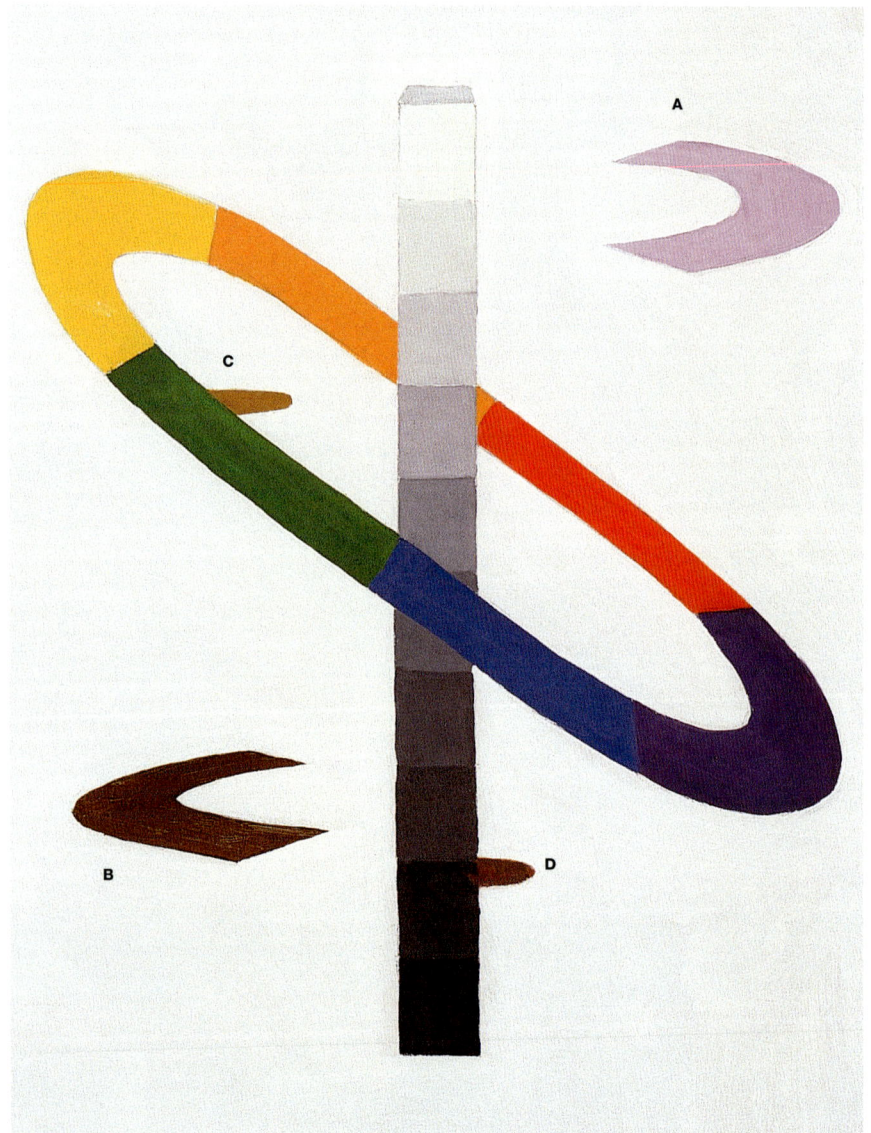

Using the Three-Dimensional Color Cylinder
To achieve a purple of the same value as the pure yellow on the color wheel you need to mix a light pastel tint of the original pure purple (A). To create a yellow as dark as the pure purple, the yellow would have to have so much of another color in it (to get it that dark) that the other color would become more dominant and you might have trouble identifying it as yellow (B). You will notice that to create both A and B, the intensity of the original hues must be greatly reduced. Cadmium Yellow would be on the outer circle, Yellow Ochre would be at C, Burnt Sienna at D. All the colors you will ever mix will rest somewhere within this three-dimensional color chart.

Expand Your Color Vocabulary

The range and effects of what you can express with pigment is a tiny fraction of what nature has at her disposal. Thus you need to be able to extract everything you can from the few pigments you have on your palette. In other words, you need to expand your color vocabulary.

Suppose you're at a painting workshop outdoors and the instructor asks you, "Is the color behind that bush lighter or darker than the bush?" or "Is the road warmer or cooler than the hedge behind it?" In my experience, students often answer with a hesitant, "Lighter?" or, "Warmer?" If you don't know the answer, you can't mix the color.

The truth of the matter is that blunt. The situation will probably occur over and over with each color shape you encounter. Multiply the problem by the number of color shapes in your whole painting and whatever you had in mind to express is likely to look very different than you'd planned—and probably not as good as you had hoped.

There are just so many notes in music and just so many colors but it's the beautiful combination that makes the masterpiece.

Charles Hawthorne

The Color Chip Exercise

This exercise will clarify the difference that value and intensity make to color. Choose color chips from a paint display at a hardware store with two things in mind. First, pick colors of medium to low intensity (middle to dark colors). Then, make sure that you have examples of all the primary and secondary colors. You will find that as the intensity gets lower and lower, it becomes difficult to decide exactly what hue it is.

Cut the six colors into strips, approximately 1½" (38mm) wide. Glue them on a board (see diagram below) with four similar-size boxes penciled in beneath the color chip so that you have the three primaries in the first row (red, blue, yellow) and the three secondaries in the second row (orange, purple, green).

Glue the edge of the chip next to the first box very flat or it will curl and skew the value.

Mix a color that matches the first color chip as accurately as you can. Let's say you start with a dull green. Then, in the two boxes below it, mix a purple and an orange of the same intensity and value as the green. Do this for each of the three primaries and the three secondaries. You are changing hues, but try to get the value and intensity as close as you can to the first color. With yellow, because it is so light in value, match either the intensity or value.

A good extension of this exercise is to take two colors opposite one another on the color wheel and mix them in ten even steps to a middle gray.

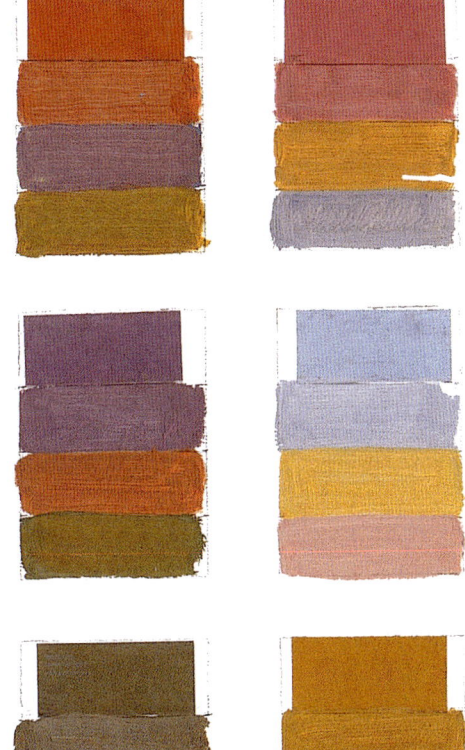

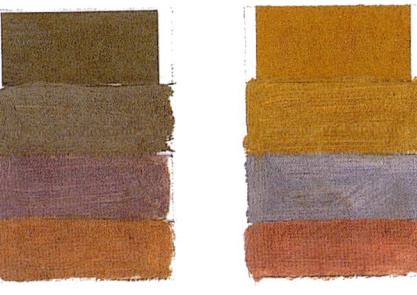

Attune Your Eye to Hue, Value and Intensity
This exercise takes color theory and, by the time you've completed it, transforms it into a conscious working knowledge of the three qualities of color.

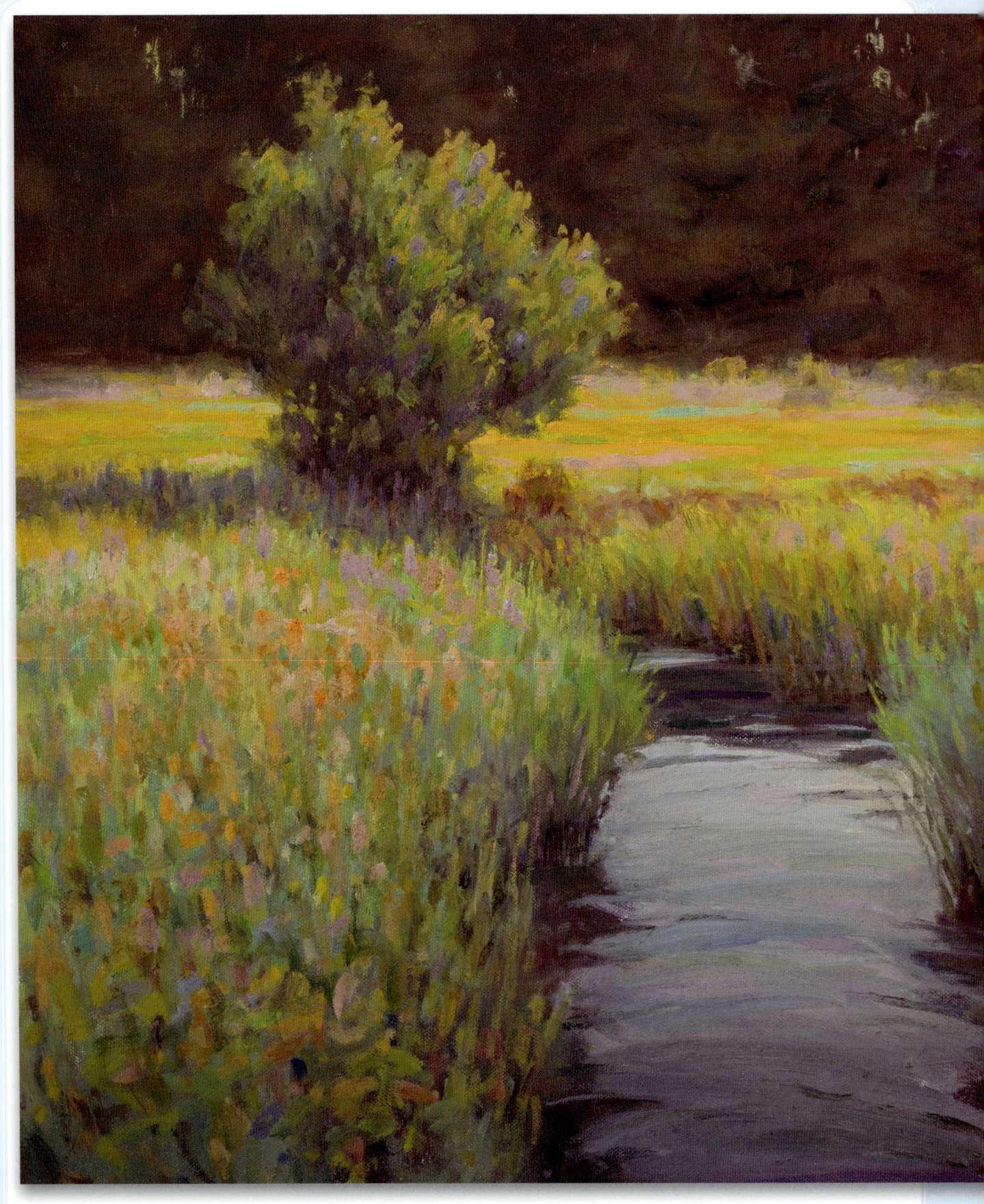

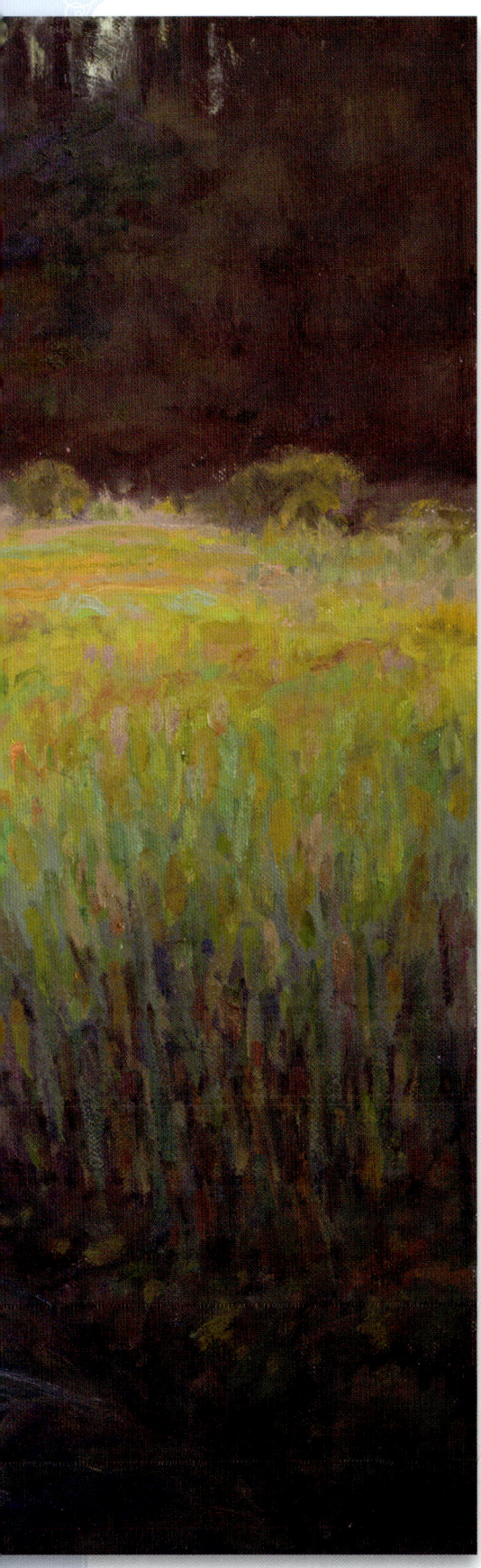

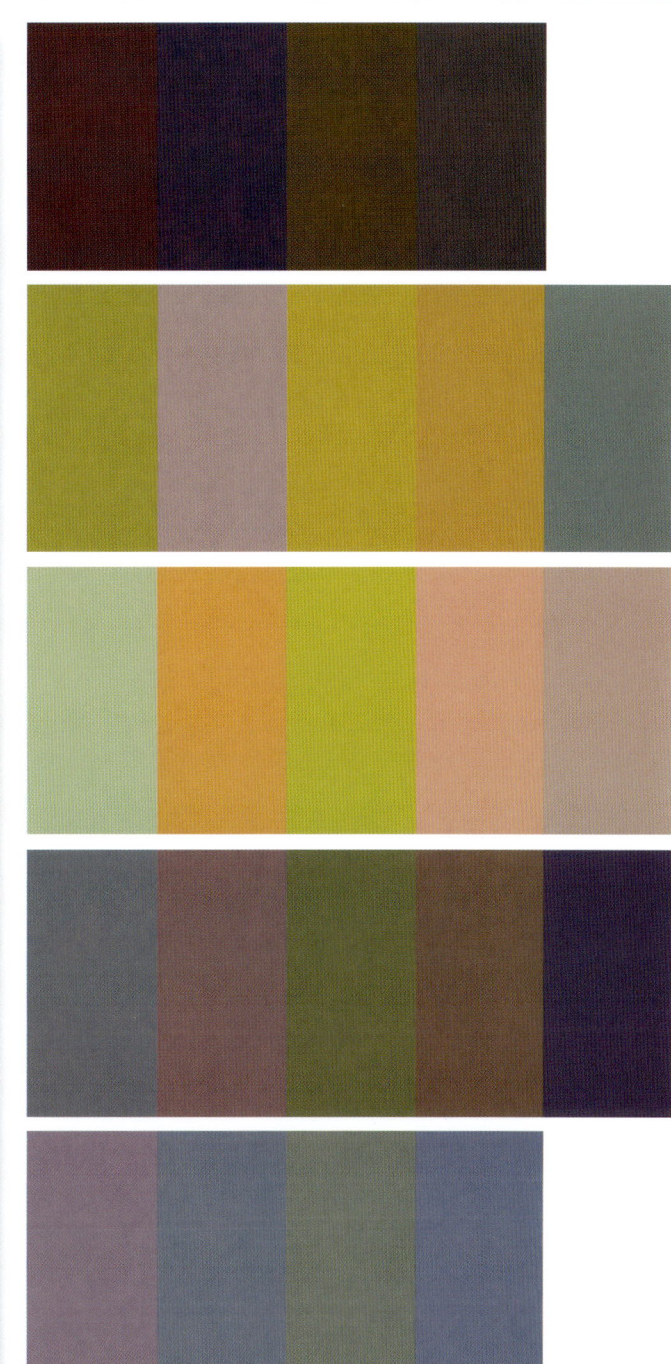

Subtle Color Intensity Creates Richness

From the color chip exercise on the previous page, you get an idea of how much variety color possesses. You can try another exercise to make this experience truly come alive for you.

Each color shape in this painting—the background, the water (which is also gradated), the background field, the shadow side of the bush, the lit side of the bush, and the foreground, left and right—has been painted to contain five hues, except the water and background, which contain four. Each of the colors has been mixed so that the value and the intensity stay the same even though the hue is different.

Try this and you will learn so much about mixing color. You might find it easier to work from a photograph for this exercise. Define a few simple value masses. Then really try to find four or five colors of different hue but similar value and intensity for each of those value masses.

Notice too how reduced the color intensity actually is in this painting. The richness comes from the nuanced variations of color. You may find your painting looks a little overworked for all the little color shapes in it, but if you are only changing the hue, it shouldn't get too edgy looking. However, you will come away from this exercise with a much richer sense of how to use color.

STREAM AT KOLAPORE
Oil on canvas · 24" × 30" (61cm × 76cm)

Color Temperature

Because the effect of mixed pigments is limited compared to the world of light around us, pushing color temperature is a very useful tool to enhance the sense of contrast, and thus light, in your paintings. Color temperature doesn't add another quality to the three we have been talking about. Pushing color temperature is imbedded in an understanding of hue, value and intensity.

The quality of the light source also influences color temperature. On an overcast day, contrasts in color temperature are minimal. On a sunny day, the warm light of the sun creates vibrant color temperature shifts between the lit areas and the shadows. How do you know the color temperature of the sun is warm? Just look at the sun—briefly. It is a warm yellow color and it bathes every-

thing it touches in that warm light. Toward evening, that light becomes more orange. If you go out on a clear, sunny, winter afternoon when everything is snow-covered and the sun is going down, the color temperature shift is clearer. You can see the obvious shift between the orange-tinged lit snow and the bluish shadow areas. When there is no snow, those same warm and cool colors blend with the local colors of the objects, making them harder to distinguish. But they're still there. In evening light, "green" trees are more likely to be a dull orange-green.

Color Temperature Exercise

It is easy to get confused when painting a temperature shift as it affects the local color. This exercise will help you focus on color

temperature so you can become more familiar with it. Paint either a sunlit landscape or a still life lit by an incandescent bulb. Focus on the color temperature and attune your eye to the warm and cool shifts; your painting will be filled with a sense of light.

To really learn about color temperature, you need to work from life. Photographs won't help you much because their range and nuance of color temperature is more limited than what your eye can perceive.

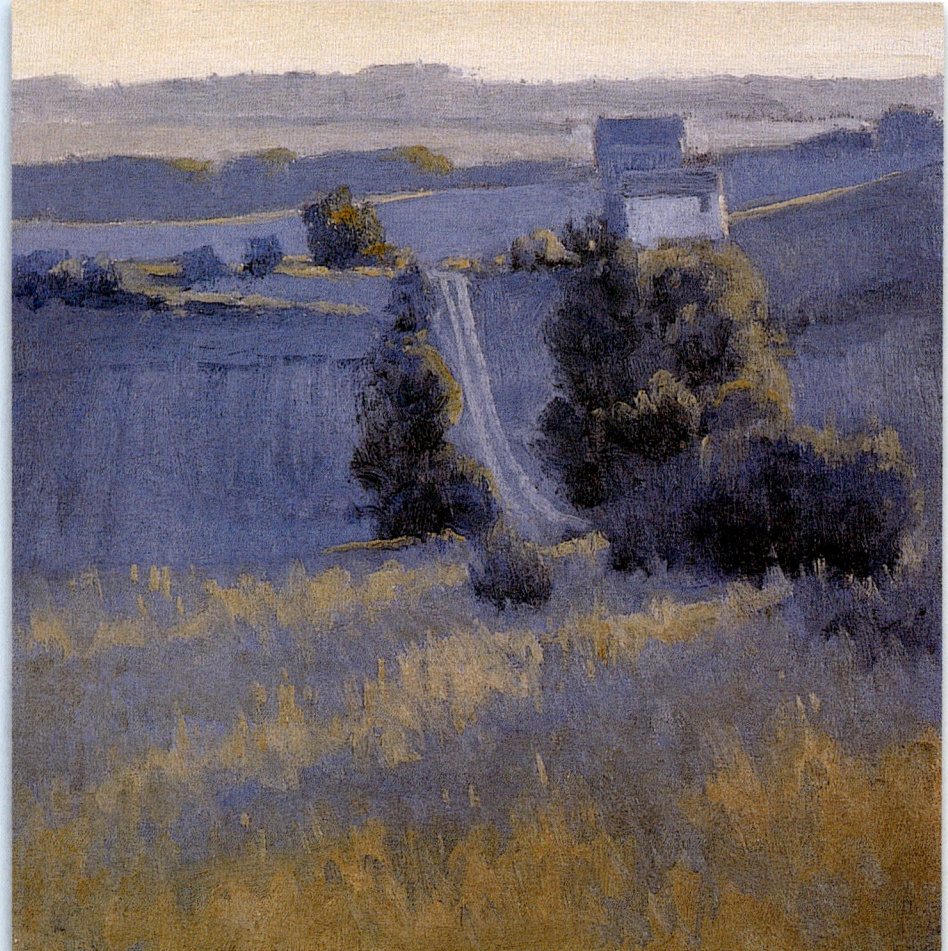

Distinguish Color Temperatures
To attune your eye to temperature shifts, try painting with only two colors plus white. Use either Ultramarine Blue and Cadmium Orange or Ivory Black and Yellow Ochre. Just as you created distinct value masses in chapter two, here you need to create distinct color shapes of warm and cool. Keep everything in the light warmer and everything in the shadow cooler. A red building in shadow may not actually be a cool color, but it will be cooler there than where it is hit by light.

THE ROAD SOUTH
Oil on board · 12" × 12" (30cm × 30cm)

Transition Colors

When you admire the color in a painting, you are probably responding to the use of *transition colors*, the colors that arise from the transition from light to shadow or when one color gets reflected into a second color.

As the light passes over an object, its color shifts. The truest color usually occurs in the mid-light. The brightest light tends to bleach or whiten color; shadows tend to obscure it—even though shadows can still be rich in color.

If you trust your eyes, you will often find wonderful nuances and hints of color. Sometimes you can see them. Sometimes you just feel the possibilities. These subtle shifts in hue or intensity create a richer, more nuanced transition from one color shape to the next.

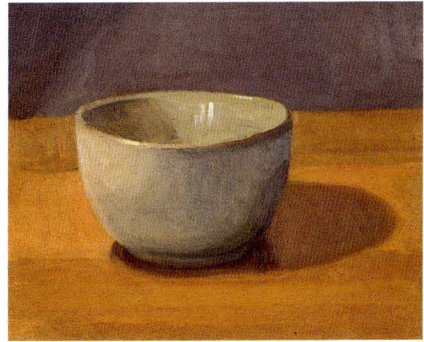 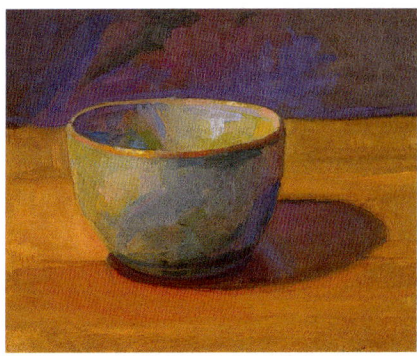

Enhance a Painting With Transition Colors
The bowl on the left was painted in a very basic, functional manner. It gets the idea across of a bowl on a table with a clear sense of light. But that's about it.

The painting on the right is the same painting with exaggerated transition colors added. They are exaggerated in that every part has some transition happening, and in some cases the color is exaggerated, too.

You can use transition colors to soften an edge or add a hint of a color. You can intensify a color to add increased richness. However, you can see that a good control of hue, value and intensity is essential, or your color transitions will draw too much attention to themselves and break the painting apart rather than add variety.

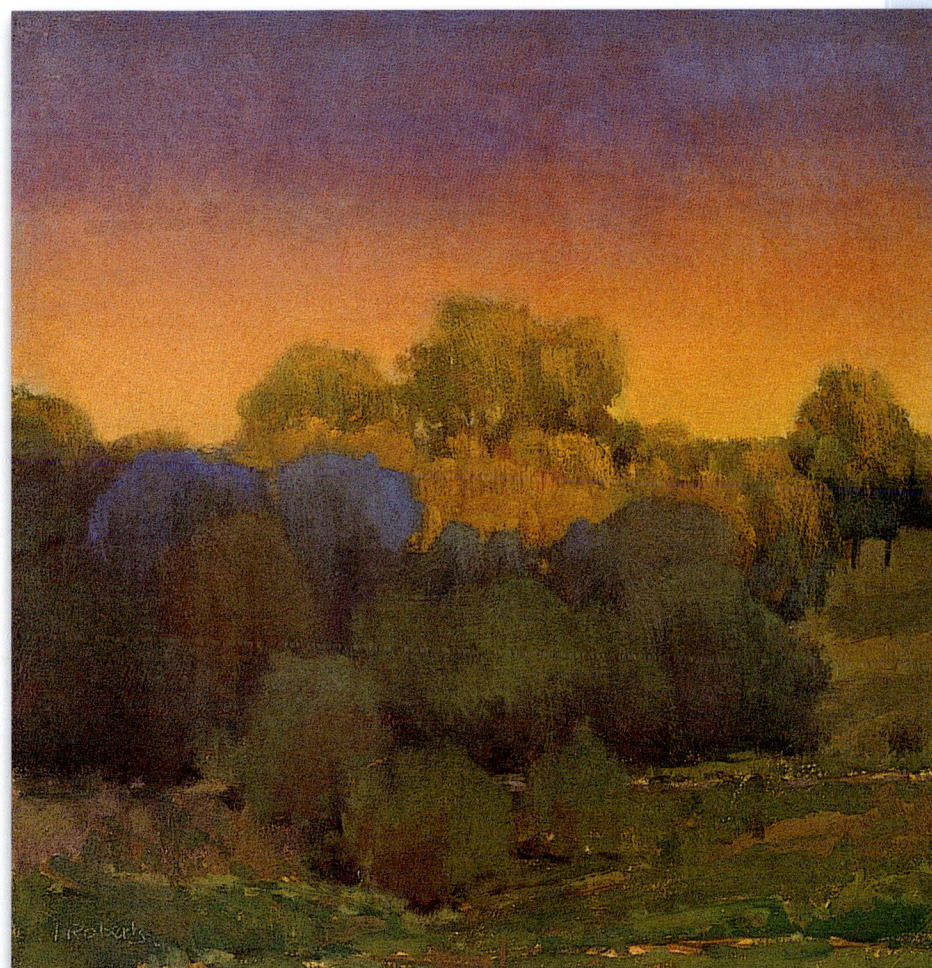

Experiment With Intensity and Value
You can see I've obviously taken some liberties with the color. It is still based on simple color shapes, but the color is exaggerated. Notice the temperature shift between the shadowed and lit trees. The contrast is made by exaggerating the intensity of both shadowed and lit areas, which necessitated reducing the value in both areas.

LAST LIGHT AT THE RESERVOIR
Oil on canvas · 16" × 16" (41cm × 41cm)

Palettes and Pigments

Your Palette

To master color, and particularly color temperature, you must start with the arrangement of the colors on your palette. This is really important. Without a sensible layout, your chances of mastering hue, value and intensity and keeping your warm-cool contrasts clean are slim.

If you watch an experienced painter move his brush around the palette, you'll notice that his movements are so fast and sure that he looks like a pianist at a keyboard. You can imagine how confused a pianist would be if the notes on the keyboard kept changing each time he played: he'd be lost.

In the same way, the experienced painter is so fast and sure because he puts his paints in the same place and the same order each time he paints. He becomes so familiar with their placement that he's often moving toward a color before he's even thought about which one he needs.

The simplest arrangement is to lay your pigments out as a color wheel. Start with white, then add yellows (either in the bottom right or left, depending on whether you're right- or left-handed), then orange, reds, purples, blues and finally greens on the far side of the palette.

The paint is laid out in a U-shape so that you can easily enter the palette to paint, but, if you took the green and pulled it around to the yellow to create a circle, you would have your colors laid out in the same order as the color wheel—logical, both for finding colors and for mixing.

What's on Your Palette?

Experiment with your color choices to determine what works for you. You might begin with a basic palette, adding or changing a color or two depending on whether you're painting a landscape or figures. Here are two palettes you could try.

Palette 1

This is a fairly standard, all-round palette.

- Titanium or Titanium-Zinc White
- Cadmium Yellow Light
- Cadmium Yellow Deep
- Yellow Ochre
- Cadmium Orange
- Cadmium Red Light
- Alizarin Crimson
- Ultramarine Blue
- Cerulean Blue
- Viridian
- Chrome Oxide Green

Here you have both warm and cool versions of yellow, red, blue and green.

Palette 2

This palette uses some of the newer synthetic pigments.

- Titanium White
- Cadmium Yellow Light
- Cadmium Yellow Deep
- Yellow Ochre
- Cadmium Orange
- Cadmium Red Light
- Alizarin Crimson
- Quinacridone Violet
- Dioxazine Purple
- Ultramarine Blue
- Phthalo Blue
- Phthalo Green
- Chrome Oxide Green

This is the palette I use. It is arranged as a color wheel and has warm and cool pigments for yellow, red, purple, blue and green.

The synthetic pigments are potent. If you've used Phthalo Blue or Green, you understand. They'll get into everything if you're not careful, so use them very sparingly or in tertiary mixtures (three colors mixed together) to push the intensity down. Nevertheless, these pigments give you wonderful nuancing possibilities. For example, if you have mixed a color—say, a warm blue—with the first, more traditional palette and you wish to cool it a bit toward green, you can't just add Viridian; it will disappear in the mix. With a color like Viridian you have to start cleanly, adding one other color to determine whether it's what you want. Otherwise, it just grays out. When you add Phthalo Green, you can always see the shift toward green. But, for that very reason, you have to be careful with it.

Neither of these two palettes is better than the other; they just behave differently. Personally, I like the stronger pigments. Whatever pigments you choose, put them in a logical and consistent order from warm to cool.

In order to use color effectively it is necessary to recognize that color deceives continually.

Josef Albers

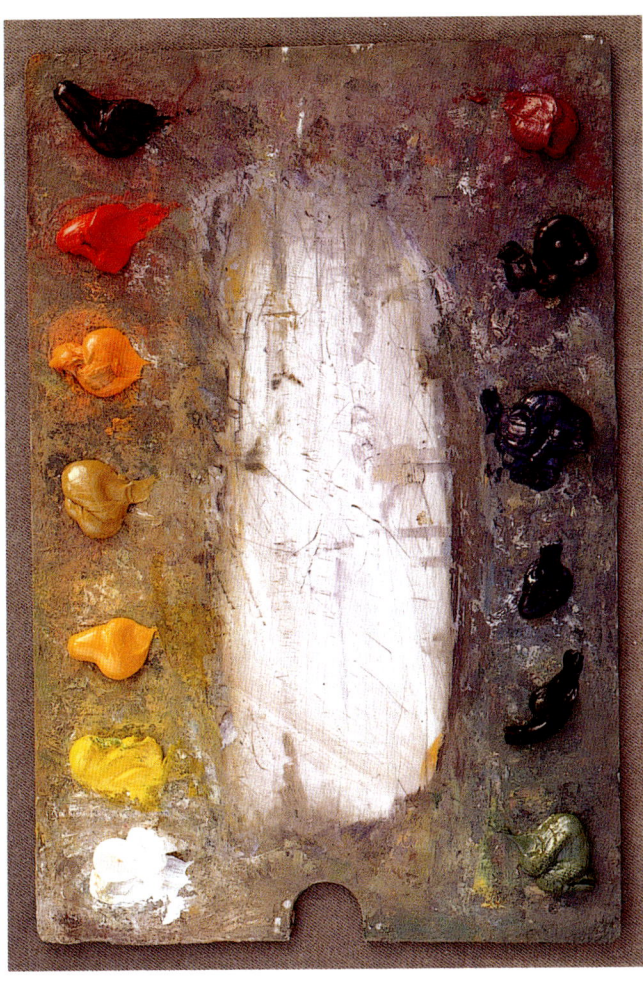

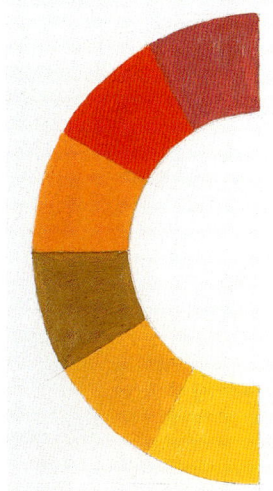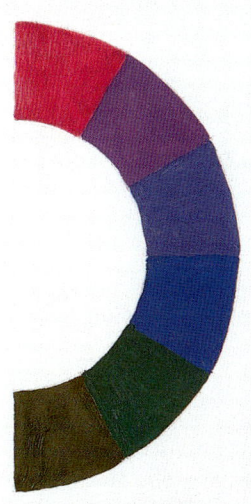

Palette Layout

I lay my colors out in a color wheel, six warm and six cool. My *plein air* palette demonstrates this clearly, although it's partly because of the easel design that it's configured like this. I'm left-handed, so your colors might be reversed. For my studio palette, the paint is laid out in the same order but in a large semicircle. If you were to pull the last color on the right, a warm green, around to the left near the cool yellow, Cadmium Yellow Light, you would have a color wheel of pigments.

Setting up the palette as suggested here keeps the whole idea of color temperature alive for you visually while you are working. When you're mixing a warm color, you pull colors from the warm side with hints of the cools to make adjustments and reduce intensity. For the cools, you do the opposite.

You can see how useful this idea is for mixing clean color. You will find that with a little practice, your color mixing becomes automatic and intuitive. Yes, you still have to go though the steps of hue, value and intensity, but where you move on the palette becomes second nature.

Three other points about your palette: (1) Place enough paint on your palette so that you don't need to think about putting out more while you're painting. Forget the pea-sized dabs on the palette. (2) If, while you're painting, you do run out of a color, put more out immediately. Don't try to squeak by on what's left. (3) Put out all your colors all the time. Just because you're painting an orange and blue bowl doesn't mean you'll just use orange and blue. You'll need all your pigments all the time if you really want to find the nuanced colors in the things around you.

Using Black

You have probably heard that you shouldn't have black on your palette. If, when you use black, your reasoning is: "I need to make this color go darker so I'll use black because it's dark," keep black off your palette or it will turn your whole painting into a lifeless gray. You need to mix your shadow colors as carefully, maybe more carefully, than you do your lights. But, with that in mind, if using black will neutralize a color in a specific situation to the right intensity and create the right relationship to the colors next to it, then use black.

Master Those Troublesome Greens

In landscape painting, no color seems to give students more trouble than green. The greens that come out of paint tubes are harsh and raw and very unnatural looking. You must neutralize them before you can use them in a landscape.

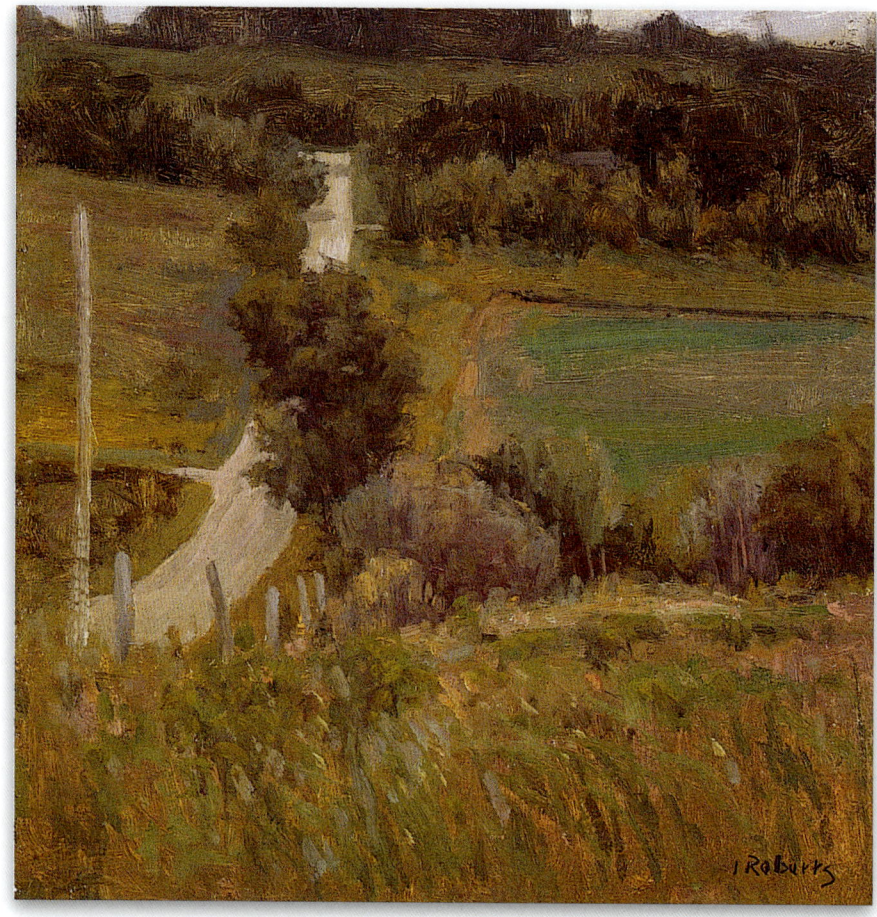

Variations on a Theme in Green
In midsummer, the greens in a landscapes can become pretty relentless. Try to create interest with the variety of your greens.

ABOVE LOREE
Oil on canvas · 12" × 12" (30cm × 30cm)

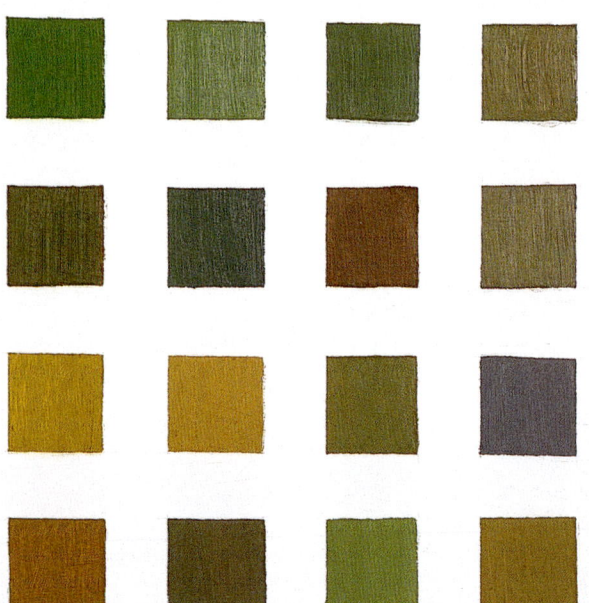

Exercise

Experiment to Create a Variety of Neutralized Greens

Try making color charts to see how varied you can make your greens without using any greens from the tube. Try using Ultramarine Blue with Yellow Ochre, and Ivory Black with Yellow Ochre. Try mixtures with Cadmium Yellow, too. Ultramarine Blue and Cadmium Yellow can make some pretty intense greens, so you will need to neutralize them. Create a wide variety of greens that are neutralized with orange or red or purple, then push the temperature toward warm or cool from those mixtures. Spend an afternoon in a museum that has lots of good landscapes just looking at the use of green. You'll quickly see how grayed out most of the greens are. If a painter has used too harsh or raw a green, it will look unnatural and garish.

Control Edges

The control of edges in representational painting is crucial, yet seldom receives enough attention. A painting is a group of color shapes on a canvas, and because every color shape has to join every other shape along an edge, you can see this is not something that can be left to chance. The movement of the eye along the armature and the way you pull the eye to the center of interest depends on the quality of your edges.

Try to visit a good museum, or look at some books with paintings by Velázquez, Titian, Vermeer, Rembrandt, Caravaggio and Chardin. Observe how they control your eye movement with the degree of contrast they create along their edges.

Edges are so important because they are where the contrasts occur: between shapes, not within them. Your eye, magnificent and sensitive as it is, essentially responds to contrast, so the stronger the contrast, the more your eye is attracted.

This is a "make it or break it" concept in painting. You want to attract and release the viewer's eye throughout the painting. You structure the armature to guide the eye toward a center of interest, which exists as a center of interest because it has the strongest contrast—of edges. The armature and the center of interest succeed only when your edges are effective.

Edges don't have to be hard to define an object. Look at the trees in the painting on pages 42–43. The edges of the trunks are lost as often as found, but because several vertical reference points have been included, the whole tree appears to be there without being overstated. This is a good example of a skill that is as much or more a perceptual one as it is a painting one. Until you learn to perceive the nuances of color and value, the tendency will be to overstate the edges.

Think of edges as existing on a scale, perhaps of one to seven, like a gray scale for value. You then have a perceptual vehicle for "seeing" edges.

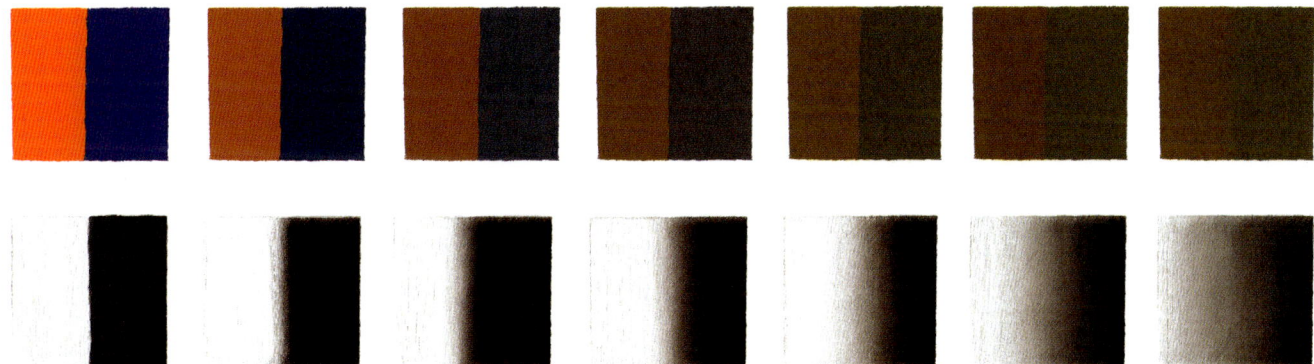

Two Scales Showing Edge Transitions
The top scale shows what happens to the edges between two colors when the intensity of both the orange and the blue and the value contrast between them are reduced. Although the actual edges remain hard and crisp, the transitions are less and less distinct. By step 7, the edge is almost completely lost.

In the bottom scale, the value contrast between the black and the white remains the same, but the edge quality itself changes and becomes increasingly softer. Notice how the harder edges and sharper contrasts draw your attention more than the soft edges and gradual transitions. As you paint, look for ways to incorporate both kinds of edges to guide the viewer's eye around your composition.

Edge Control Is Fundamental to Success

Try studying a painting just for its edge quality. Using the edge transition scales (see page 87), examine the range of edges in this painting. The process of evaluating an edge and labeling it 1 to 7 may seem clumsy at first, but you'll quickly get the idea. Eventually your awareness of edges will increase, and you will be able to leave the numbering behind as you integrate edge control into your own painting.

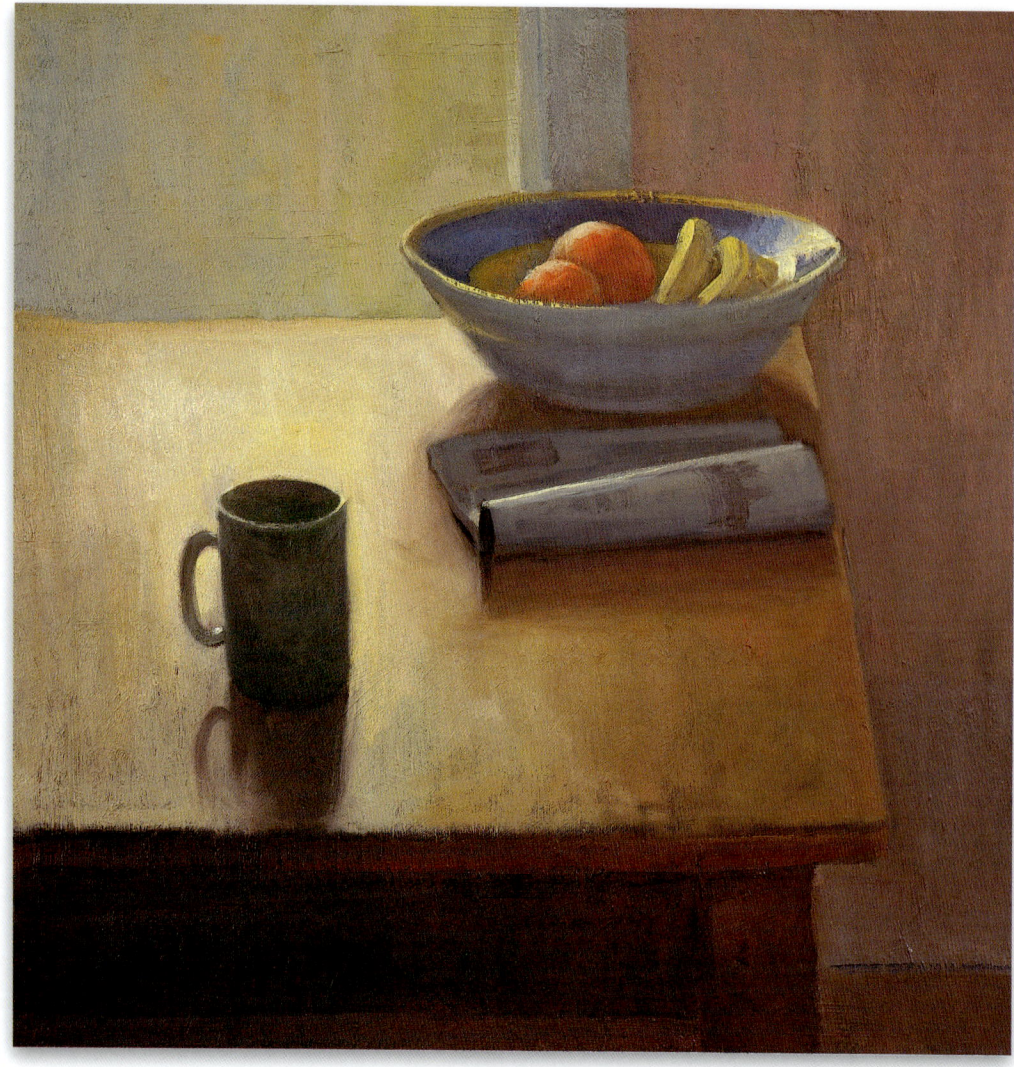

THE DINING TABLE
Oil on canvas · 24" × 24" (61cm × 61cm)

A Study of Edges

Start by looking at the edge of the table along the back, side and front. It rarely stays the same for long. The edge along the back of the table is softened on the left side to make sure the eye moves into the painting toward the stronger edge on the right. Notice the transition along the edge of the right side of the table from a distinct hard edge (say, a 4) to a lost edge where the shadow of the bowl meets it (7), to a distinct but not strongly contrasted edge in the lower right (5). The lit area of the table to the right of the mug and the darker area to its right can be seen as two distinct color shapes joined by a long, gradated edge.

Notice that the long, straight edges of the table are not painted cleanly. A long, straight, clean edge in a painting will, just by virtue of its clarity, pull the viewer's eye along its length and probably away from where you want the eye to go.

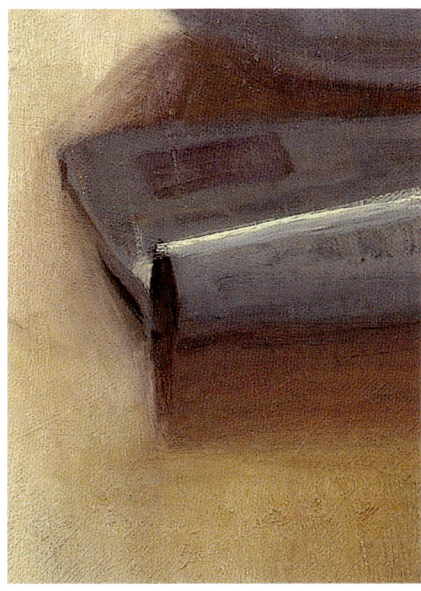

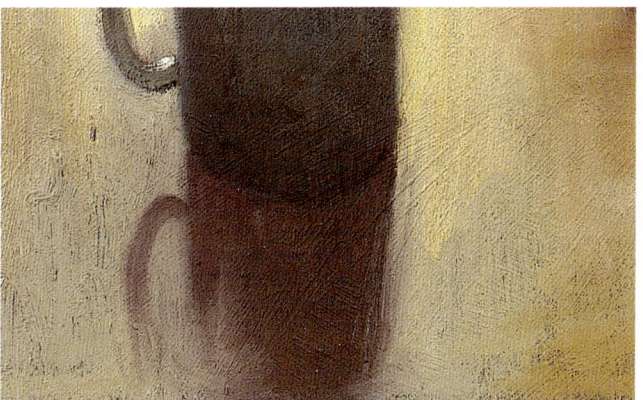

Detail B

The shape of the reflection of the mug is again primarily made of value shifts. It ranges from a 2 on the right side next to the mug to a blended out edge at the end of the handle (7). Because there is less contrast there, your eye is released from the reflection at the table edge and moves up to the mug.

Detail A

This detail contains a wide variety of edges, hard to soft, achieved mainly through contrast of value.

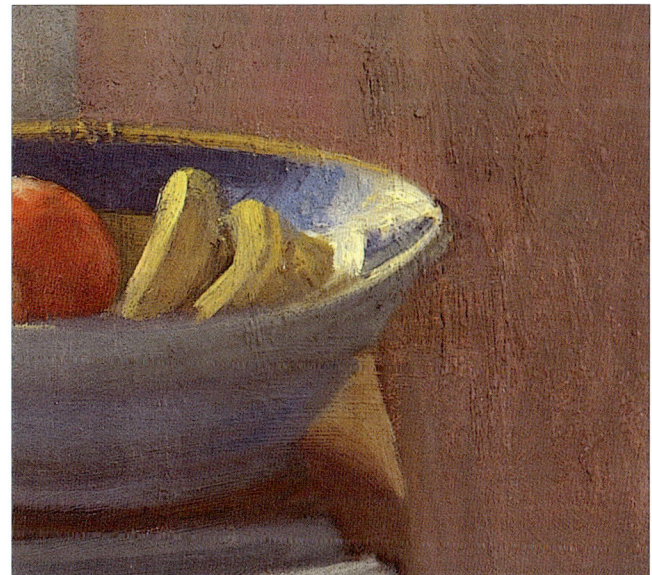

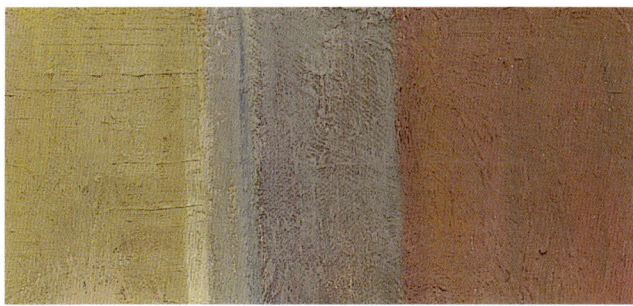

Detail D

Here the edge quality is consistent: all low contrast. You can see shifts in hue, value and intensity, but because the contrast is low, they add life and variety, but they do not detract from the more emphasized areas in other parts of the painting. The same can be said of all the color modulations in the top left of the painting. You can see pink, blue, purple, orange and green. Because the intensity and value are similar, the hue modulation creates edges of 6 or 7. The whole color shape reads as one, gently moving us from the cooler left side to the warmer right to the lighter shape above the top edge of the bowl.

Detail C

Here we see changes in hue and intensity as well as in value affecting the edges. There are four distinct color shapes along the blue band on the bowl, shifting in value, hue and intensity. The edge of the underside of the bowl is almost lost against the background. The value is the same, and the intensity is almost the same. Just the hue is changing. Look at the highlight along the rim of the bowl as it passes in front of the bananas. It is crisp and defined on the right and fades to nothing as it moves left along the rim.

Brushwork: Your Personal Calligraphy

Two things seem to entice students more than anything else in painting. One is color; the other brushwork. With color, it's the careful modulation of intensities that signifies mastery, not the use of bright color. Similarly, bold brushwork does not necessarily indicate mastery.

Brushwork is a personal thing, like handwriting. At first it may be tentative because you have to juggle so many ideas and possibilities as you paint. Think about when you first learned to write. It was awkward and took all your attention to just form the letters. Once you'd learned, however—assuming your handwriting was legible—you didn't think much about it. It's the same with brushwork. It becomes a tool to express what you want to say.

Some people start off with bold brushwork. The problem with bold brushwork in most student painting is not actually the brushwork, but the color of each stroke. If the value is too dark or the intensity too bright, we become too aware of the marks of paint. Bold brushwork that succeeds comes with experience and relaxed confidence.

Think of your brushwork the same way you think of your handwriting. As your experience as a painter grows, you will develop your own natural expression of how to put paint on a canvas. Concentrate on good abstract design, learning to see and paint in color shapes. The brushwork will take care of itself as an extension of your personal expression. It will come naturally and uniquely, just like the calligraphy of your own handwriting.

Illusion vs. Painterliness

Each representational artist, particularly over the past 150 to 200 years, has had to come to terms with two aspects of brushwork: the illusion created by the brushwork and the physical strokes themselves. Some artists, such as Jean-Auguste-Dominique Ingres, focus on illusion, de-emphasizing the tactile quality of the strokes, which would interfere with the illusion they seek to cre-ate. For these artists, brushwork is a vehicle for creating an illusion, not an end in itself. Other artists, such as Chaim Soutine, are more entranced with the process of applying the paint itself than with trying to create an illusion. The "painterly" technique calls attention to the play of the brushstrokes on the canvas surface.

In the past 150 years or so, there has been a definite bias toward a more painterly expression. Most of the painters in the "Gallery of Greats" in chapter five, however, are masters at achieving a marvelous blend of representational illusion and painterly brushwork. Where you decide to stand between those two poles is no one's call but your own.

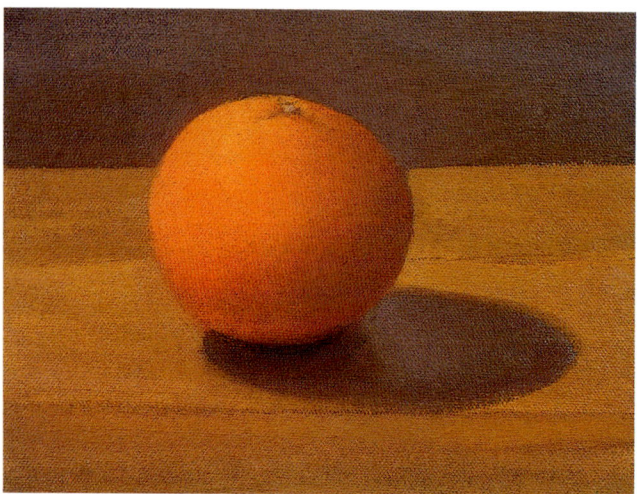

Focus on the Illusion
It's a good exercise to try painting really illusionistic form, even if it isn't your natural inclination. Use softer brushes. One thing that becomes apparent when you paint this way is how attentive you must be to tiny shifts in color that disturb the illusion. You are, in a sense, locked in by the convention. That's not bad—any more than being locked in by Bach's notes when you play one of his fugues on the piano is bad. It's just the nature of creating that degree of illusion with paint.

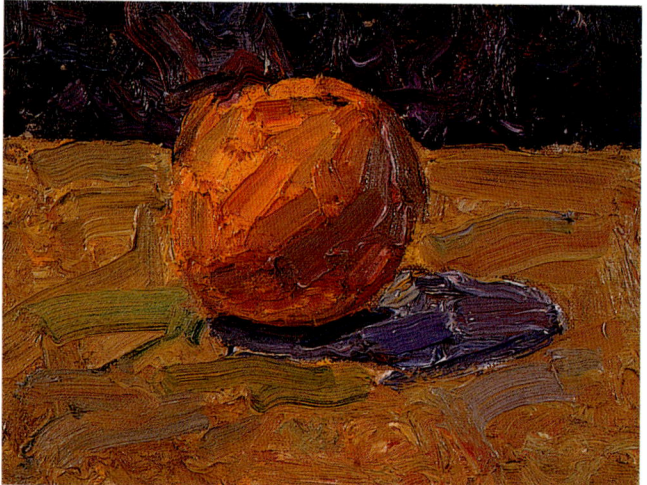

Focus on the Paint
You might try this exercise too. Paint something simple. Apply a lot of paint so the process of actually moving the paint around is your main focus. Keep your color shapes distinct, but, for the sake of the exercise, don't worry whether it's a good painting or not. Just experience what it's like to have that much paint moving around.

Surfaces and Grounds

An important consideration when discussing brushwork is what ground you are painting on. Surfaces may include canvas (cotton or linen), Masonite and plywood. Linen, because it is stronger than cotton, can be woven more tightly to create a smoother surface. But the surface ultimately is less important than the ground on that surface. This is a very personal choice that you can make only after some experimentation.

The cheap canvas-covered boards you find in art stores are the worst surface and ground imaginable to paint on. They are very "slow," meaning that if you wipe a brushful of paint across them, you see about 50 percent color and 50 percent little white spots of uncovered canvas. You have to really work at it, scrub the paint, to get rid of the white canvas. That's a "slow" surface.

Smooth, oil-primed linen is a "fast" surface for oil painting. You can run a brush over it and immediately manipulate the paint right on the surface. Because the surface is responsive, those early brushstrokes can become a significant part of the finished painting. Fredrix, Utrecht and Gamblin all make good oil primers.

You can use acrylic gesso as a ground for oil painting, but it tends to be absorbent and therefore slow. A thin coat of shellac wiped on the gesso will make it less absorbent and therefore faster. Acrylic painters can apply a thin wash of medium if they want a less absorbent surface. Watercolor painters, for whom surface and ground are the same, usually come to terms with this idea early since it's fairly normal to try out different papers to see what you prefer.

Try a variety of surfaces and grounds. Eventually you will choose a surface that allows the most natural play of your brush as you paint.

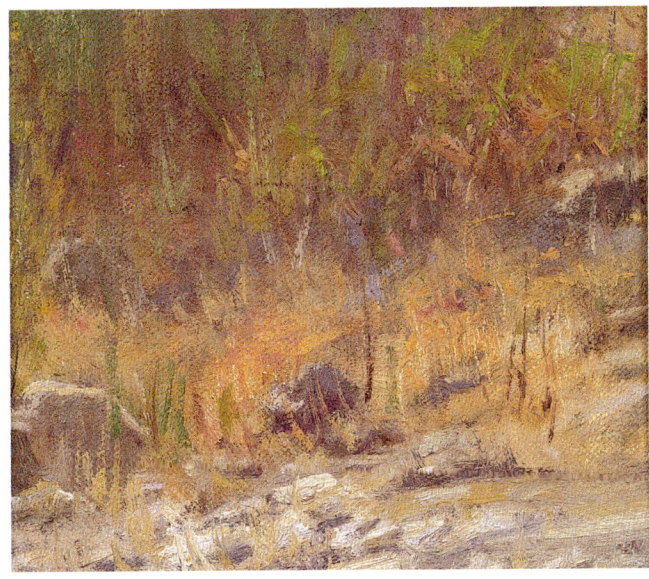

Engaging Brushwork
In this detail of a painting, a variety of brush marks combine to form an intricate and engaging blend of effects. The variety is interesting but won't conflict with the path the eye takes though the entire painting.

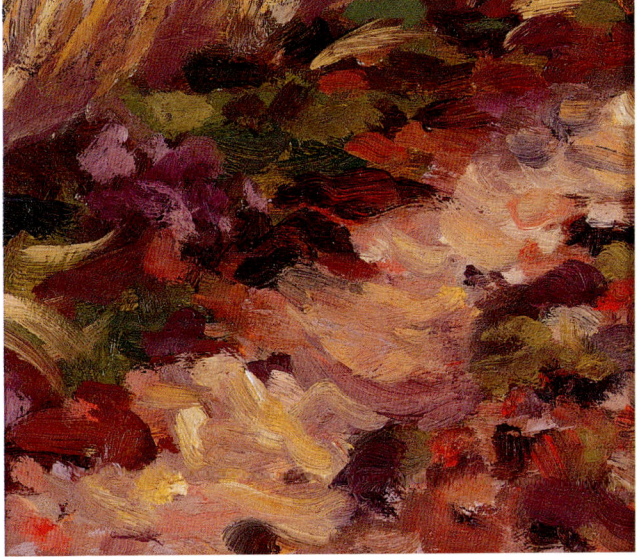

Distracting Brushwork
In this detail of a work by a student, the abrupt changes in value, hue or intensity call too much attention to the brush marks themselves. If a brush mark is too light or dark, or too intense in color, its edges will compete for attention with the armature and areas of emphasis you've tried to establish. Look at paintings by Sargent and Sorolla (see pages 128 and 129) to see bold brushwork. Each of their brushstrokes adds beautifully to the whole composition and aids in leading the viewer's eye along very specific paths of attention.

Brushes Are Not Very Smart

If you want one word to describe good brushwork, it would be *deliberate*. It doesn't matter whether you paint thick or thin, loose or tight. Over time, you'll naturally gravitate toward what works best for what you want to say and how you want to say it.

But deliberate brushwork, with attention, is crucial. When I was in art school, I had a figure-drawing teacher who, when he came around to look at your work, would comment: "Here, along the shoulder, you've really seen that. You can feel it in the quality of your line. Over here on the forearm, there's nobody home." And he was always right. The quality of attention clearly affected the quality of the drawing.

I often find the same thing when I come up to students during a workshop. The brush is moving back and forth, back and forth—but "there's nobody home." You obviously can't expect the brush to do the work for you. Brushes just aren't that smart. If your brush is moving but your attention has wandered, stop and regroup.

"Deliberate painting" means seeing what you want to paint—the shape and the color—and putting that down on the canvas. See each color shape, then, mark by mark, put it down and leave it. This means slowing way down and being really attentive. Often you lose deliberate painting when you confront something you think looks complicated, something you can't interpret as shapes of color, such as a reflection in moving water or sunlight coming through a glass jar in a still life. So you just plunge in, hoping that something will work out. Before you do that, stop and squint and really spend time "seeing" what you are looking at and deciding how you can simplify it into several color shapes that will get the idea across. Then paint those shapes. Don't start until you can see it.

If you have really concentrated on great color shapes and you can get them to carry the painting, you are less likely to get sidetracked or derailed by details. Try to resist adding any details until the very end. That way you are freer to keep adjusting the relationships of the larger shapes. Once you've put in details, you're likely to be reluctant to paint over them if you see the need to make broader adjustments. You will get boxed in too early, and it will handicap you. If you see that you need to adjust the big shapes, no amount of detail will ever take the place of those adjustments.

I don't close my eyes and hope for the best. I want to know what my brush is doing. I "stop, look and listen." I really want to be accurate.

Joan Mitchell
(And she's an abstract expressionist!)

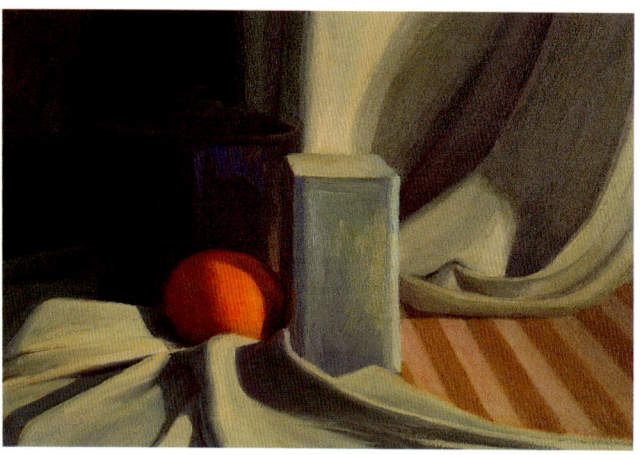 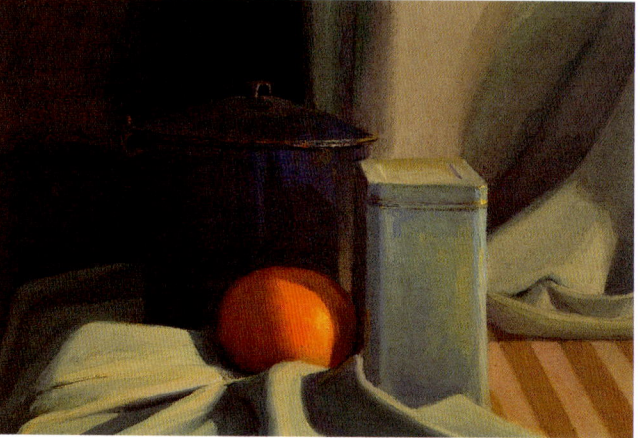

Think of Details As Just Smaller Color Shapes
Look at the example at the left above, which includes some of the large shapes from the demonstration on pages 37–41. There are no details, yet the illusion is already created. Color modulations add richness, but the basic shapes carry the painting. In the example on the right, twelve, maybe fifteen, marks were done right at the very end using a no. 6 synthetic rigger. They are simply embellishments on top of the color shapes. Restrain yourself and try to leave all details to the very end like this so you're forced to work with the structure of the painting. Details are charming but tend to be superficial and distracting if they aren't resting on a sound foundation.

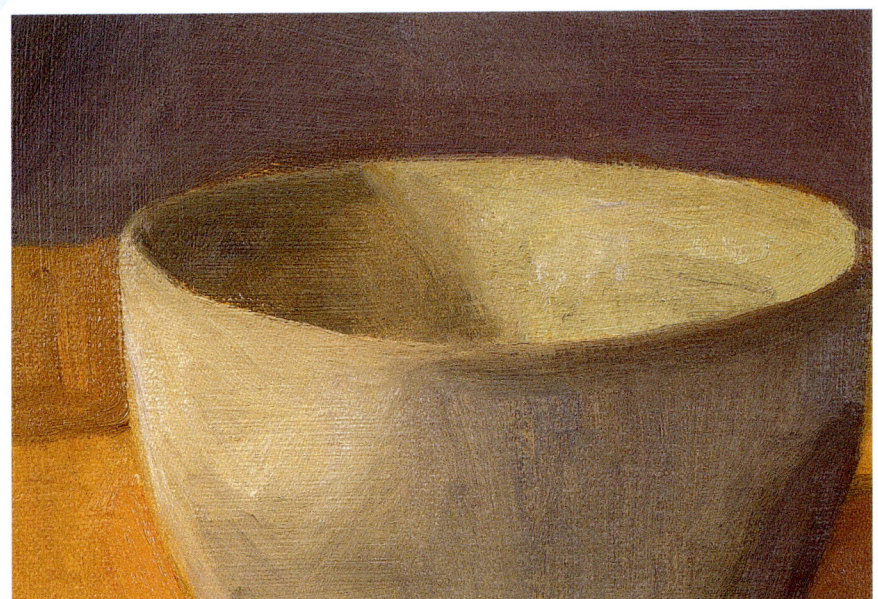

Establish the Color Shapes
Here the color shapes are already creating the sense of form.

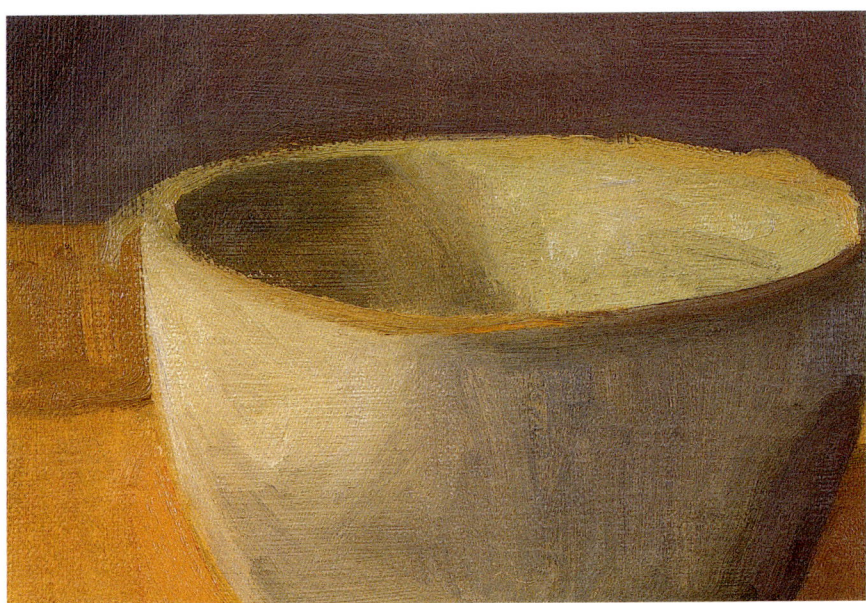

Add Details Confidently
When it's time for details, don't tighten up. Decide where you want a line of paint to go and put it down. It doesn't matter if it's perfect. Paint it in and leave that brushstroke alone.

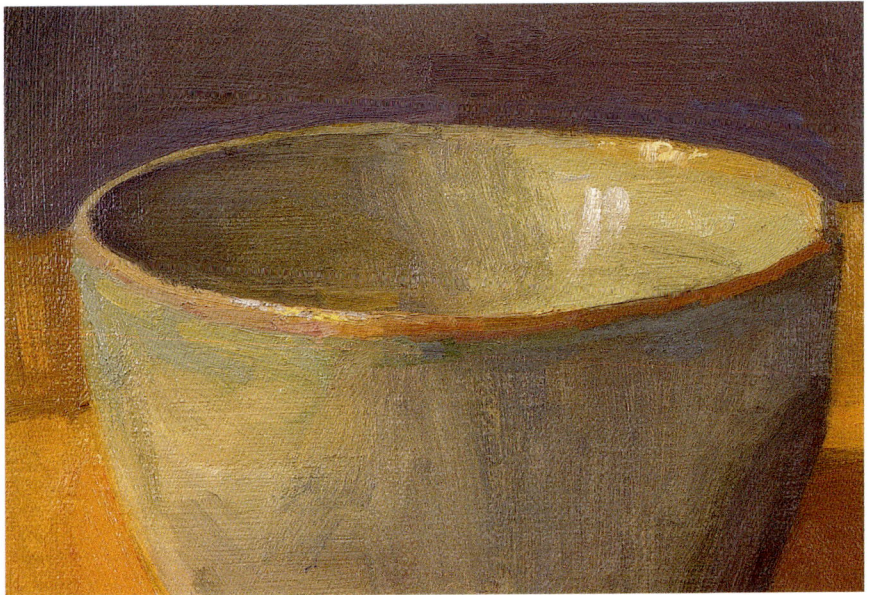

Refining Details
If you keep your paint fairly thin, you will be able to add "cleanup" strokes to adjust a shape that got too wide, or add interesting transitional colors without building up too much thickness. Don't overwork the details so your painting will remain fluid and painterly.

focus on abstract shapes

If you focus on the abstract value shapes of your painting, laying them in simply, you won't find the need for fussing and repainting when you've finished your block-in. You may need to make adjustments here and there for emphasis, but a good basic design carries the painting as a whole.

This demonstration was done with that focus in mind. Create good abstract shapes, block them in simply and leave it.

MATERIALS

Surface
Oil-primed canvas, 30" × 24" (76cm × 61cm)

Brushes
Nos. 4, 8 and 10 hog bristle filberts, no. 6 sable or synthetic rigger

Pigments
Zinc White, Cadmium Yellow Light, Cadmium Yellow Deep, Yellow Ochre, Cadmium Orange, Cadmium Red Light, Alizarin Crimson, Quinacridone Violet, Dioxazine Purple, Ultramarine Blue, Phthalo Blue, Phthalo Green, Chrome Oxide Green, Terra Rosa, Ivory Black

Other supplies
Smooth drawing paper, B and 2B pencils, viewfinder, L-shaped cards, tracing paper, kneaded eraser, mineral spirits

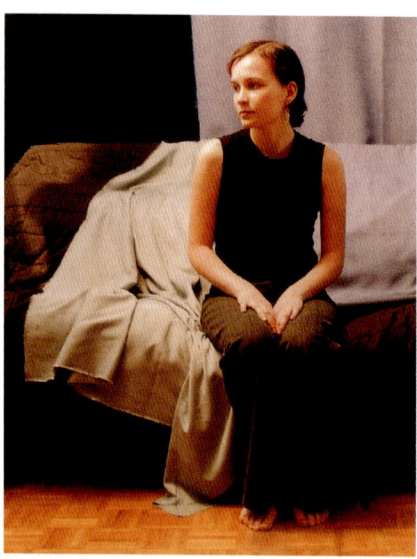

Crop to Create Drama
Notice the cruciform armature here as well as the strong abstract value shapes. Use your L-shaped cards for cropping your photograph, or use your viewfinder when painting from life. Crop into your idea for a painting until it becomes design driven, not just an obvious expanse of subject matter. This is such a critical moment in the life and success of a painting. If you can't seem to find good dramatic value masses in what you've chosen to paint, try another idea. Move on. But don't start painting until you can see how you will express your idea in dramatic abstract masses.

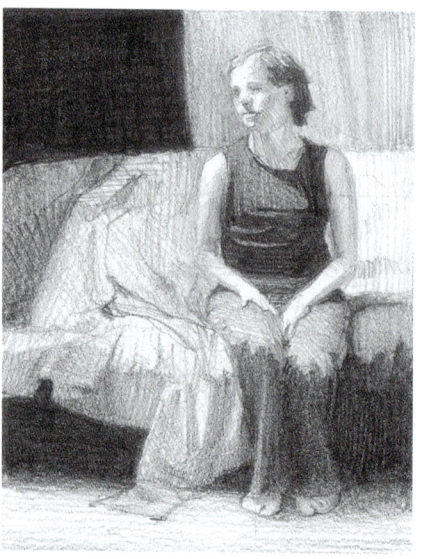

Thumbnail
A thumbnail can save you hours of frustration by identifying the strengths and weaknesses of an idea right at the start. You can emphasize the strengths and find solutions to problems before you start to paint.

If you avoid doing thumbnails because they seem to create as many problems as they solve, do spend time learning to draw in flat value masses (see pages 62–64). That one skill, as well as laying in your initial drawing using one-third divisions so the proportions of your masses are accurate, will change your experience of drawing and will create an invaluable tool as you prepare to paint.

Which White?

Notice here the use of Zinc White instead of Titanium White. Titanium White has a very high tinting strength that makes it a useful all-purpose white. However, I find Zinc White is less harsh when you need more subtle tint gradations, as you often do when painting skin.

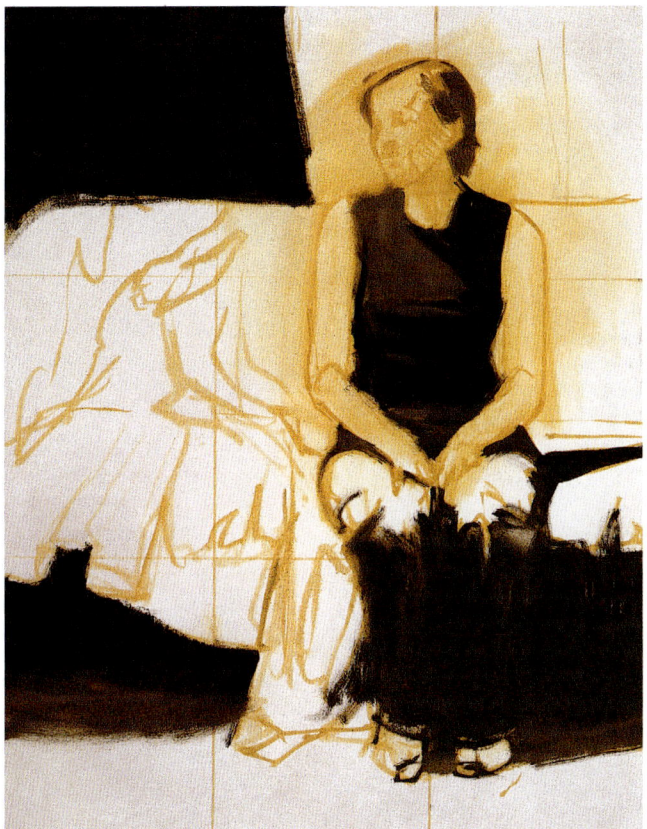

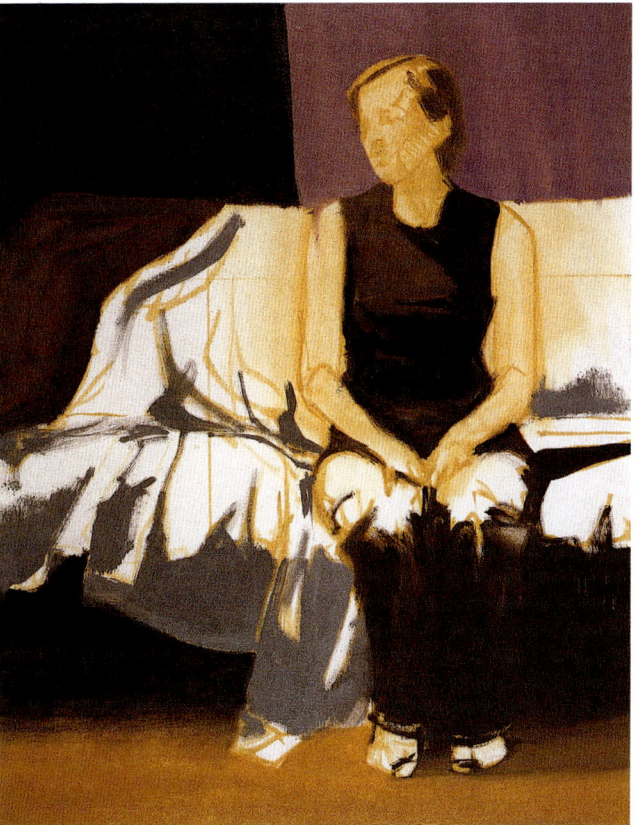

1 Lay In Value Shapes

Grid the canvas in thirds. Look through a viewfinder marked with thirds or use tracing paper marked in thirds over your photo.

The main idea in this demonstration is to lay in each value shape and leave it, letting the abstract shapes carry the painting. Start by painting in all the darks with a mixture of Ivory Black and Yellow Ochre. The bottom edge of the dark as it meets the lit part of floor is softened and has more Yellow Ochre added. Add a touch of Cadmium Orange to Ivory Black for the hair.

Add more Yellow Ochre and a touch of Chrome Oxide Green to the Ivory Black for the lit part of the shirt. Both the lit and shadow shapes of the shirt are integrated within the darks of the painting. Establish your light and shadow shapes carefully as you proceed and you will find the painting coming to life as you go.

2 Block In Simply

For the shadows on the cloth over the couch, use Yellow Ochre, Chrome Oxide Green, Ultramarine Blue and Zinc White to create a cool gray-green. Overpaint the shadow shapes so that you can paint the light shapes into them later. Don't worry about carefully painting right up to the edges of your drawing. Overpaint them, then create a variety of edge qualities (sharp, soft, lost) when you come back in with the second color.

Use Ultramarine Blue, Quinacridone Violet, Yellow Ochre and Zinc White for the backdrop in the right background. Add a bit more Ivory Black and Ultramarine Blue, then paint the right side of the backdrop darker so that the whole shape is gradated and visually pushes us into the painting.

Use Cadmium Orange and Ivory Black for the floor, softening the edge where the light trails into the dark.

Additional Pigment Placement

Terra Rosa and Ivory Black are "guest" colors to my standard palette. I place them next to the greens so as not to disturb my usual layout.

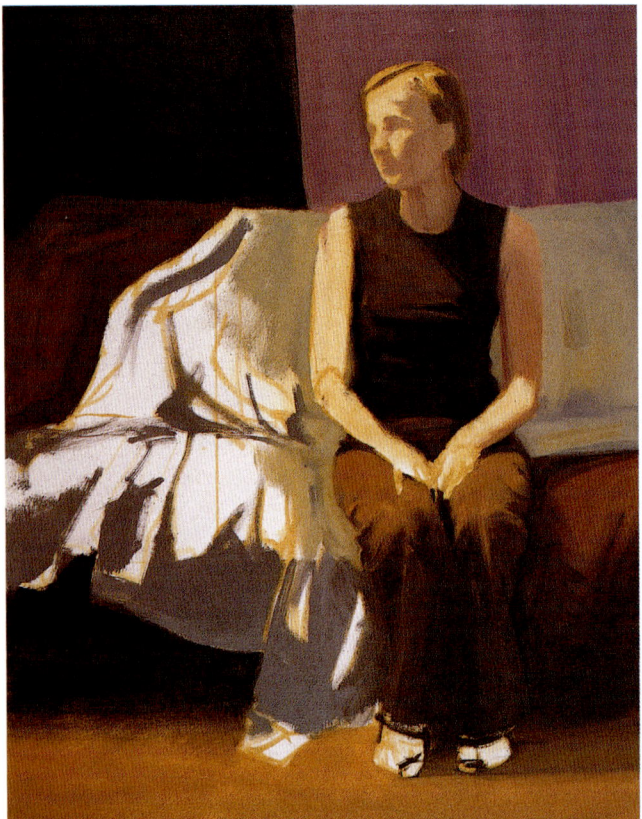

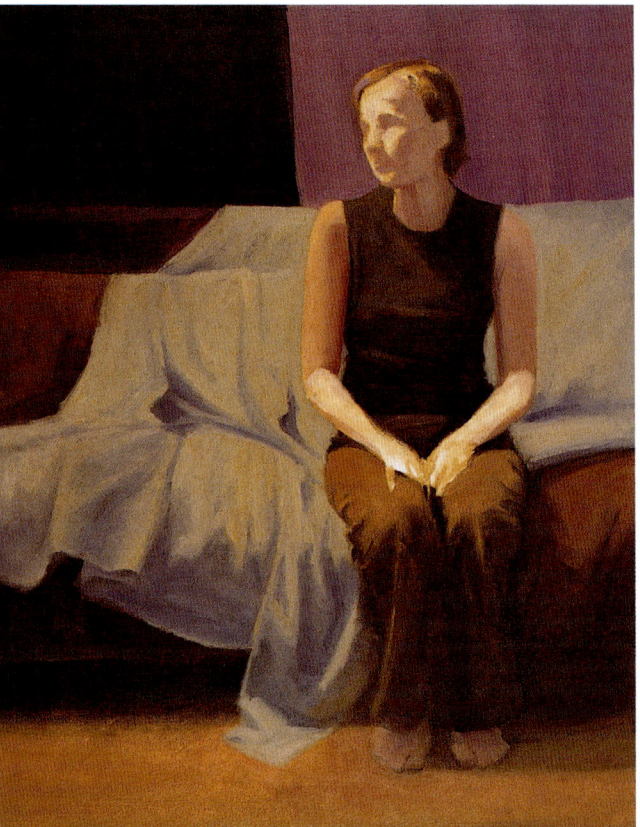

3 Integrate Edges and Add Skin Tones

Be conscious of the edge quality as one shape joins the next. Brush one shape into the next. Look at the lit shapes of the pants and the couch on the right; paint their edges to create a transition between the two shapes. Some edges will be soft as they wrap around the form; others will be crisper where a fold in the material catches the light.

For skin tones, try using Terra Rosa—but don't just call it "flesh color" and add white. It is a "softer" pigment, so it is good for creating nuanced gradations and transitions.

For the left arm and face in shadow, use Terra Rosa, Ultramarine Blue, Yellow Ochre, Ivory Black and Zinc White. For the shadows on the cheek and the inside edge of the arm, add more Terra Rosa. For the top of the shoulder, which is cooler and lighter, add more Yellow Ochre and Zinc White. Notice the edge of the arm against the lit cloth behind it. At the top the value is the same, the edge is almost lost. A soft shift in hue is all that separates the two shapes.

When painting the skin, mix enough of the basic Terra Rosa mixture for the whole block-in and modify it slightly to get subtle changes in color within each shape. Don't try to keep remixing the color from scratch each time; the color shifts will be too dramatic.

4 Paint Shapes, Not Details

Use four values for the cloth: two for the light and two for the dark. Paint your main light and dark shapes in the cloth distinctly. Take your time getting the shapes right before you start to paint, then paint them in simply. You may find that they're done without any need to fuss. Notice the warm reflected light bouncing warm from the floor onto the cloth next to the right foot. Add a small amount of Yellow Ochre to warm the shadow. The feet are in shadow. Put them in very simply so that they won't attract a lot of attention.

Start With Drama

I keep emphasizing the importance of dramatic abstract masses. That doesn't mean those masses can't be subtle in nuance or that you should paint only in big black and white shapes. No matter how dramatic you conceive of something, you will lose some of that drama in the execution. It just happens. So start with drama.

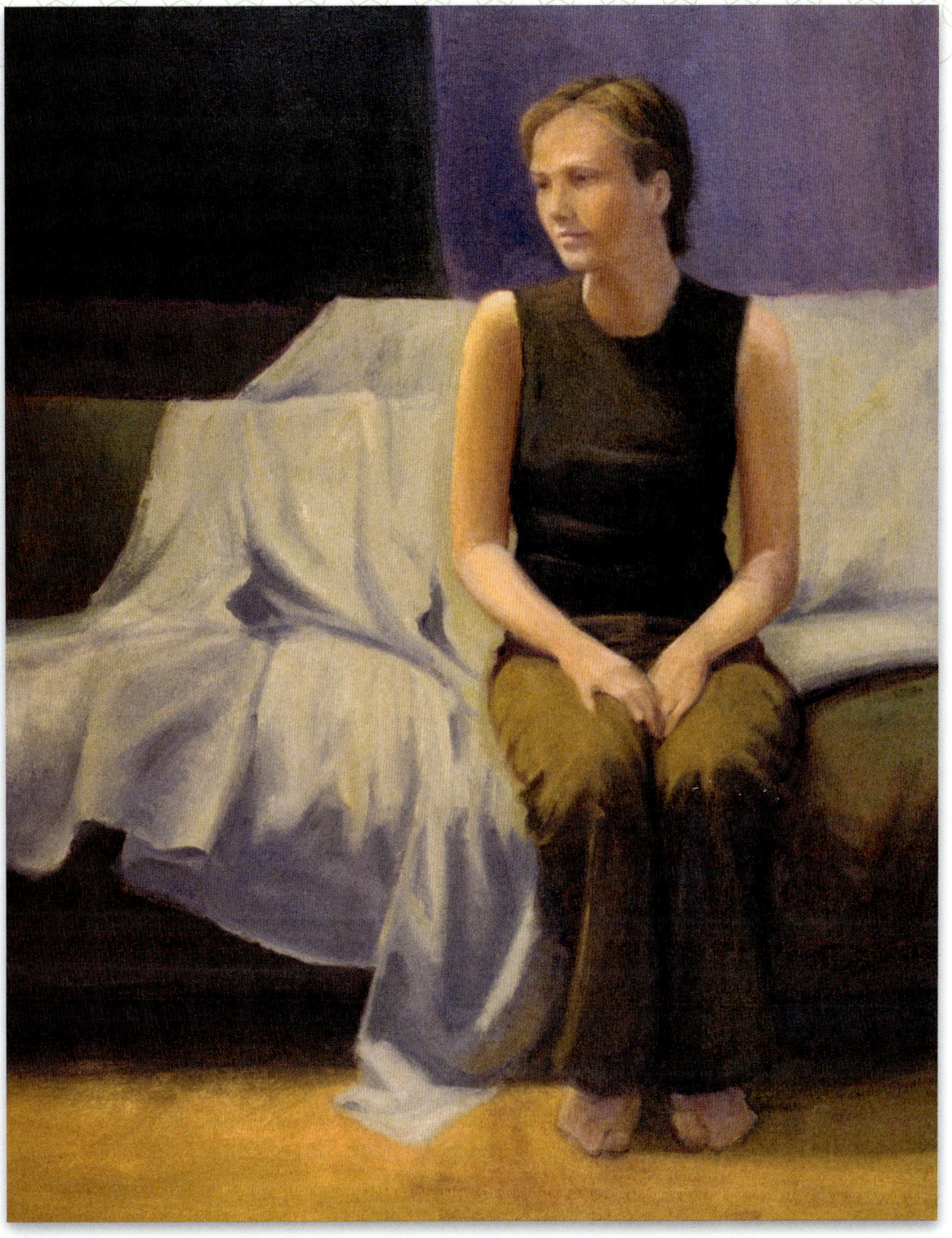

HAILEY
Oil on canvas
30" × 24" (76cm × 61cm)

5 Make Final Adjustments

Paint the lit side of the face and arms with Cadmium Yellow Light, Yellow Ochre, Cadmium Orange and Zinc White, using small amounts of Ultramarine Blue and Terra Rosa for darker gradations within the lit area. Keep it simple. Paint the lit side. Paint the shadow side. Be attentive to changes in edges between the two. Then leave it.

When you've finished blocking everything in, you will always have an edge to soften or a gradation or two to enhance. Notice two changes. First, the left edge of the green cloth against the couch has been made darker, so it holds less attention. Also, the contrast between the purple and black background shapes is reduced, so that area, too, holds less attention. The purple was darkened, which creates less contrast with the black but more contrast—and therefore more interest—on the face.

If you've spent time designing the abstract shapes of light and dark well before you start, and if you've painted them simply, the need for lots of adjustments and repainting and fussing is reduced dramatically. Your shapes carry the composition, and you can stop while the painting still feels fresh.

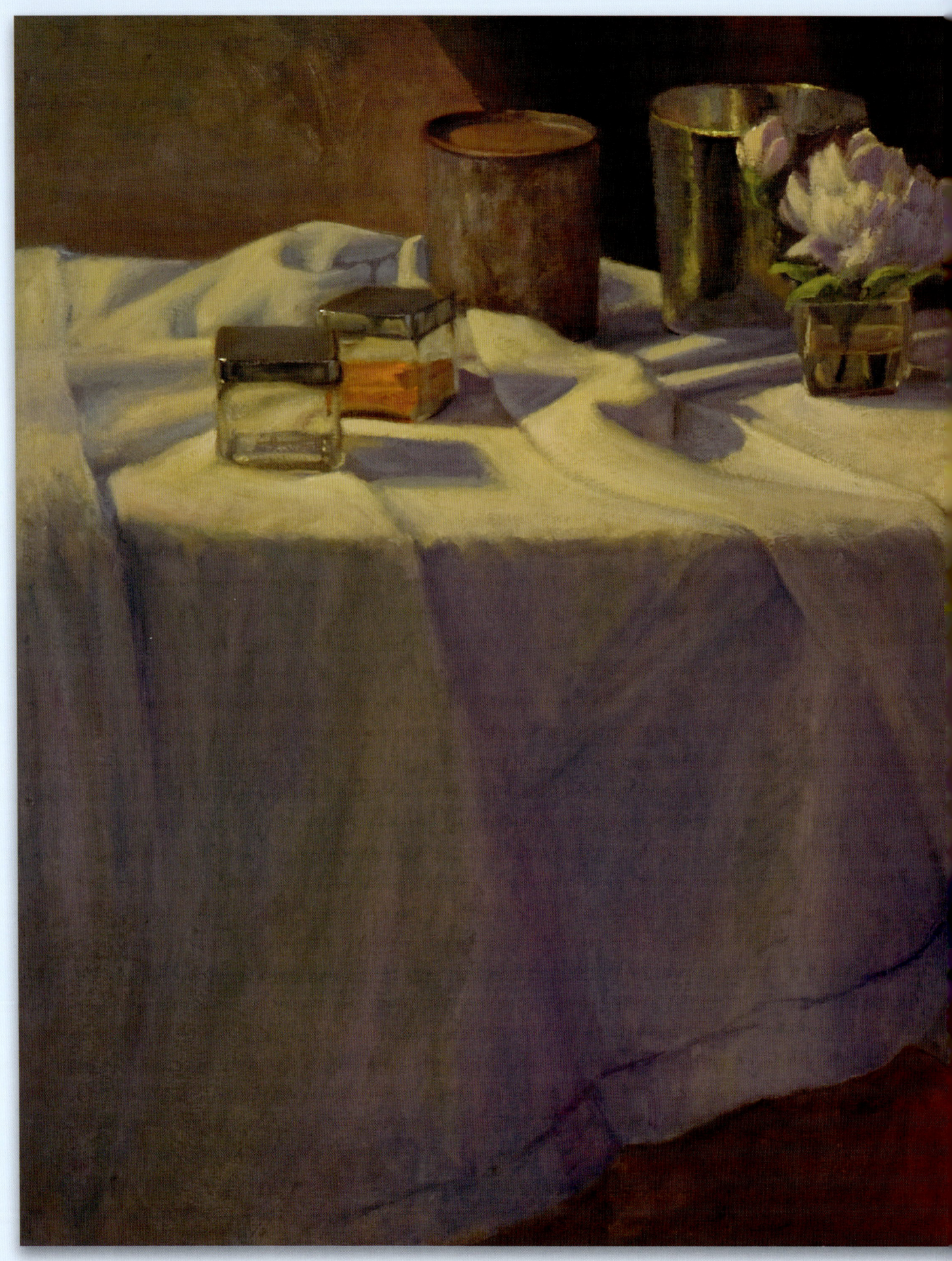

CHAPTER FOUR

Guiding the Eye Through the Picture Plane

Most art forms—opera, dance, film, literature, theater, poetry—are expressed over time. Even sculpture and architecture, because they exist in three dimensions and need to be viewed from different angles to be fully seen, demand time. Painting is one of the very few art forms that doesn't. It exists fully realized in front of us, right now. All of it. That's why composition is so important. Everything is apparent to the viewer at once. There's no second act, no better angle.

I'm not saying we don't need time to view a painting. In fact, the better the painting, the more time it takes. We are still looking at paintings hundreds of years old because there is so much they continue to reveal to us. But it takes careful planning to produce a picture that will hold a viewer's attention for more than that brief moment when she first encounters it. The purpose of this chapter and the accompanying video (ianroberts.com/video-bonus) is to address the question of how to keep a viewer enthralled with your image. The visual dynamics of your painting can invite the viewer's eye to come inside and stay for a while, to explore interesting corners and linger over subtle nuances. Or they can literally drive the viewer's eye right out of the picture. Once you learn how to use those dynamics effectively, you can create paintings that will captivate viewers and encourage them to spend more time with your work.

EARLY LIGHT
Oil on canvas
36" × 36" (91cm × 91cm)

Evaluate Your Composition As a Whole

Many of the ideas in this book—armatures, emphasized-edge sketches, designing value masses, using viewfinders—are about what to do before you put brush to canvas. The point is that the more time you spend planning the composition, the greater your chance of success. You need to slow down and feel your way into a painting.

When you've finished blocking in all the major color shapes, stop painting and evaluate how your block-in looks compared to your thumbnail and initial conception.

Slow down again toward the end of a painting. All the way through the painting process you must think of the parts and how they fit into the whole. The closer you get to finishing, the more important this becomes. All the parts get submerged as the whole takes over—or doesn't.

That's why it's so important toward the end of the painting process to spend more time looking and less time painting. Let the painting speak to you. I don't mean you will

start to hear voices. Or at least I hope not. If you sit quietly and patiently and feel how you are responding, impartially, you'll become aware of how the composition is directing your eye around the picture plane.

Are you in control of that movement? Or not? Is your eye moving toward your center of interest? Is it pulled there too quickly? Do you get distracted by too much information and detail somewhere else in the painting? The dynamic relationships are now right before your eyes, so you need to learn to recognize the dynamics you have created in your painting.

The eye responds to contrasts. The stronger the contrast, the stronger the attraction. This is a fact of optical mechanics. So your center of interest—no matter where you think it should be—will be in the area with the greatest contrasts. It's crucial, therefore, to make sure that your strongest edges and values and more intense colors are in the area you want to draw the most attention.

Yet, because you're so caught up in the painting process and trying to express your idea, you may not notice all the contrasts you've created. That's why it's essential to slow down, put away your brush, step back and evaluate your painting with fresh eyes and an open mind.

Take a Break and Look Again

Find a way to see your painting anew. Go out for a walk or have some lunch. Try looking at your painting in a mirror or upside down. Or you can just sit quietly in front of it and let the painting tell you what is working and what isn't. It will—if you are patient.

Putting your brush away also prevents you from blobbing paint on a problem area before you understand exactly what the problem is. I can't tell you the number of times I've seen students who have been careful and attentive all morning suddenly, in a kind of wild fury, ruin their painting in ten

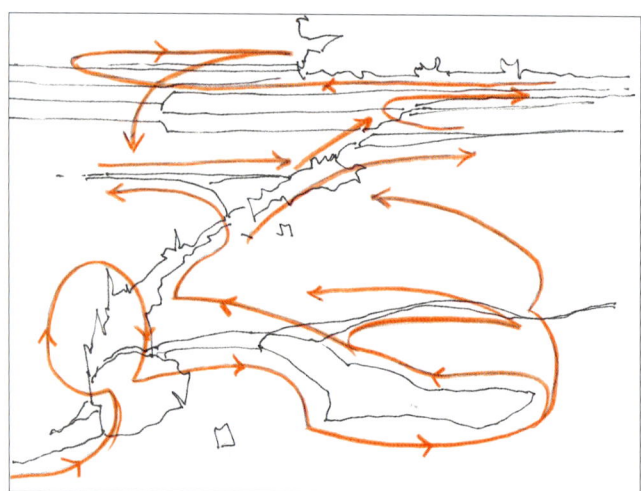

Analyze the Eye's Movement Through a Painting
This diagram gives you some idea of how the eye is pulled around the picture plane of the landscape. Your eye may not move in exactly the same order, but it will seek out these primary and secondary cycles of interest as it responds to the contrasts within them. Look at paintings you like and monitor the movement of your eye around the picture plane. Mastering the way to consciously lead a viewer through your painting is an invaluable, essential skill, and, ultimately, what composition is all about.

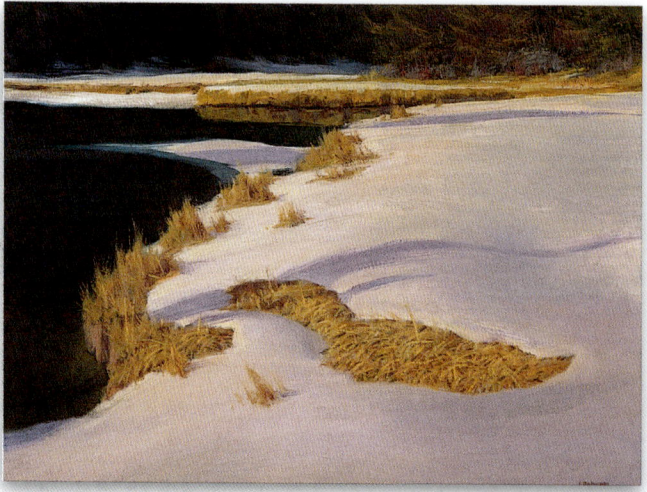

Primary and Secondary Viewing Cycles
Although you set up armatures and lines of direction to pull the eye into a composition, paintings often have secondary viewing cycles within them. This landscape has an L armature, but you'll notice that your eye is pulled to other areas of the painting, circling out and then back into the main line of the armature. It is important to adjust the contrast of each secondary viewing cycle so that it doesn't override the primary cycle.

SPRING ON THE BEAVER RIVER
Oil on canvas · 30" × 40" (76cm × 102cm)

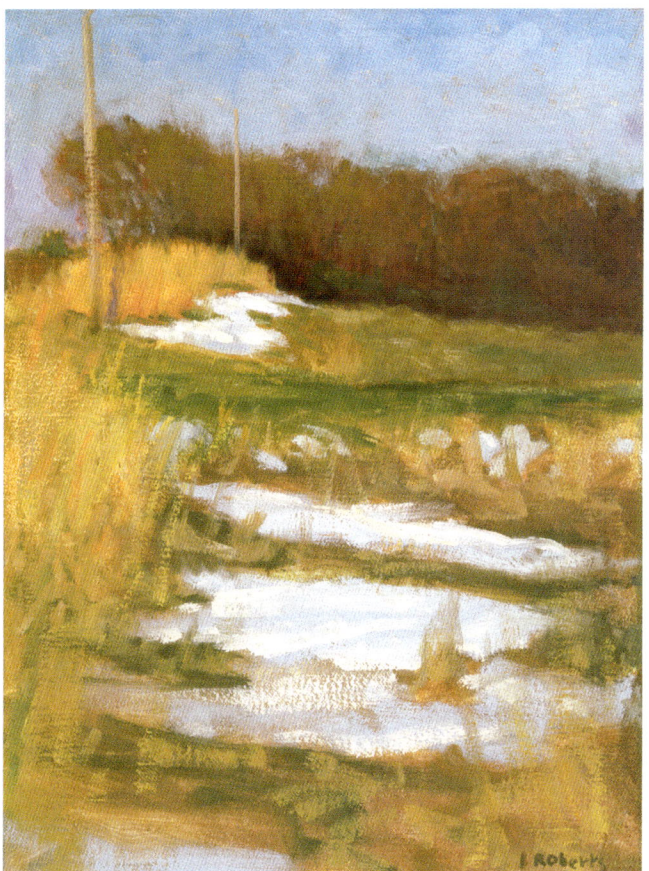

Watch for Eye Traps
It is one thing to lead the viewer to a center of interest. It's another to lead the eye into a trap—a place you visually can't get out of. In this example, the eye goes to the center of interest and gets stuck because there is nowhere else to go, no flow back into the painting.

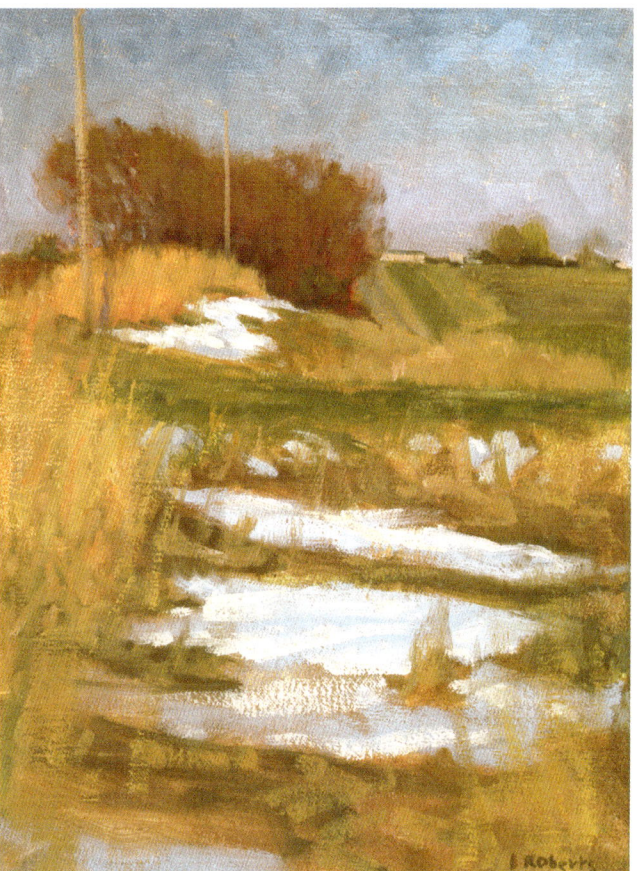

Keep the Eye Moving
Here the eye is released from the center of interest because it gets pulled into the background at the right. You want to keep the viewer's eye moving around and through the picture plane, leading it here, pulling it there, but never directing it out of the picture plane.

minutes by rashly applying a bunch of ill-considered blobs of intense color.

You will always find adjustments you want to make as you are completing a painting. It's inevitable. However, don't try to repaint too much or you're likely kill everything that is fresh and exciting. Usually, there is a hierarchy of problems in a painting that is nearing completion. Some will be fundamental to its success; others may be incidental. Identify the fundamental elements that are currently disrupting your intended flow around the composition, find the simplest way to remedy them and leave the rest.

You may wonder, "How can I be sure that everything is working?" Just relax and let your eye and the painting tell you. You may not always see what you need to see at first. Perhaps you won't see it until you come back the next day, or even the next week or next month (an advantage of not painting to deadlines). With practice, you will see it. The accompanying video (ianroberts.com /video-bonus) focuses on how your eye is pulled by contrast and will help you evaluate your composition as a whole.

Attune Your Eye to the Role of Contrast

A relatively minor change in color intensity or value somewhere in a painting can completely disrupt a composition. On the next few pages you will see four of my paintings. Each painting will be shown in four different versions. The first will be as I painted it, with a successful composition that leads the eye through the picture plane. In each of the other three versions some change will distract your attention from the original composition. Notice how your eye is attracted by that change. Notice, too, how your eye can get pulled right out to the edge of the picture plane, and even beyond it. Once the eye has left the arena, the viewer is gone, on to the next painting—which is pretty much the kiss of death for a painting in a show.

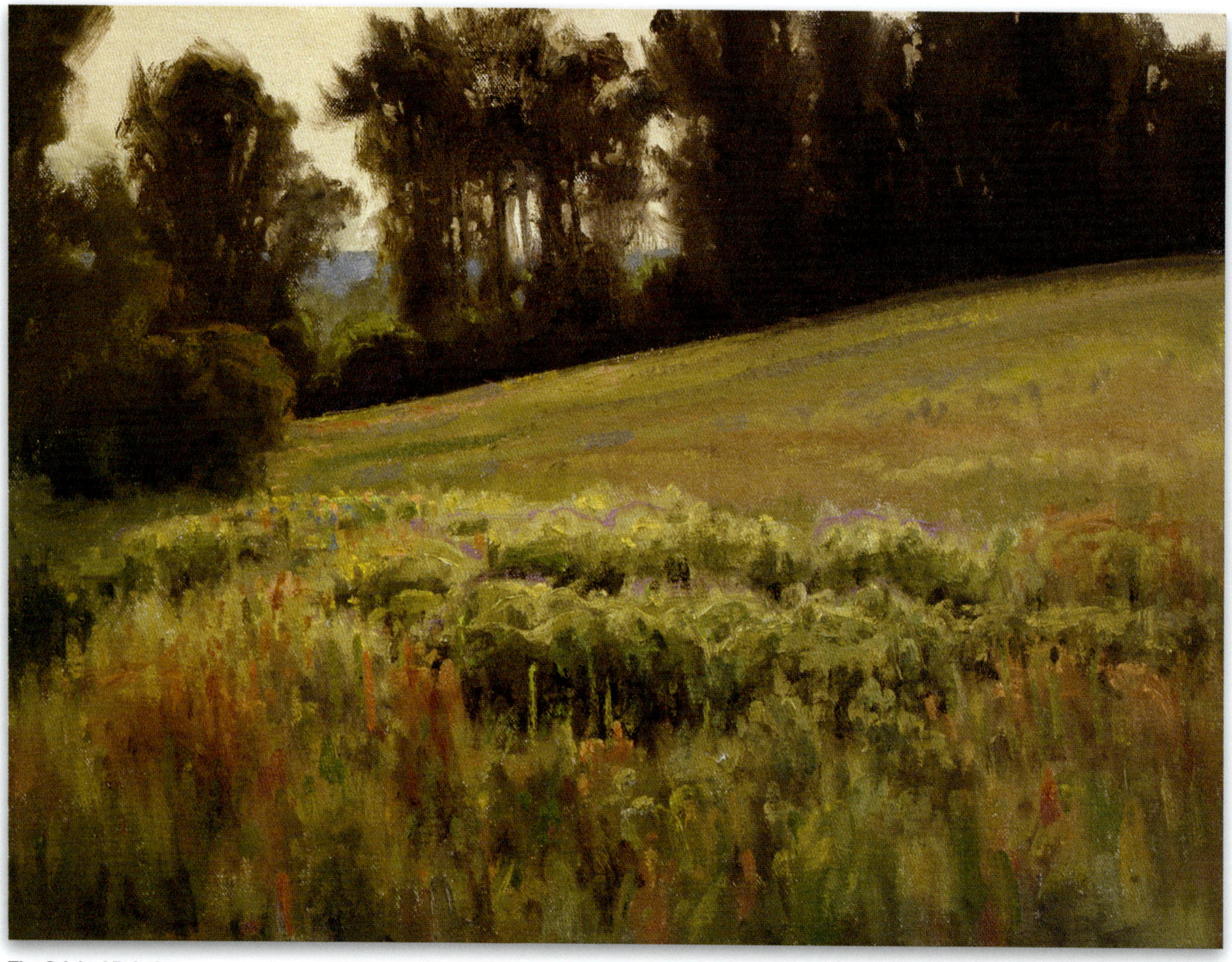

The Original Painting
The eye is drawn from right to left along the long line of the dark row of trees. That line is de-emphasized on the right and sharpened at the left end. The bush at the end of that line halts the movement and draws our attention. The color intensities are heightened here, too, in the grasses and the purple shadow. The foreground has a lot of implied information, but none that competes with the movement of the eye back into the painting to the left end of that long line of trees. You can see secondary cycles of interest in the foreground, in the distance, and in the silhouetted tree shapes.

FALL IN THE VALLEY
Oil on canvas · 12" × 16" (30cm × 41cm)

Rule #1

Keep the viewer in the picture plane.

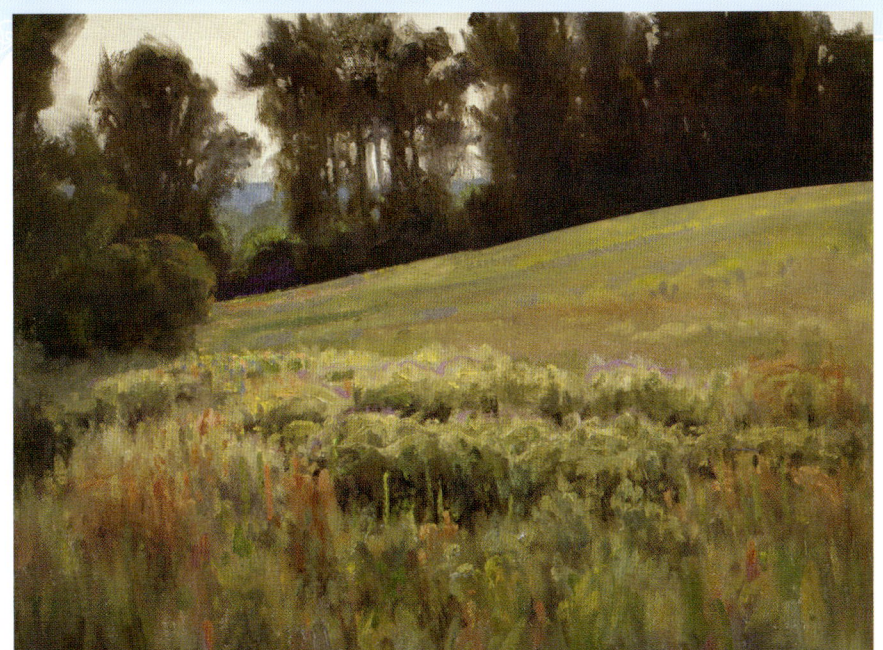

Change 1: Pulled to the Right
The only change made here is the quality of the edge along the entire length of the bank of trees. In this version, it remains hard from one end to the other. The eye is now confused. It still goes down toward the center of interest at the left, but you can also feel the pull of that line out toward the right edge of the painting.

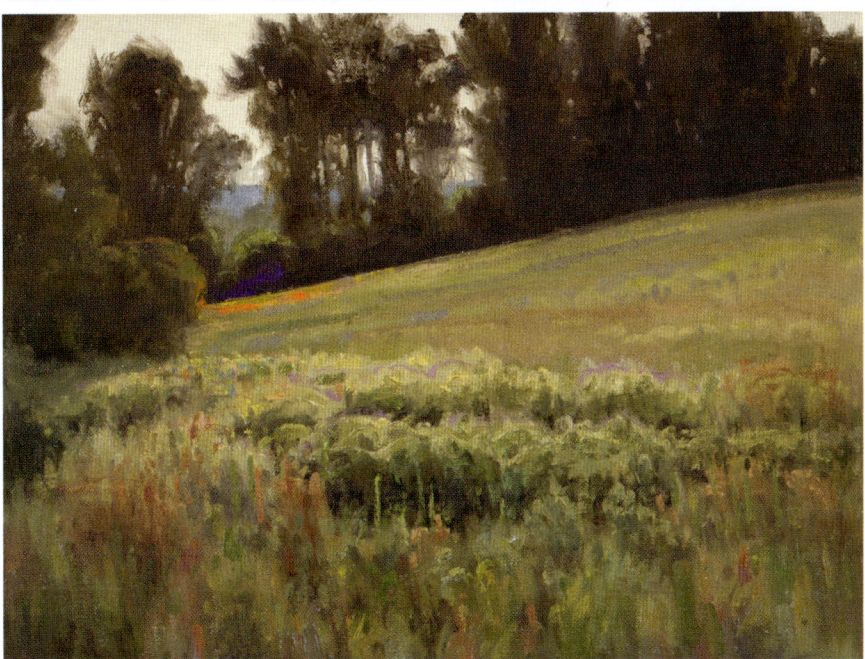

Change 2: Stuck in the Center of Interest
The enhanced color intensity at the center of interest attracts the eye and glues it there. None of the secondary cycles of interest get a chance now because the eye keeps getting pulled back to those heightened colors.

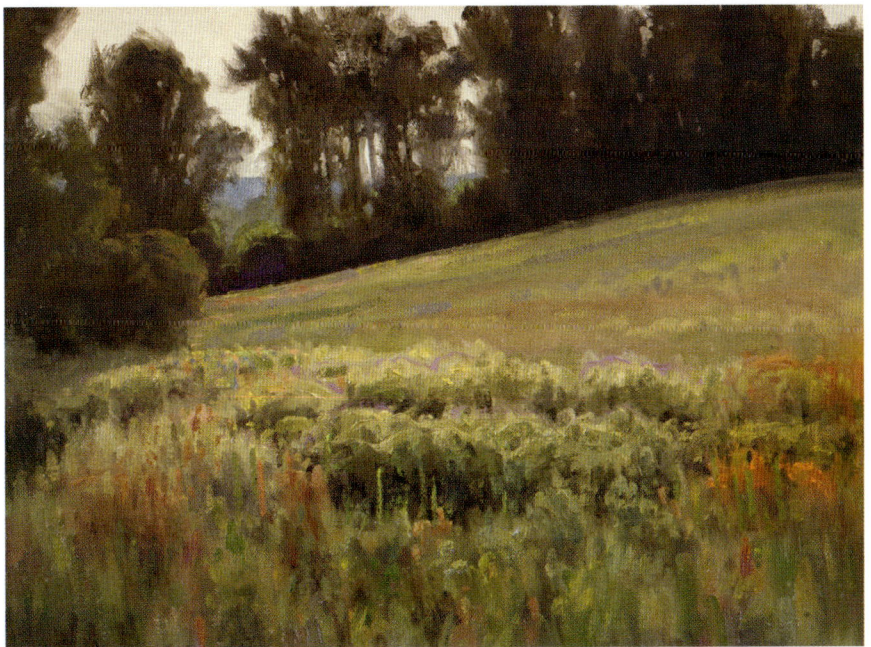

Change 3: Pulled to the Right Again
This time, the enhanced color intensities in the far-right foreground pull the eye in that direction. The eye wants to follow the armature into the intended center of interest, but the new color keeps pulling the eye to the right.

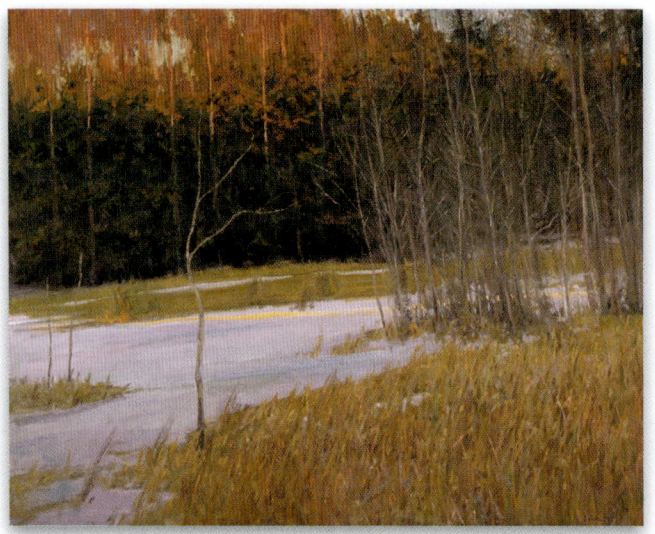

The Original Painting
Although your eye does get pulled to the top left of this painting, the verticals and dark shadows of the trees in that area, the shaft of sunlight across the midground, the variety of foreground grasses, and the foreground and midground trees all keep your attention moving throughout the composition.

DUSK IN THE VALLEY
Oil on canvas · 48" × 60" (122cm × 152cm)

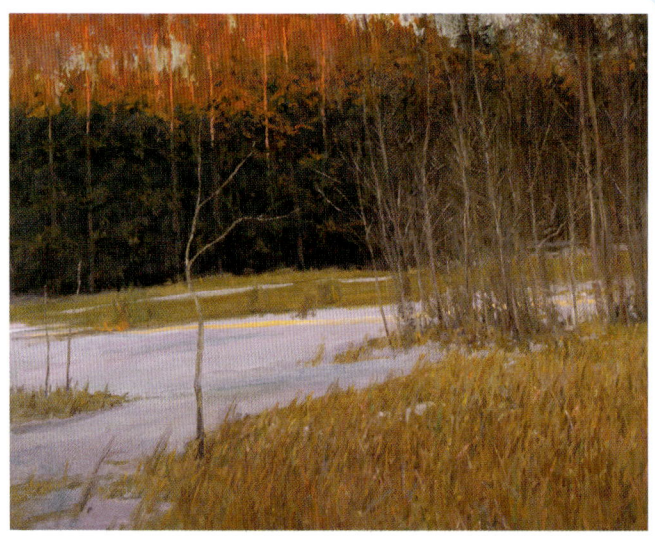

Change 1: Stuck at the Top
The intensified color of the last sunlight on the trees at the top left overrides all the other balancing factors, so your eye gets stuck there.

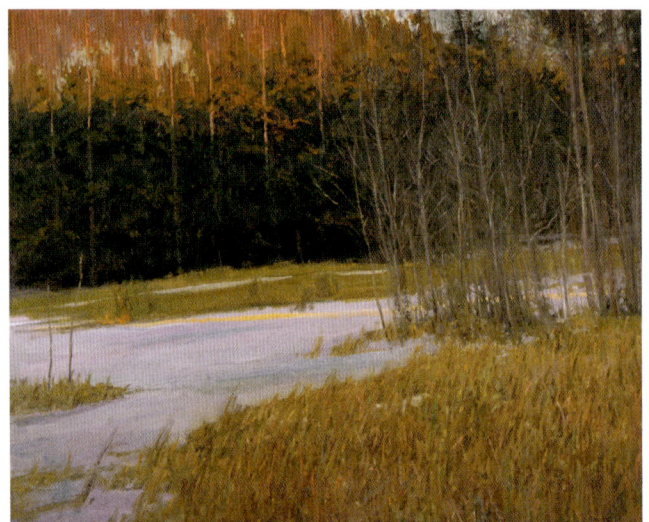

Change 2: Sliding Into Space
Removing the foreground tree leaves a strange empty space to fall into. You find yourself sliding to the bottom left—or else getting held by the dark shadow shape in the center of the painting.

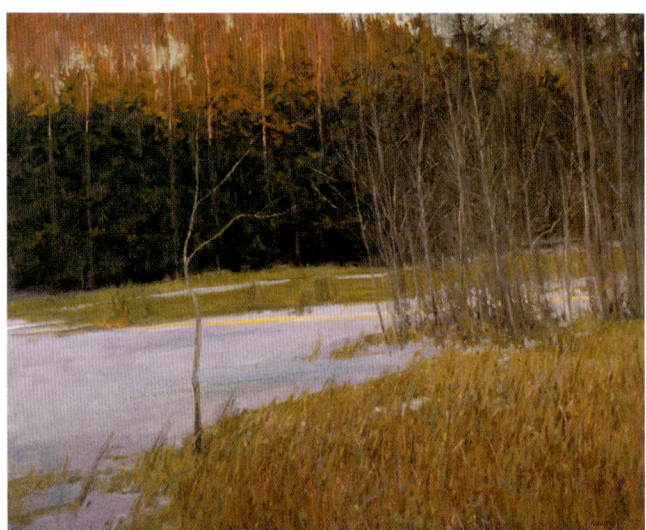

Change 3: Pulled to the Left
Without the little stand of grasses and twigs on the left of the painting, you can feel the gentle pull in that direction. Even though you try to stay in the composition, that space on the left keeps pulling your attention left.

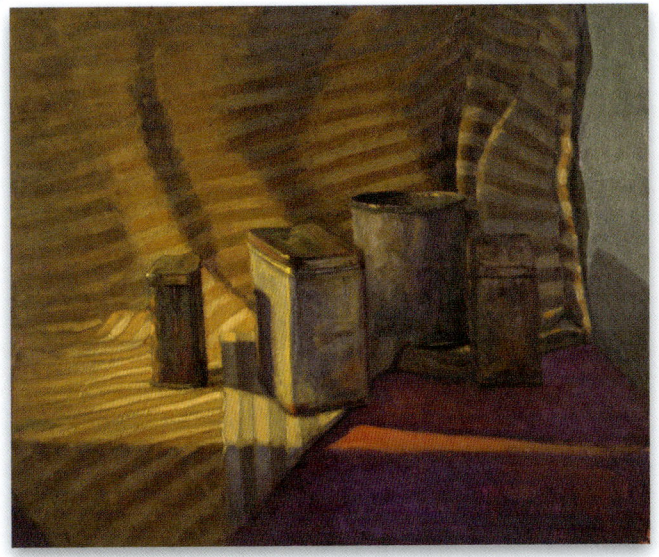

The Original Painting

Notice the major armature, a sideways V culminating in the tin on the left. A lot of other things are going on, but that structure dominates the painting.

EVENING LIGHT ON OLD TINS
Oil on canvas · 20" × 24" (51cm × 61cm)

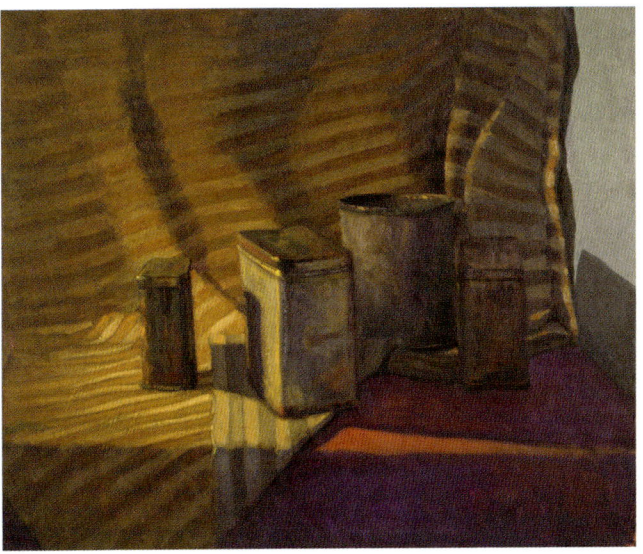

Change 1: Pulled to the Right

Although the main structure of the painting is still intact, you can't help but have your attention pulled right to the heightened color of the green wall.

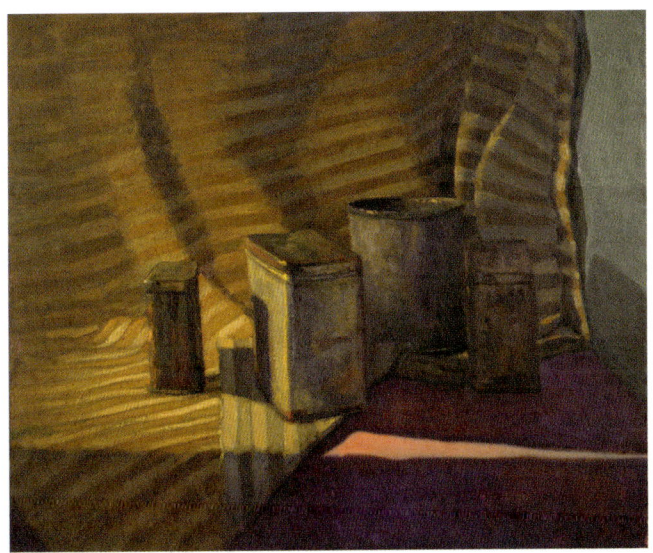

Change 2: Pulled Forward

This change follows the bottom arm of the armature and completely disrupts the composition. Now you get the feeling that all the tins are being pulled forward to march along that line of pink light right out of the painting.

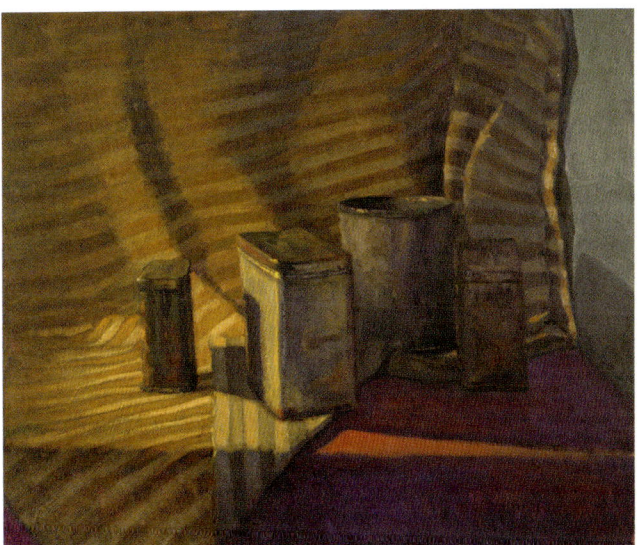

Change 3: Overwhelming Intensity

One tiny color shape (the small purple triangle in the bottom left) can subtly undermine the stability of a whole composition if it's too intense.

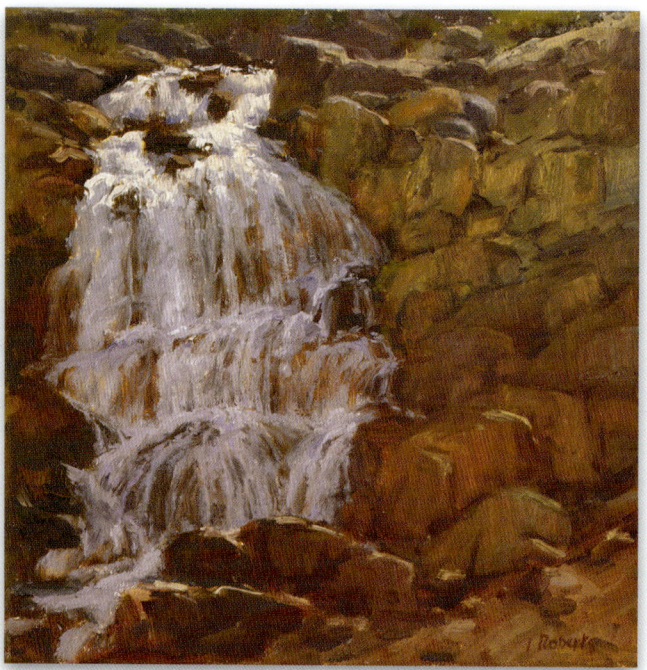

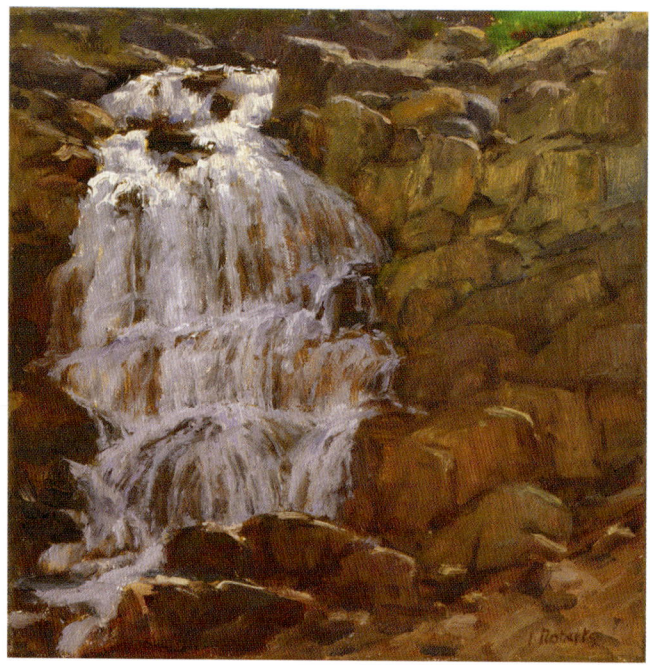

The Original Painting

This example has an S-armature running from bottom left to the top right, with the center of interest in the top left where the sunlight hits the cascading water. There's lots to look at here. The rocks on the right seem varied and delineated but they never pull your attention out of the main flow of the composition.

SIERRA RUN-OFF
Oil on canvas · 12" × 12" (30cm × 30cm)

Change 1: Pulled to the Right

One overly intense color shape and your attention follows the armature up to the top right and out of the painting. If you allow your eyes to innocently be with the painting you find you are struggling now to stay within it. Just one small color shape can do that.

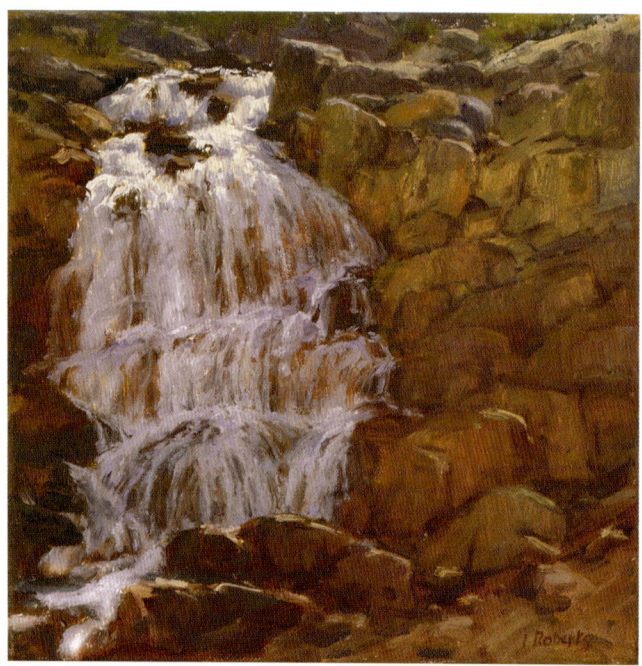

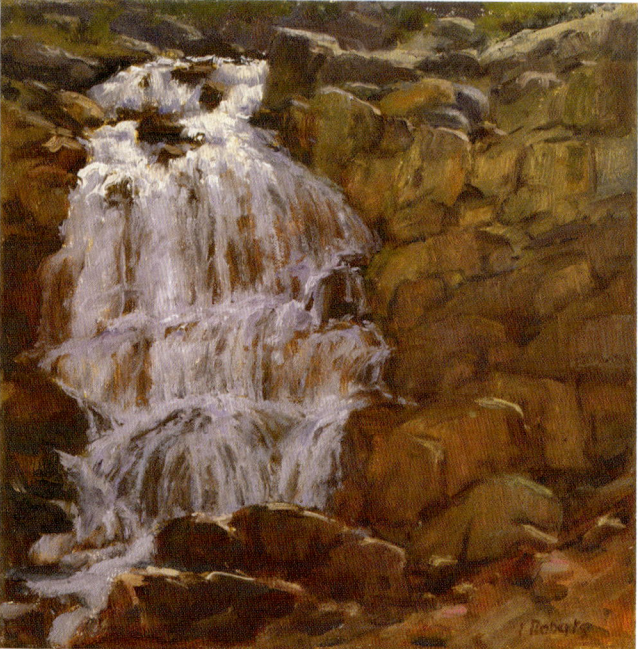

Change 2: Pulled to the Lower Left

Now the same thing is happening in the bottom left. Interestingly the sun was hitting the water there when I painted the painting and it was at least this bright. But in order to move the eye into the painting I had to tone it down. Although you can look at the painting and see it as a whole, that spot of white in the bottom left is subtly disrupting the balance.

Change 3: Pulled to the Lower Right

Again you can look at the painting as a whole, but your eye has this relentless pull to the bottom right which you're always fighting visually. Wherever this change would be it would be distracting. By placing it on the edge of the picture plane, just how distracting becomes more obvious. But place it anywhere and the same disruption, if not the same movement, will be present.

You might ask, "What exactly am I looking for when I slow down and look at my painting?" If you planned an armature with lines of direction to pull us toward a center of interest, then you are looking for visual distractions to the movement you planned. Do you want the eye circling around the canvas, pulled into the center of interest, then pulled out into another loop of visual interest, then circling back again? Visual distractions are those areas that pull your eye away from the natural path you had intended.

Part one of the video presents a series of my paintings along with the intended armature and center of interest for each. Next, it shows a small adjustment (the color intensity heightened or a value exaggerated) to part of the painting. An arrow will indicate how the change pulls your eye away from the original flow of the composition.

In part two, you will see the same changes in the paintings (three or four adjustments per composition), but this time there will be no commentary or arrows. So as you sit there, innocently watching the paintings, many of the kinds of distractions you may have created in your own paintings will present themselves. Your eye will get pulled by one up to the top left, by another to the middle right, and so on. You will become more sensitive to the visual dynamics of the picture plane, so when you look at your own paintings you will be better attuned to the role contrast is playing in your work.

You might want to play part two from time to time to keep that sensitivity lively until you find that you have mastered the skill.

If you miss one of the changes in a composition shown on the video, don't worry. Some are more subtle than others. Don't try too hard to find them. Just be really relaxed and let your eye tell you.

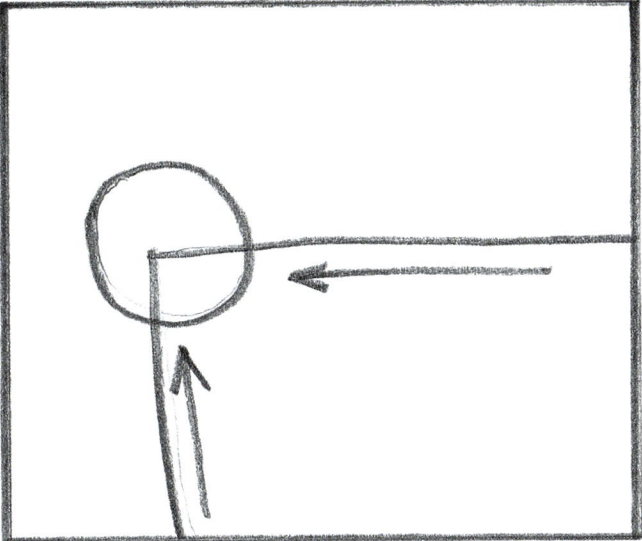

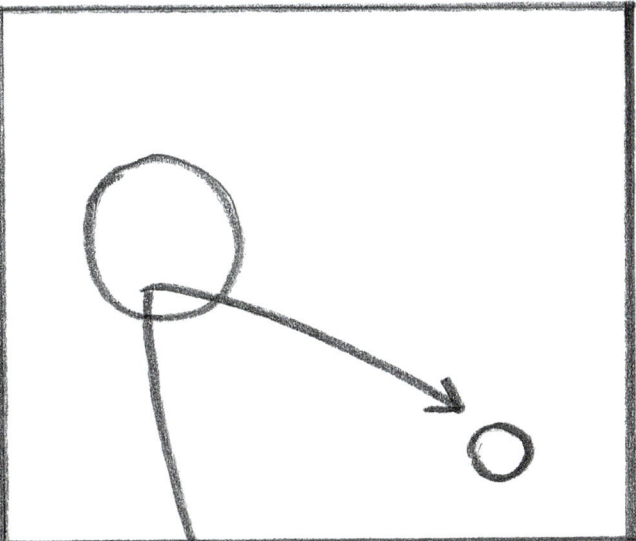

Noticing How the Eye Gets Distracted
In the Video, you will see a painting that works compositionally. You will see the natural flow of the composition along lines of direction to a center of interest. Then you will see how your eye is pulled away from that flow by a digitally altered contrast somewhere in the painting.

Learn From Student Work

If you spend time looking at a painting you have had trouble with, you can find the foundation for a good painting. In execution, distracting edges, too-vibrant color intensities and busy brush marks have created a confusing jumble on the canvas. You can see from the examples on the preceding pages how one change can disrupt the flow of a composition. If you're not attentive to what is happening, a number of such distractions will ruin it.

You often don't have to do much to pull the painting around. Generally, some parts will be working well. Figuring out what isn't working is almost always a perception issue. You have to "see" the problem, and be able to articulate it to yourself: That shape in the top right is too dark and the intensity of the blue is too strong. Once you can see the problem, the solution is usually pretty logical and straightforward.

The next several images are student paintings. They were done by friends who were kind enough to allow me to use the paintings to illustrate different points. Each has composition potential, but something got out of hand in execution. Brushwork, edges, color intensity or lack of gradations conspired against them.

In each case I have adjusted the painting to let the implied but largely buried composition reassert itself. I made a point of staying within the ideas and structure the student was actually wrestling with. I used the exact shapes and structures already in the painting, adjusting them for emphasis so that the eye is led through the composition more effectively.

Tip

If you become aware of an area that might be causing a problem, try blocking that area with your hand or your finger while you view the painting. If that area is indeed causing a problem, you'll probably find that blocking it from view will make the relationships in the rest of the painting suddenly gel much better.

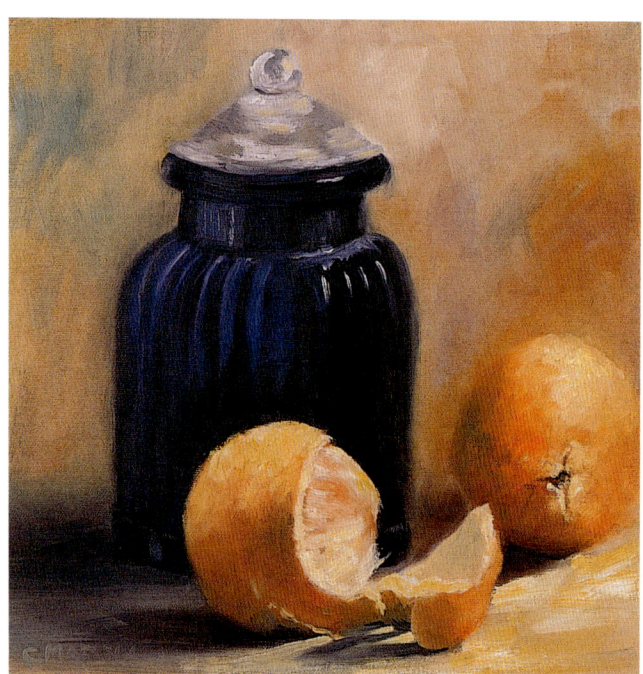

Original Student Painting
The orange in the foreground, with its peel and shadows, is nicely painted. However, the strong edge of the blue jar and the light background pull your attention away from the center of interest (the orange). You're left looking at highlights on a jar.

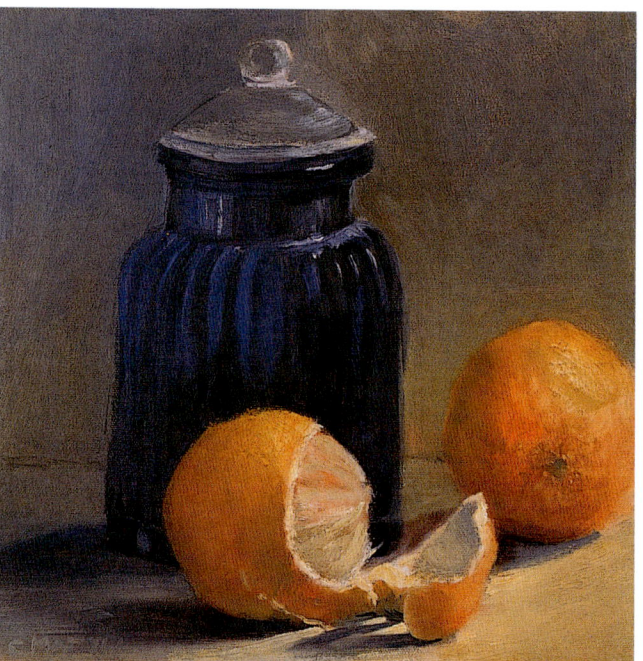

Adjusted Painting
Adding a simple gradation in the background de-emphasizes the jar and pulls your attention down to the orange. Reducing the highlights on the right orange and on the table and adding a stronger value of shadow on the orange peel give the composition a more natural flow.

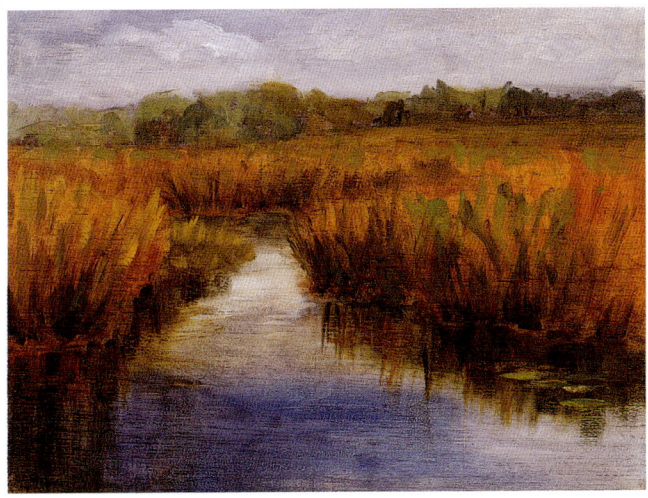

Original Student Painting

The most intense colors and strongest edges are in the foreground. The viewer can't move back into the landscape because the foreground demands all the attention.

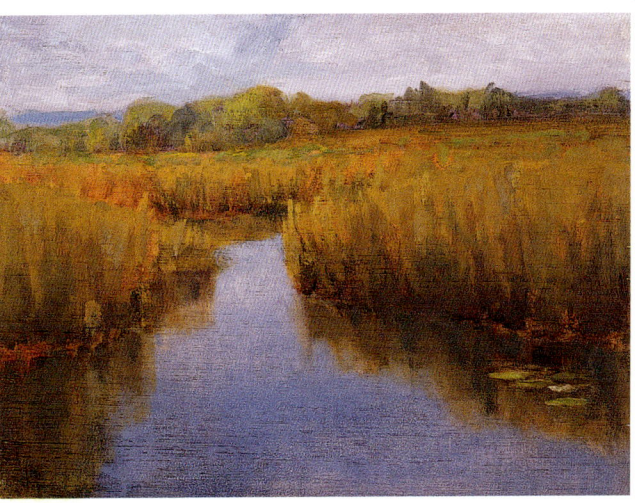

Adjusted Painting

I reduced the color intensity of the foreground rushes on both sides, created a simple gradation in the water and added a small amount of interest in the trees in the distance by modulating the hue and intensity of color there and a bit of blue hill. The viewer can now move back into the landscape. The structure, which had been buried, becomes apparent.

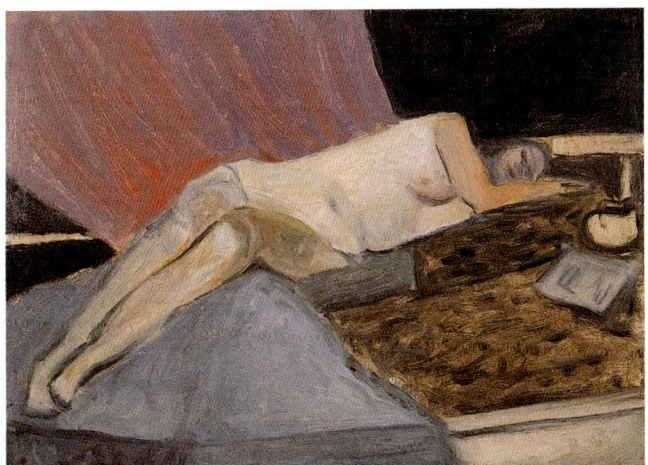

Original Student Painting

A friend told me she had done this In an evening class in an hour or an hour and a half. Although there are problems, the shapes and simplicity work—almost. The shape of the red cloth draws too much attention, as do the darks in the calves and feet, pulling the eye into the bottom left of the painting.

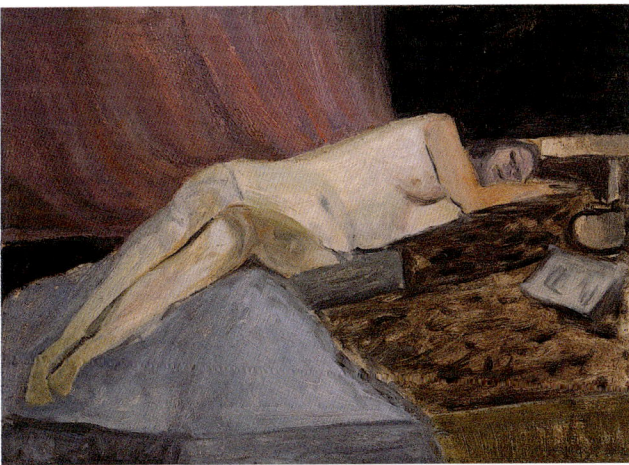

Adjusted Painting

I softened the edges of the red cloth and the shadows around the feet. Now your attention moves through the painting to the center of interest (the head and upper torso of the figure).

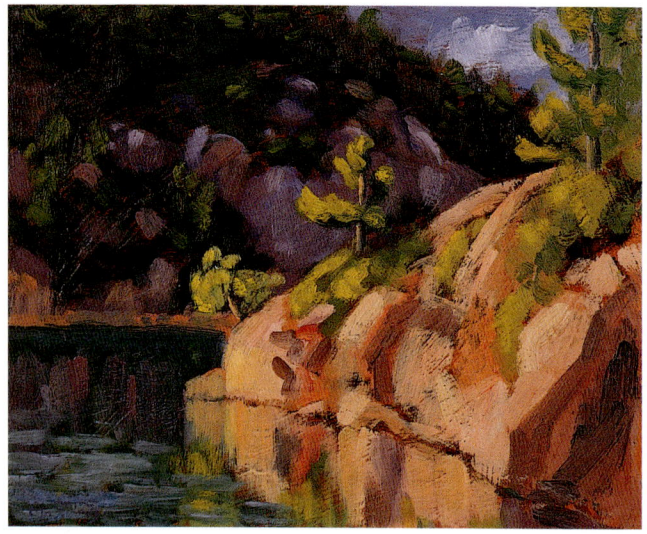

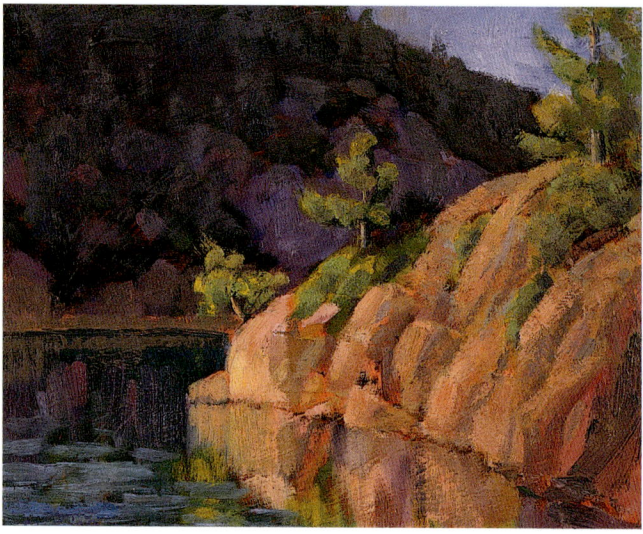

Original Student Painting

This painting has a fresh, lively feeling, but notice how the highlights in the background hill compete with the foreground. The highlights are too light and therefore come forward too much. The color intensity of the foreground rocks is too much the same. Also, the line of shadow on the rocks on the far right pulls us out to the right.

Adjusted Painting

I reduced the contrasts in the background and gradated the color intensity of the foreground from low on the right to high on the left. The structure of the composition is now more apparent. You move across the foreground to the end of the point, set against a distinct background.

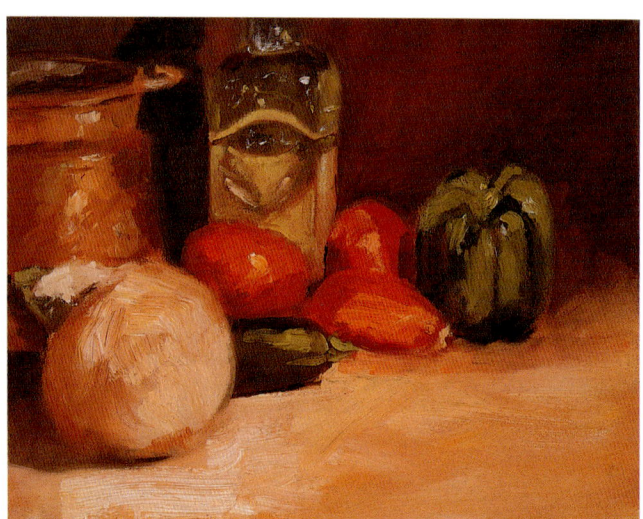

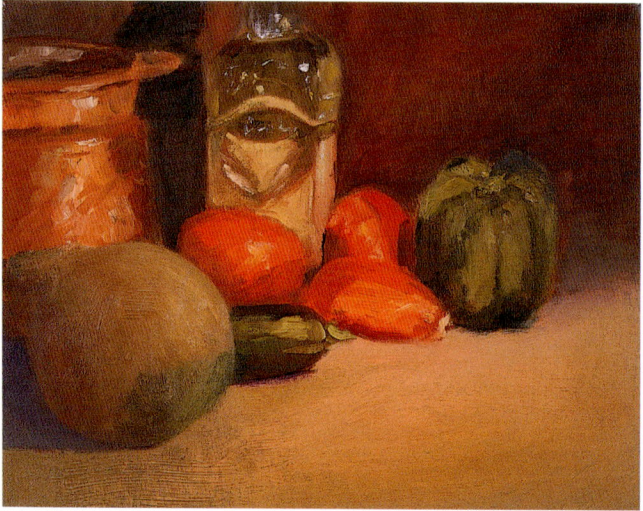

Original Student Painting

You can't really see the parts of this painting that are working because the onion and the foreground in front of it are much too overpowering.

Adjusted Painting

I reduced the onion's dominance in the still life and created a dark gradation in the bottom-left corner. You now move into the painting and find you're looking at some nicely painted parts in the middle ground that had been almost unnoticeable before.

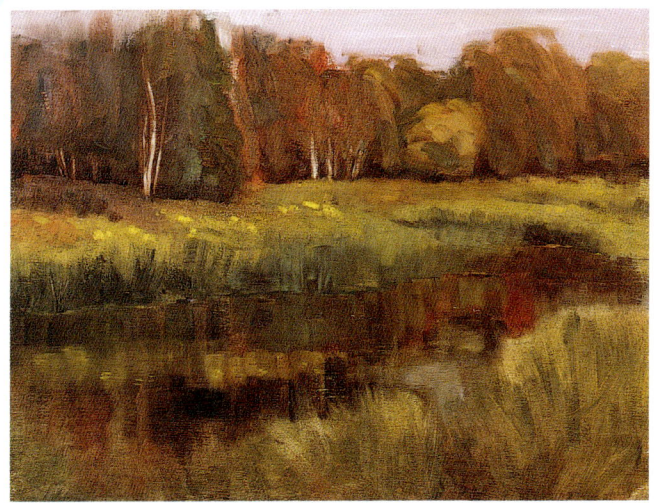

Original Student Painting
The intended structure here is clear, but there are too many distractions to allow it to work.

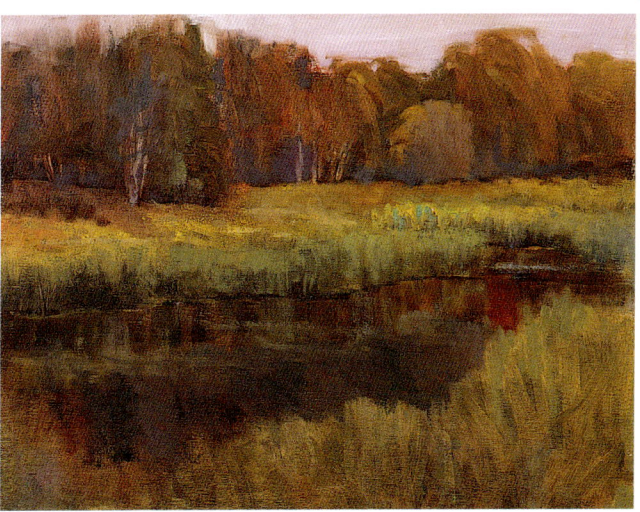

Adjusted Painting
I reduced the value of the foreground weeds, simplified the water, reduced a few of the details (yellow flowers and tree trunks) and heightened a couple of shifts in hue and intensity in the center of interest in the right middle ground. You can now see the structure and the illusion of depth.

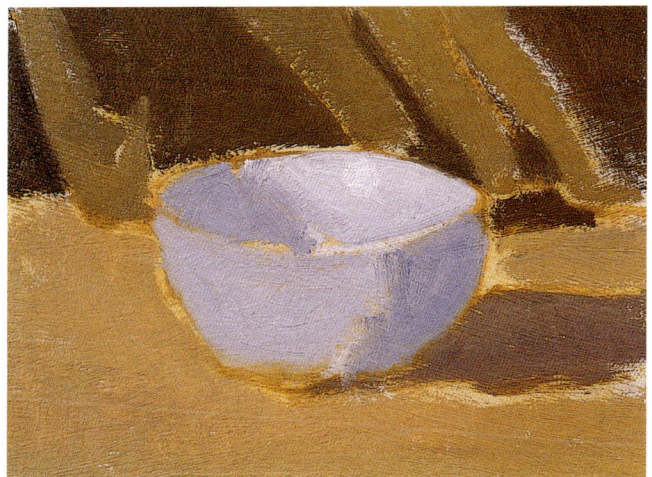

Original Painting
When blocking in, paint each color shape right up to the next; don't leave gaps of bare canvas. You won't be able to see the color relationships between each shape or sense the illusion of depth because the gaps will remind your eye of the picture plane itself.

Notice that the value of this painting is keyed too high and needs to be darker so the highlight can stand out. If you find yourself smearing larger and larger blobs of white paint to create a highlight, stop and darken the value shapes around it.

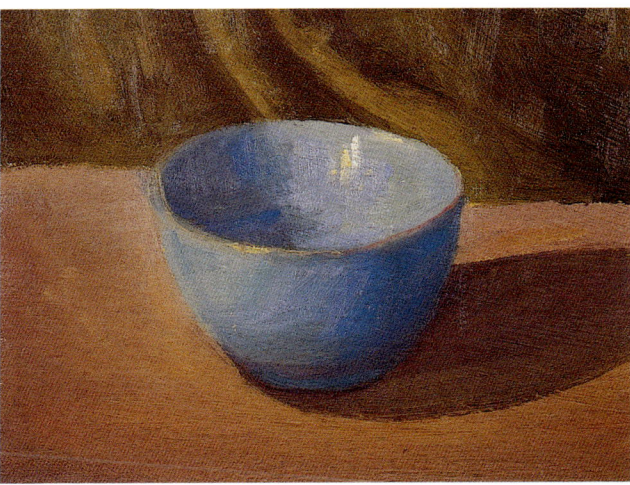

Adjusted Painting
The mark of lighter paint now shines like a highlight against the darker value of the lit side of the bowl. Notice how dark the shadow side of the bowl has become to support the other values. The first two or three colors of your block-in are so important and worth taking some time over.

lead the eye around the picture plane

The method I'm suggesting for these demonstration paintings is obviously pretty controlled. So much happens when you paint. So much is about acting and responding and reacting. This method will help you develop consistency and an awareness of picture-plane dynamics. Then you will have a foundation on which to build a more personal form of expression.

MATERIALS

Surface
Oil-primed canvas, 30" × 30" (76cm × 76cm)

Brushes
Nos. 4, 8, 10 and 12 hog bristle filberts, no. 6 sable or synthetic rigger

Pigments
Titanium White, Cadmium Yellow Light, Cadmium Yellow Deep, Yellow Ochre, Cadmium Orange, Cadmium Red Light, Alizarin Crimson, Quinacridone Violet, Dioxazine Purple, Ultramarine Blue, Phthalo Blue, Phthalo Green, Chrome Oxide Green, Ivory Black

Other supplies
Gray-toned paper, white chalk pencil, 2B pencil, kneaded eraser, viewfinder

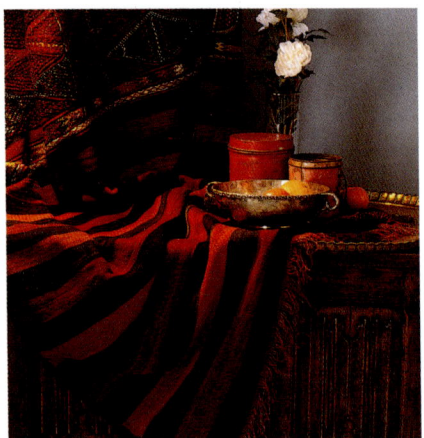

Photo of a Still-Life Setup
Arrange your still life using a viewfinder with the idea of finding a movement through the various shapes around the picture plane. If you're using a piece of fabric, take the time to adjust the folds so it actually works for you in the composition, as this does here.

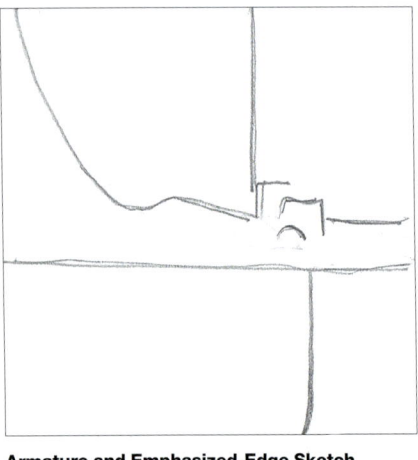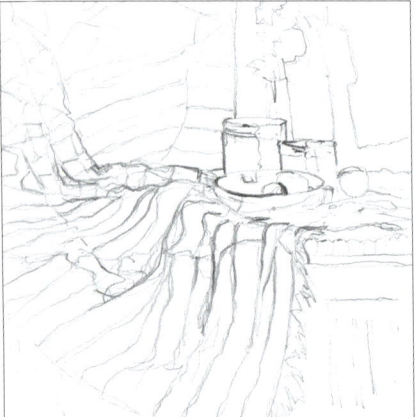

Armature and Emphasized-Edge Sketch
The various elements have been consciously arranged to draw the eye to the center of interest. Notice how the strips in the carpet support this movement. Compare the reference photo to the drawing. The fringed edge of the carpet, the sweep of the cloth up to the top left, the design in the carpet in the top left and the flowers are all de-emphasized, bringing your attention toward the center of interest at the silver bowl and the metal tins.

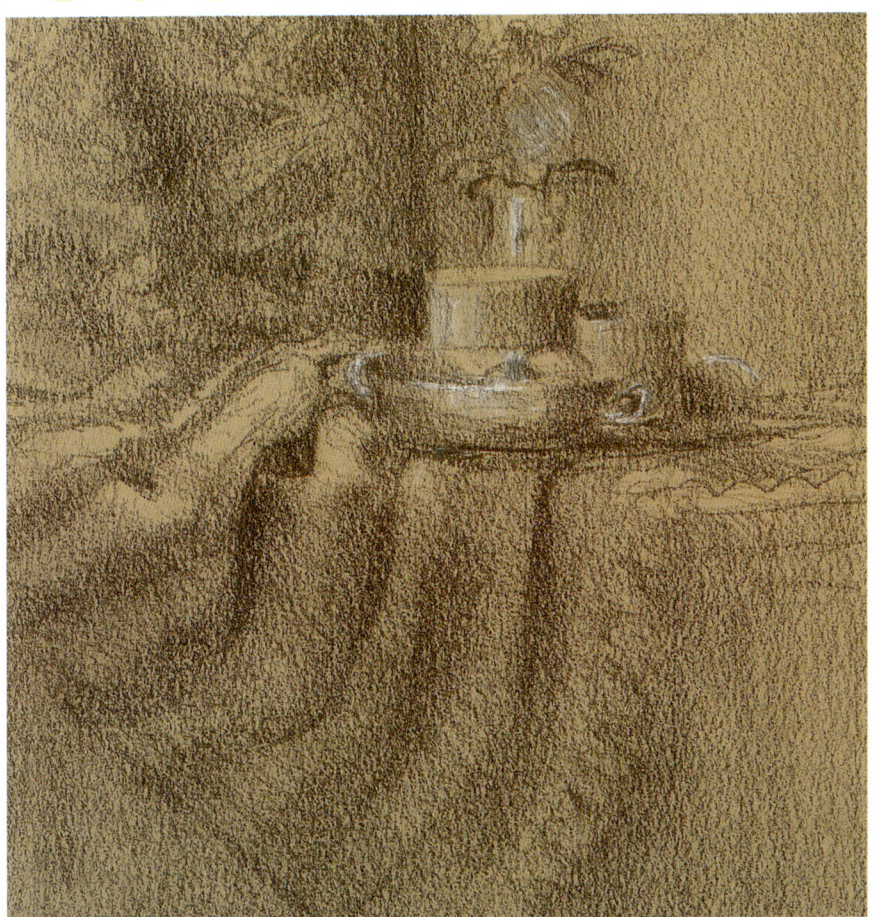

Very few things are truly white, unless they're in very direct strong light. So, if you're using white paper, you'll need to darken most of the paper to approximate the values of what you see. If you use toned paper, a lot of that toning is already done for you. You just use the white chalk pencil to indicate highlights. Make use of the tone of the paper as much as possible. You don't need to completely cover it with pencil and white chalk; that defeats the purpose. If you look at a good book of Old Masters' figure drawings, you'll see that they used toned paper, indicating only shadows and highlights and letting the untouched tone of the paper read for most of the figure.

You may or may not enjoy using toned paper this way. But it's worth trying as an exercise to make sure that you're clear about isolating shadows, mid-tones and highlights.

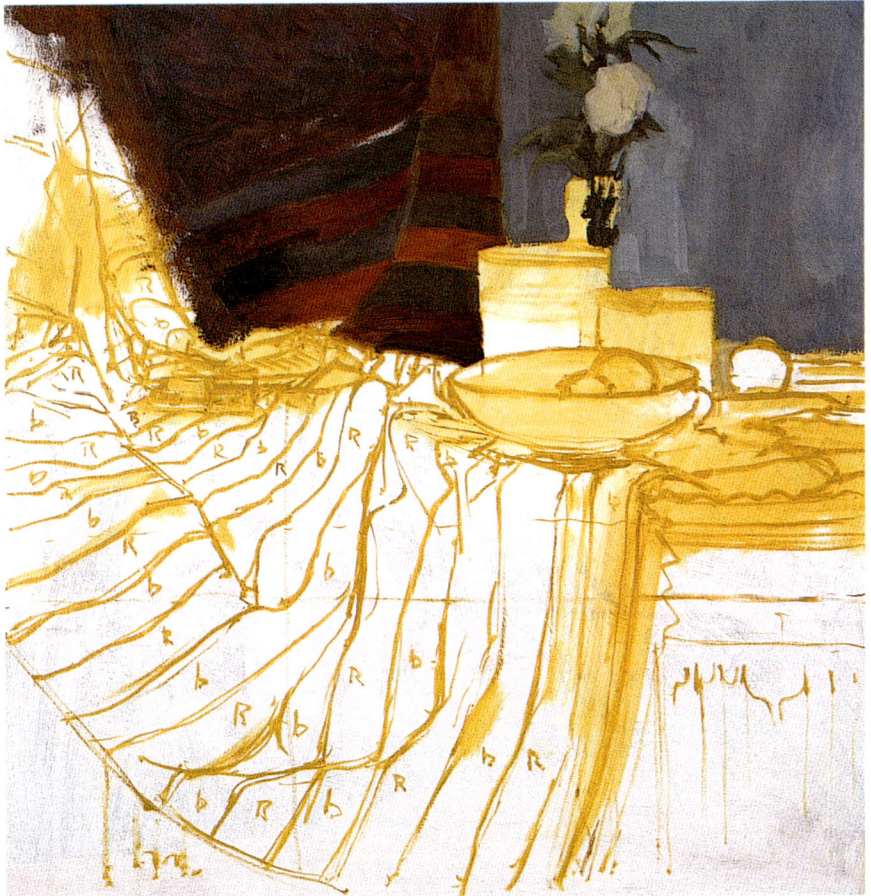

1 Start the Block-In

Using your viewfinder divided in thirds, paint the major shapes of your composition with Yellow Ochre. Drawing lines to divide the canvas in thirds will help with placement. Note: stripes define the folds in striped fabric, so pay careful attention to their shapes and keep their width consistent.

Start with the easiest color: the background gray. Use Ultramarine Blue and Cadmium Orange, pushed with Yellow Ochre and Cadmium Red Light, for the lit part and more Ultramarine Blue and Dioxazine Purple for the shadow.

Keep the material to the top left in the background simple. Ignore most of the design.

Even though the shapes in the top left are dark in value, look for the color of each shape. Here use a base color of Ivory Black and Alizarin Crimson, and then shift that with Cadmium Red Light and Cadmium Orange to block in the shapes.

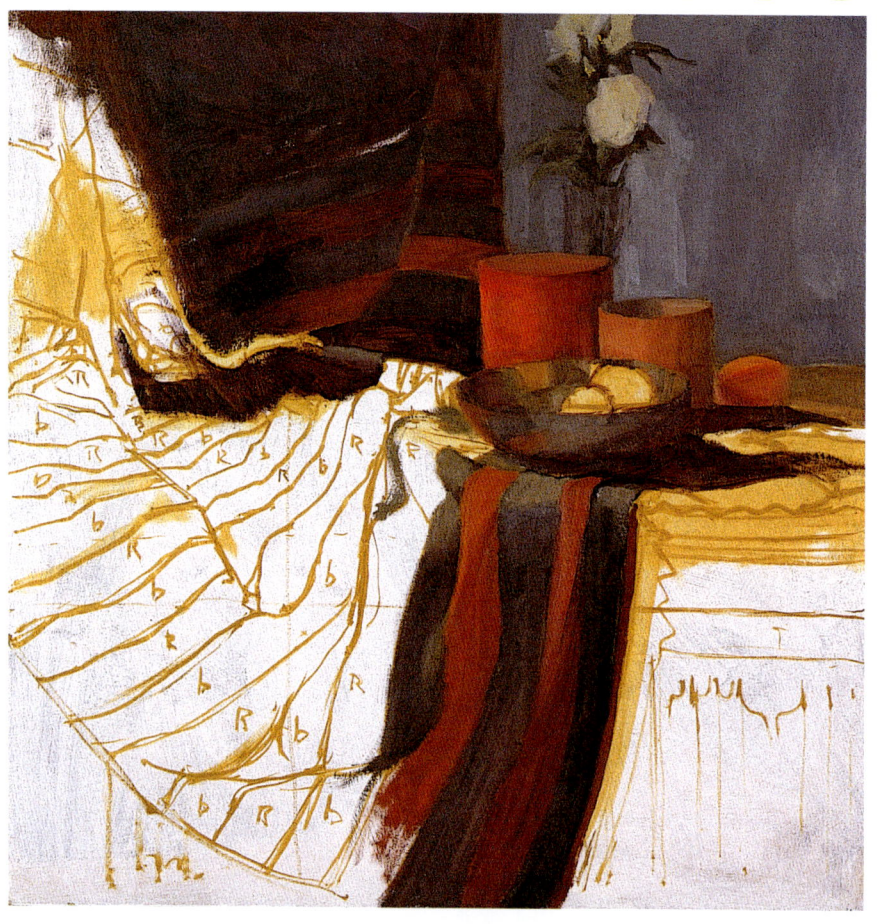

2 Create Edges With Deliberation

Block in each shape simply at first, being sure to establish the lit side and the shadow side of each object carefully as you go. As you block in each shape, paint over the line of your Yellow Ochre drawing. Then, if necessary, paint back over that again as you block in the color shape next to it. The line is only for reference. Paint over it and back over it so that you are painting the quality of your edges. You don't want to create your edges by default as you carefully paint up to but not over your reference line.

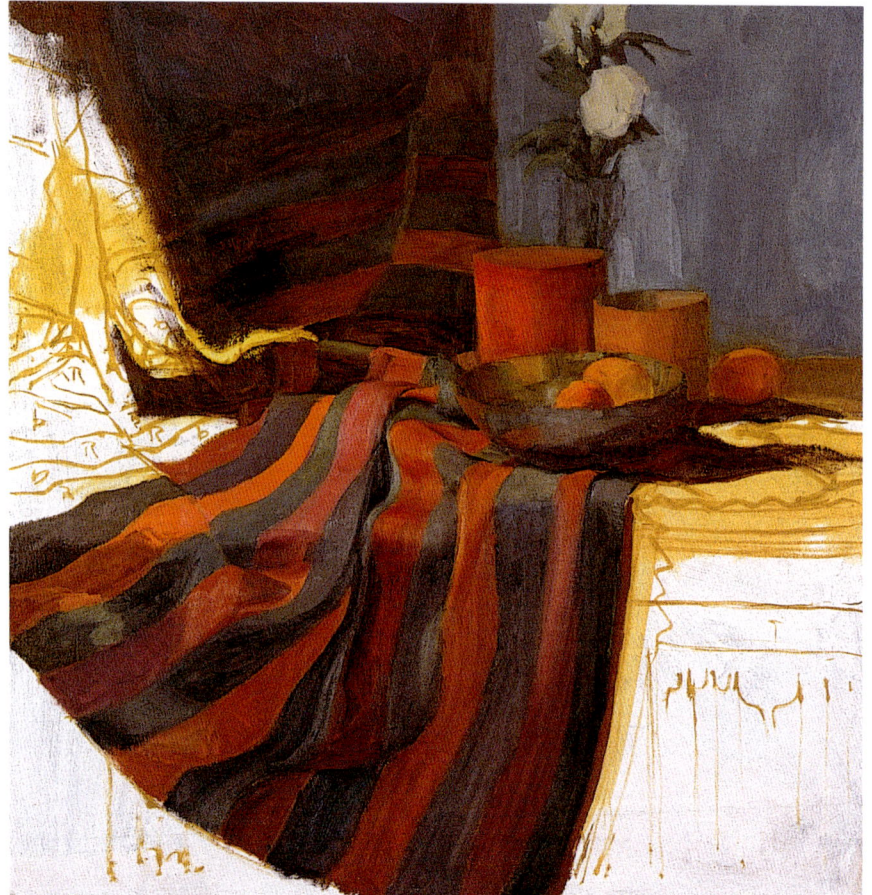

3 Pay Close Attention to the Stripes

The stripes on the cloth alternate between red, orange, dark gray and black. Each stripe has sections that are lit, in half light and in shadow. If you choose a complex subject such as this, you must be attentive and careful. It's not that it's necessarily all that difficult, but it won't come together and happen by itself. If you do block in each color shape, paying attention to the color shapes of the lights and darks, it's amazing how the representational illusion just seems to pop into place.

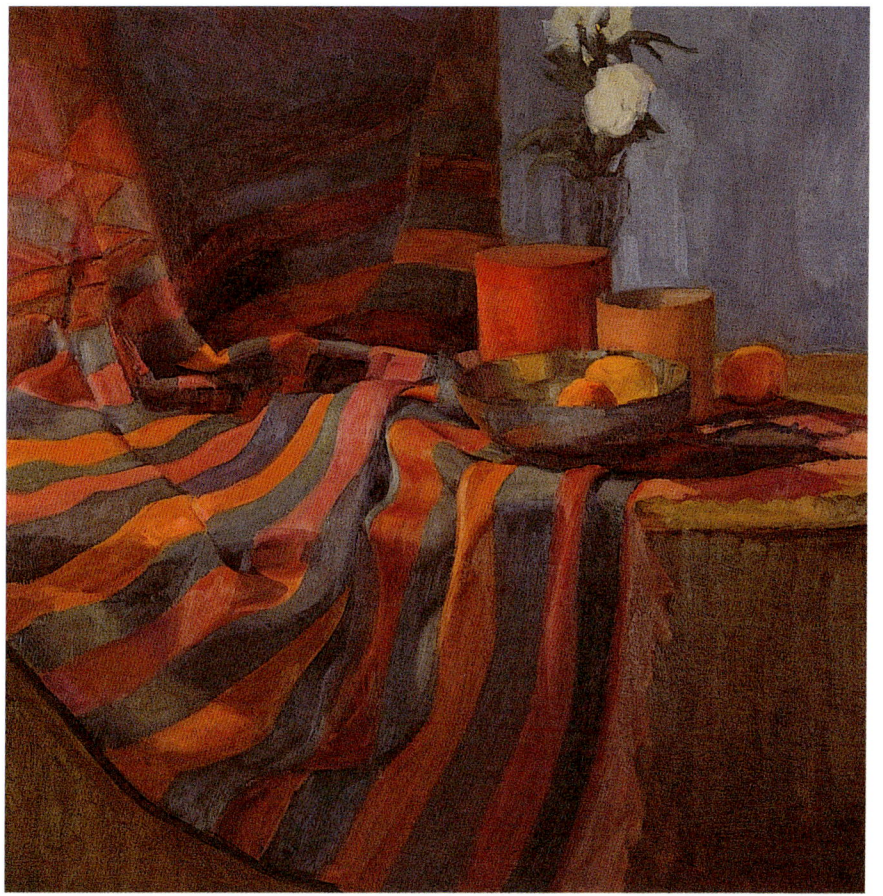

4 Evaluate the Block-In

When you finish the block-in, stop and take stock. Sit quietly and observe patiently. See what's working and what needs adjustment. Refer to your emphasized-edge sketch, your thumbnail and, of course, the still life itself. What's already working, and can perhaps even be left as it is? What's drawing too much attention and needs adjusting? Are any colors too intense or edges too sharp? Does the sweep of the armature pull the eye away from the center of interest? Get the feel of the armature and the color shapes in relation to the picture plane.

At this stage, two things need work. First, the flowers pull the eye up to the top of the picture plane, away from the center of interest. Second, the foreground drape of cloth draws too much attention, particularly on the left side where the lit areas grab the eye.

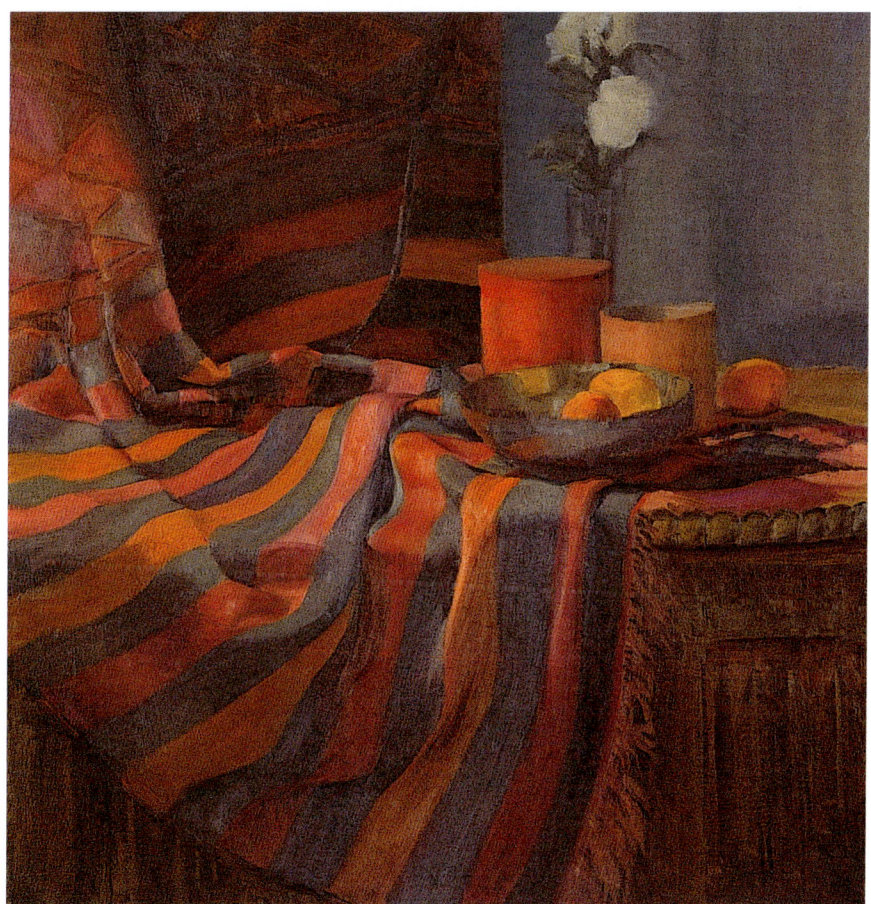

5 Make Broad Adjustments

Before thinking about any specific refinements of the block-in, keep standing back and evaluate the overall flow of the painting. Look at the painting in a mirror. That will reveal things you might not otherwise see. Then make necessary adjustments, feeling where your eye is getting pulled or distracted, until you're satisfied with the flow of the whole composition. Don't, at this point, think at all of finishing. Work with the shape relationships and flow around the picture plane.

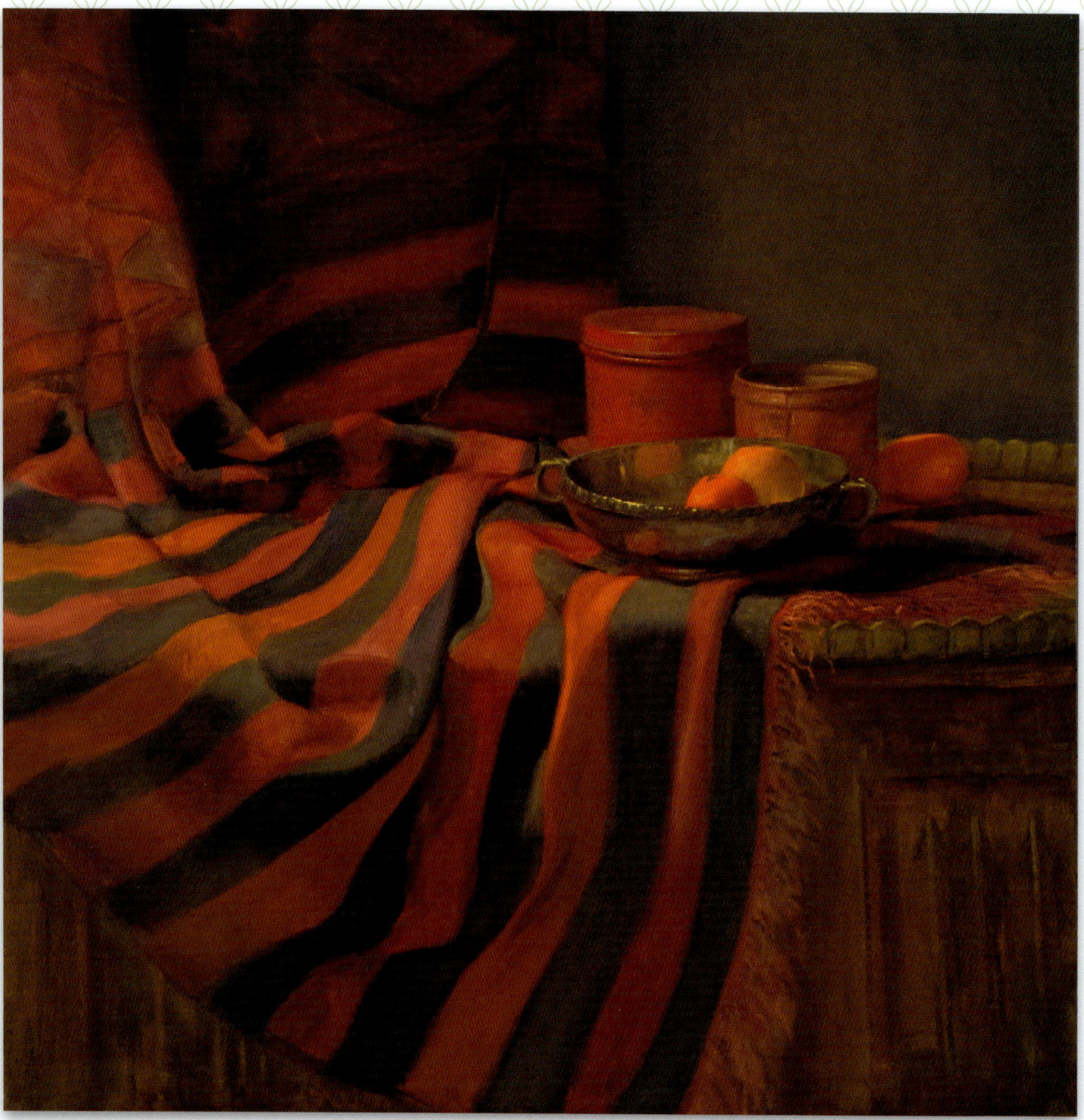

6 Add Refinements

When you're feeling satisfied with how your eye responds to the major shapes and their relationships, start to make refinements. These should be primarily around the center of interest. If the flow of the painting is working, you may be close to being finished. You may continue to find adjustments you need to make to enhance or diminish an area, but now you mainly want to draw us into your area of greatest interest.

Make adjustments to each color shape by looking for shifts in color and value, in the quality of edges, in the transition from light to shadow. Develop the form, its nuances of light, half-light and shadow. Don't think of details, just of smaller color shapes and the transition quality of the edges between them. Save highlights until the very end

when all the nuances of color and form are already in place. When I was first imagining this still life, I wanted to use a plant with red-edged leaves to sit darkly in the background. By the time I came to paint it, the plant didn't look very healthy, so I put in the vase of flowers. By the time the block-in was finished, I knew the flowers were causing problems, but I thought I could de-emphasize them until they, too, would sit unobtrusively in the composition without drawing our attention too much to the top edge of the picture plane. In the end, it worked better just to eliminate the flowers and let the eye focus naturally on the center of interest below them. Notice the soft gradation in the background gray from the top right down into the center of interest.

LAURA'S CARPET
Oil on canvas · 30" × 30" (76cm × 76cm)

think flow on the picture plane

This is an area I often paint from life. I took this photo on one of my painting trips. It's one of those "one in thirty-six" photos that I mentioned in chapter two (page 52). The big shapes caught my attention: the clear flow down the river to the sunlit background.

MATERIALS

Surface
Oil-primed canvas, 20" × 20" (51cm × 51cm)

Brushes
Nos. 4, 8, 10 and 12 hog bristle filberts, no. 6 sable or synthetic rigger

Pigments
Titanium White, Cadmium Yellow Light, Cadmium Yellow Deep, Yellow Ochre, Cadmium Orange, Cadmium Red Light, Alizarin Crimson, Quinacridone Violet, Dioxazine Purple, Ultramarine Blue, Phthalo Blue, Phthalo Green, Chrome Oxide Green

Other supplies
Mineral spirits, drawing paper, B and 2B pencils, kneaded eraser

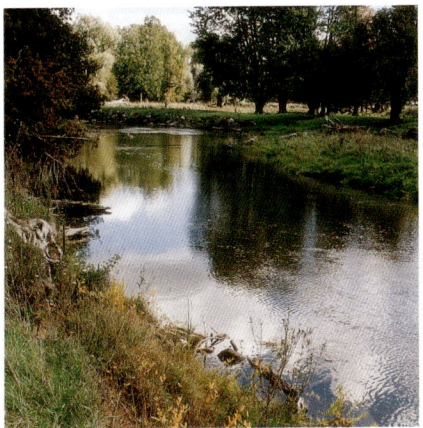

Cropped Reference Photo
If you look at this photo in terms of details you'll find twigs and stumps and fallen trees and all manner of distracting stuff.

However, if you pull back a bit visually and see the big shapes, you see some very interesting value masses pulling the eye back into a clear center of interest where the sunlight hits the trees in the background.

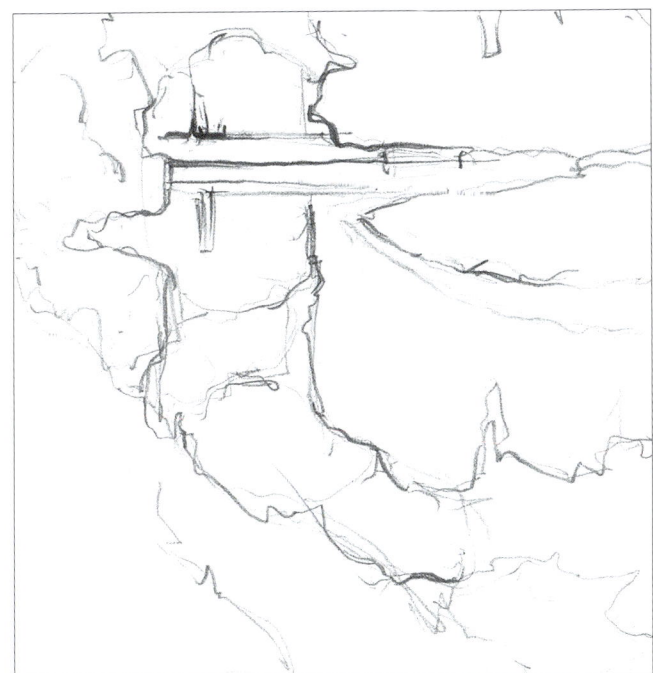

Emphasized-Edge Sketch
The value of the emphasized-edge sketch is that it forces you to think of the contrast along the edges of the major value masses and color shapes of your painting before you start to paint. If you've given some thought to it, and keep that drawing hanging by your easel while you paint, you can refer to it and adjust edges to fit your initial idea. Possibilities you hadn't thought of when you started may come up, so you can refer to the emphasized-edge sketch and think through whether to go in that new direction or stay with your original idea. Either way, you will have a frame of reference for any changes you decide to make.

Notice the lines of emphasis in the reflected trees and cloud shapes in the bottom middle of the drawing. This was an idea for a secondary cycle of interest in that area, so the whole movement wasn't directed straight into the background. This provides the possibility of getting pulled forward again into the cloud shapes in the water and then looping into the background again.

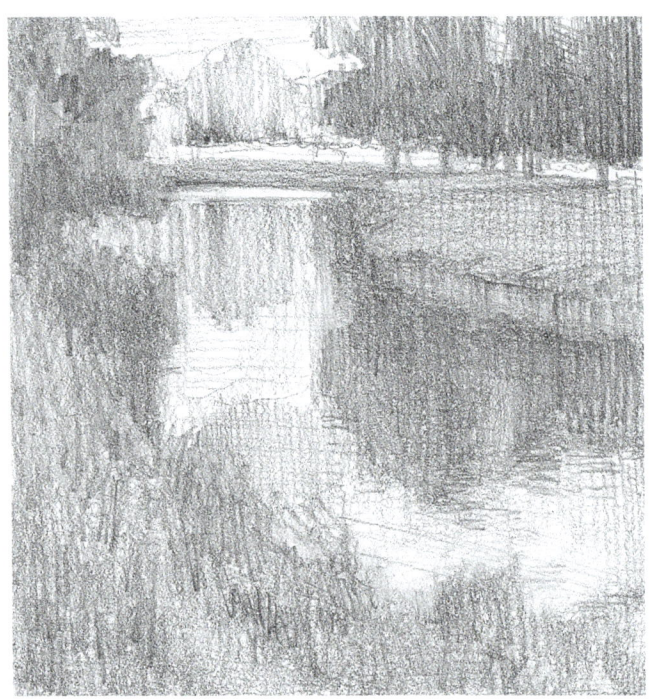

Thumbnail
By eliminating all the detail and concentrating on the main value masses, you can feel how the shapes will be able to carry this painting.

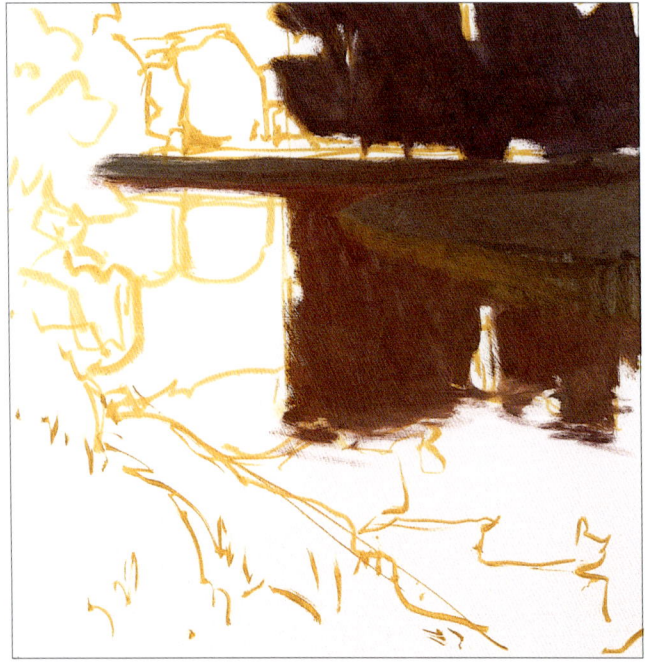

1 Start With the Easiest Color

Draw in the major shapes with Yellow Ochre mixed with some mineral spirits. When you're happy with the placement and your proportions (remember, this will affect everything all the way through to the finished painting, so take your time), choose the largest color shape with the easiest color to find. The large shape of the trees in the right background is good. It is dark, but the actual color is not especially clear (i.e., the intensity is very low). The shape of the grass banks below it is slightly lighter and greener. The color of the reflection of the trees is darker and warmer than the bank. Paint each shape right up to the next. If, as you block in each shape, it becomes clear that it is not the right color and needs adjusting, do it as soon as you notice it and then adjust the other colors around it to maintain the proper relationships. If you say, "I'll adjust it later; I just want to keep painting," you will find as you continue, you'll have more and more trouble establishing each new color relationship because you'll be using a poor reference point for each new color. By the time you've finished your block-in, you'll have no real indication of how the whole composition will work.

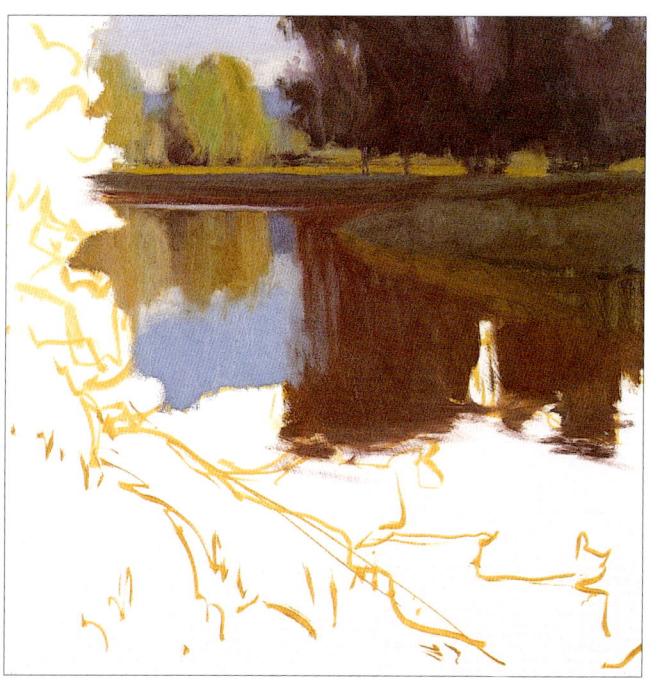

2 Add Some Lights and Establish the Value Key

Up to now all the color shapes have been dark. The white shapes under the trees on the canvas are leaping forward. Although you could now continue down farther into the water, for example, it makes sense to paint in the main lights against the dark shapes to establish the value key of the painting. If those two areas—the dark trees and the sunlit background—are working together, the relationships of the rest of the shapes can be adjusted to them.

This area will be the center of interest, so you want to use colors that will pull your eye here, but keep them somewhat muted so you can later give greater emphasis to the color where you need it.

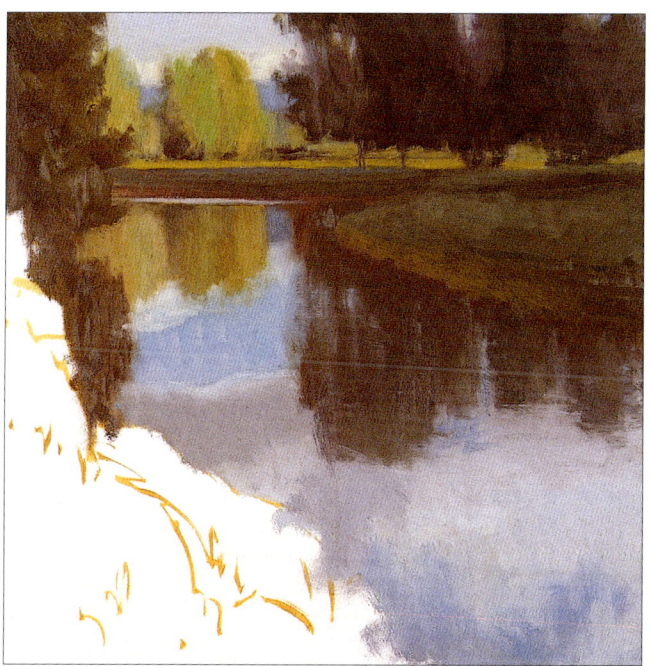

3 Paint Each Shape in Relation to the Next

Notice that each shape is painted in relation to the one next to it. The dark shape of the tree and its reflection on the left are warmer than, but about the same value as, the dark tree shapes on the right. The clouds reflected in the water are painted even in value; later you can add emphasis to create secondary movements through that area. The bottom of the edges of the tree reflections are softened to ensure that they don't attract too much attention. Later, those edges will be painted more carefully, but, for now, keep them softer.

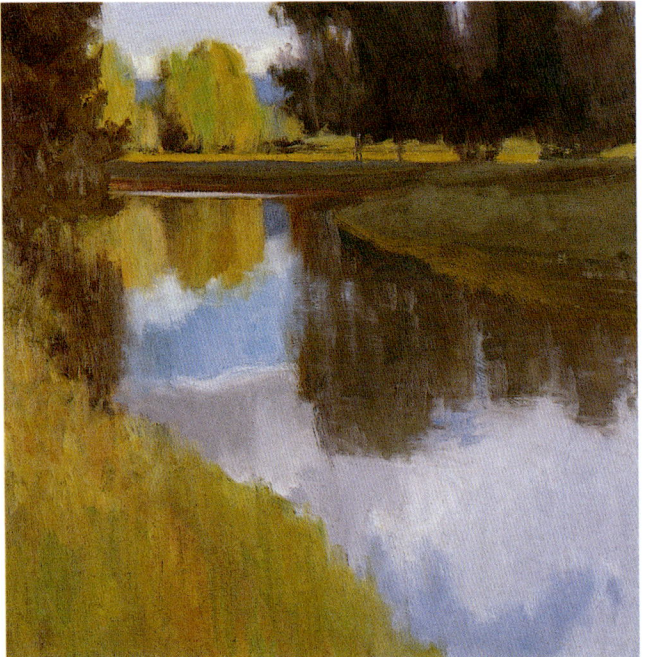

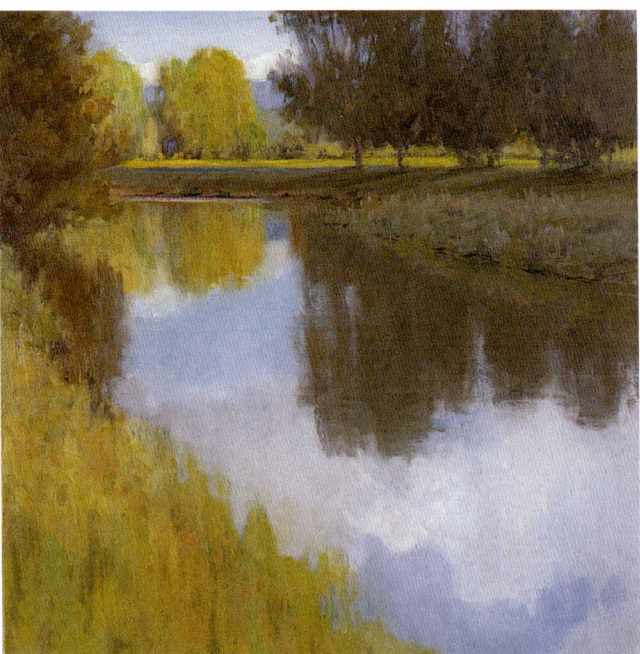

4 Evaluate the Block-In

When you've finished the block-in, stop and take stock. You can see the general flow of the painting down the river toward the lit trees in the background follows the plan in the emphasized-edge sketch. The other simple shapes support that movement.

Now, as you enhance color, refine edges and continue to study how the eye moves on the picture plane, you are building a sound foundation to work on. If you add a color or an edge that starts to draw your attention away from the movement you establish in your block-in, you will see it.

5 Refining Color Shapes

Begin refining the color and edges. Notice the new color slightly lighter in value and more intense added to both dark tree masses, left and right. It provides more definition, but the general feel of both masses remains the same. The sky holes in the trees on the right create greater interest but don't attract too much more attention than they did at the block-in stage.

Compare the edge that separates the shadow and the sunlight on the field in the background with the same edge in step 4. If you have a warm color shape that you want to contrast strongly with a cool shape, paint the two shapes as closely as you can to the colors you see. Then, where the two shapes meet, exaggerate the color temperature a bit more. You will create the vibrancy of the color contrast without having to shift the temperature of the whole color shape.

Stop and Evaluate

Every ten or fifteen minutes, stop, stand back and evaluate what is happening on your canvas. Look at your painting in a mirror. Does the eye remain in the picture plane? Is it drawn to a specific area of focus? Is there too much detail or information in areas of less focus? Make necessary adjustments to the overall flow of the composition that you had originally intended. Keep that intention alive as you proceed; otherwise, you may stand back after an hour or two of painting and find that you can no longer see the structure you had intended and have no idea where to start to get back there.

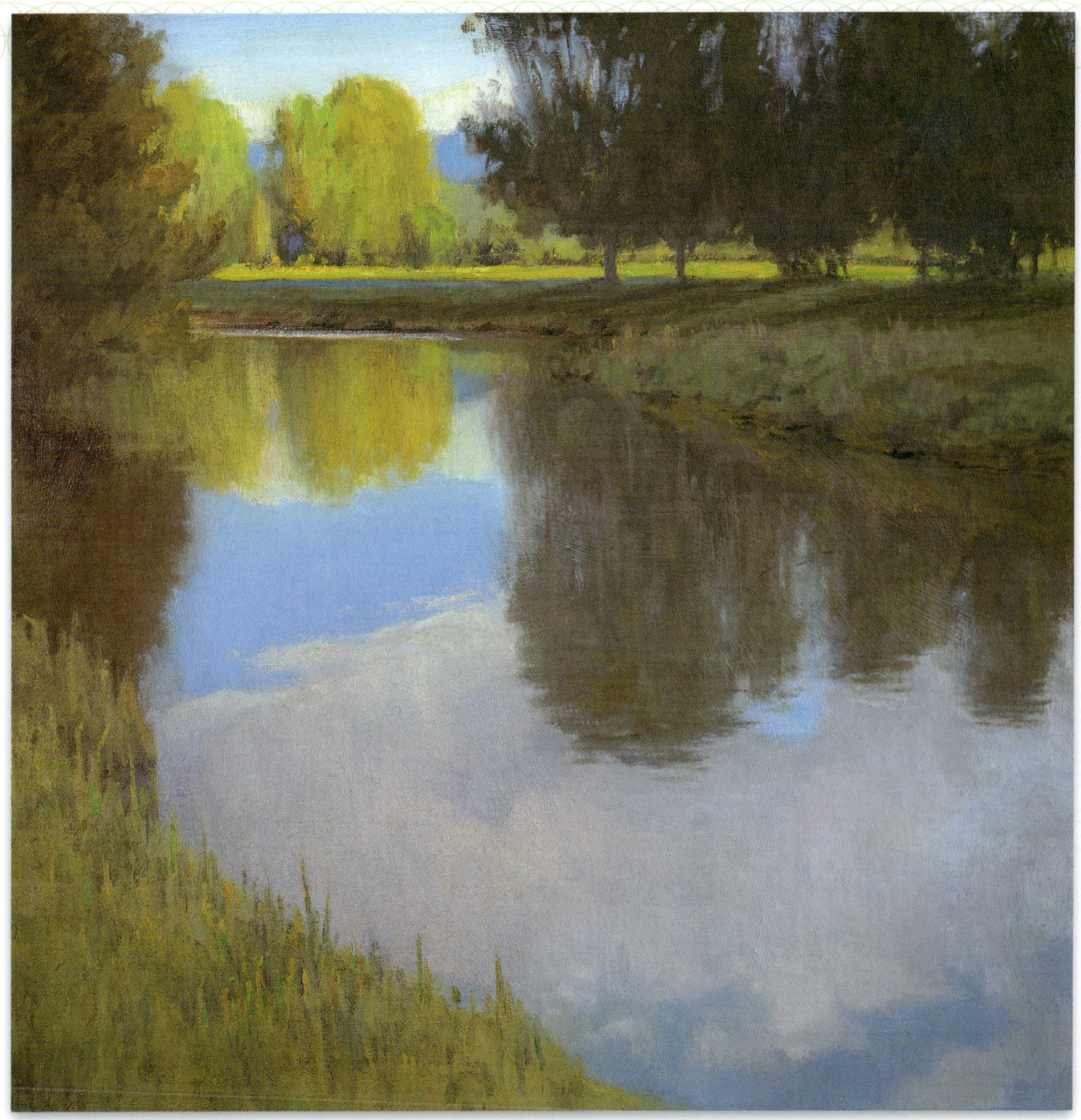

6 Final Adjustments

The whole painting up to step 5 took about three hours. From that stage to this one took about another three hours. I spent all that time adjusting the angle of the shoreline in the foreground and figuring out how the secondary movement down into the reflection of the clouds would work. Sometimes everything comes together quite effortlessly; sometimes a small area of a painting will continue to elude you. You may not always enjoy the process of looking at the painting, trying to determine how to proceed, getting an idea, trying it, adjusting it. The adjusting and refining process can go on for a while.

The thing to keep in mind: Don't lose sight of your overall plan and start making exaggerated adjustments in an attempt to get the painting to work. Look at the painting calmly, get a feeling for what it needs, then try it, one thing at a time. Stand back again and reassess. Be patient and proceed one step at a time until you pull the composition together.

SUMMER ON THE BIGHEAD
Oil on canvas · 24" × 24" (61cm × 61cm)

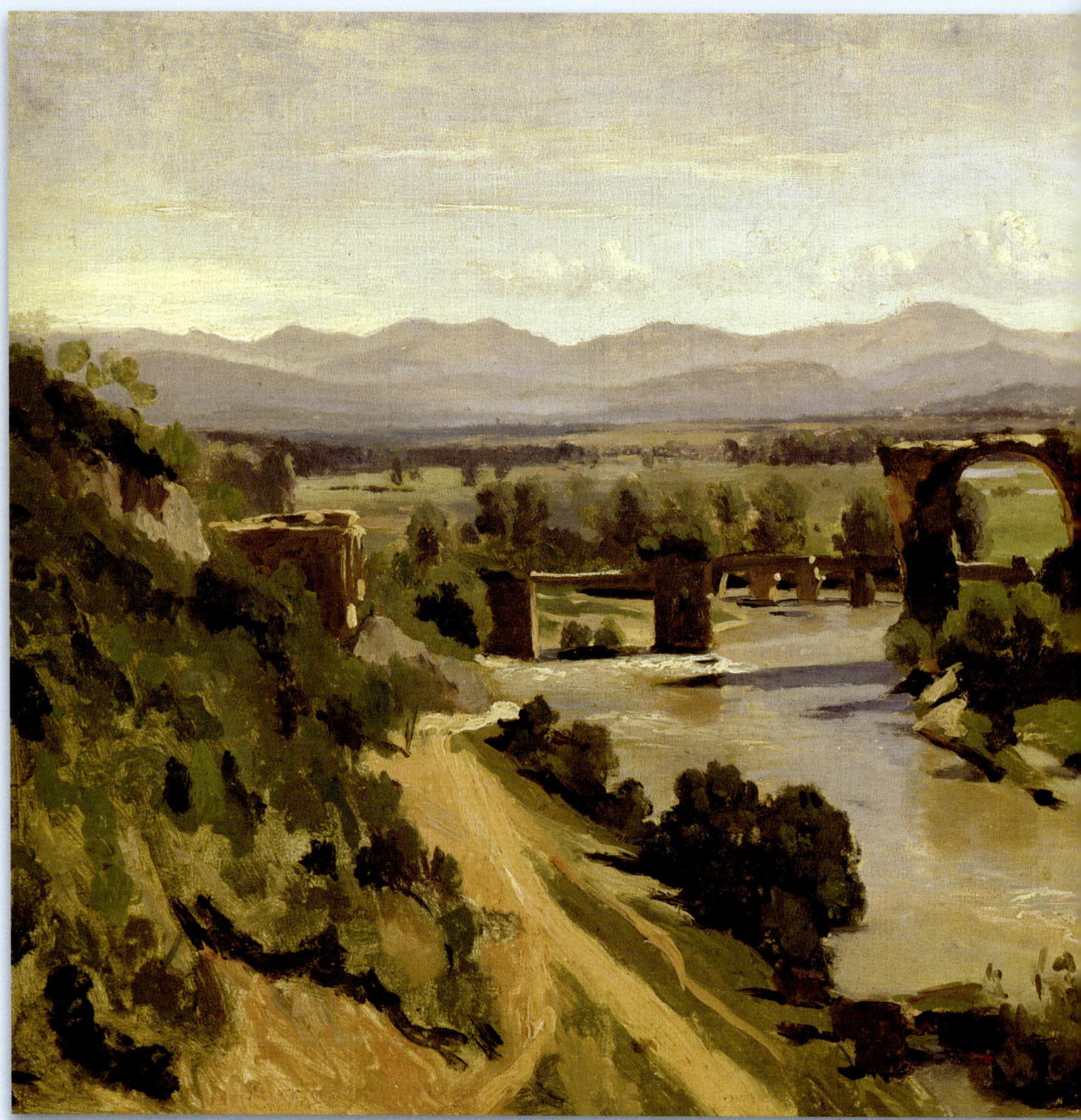

Jean-Baptiste-Camille Corot. *Narni, The Bridge of Augustus Over the Nera* (1826). Oil on paper mounted on canvas, 13¼" × 18⅛" (34cm × 48cm). © Louvre, Paris, France, Giraudon, The Bridgeman Art Library

Jean-Baptiste-Camille Corot (1796–1875)

Over the course of his career, Corot produced many different kinds of paintings. His *plein air* studies were not always regarded as his most important work. However, during the twentieth century, these studies were viewed as the high point of his diverse output. He freely lent them to other painters to study. They hung on the walls of his studio all his life.

Look at how the artist translates the whole landscape into shapes. The sky and distant mountains are cool and very close in value. The larger, simpler shapes in the foreground lead to the smaller, more complex shapes of the bridge. You cannot help but get drawn to the base of the bridge on the right with that gorgeous blue shadow across the water, then over to the left side of the river and back again. In 1853, Théophile Silvestre, a very perceptive critic, wrote of Corot's *plein air* landscapes: "By transposing one by one to the canvas the colored masses as he had observed them, he was able to establish accurately the ensemble of a landscape, absolutely as if it were a matter of assembling the various pieces of a mosaic."

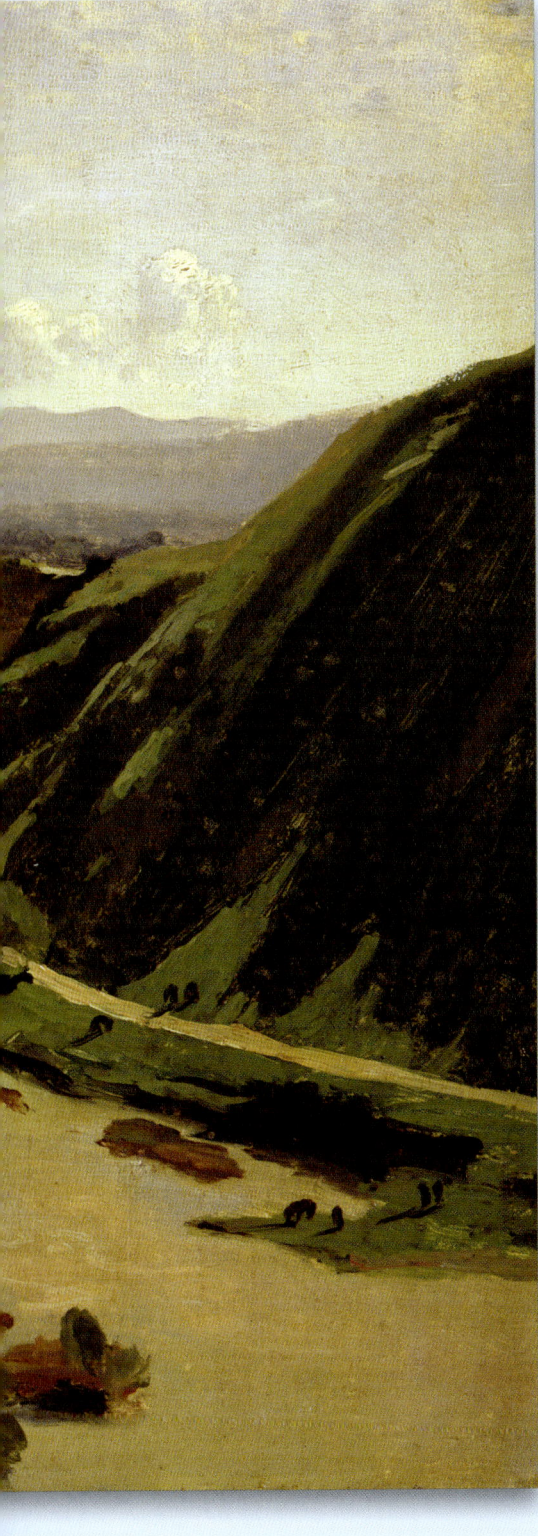

CHAPTER FIVE

Gallery of Greats

One of the best ways to improve at anything is to study the best in your field. This method is particularly true for painting. In fact, until recently, copying the masters was considered fundamental to learning to paint.

A master has "mastered" every technique he needs to get all the parts of a composition working in a coherent and integrated way. Within a single masterpiece, you can see structure, clarity, great shapes, nuanced color and edges—all of which pull and release the viewer's attention.

During workshops, I always show slides of great compositions. After painting all day and wrestling with the challenges yourself, it's very instructive and engaging to see how other painters have wrestled with them—and won.

Although I love the work of many Old Masters—Velázquez, Vermeer and Chardin immediately come to mind—I decided to share with you several more modern painters who lived around the end of the nineteenth century and into the beginning of the twentieth.

Representational painting thrived during this period. Strict academic painting, with its emphasis on a high degree of finish and classical or religious subject matter, had given way to more painterly and personal expression. Many of these artists had received a sound academic training. Their mastery is still relevant and exciting for a representational painter today.

So let me share with you the paintings of a number of my favorite artists. Some you will know. Others may be less familiar. All had—or have—a wonderful grasp of composition and a seemingly unlabored, fresh way of expressing themselves.

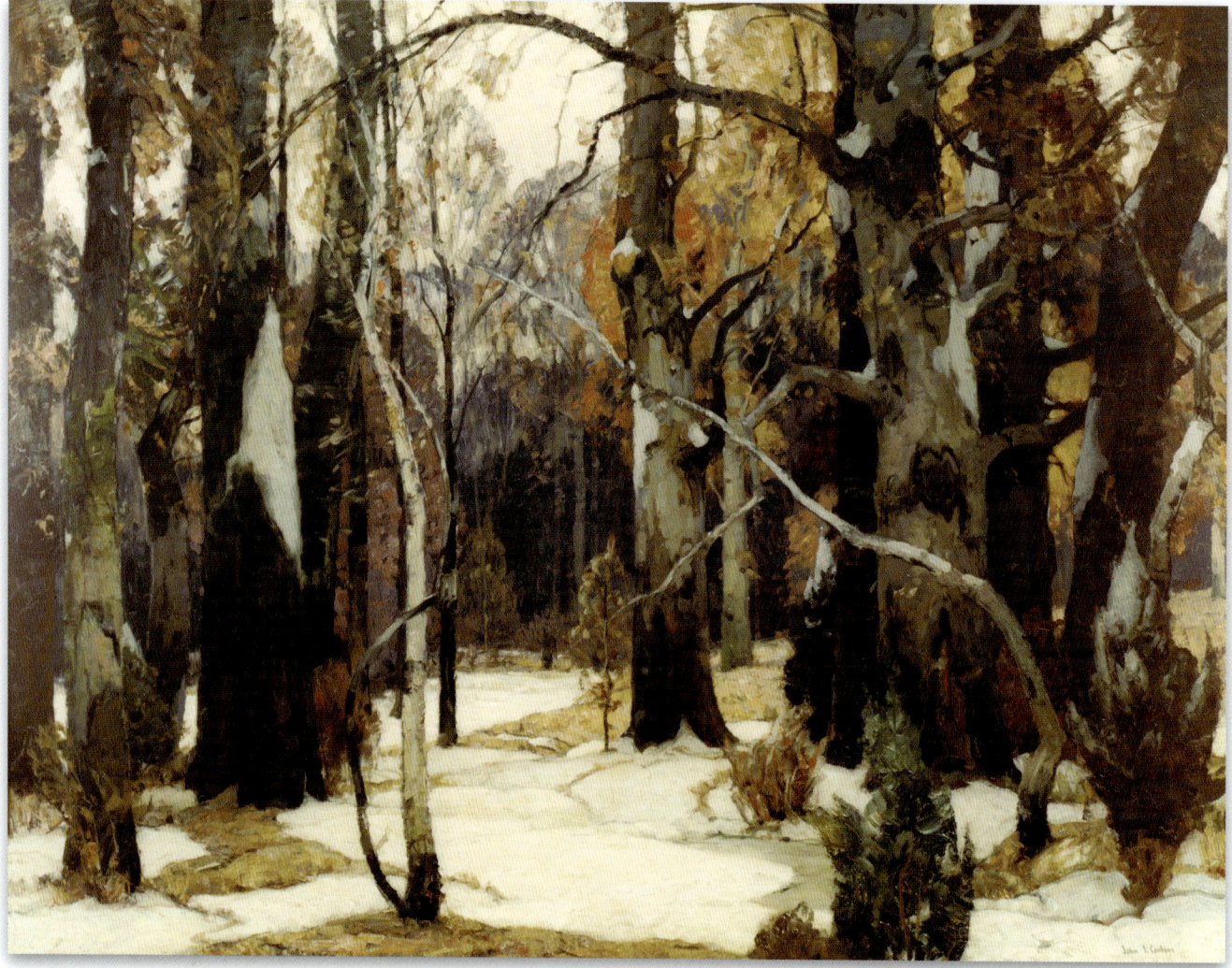

John Fabian Carlson (1874–1945)

The most dog-eared book in my library is a copy of *Carlson's Guide to Landscape Painting*. In my copy, the text is underlined, circled and starred in three different colors. This book has helped and influenced a lot of contemporary landscape painters. Unfortunately, the black-and-white reproductions of his paintings are of medium quality. You can see the main abstract value masses, but that's about it.

So I was surprised when I stumbled upon a really good John Carlson while I was in Washington, D.C. The richness and nuanced modulation of color was exquisite. I got the feeling that Carlson was someone who loved the process of lavishing attention onto the surface of his painting.

This painting has maybe four values. Yet, by weaving one into the next, the foreground trees become intricate and complex. However, spacially, it's always clear what and where everything is. There is a clear lead-in with that little pine in the bottom right that then allows us to move straight back to the background. But we don't go there immediately. We are pulled left, then right, then stopped, then released, as we move back through this painting. It is a complex subject executed with a lot of attention and control to how the eye moves through the painting.

John Fabian Carlson. *Forest Vistas* (ca. 1932). Oil on canvas, 40" × 50" (102cm × 127cm). © Private collection, The Bridgeman Art Library

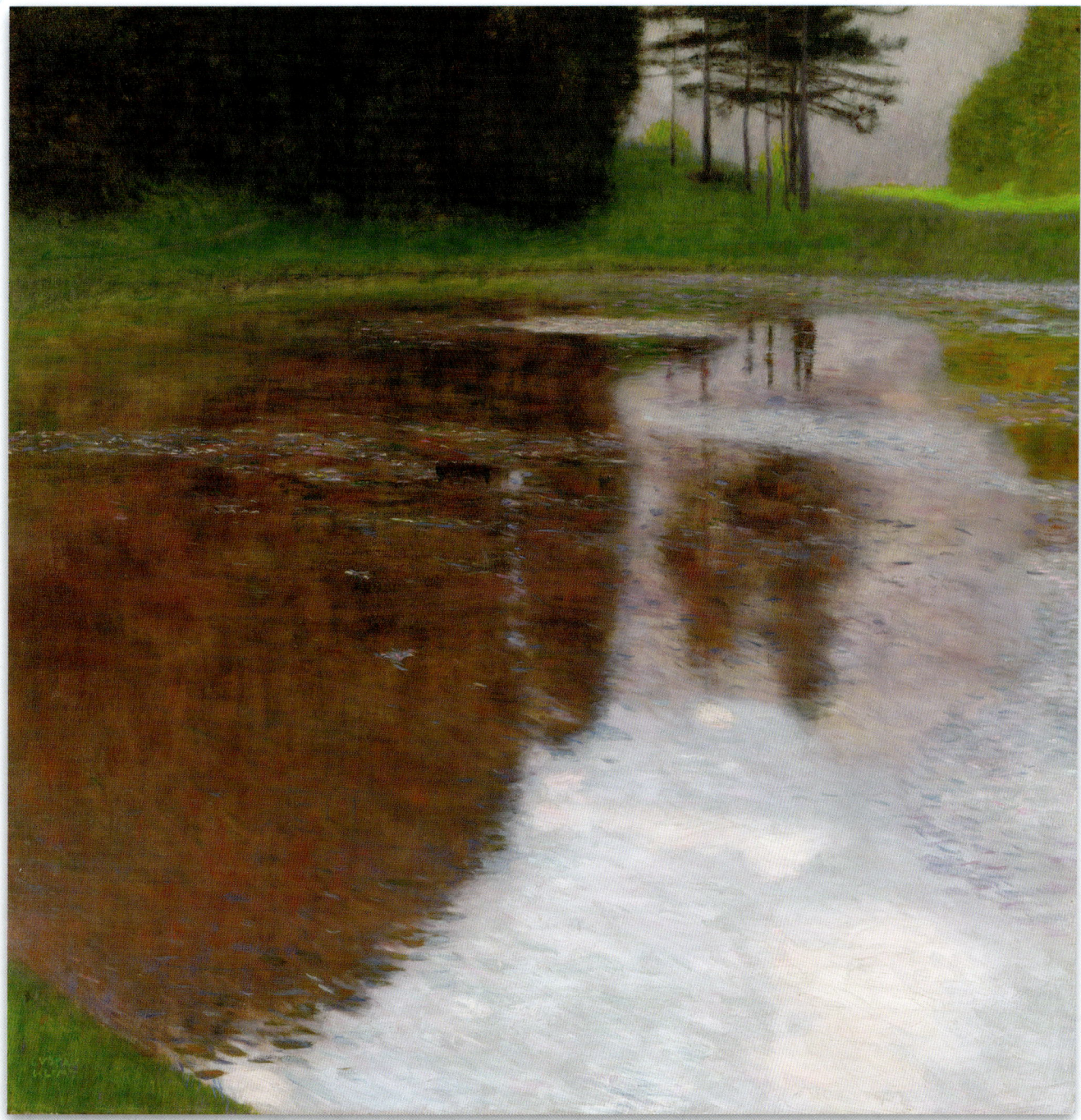

Gustav Klimt (1862–1918)

Klimt started painting landscapes late in his career, so he isn't that well known for them. Nevertheless, the dramatic sense of design in these works is worth a closer look.

Notice the placement and drama of these shapes. The detail and edges on the small pine trees clearly create a center of interest, and yet you can see the pull of the secondary lines of interest in the water. The reflections in the pond have a wonderful range of color and contrast between very large and very small shapes. Wherever you look, you find engaging color shifts and nuances, but the composition—the design—is carried by the abstract value masses—the big lights and darks.

Gustav Klimt. *Still Pond* (1899). Oil on canvas, 29½" × 29½" (75cm × 75cm). © Leopold Museum, Privatstiftung, Vienna, Austria

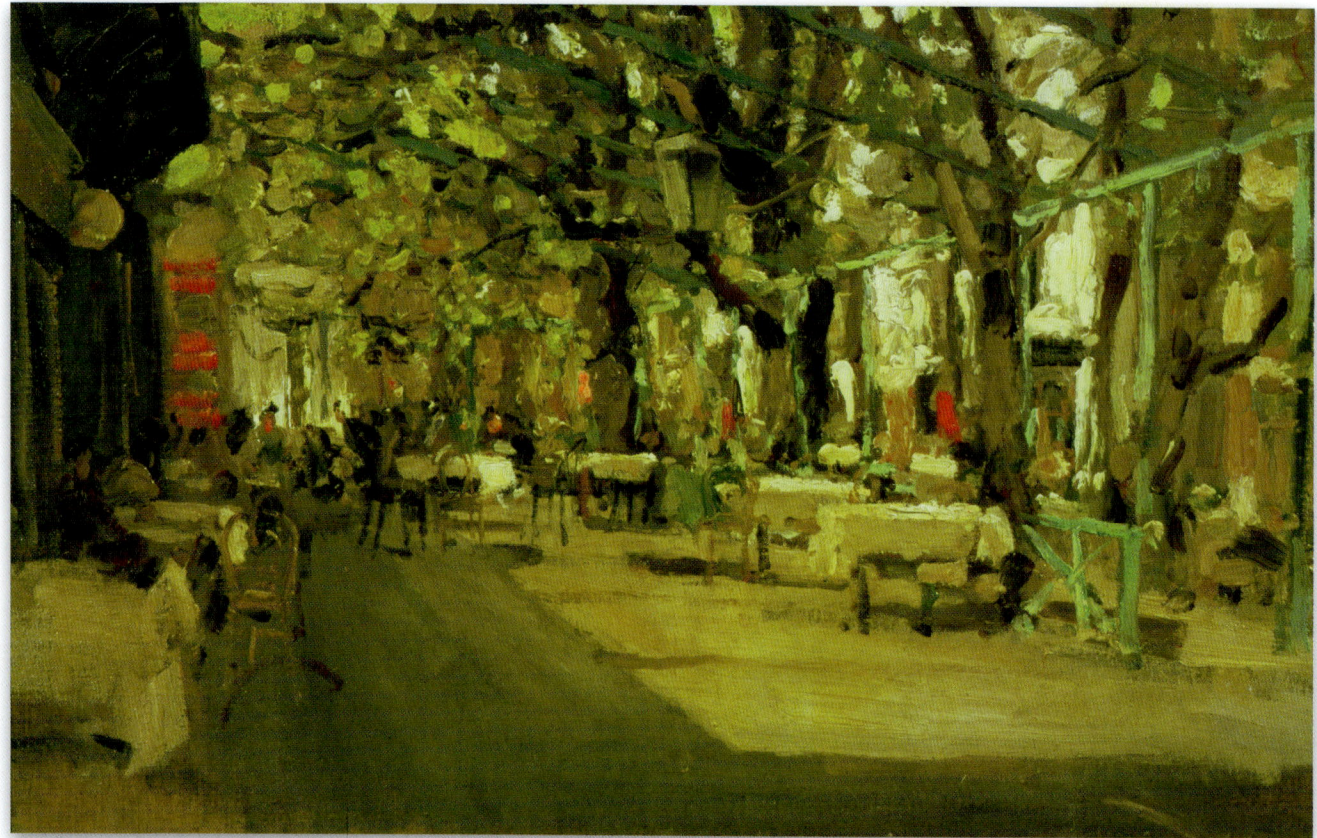

Konstantin Korovin (1861–1939)

I studied the paintings of the great Russian representational painters of the last century—Il'ya Repin, Valentin Serov and Isaak Levitan—in books, since their paintings never seemed to come to the West. Eventually, I went to Russia to see them in the State Tretyakov Gallery in Moscow and the Russian Museum in St. Petersburg. While there, I discovered Korovin, whose paintings were a wonderful surprise—fresh, loose and alive.

Look at the way Korovin has let the structure of the shadow lines and the one-point perspective pull us into the depth of the painting. This keeps the eye moving back to the bottom of the patch of white in the left distance. On top of that structure he has translated everything into simple marks of paint. There is a lot of implied complexity. We are pulled all over the canvas, but that one-point perspective quietly imposes order and structure to hold it all together.

Look at the way Korovin painted the foliage and the buildings on the left background of the painting. The value is similar; the intensity is similar. He feels no need to carefully define it. He's responding to both what he actually sees and the needs of the painting.

Konstantin Korovin. *Café in Yalta* (1905). Oil on canvas, 17½" × 28" (44cm × 71cm). © Tretyakov Gallery, Moscow, Russia, The Bridgeman Art Library

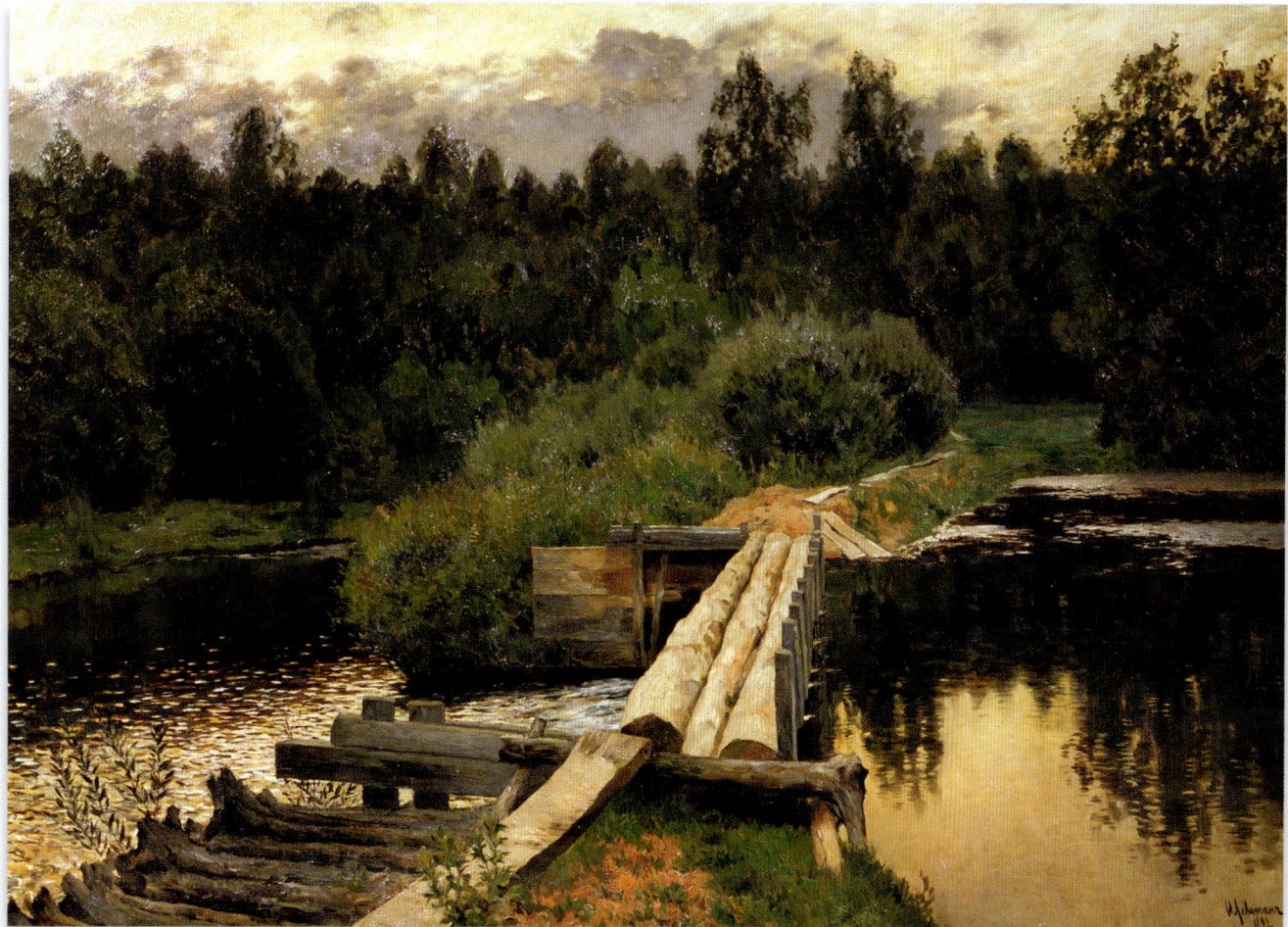

Isaak Levitan (1860–1900)

Levitan was one of the painters who inspired my trip to Russia. You can feel silence in his painting, a strong spiritual communion. Imagine him on a walk, stopping in his tracks when he saw this scene, riveted by that wonderful set of shapes pulling him into the background amid the play of the larger masses of light and dark. That structure allows the movement of the eye all over the canvas to look at details and nuance, but it is always brought back to the main structural theme.

Notice the gradation in the water in the bottom right pushes your attention up into the painting. It doesn't allow you to exit down there. You can also see Levitan's subtle use of value transitions in the midground bushes. Look at how close in value the bushes at the end of the bridge are compared to the bushes behind it, farther down the dam. The value shift at the tops of the bushes at the end of the dam anchors the entire painting before releasing your attention to the small field to the right. From that field Levitan gives you two paths to follow: The first pulls you forward on the right to the water and then into the foreground. The second pulls you to the large dark bush on the left and then forward into the foreground. He creates a flow around the entire picture plane.

Isaak Levitan. *At the Shallow* (1892). Oil on canvas, 59" × 82" (150cm × 208cm). © Tretyakov Gallery, Moscow, Russia, The Bridgeman Art Library

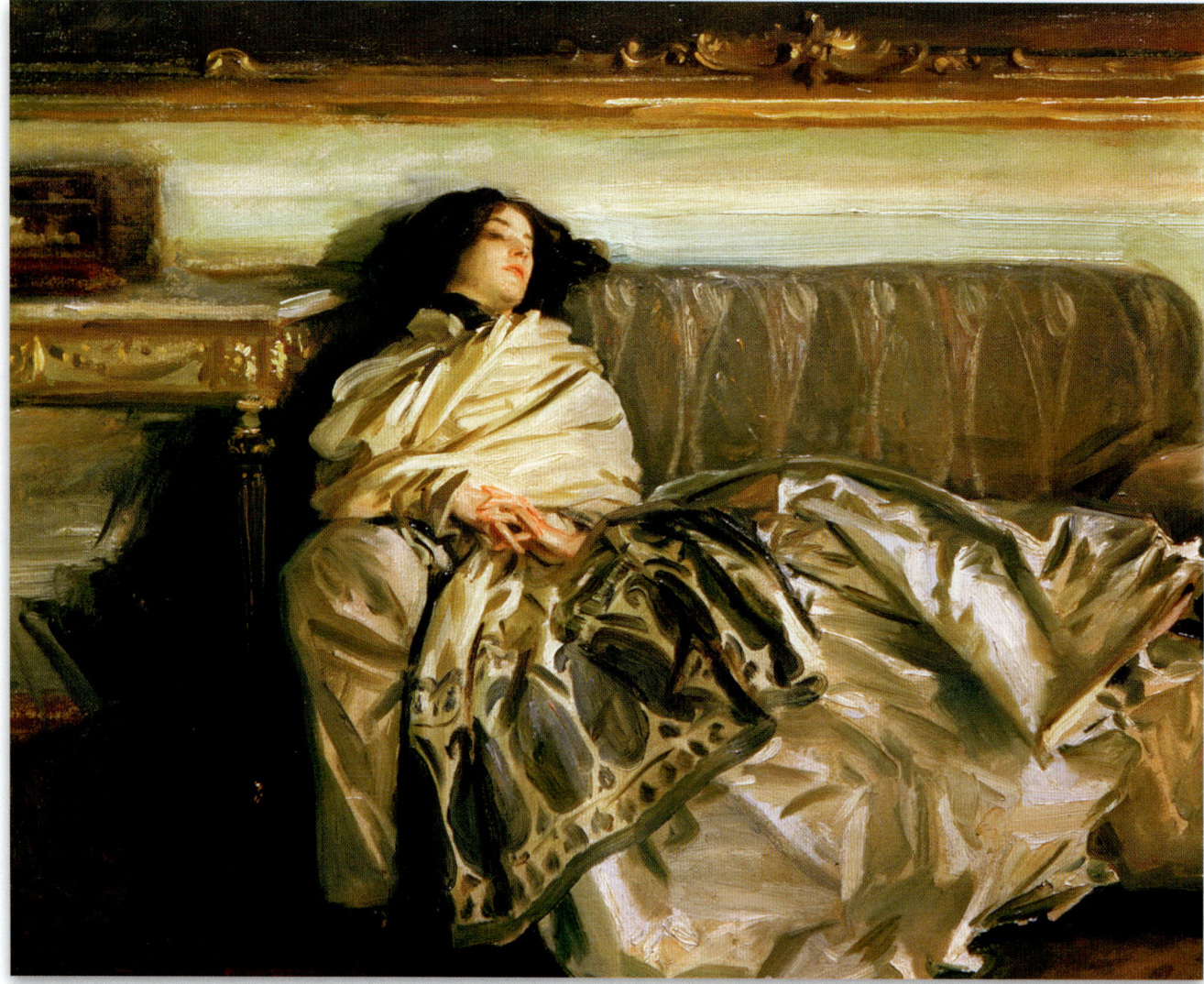

John Singer Sargent (1856–1925)

It's hard not to love this painting. This is Sargent at his best, at his most virtuosic, not constrained by a commission.

Notice the difference in edge quality on either side of her face. Our eye is pulled to the hard edge between the woman's hair and the right side of her face. The left side is much softer. Look at the armature of the horizontal that leads to the face, the vertical down her right side and down the couch and the wonderful shape of the curves of her dress, as well as the three dark lines that lead to her hands and then up her right side to her head. It is a beautifully orchestrated composition. Other shapes catch the eye: the box on the far left, the details of the light hitting the table, the frame's gilded edge, the folds and decorative patterns in the dress. But nothing interferes with the main movement. Sargent has painted a marvelous balance between the quiet relaxation of the pose and the vigorous energetic brush marks of the dress.

John Singer Sargent. *Repose* (1911). Oil on canvas, 25⅛" × 30" (64cm × 76 cm). © National Gallery of Art, Washington, D.C., U.S.A., The Bridgeman Art Library

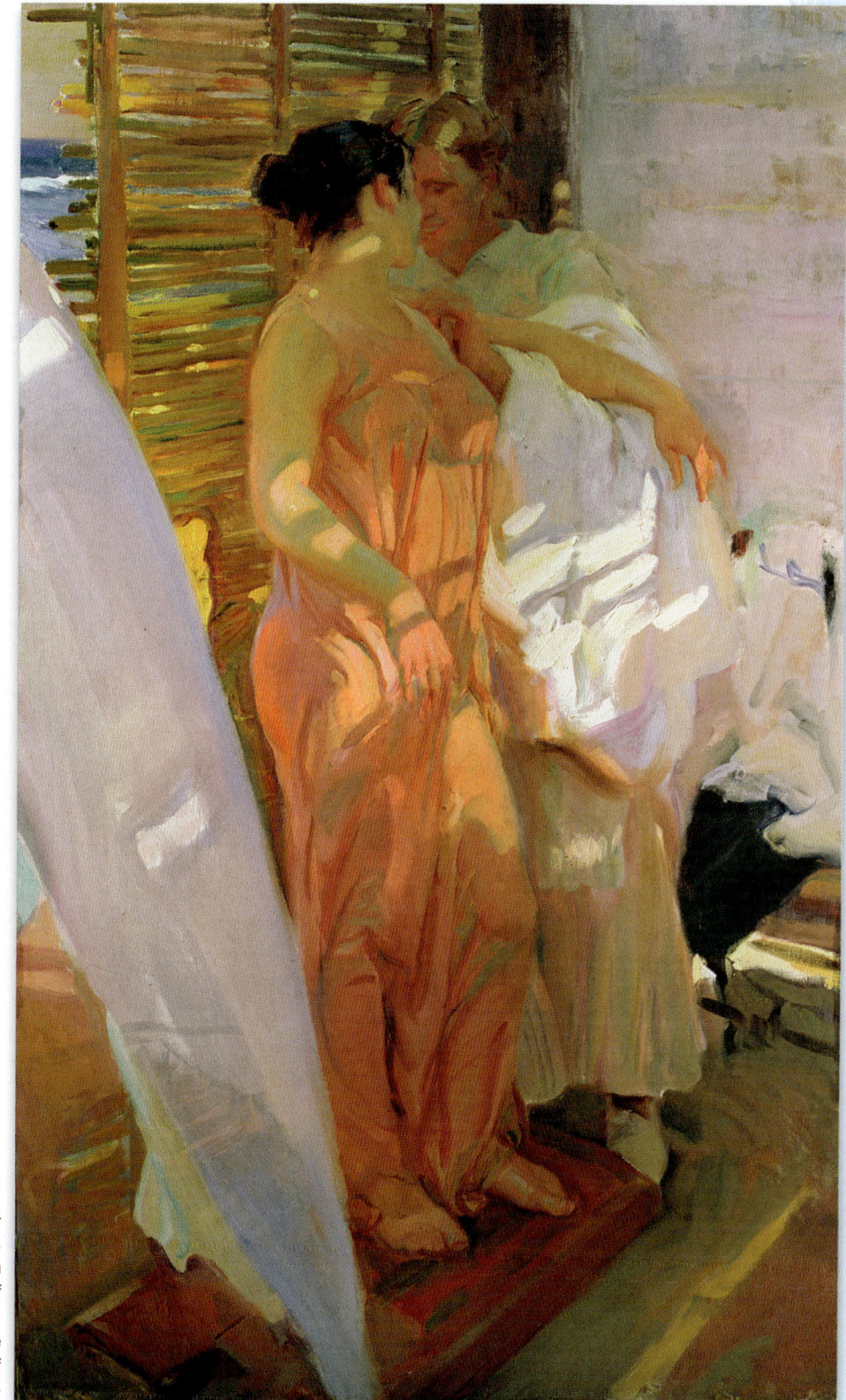

Joaquín Sorolla y Bastida (1863-1923)

I don't know any painter who had a better command of warm and cool coloration than Sorolla. In fact, you can't fully appreciate it in reproduction because the printing process will dull one end of the spectrum or the other.

This is a big painting, over 6' (2m) high. He makes it look so easy to paint in big strokes of clean, fresh color. Notice the facility of his drawing, the confidence of his brushwork, the wonderful shifts in color within a color shape. They move back and forth on the color wheel, enriching but not disturbing the integrity of each shape.

If you get a chance, visit his home and studio (now a museum) in Madrid. You'll be enchanted. You also can see a series of enormous paintings (15' × 227' [4.6m × 69.2m]) of *The Provinces of Spain* in the Hispanic Society in New York. He doesn't seem to have a hesitant brush mark in the whole series. They are a national treasure; yet, whenever I've been there, there's never been anyone else there to see them but me and the staff.

Joaquín Sorolla y Bastida. *After the Bath* (1916). Oil on canvas, 79" × 49½" (201cm × 126cm). © Museo Sorolla, Madrid, Spain, The Bridgeman Art Library

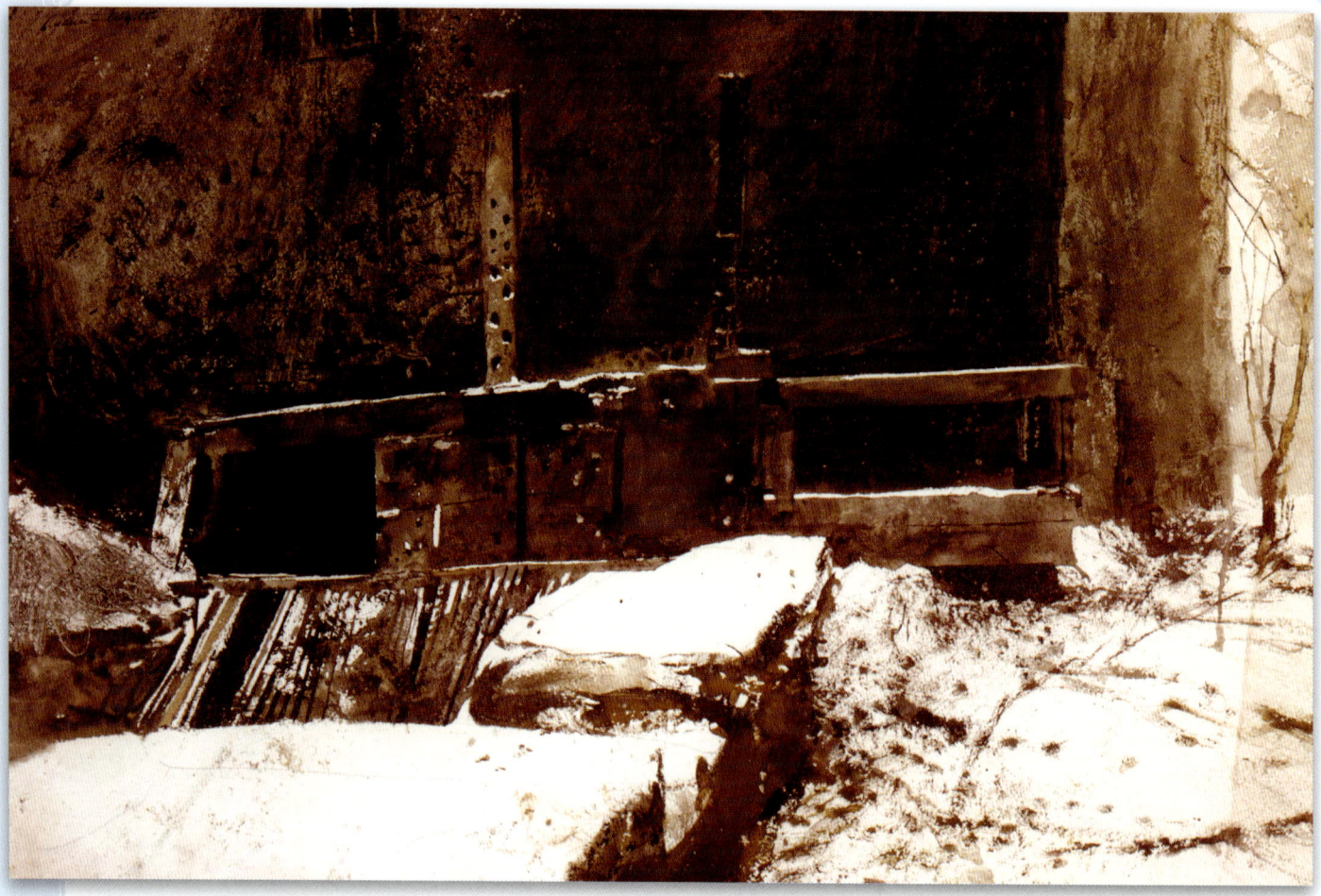

Andrew Wyeth (1917– 2009)

A friend of mind said to me some years ago that Andrew Wyeth is the best abstract painter in America. If you take "abstract" to mean "nonrepresentational," this comment will be confusing. But, if you recognize that any painting is an abstraction into two dimensions, and that the quality of the painting is about the quality of the abstract shapes in the painting, you'll see how dramatic and abstract Wyeth's work really is, particularly the landscapes.

Stop for a second and imagine him "seeing" this scene, being held by it. Think of Paul Valéry's statement, "To see is to forget the name of the thing one sees." This is definitely seeing in abstract value masses. This is real vision, combined with a masterful skill.

Andrew Wyeth. *Race Gate* (1959). Watercolor on paper, 14" × 20" (36cm × 51cm). Private collection. © 2020 Andrew Wyeth/ Artists Rights Society (ARS), New York

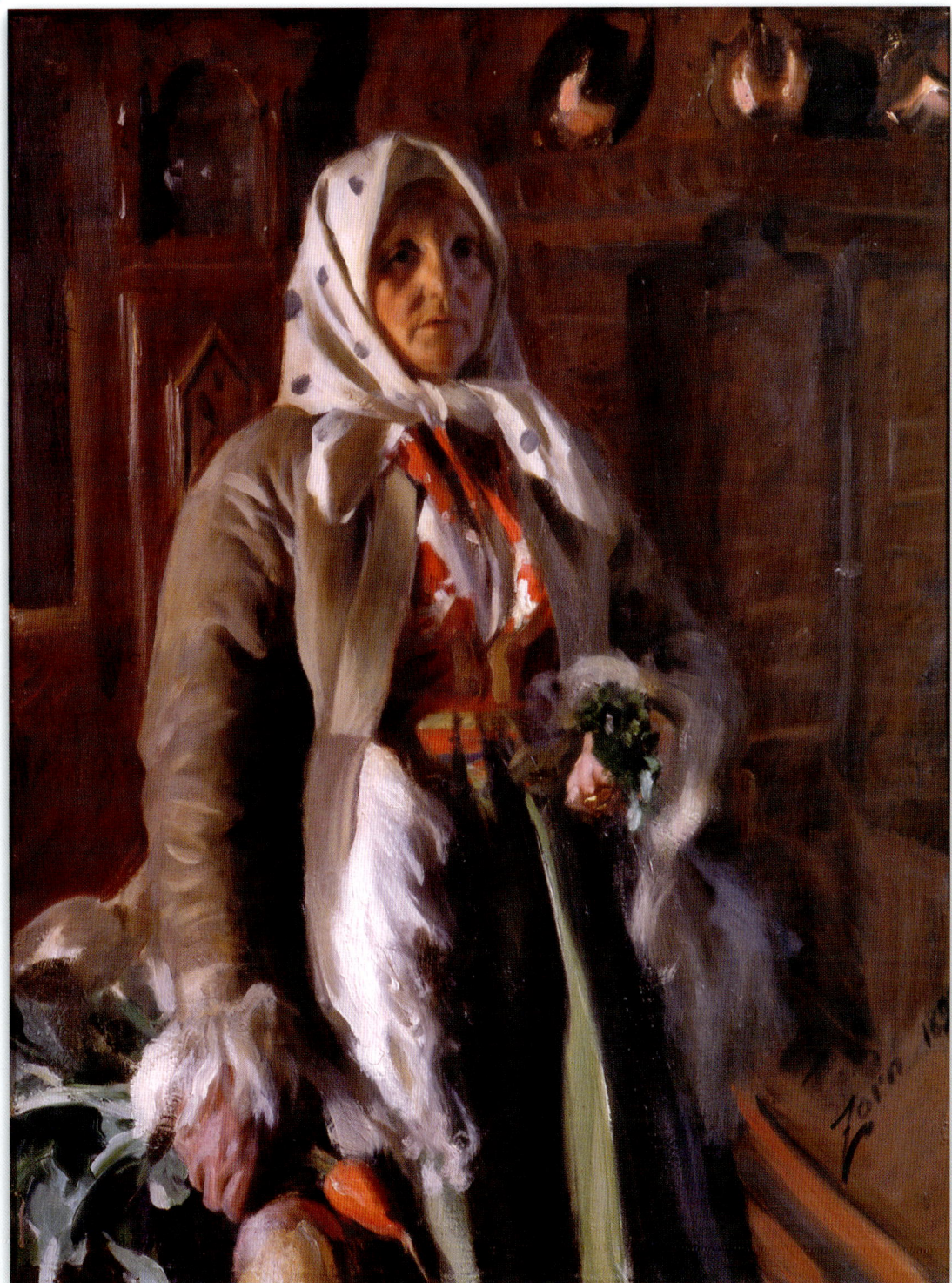

Anders Leonard Zorn (1860–1920)

Zorn is not well known in North America today, but at one point this Swedish painter had a very successful portrait career in the U.S., painting, among others, three presidents. At the turn of the last century, the expression "Zornish" was used in Russia to describe the effect many of the Russian painters were after. Like Sargent and Sorolla, Zorn creates an apparently effortless display of brushwork coalescing with the illusion and form in the painting.

Wherever you look in this painting, you see an absolute mastery of edges. Look at the green leaves of the vegetables and the two values of the handkerchief around the head. Simple shapes. The head is remarkable with its two sets of contrasts, light and dark and warm and cool.

The Isabella Stewart Gardner Museum in Boston has a couple of good Zorns in its collection. It also has dozens of his etchings, whose lines give the same sense of bold painterliness and control of form as his paintings.

Anders Leonard Zorn. *Mona* (1898). Oil on canvas, 42½" × 32" (108cm × 81cm). © Zornsamlingarna, Mora, Sweden

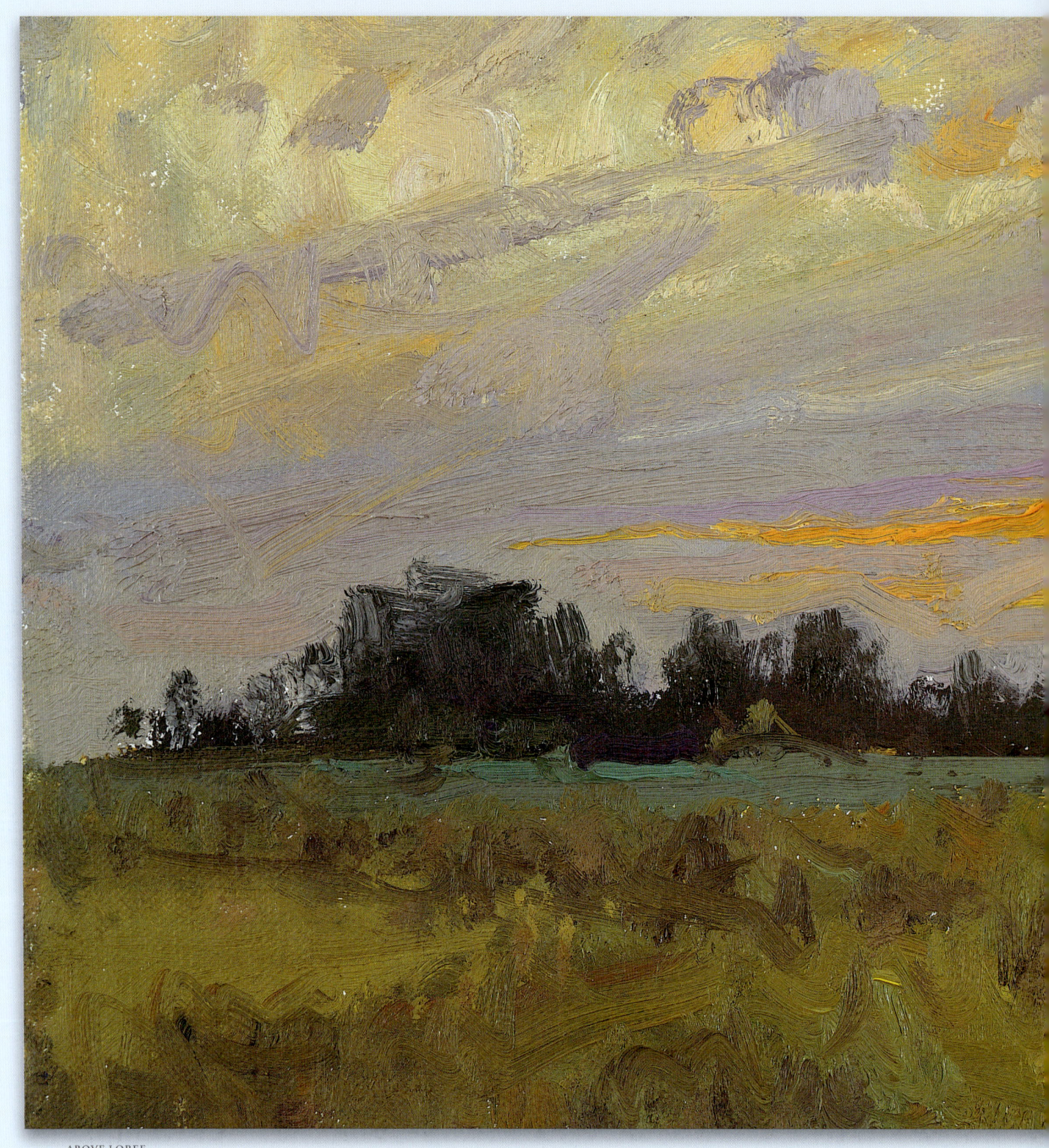

ABOVE LOREE
Oil on panel · 6" × 8" (15cm × 20cm)

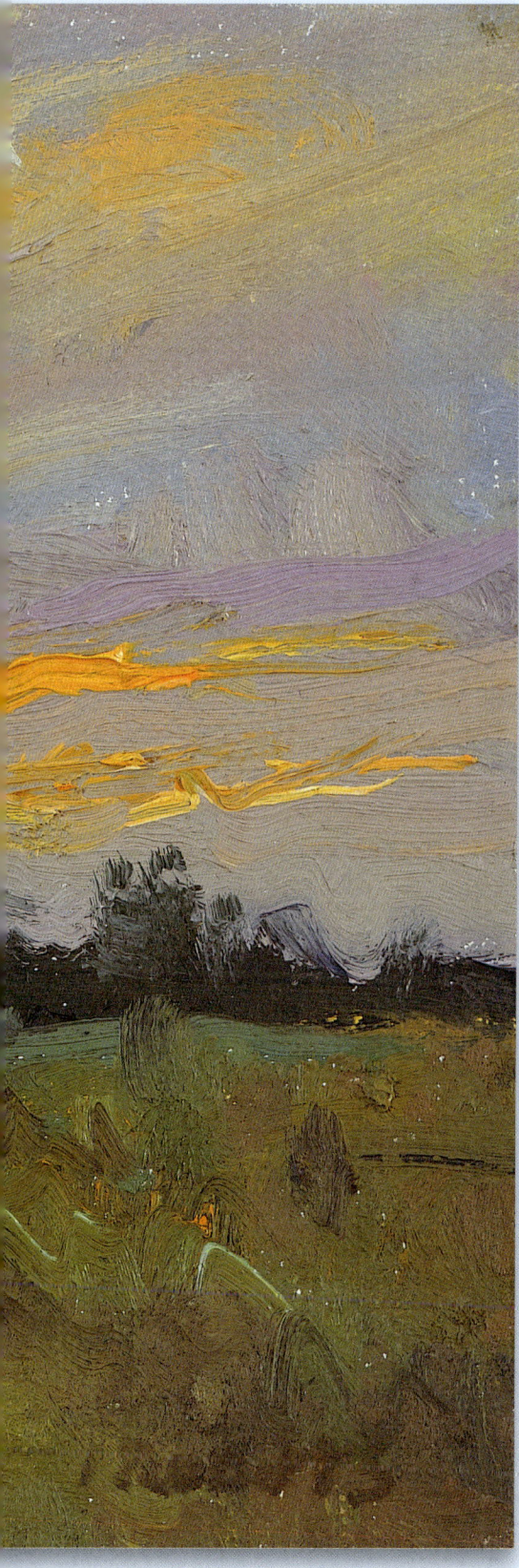

Expressing Your Artistic Voice

The history of art is not the history of who is most skilled at making things look the most real. The history of art is a history of artistic voice. We don't remember Rembrandt's self-portraits, Monet's garden or Chardin's still lifes because they are the most realistic; we remember them because we are gripped by the truth and strength of the artist's vision.

No one can show you what inspires you or tell you what you want to give expression to. You could choose to paint water lilies or ballet dancers, and paint them with such connection and authenticity that no one will ever think of Monet or Degas. Or you could paint them so that's all anyone will think of.

Voice is not about "finding a style." Find something to say and style will take care of itself. Discover what fascinates you. Look for the poetry of shapes and color and for those few themes that you can paint again and again, "going as far and as deep as your love goes."

But there's another side of giving expression to your voice. That's craft. You've got to build your expression on the foundation of sound skills and sound structure. No matter how lofty the vision, it cannot find wings without craft, without structure and (yes, you saw it coming) without composition: that holistic blending of the parts into a radiant whole.

As we change, our voice changes. We leave behind the known and tested to move into uncharted territory. All artists wrestle with this one. Experience doesn't necessarily make it any easier. I almost always feel what I really want to say is still way out there ahead of me, still unexpressed, still elusive. The following pages are a gallery of some of my more recent work, work that seems sometimes to be getting close to what I want to say.

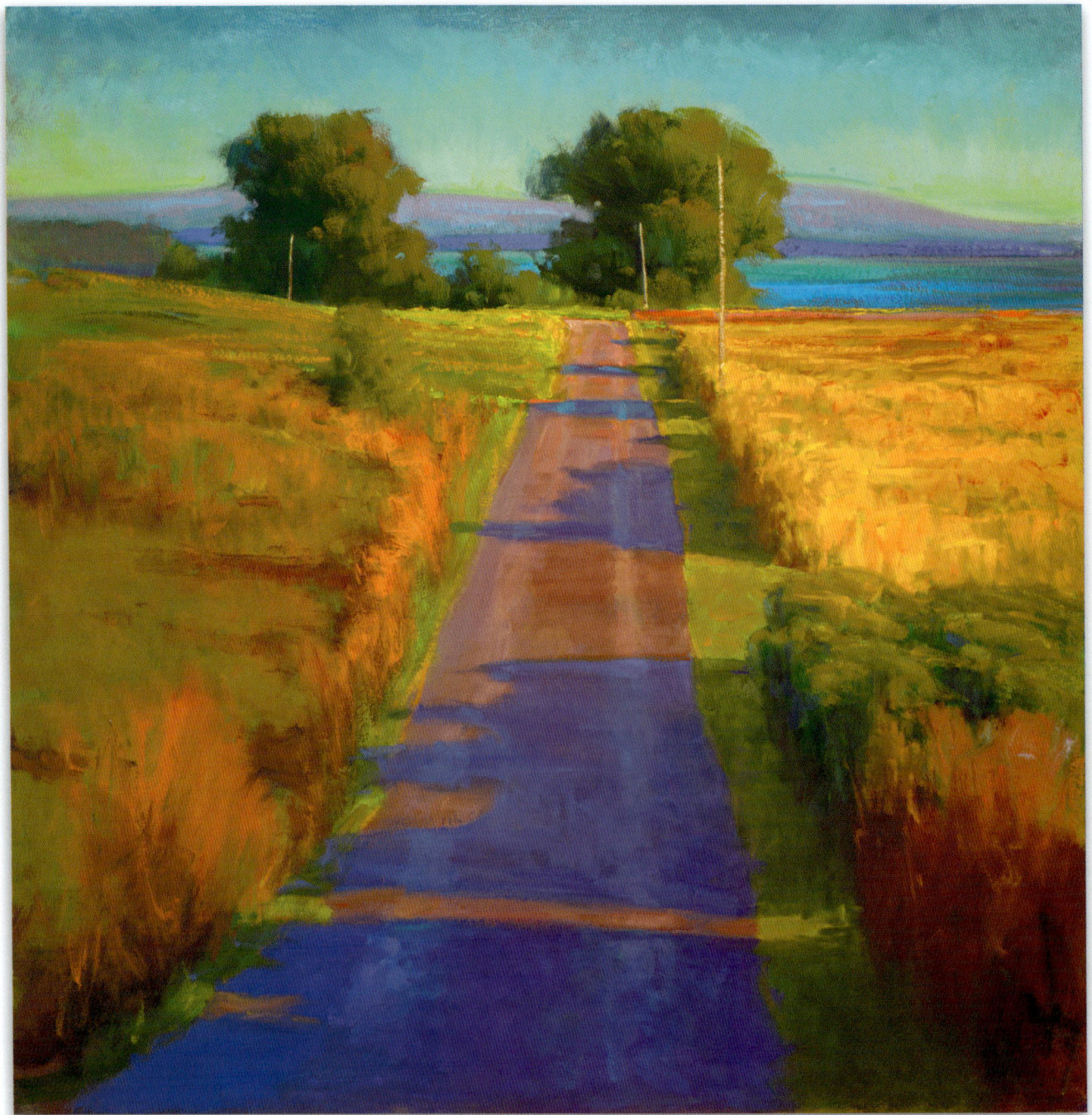

Pushing Intensity

This was the first in a series of paintings where I significantly pushed the color. Although it looks like a dirt road, it's actually Highway 1 in northern California. I drove this section over and over on a painting trip, and every time I came to this spot, I realized that this could be a great painting. The color is intense compared to most of my work, but the whole painting is keyed to the same intensity.

TOMALES BAY, EVENING
Oil on canvas · 36" × 36" (91cm × 91cm)

The bird's song would then strike our retina as a pageant of color: we should see the magical tones of the wind, hear as a great fugue the repeated and harmonizing greens of the forest, the cadences of stormy skies.

Evelyn Underhill

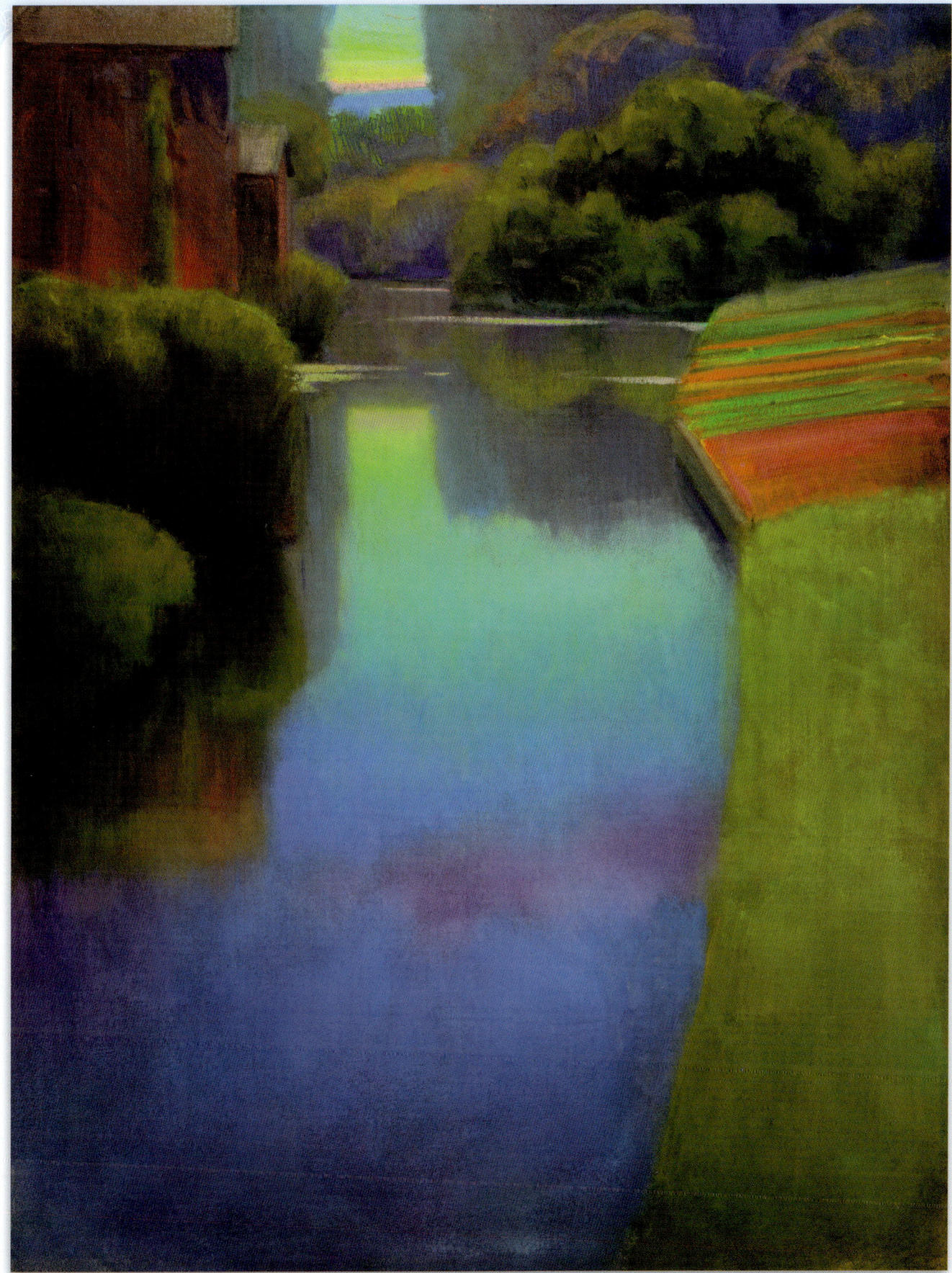

Simplifying Shapes

I painted the *plein air* sketch for this painting in a small village in the Loire Valley in France. I wanted to do a larger studio painting and liked the main shapes, so that's what I focused on. The river was full of lily pads, there was a bridge across it in the middle ground and both sides of the river were thick with tall grasses and rushes in the foreground. All of that detail had to go so I could I focus on simple shapes alone. Notice the gradations in the foreground, leading the eye back into the tall vertical of the picture plane. I decided to keep this one; it hangs in my dining room.

DUSK AT CONTEVOIR
Oil on canvas · 40" × 30" (102cm × 76cm)

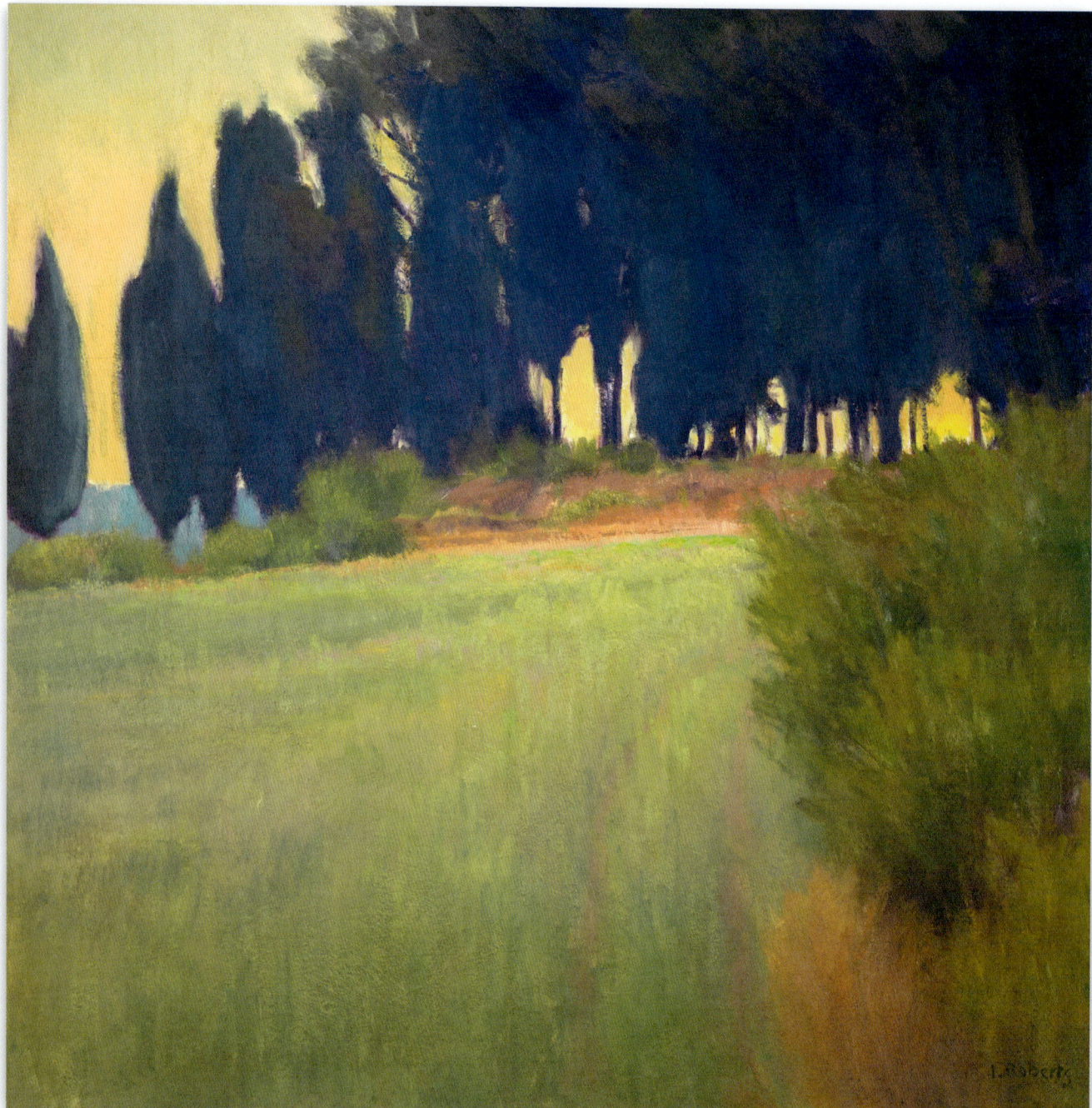

Leading the Eye

I painted this from a photograph that I took at the end of a day in Tuscany while I was teaching a workshop there. Cypresses are so dark and create the most wonderful shapes and masses in the landscape. I could have painted for a month at this spot, just turning to the left, looking to the right, observing the shapes and relationships and the play of light and shadow at different times of the day.

ROAD TO ASCIANO
Oil on canvas · 36" × 36" (91cm × 91cm)

A person's work is nothing but the slow trek to rediscover through the detour of art, those two or three great and simple images in whose presence his heart first opened.

Albert Camus

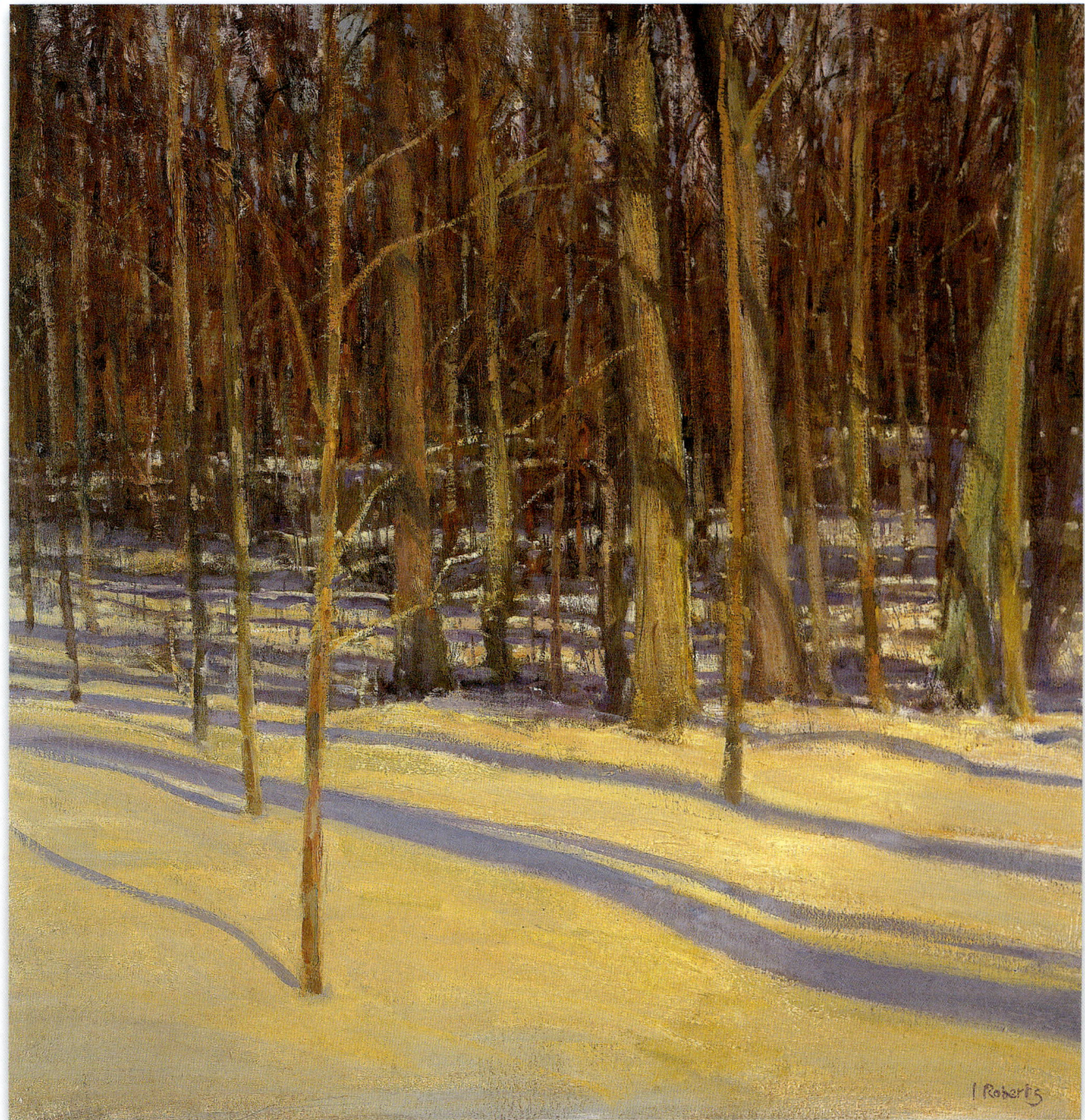

Contrasting Simplicity and Complexity

I loved the contrast between the simplicity of the foreground and the dense complexity of the forest. I wanted to get the feeling of the complexity and rich modulated color of the trees moving into the background without thinking about one tree, then the next, and so on. I hoped to provide enough information to indicate the complexity and then let the eye make sense of it. That is so much of what painting is about: learning to see what needs to be included and what can be left out.

INTO THE WOODS
Oil on canvas · 36" × 36" (91cm × 91cm)

I think one's art goes as far and as deep as one's love goes.

I see no reason to paint but that.

Andrew Wyeth

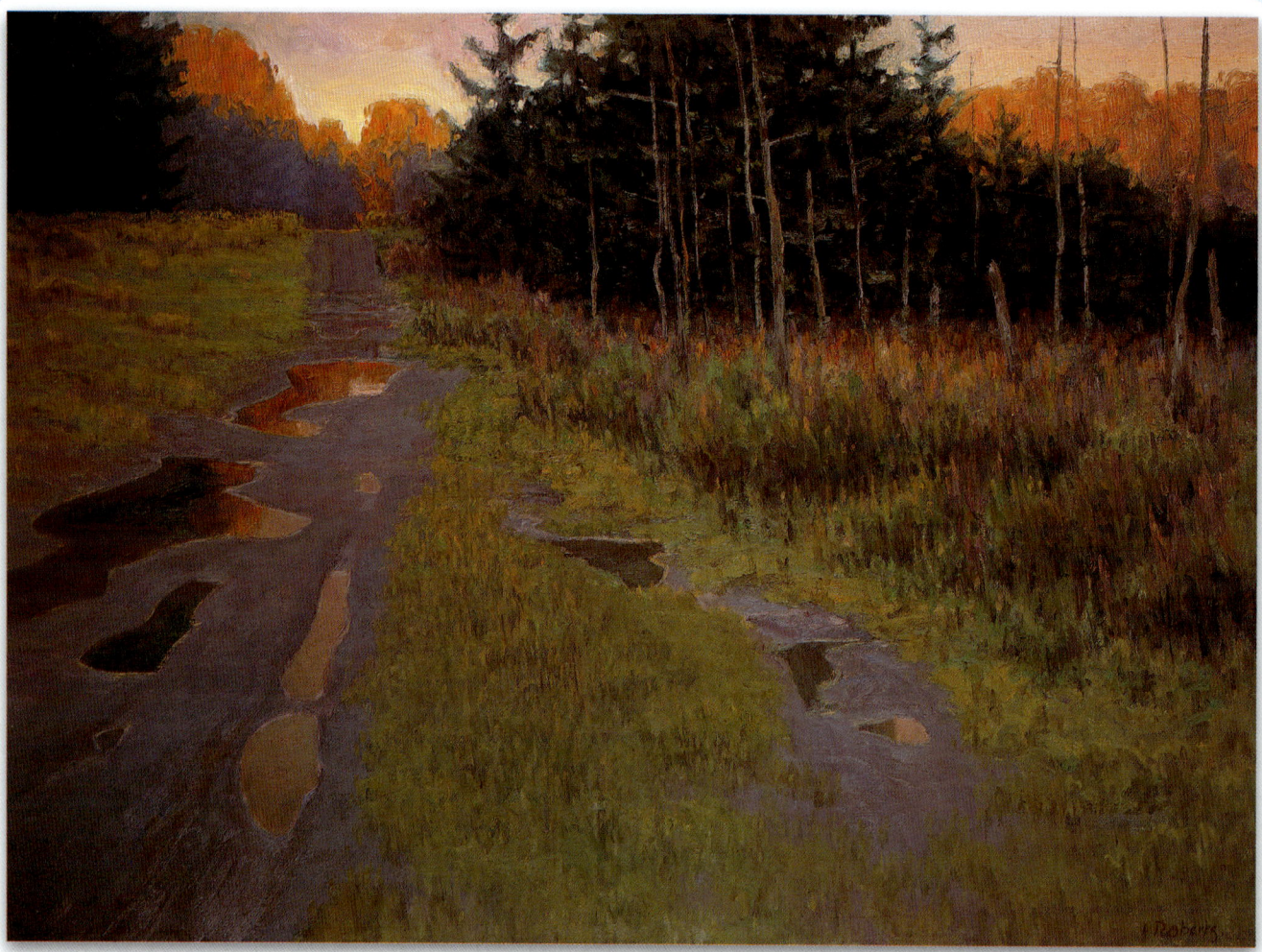

Pushing Color Temperature

I love that moment when the last warm light of the day hits the tree tops and the rest of the landscape is cool and dark.

LITTLE EGYPT MARSH
Oil on canvas · 48" × 60" (122cm × 152cm)

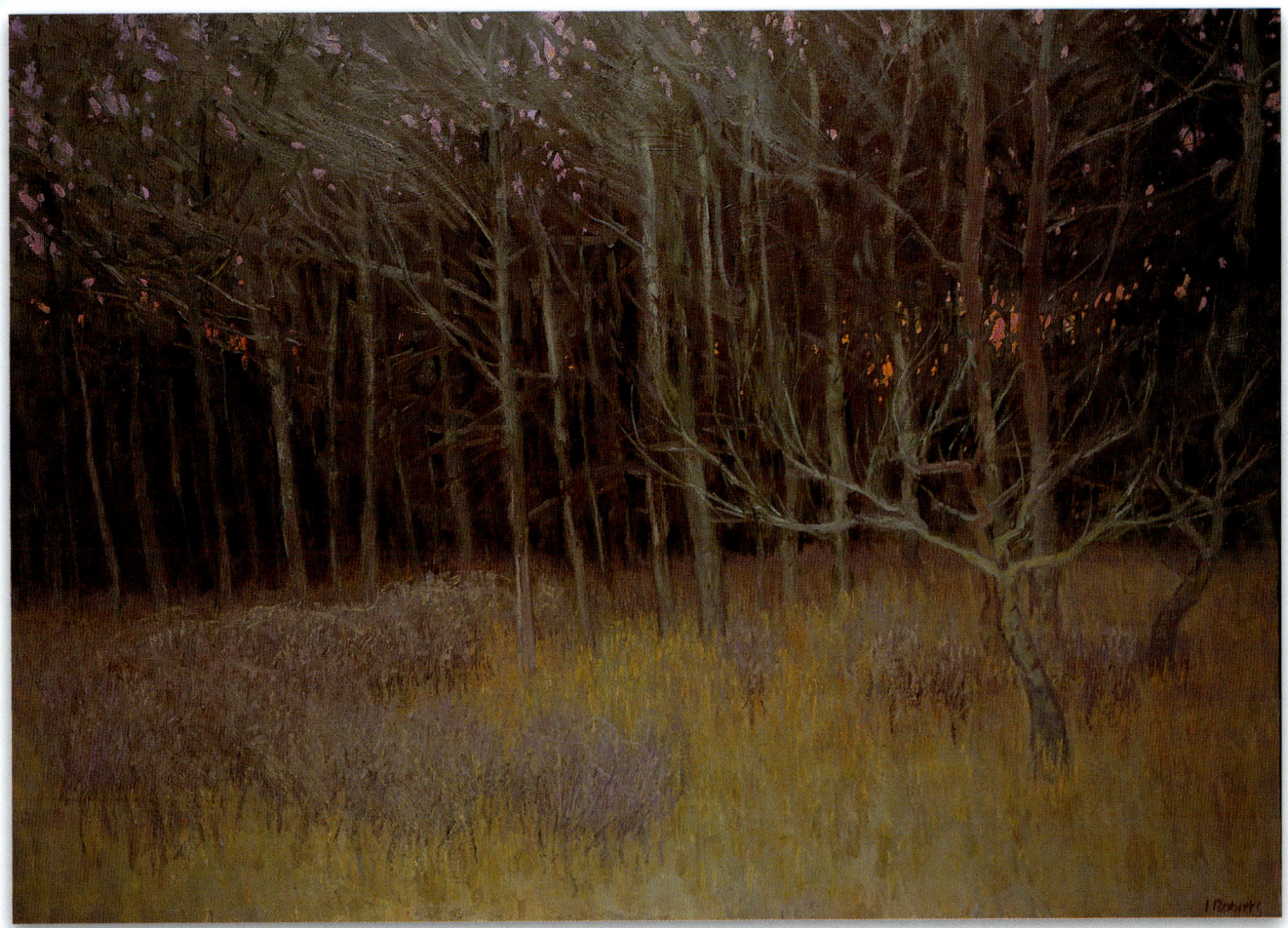

Pushing and Pulling Negative and Positive Shapes

At dusk, most of the color drains out of a photograph. The foreground and trees in the photograph I used for this painting were mainly just two value masses. Even the rich color in the evening sky was pretty flat. I made some color notes at the time, but, for the most part, it was all invented. Painting from life is a great teacher and gives you a huge storehouse of knowledge that you can bring to the studio.

TWILIGHT
Oil on canvas · 40" × 60" (102cm × 152cm)

I should paint my own places best.

John Constable

Conclusion

During a composition workshop, a diligent student who was setting up her still life said to me, "I want to set this up so it is really outstandingly good." I think that is a very good attitude to have when approaching any painting. So much can happen in the painting process to lessen a painting's final impact. But that positive attitude might mitigate the usual diminishing drag. It is so easy to make tired paintings.

Really great compositions, however, seem to come to us through grace or some other mysterious intangible. Sometimes the shapes, proportions and colors just come together, and the painting sings. You could sell that image ten times over. The magic doesn't happen every time, but I think you can put the pieces in place every time, structuring each painting as if this is the one. You will then have a consistently improving body of work, and your skills will become so honed and lively that you'll be ready when that moment of "composition grace" presents itself.

Often, keeping your skills lively is the hardest part. Having the discipline to complete a composition-a-day drawing, for example, can be difficult. You know you want to do it, but one thing comes up and then another, and before you know it, it's dinnertime. If you intend to practice daily, remember one thing: it is the starting that is the most difficult. Once you've started, you've got the paper and pencil in your hands, you're drawing, you're engaged, and you'll wonder what all the resistance was about.

I have presented a lot of ideas in this book. I don't mean to burden you with rules and restrictions in any way. I remember reading a quote once that said, "There's no God-given right and wrong. Only what works." Art is full of examples of that.

From my experience, however, I've learned that devoting a period of time to think about and practice the ideas here will give you a strong foundation of competence as well as confidence. Then you can follow or break the rules as your vision dictates.

When I was ten, my father gave me a good book on oil painting. Inside he inscribed, "May this bring you many happy hours." It did. I hope this book does the same for you. Good luck!

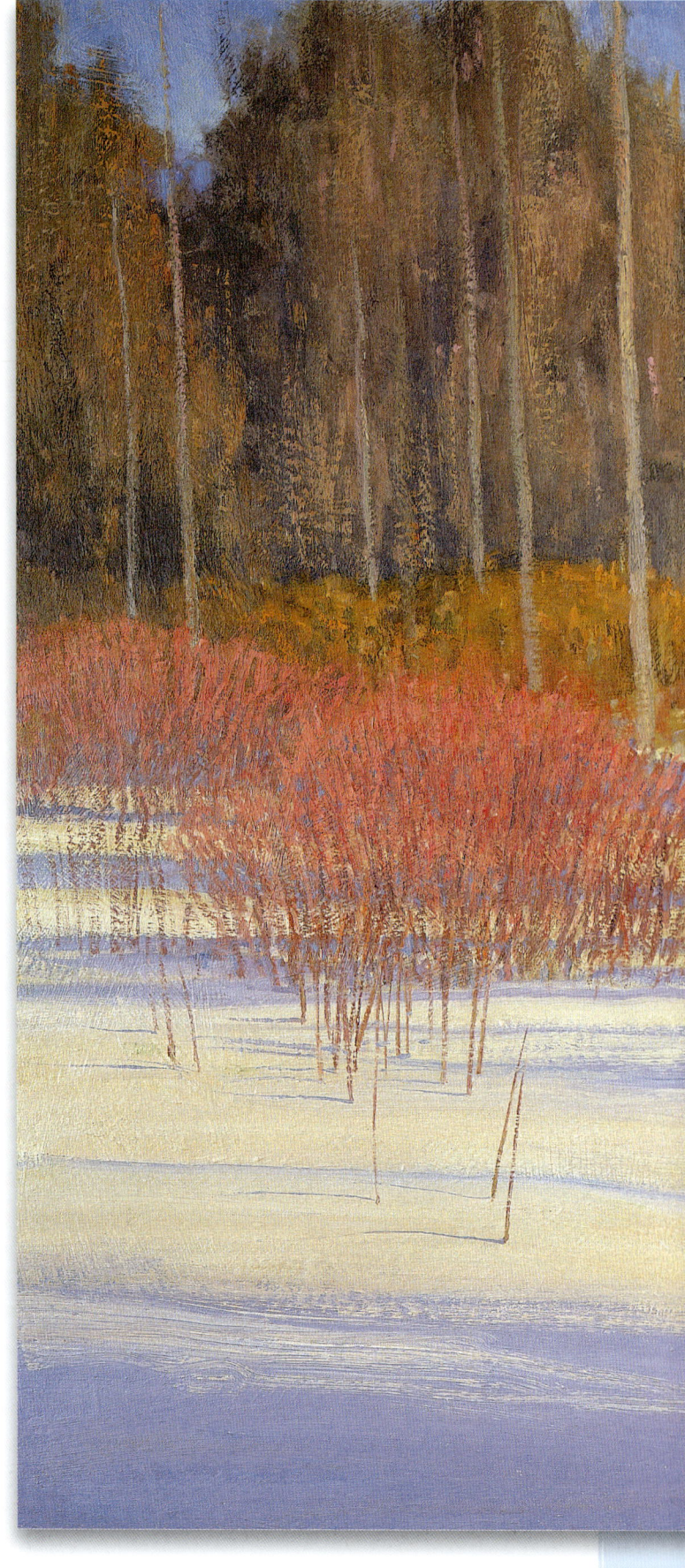

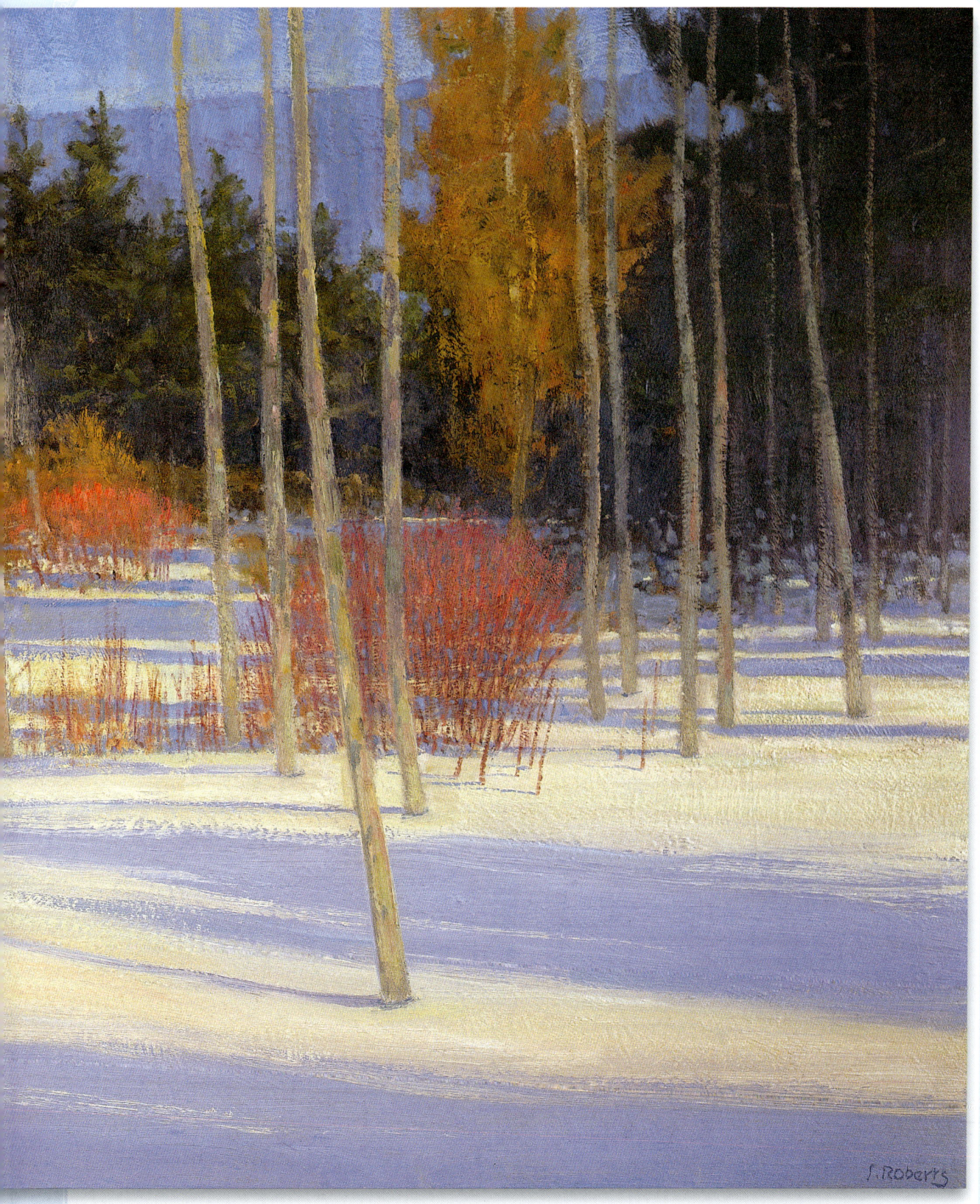

DOGWOODS ON THE BIG HEAD
Oil on canvas · 36" × 48" (91cm × 122cm)

Index

Also available from Ian Roberts

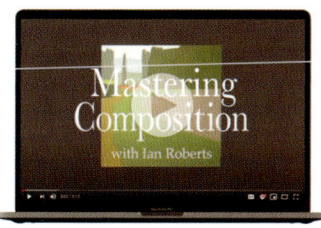

Live Online Training

Mastering Composition: Drawing

Mastering Composition: Brushwork and Vibrant Color

"Inspirational, generous with his time, and tireless in his devotion to all his student's questions. If you take one of his courses - you will leave a better artist!"

Go to ianroberts.com to view more information about the online courses.

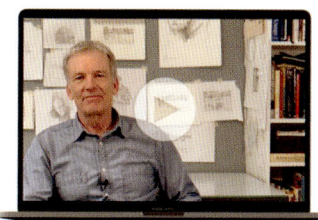

Free Weekly YouTube Video

Each week I host a 5-10 minute video on my YouTube Channel *Mastering Composition: The Laboratory of the Painting Process.*

We cover compositional structure, I do demonstrations, talk about finding our own unique voice as an artist, and sometimes I will talk about an interesting painter or painting worthy of attention.

Join me next Tuesday on YouTube. You can go to YouTube and search for Ian Roberts - Laboratory of the Painting Process.

Or, sign up on my website to receive the video to your inbox each Tuesday morning.

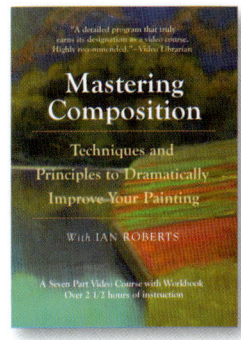

Video Course

Mastering Composition:
Techniques and Principles to Dramatically Improve Your Painting

A two-hour, seven-part video course with workbook, packed with ideas, critiques, demonstrations, animated sequences, insights and exercises. View video clips of each of the seven parts online at **ianroberts.com/videos**

"A detailed program that truly earns its designation as a 'video course'. Highly recommended."
— Video Librarian

"Your video is excellent. First rate."
— Kevin Macpherson

A great supplement to the book *Mastering Composition*.

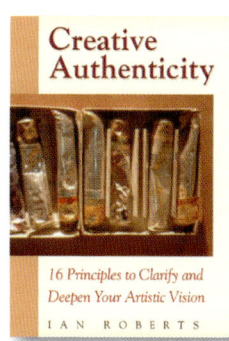

Creative Authenticity:
16 Principles to Clarify and Deepen Your Artistic Vision

ISBN-13: 978-0-9728723-2-4
Paperback, 184 Pages

"Offers spare, direct insights that are timeless and resonant for artists in any medium."
— Fearless Reviews

"How-to goldmine."
— New Age Retailer

"Enthusiastically recommended."
— Midwest Book Review

The book helps you answer the questions each one of us needs to address if our work is to be true, deep and meaningful.

Read a sample chapter and other reviews at ianroberts.com/books

To see paintings, order books and videos, or to find out more about online training, go to **ianroberts.com**